EU ANTI-MONEY LAUNDERING, DIGITAL CURRENCIES AND PRIVACY

Through an examination of the underlying technology driving digital currencies, this book offers a comprehensive understanding of the mechanisms governing their operation, clarifying complex legal concepts and confronting the pressing issue of anonymity inherent in digital currency transactions.

The book focuses on two categories of digital currencies: cryptocurrencies (eg, bitcoin) and in-game currencies (the currencies used in the closed virtual environment of a game). Despite their differences in governance – cryptocurrencies being decentralised and in-game currencies being centralised – they share significant similarities in terms of anonymity, which presents a notable issue within the anti-money laundering (AML) framework.

Against the backdrop of both the international AML standards developed by the Financial Action Task Force (FATF) and the European Union AML regime, the book examines the AML compliance stage of the private sector and, specifically, the collection and retention of data relating to digital currency users. It analyses the new AML Regulation, alongside the 5th AML Directive, the Market in Crypto-Assets (MiCA) Regulation and the 'Travel Rule' Regulation, to construct a complete picture of the obligations imposed on virtual asset service providers and to assess whether the new framework disproportionately interferes with the right to privacy and data protection of the end user. In doing so, the book offers the first legal assessment of the proportionality of private-sector AML obligations in the field of digital currencies based on the argument that, in this context, EU AML law is increasingly transforming into a surveillance regime.

Volume 26 in the series Hart Studies in European Criminal Law

Hart Studies in European Criminal Law

Since the Lisbon Treaty, European criminal law has become an increasingly important field of research and debate. Working with the European Criminal Law Academic Network (ECLAN), the series will publish works of the highest intellectual rigour and cutting edge scholarship which will be required reading for all European criminal lawyers.

The series is happy to consider both edited and single authored titles. The series defines 'European' and 'criminal law' in the broadest sense so books on the European criminal law, justice and policy will be considered. The series also welcomes books which offer different methodological approaches.

Volume 1: *EU Criminal Law after Lisbon: Rights, Trust and the Transformation of Justice in Europe*
Valsamis Mitsilegas

Volume 2: *Challenges in the Field of Economic and Financial Crime in Europe and the US*
Edited by Vanessa Franssen and Katalin Ligeti

Volume 3: *Chasing Criminal Money: Challenges and Perspectives On Asset Recovery in the EU*
Edited by Katalin Ligeti and Michele Simonato

Volume 4: *Limits to EU Powers: A Case Study of EU Regulatory Criminal Law*
Jacob Öberg

Volume 5: *The Needed Balances in EU Criminal Law: Past, Present and Future*
Edited by Chloé Brière and Anne Weyembergh

Volume 6: *Redefining Organised Crime: A Challenge for the European Union?*
Edited by Stefania Carnevale, Serena Forlati and Orsetta Giolo

Volume 7: *White Collar Crime: A Comparative Perspective*
Edited by Katalin Ligeti and Stanislaw Tosza

Volume 8: *Criminal Liability of Managers in Europe: Punishing Excessive Risk*
Stanisław Tosza

Volume 9: *The European Union and Deprivation of Liberty: A Legislative and Judicial Analysis from the Perspective of the Individual*
Leandro Mancano

Volume 10: *The Legitimacy of EU Criminal Law*
Irene Wieczorek

Volume 11: *The Fight Against Impunity in EU Law*
Edited by Luisa Marin and Stefano Montaldo

Volume 12: *Controlling Immigration Through Criminal Law: European and Comparative Perspectives on 'Crimmigration'*
Edited by Gian Luigi Gatta, Valsamis Mitsilegas, and Stefano Zirulia

Volume 13: *The Principle of Mutual Trust in EU Criminal Law*
Auke Willems

Volume 14: *Surveillance and Privacy in the Digital Age: European, Transatlantic and Global Perspectives*
Edited by Valsamis Mitsilegas and Niovi Vavoula

Volume 15: *The External Dimension of the EU's Policy against Trafficking in Human Beings*
Chloé Brière

Volume 16: *Criminal and Quasi-criminal Enforcement Mechanisms in Europe: Origins, Concepts, Future*
Edited by Vanessa Franssen and Christopher Harding

Volume 17: *Data protection, Migration and Border Control: The GDPR, the Law Enforcement Directive and Beyond*
Teresa Quintel

Volume 18: *Corporations and the Privilege against Self-Incrimination*
Stijn Lamberigts

Volume 19: *EU Enforcement Authorities: Punitive Law Enforcement in a Composite Legal Order*
Edited by Michiel Luchtman, Katalin Ligeti and John Vervaele

Volume 20: *Admissibility of Evidence in EU Cross-Border Criminal Proceedings: Electronic Evidence, Efficiency and Fair Trial Rights*
Edited by Lorena Bachmaier Winter and Farsam Salimi

Volume 21: *Proportionality of Criminal Penalties in EU Law*
Edited by Stefano Montaldo, Valsamis Mitsilegas and Lorenzo Grossio

Volume 22: *Stronger Victims' Rights in EU Law?: Assessment and Prospects*
Edited by Julia Burchett and Anne Weyembergh

Volume 23: *Proportionality of Criminal Offences and Penalties in EU Law: A Hybrid Principle*
Lorenzo Grossio

Volume 24: *UK-EU Police and Judicial Cooperation Post-Brexit: Implementing the Trade and Cooperation Agreement*
Edited by Gemma Davies and Helena Carrapico

Volume 25: *AI Evidence and Criminal Proceedings*
Edited by Katalin Ligeti

Volume 26: *EU Anti-Money Laundering, Digital Currencies and Privacy*
Andreas Karapatakis

EU Anti-Money Laundering, Digital Currencies and Privacy

Andreas Karapatakis

• HART •
OXFORD • LONDON • NEW YORK • NEW DELHI • SYDNEY

HART PUBLISHING
Bloomsbury Publishing Plc
Kemp House, Chawley Park, Cumnor Hill, Oxford, OX2 9PH, UK
1385 Broadway, New York, NY 10018, USA
Bloomsbury Publishing Ireland Limited, 29 Earlsfort Terrace, Dublin 2, D02 AY28, Ireland

HART PUBLISHING, the Hart/Stag logo, BLOOMSBURY and the Diana logo are trademarks of Bloomsbury Publishing Plc

First published in Great Britain 2026

1

A catalogue record for this book is available from the British Library.

Library of Congress Control Number: 2026944708

ISBN: HB: 978-1-50998-277-6
ePDF: 978-1-50998-279-0
ePub: 978-1-50998-278-3

Typeset by Amnet

To Eleftheria

FOREWORD

Digital currencies can be seen as disruptors to established systems of financial regulation. In this ground breaking monograph, Andreas Karapatakis focuses on the place of digital currencies in the evolution of the global and EU anti-money laundering regulatory framework and casts light expertly and convincingly on the challenges digital currencies pose to established principles in anti-money laundering regulation. The book provides three main fields of analysis. The first field consists of defining and categorising digital currencies and explaining key technological features underpinning them, while also explaining how money laundering can occur through the use of cryptocurrencies and virtual worlds. The second field of analysis focuses on the regulation of digital currencies in the evolving global and EU preventive anti-money laundering framework, highlighting the prevalence of a risk-based approach and the challenges in applying such a risk-based approach to digital currency providers. The third field of analysis addresses head on the regulatory and fundamental rights challenges in applying existing anti-money laundering preventive frameworks to digital currency providers. Karapatakis compares the regulation of banks with the regulation of virtual asset service providers, and focuses on the different application of anonymity in their relationships with their customers. He further examines the impact of anti-money laundering preventive duties on virtual asset service providers in terms of fundamental rights, and in particular privacy and data protection. The book's clear analytical framework and in depth analysis leads to a number of original insights. Karapatakis elucidates a number of challenges in effectively applying existing anti-money laundering rules to virtual asset service providers stemming from the decentralised nature of cryptocurrencies and from the fact that the banking system and virtual asset service providers are underpinned by different business models. Karapatakis further demonstrates the difficulties in applying existing understandings of anonymity to the heterogeneous landscape of virtual asset service providers, and points out the divergencies in the application of the risk-based approach with regard to virtual asset service providers in comparison with the banking sector. These insights, underpinned by detailed, original, and rigorous legal analysis, render this book indispensable reading for academics, legal practitioners and policy makers with interest and expertise in anti-money laundering law and digital currency regulation.

Valsamis Mitsilegas
Liverpool, 15 February 2026

ACKNOWLEDGEMENTS

This book is a revised and updated version of my PhD Thesis I defended in February 2024 at Queen Mary University of London. This project could not have come to fruition without the remarkable and generous individuals who, in different ways, accompanied me along the way and contributed to shaping both this book and my growth as an academic. Above all, I am deeply grateful for the support of my supervisors, Saskia Hufnagel, Niovi Vavoula and Valsamis Mitsilegas. I extend my heartfelt thanks to each of them, especially for their sustained encouragement and guidance during the pandemic and the periods of isolation that made the writing process exceptionally challenging.

Since starting as a Lecturer in Commercial Law at the School of Law and Social Justice, University of Liverpool, I have had the pleasure of working with outstanding colleagues. This book benefited from the feedback provided by the Liverpool School of Law and Social Justice Pre-Publication Reading Programme. I would like to thank, in particular, Padraig McAuliffe, Rob Stokes, Mavluda Sattorova, Sarah Kebbell and Brian Christopher Jones for their insightful comments and suggestions. I am especially grateful to Niovi Vavoula for her valuable input on privacy-related issues.

Writing this book would have been a far less pleasant experience without the company of friends. Warm thanks are due to Oğulcan Ekiz, a dear friend since the first day of the PhD; we have supported each other through this journey. I am deeply grateful to my very close friends, Alexandros, Yiannis and Pavlos, who never fail to bring a smile to my face and who, in their own way, bring a little Cypriot sunshine to the rainy UK.

My sister Maria, my brother Sotiris, and my goddaughter Dimitra have been a constant source of support, regardless of the distance. Finally, I would like to thank my parents, Stavroula and Nicos, whose trust and unwavering encouragement made this journey possible. This book is, in many ways, also a product of their dedication.

Most importantly, I am grateful to Eleftheria for her love, support, and patience, as well as her feedback on the final stages of this book.

Andreas Karapatakis
July 2026

CONTENTS

Foreword ix
Acknowledgements x
Abbreviations xiv
Tables of Cases xvi
Table of Legislation xviii
European Union Documents xxii

Introduction: Anti-Money Laundering (AML) Law, Fundamental Rights and the Digital Turn **1**
1. The Application of AML Law to Digital Currencies: A Privacy Question? 1
2. Research Questions 7
3. Aim and Scope of the Book 8
4. The Book's Contribution 12
5. Methodology 14
6. Structure of the Book: Chapter Outline 15

1. Digital Currencies: An Analysis of the Technological Characteristics **17**
Introduction 17
1. The Evolution of the Concept of Money through Time 18
2. An Umbrella Concept for Digital Currencies 25
3. Digital Currencies: Types and Characteristics 29
4. The Technology behind Cryptocurrencies 41
5. The Actors in Cryptocurrencies 43
Conclusion 48

2. The Crime of Money Laundering and Digital Currencies **49**
Introduction 49
1. Money Laundering 51
2. The Process of Money Laundering: The Traditional Form 54
3. Criminal Abuse of Technology During the Money Laundering Process: Covering the Tracks in the Blockchain Environment 59
4. The Dark Side of Digital Currencies: A Quantification Exercise 60
Conclusion 63

3. The International Anti-Money Laundering (AML) Regime of the Financial Action Task Force (FATF) ... 65
Introduction ... 65
1. The International Response to the Crime of Money Laundering: The FATF ... 67
2. 'Digital' Money Laundering and the FATF Recommendations: The Timeline ... 74
3. The International AML Framework to Protect Digital Currencies from Criminals ... 79
4. FATF Guidelines for Virtual Asset Service Providers ... 83
5. Money Laundering and Digital Currencies: How the FATF Tries to Kill Two Birds with One Large Stone ... 90
Conclusion ... 92

4. The Evolution of the European Anti-Money Laundering (AML) Regime and the Policy Choice to Regulate Digital Currencies ... 95
Introduction ... 95
1. The EU's AML Regime: History, Content and Evolution ... 96
2. The Path Towards the Introduction of Digital Currencies in the EU's AML Regime ... 104
3. The Newly Adopted AML Regime and the Evolving Reality for Virtual Asset Service Providers ... 114
Conclusion ... 133

5. Revisiting Anonymity and Trust under the Anti-Money Laundering (AML)Regime: Why Structural Differences Between Banks and Virtual Asset Service Providers Matter ... 135
Introduction ... 135
1. The Preventive Side of the European Union's (EU's) AML Legislation ... 137
2. Confidentiality and Secrecy in the Bank–Customer Relationship ... 142
3. How Burdensome is the AML Regime? ... 149
Conclusion ... 159

6. The Extension of the Anti-Money Laundering (AML) Regime to Digital Currencies: A Privacy Appraisal ... 161
Introduction ... 161
1. Financial Privacy: FIUs and Existing Literature ... 162
2. The Right to Privacy and the Right to the Protection of Personal Data ... 166
3. Blockchain: An Interference with Privacy? ... 178
4. Surveillance on the Blockchain and Justification of Interference ... 184

5. An Assessment of the Necessity and the Proportionality of the AML Regulation 193
Conclusion 209

Conclusion **213**

Bibliography *219*
Index *235*

ABBREVIATIONS

AML	Anti-Money Laundering
AMLA	Anti-Money Laundering Authority
CDD	Customer Due Diligence
CFT	Countering the Financing of Terrorism
CJEU	Court of Justice of the European Union
DAO	Decentralised Autonomous Organisations
DeFi	Decentralised Finance
DLT	Distributed Ledger Technology
DPO	Data Protection Officer
EBA	European Banking Authority
ECB	European Central Bank
ECHR	European Convention of Human Rights
ECtHR	European Court of Human Rights
EDPB	European Data Protection Board
EDPS	European Data Protection Supervisor
EU	European Union
FATF	Financial Action Task Force
FIU(s)	Financial Intelligence Unit(s)
GDPR	General Data Protection Regulation
ICCPR	International Covenant on Civil and Political Rights
IP	Internet Protocol
KYC	Know Your Customer
LED	Law Enforcement Directive
MiCA	Markets in Crypto-Assets Regulation
MMORPGs	Massively Multiplayer Online Role Playing Games

OECD	Organisation for Economic Co-operation and Development
PNR	Passenger Name Record
SAR	Suspicious Activity Report
TEU	Treaty on European Union
TFEU	Treaty on the Functioning of the European Union
TOR	The Onion Router
UDHR	Universal Declaration of Human Rights
VC	Virtual Currencies

TABLE OF CASES

Court of Justice of the European Union

Case C-264/14 *Skatteverket v Hedqvist* ECLI:EU:C:2015:718 34

Case C-623/17 *Privacy International v Secretary of State for Foreign and Commonwealth Affairs and others* ECLI:EU:C:2020:790 191–92

Case C-362/14 *Maximillian Schrems v Data Protection Commissioner* ECLI:EU:C:2015:650 .... 195, 200

Case C-817/19 *Ligue des Droits Humains v Conseil des Ministres* ECLI:C:2022:491 205

Case C-207/16 *Ministerio Fiscal* ECLI:EU:C:2018:788 196

Joined Cases C-37/20 and C-601/20 *WM and Sovim SA v Luxembourg Business Registers* ECLI:EU:C:2022:912 .... 174, 194

Joined cases C- 293/12 and C-594/12 *Digital Rights Ireland Ltd v Minister for Communications, marine and Natural Resources and others and Kärntner Landesregierung and others* ECLI:EU:C:2014:238 .... 183, 190–91, 193–96, 199–201, 204–05

Joined Cases C-203/15 and C-689/15 *Tele2 Sverige AB v Post- och telestyrelsen and Secretary of State for the Home Department v Tom Watson and Others* ECLI:EU:C:2016:970 ....191, 193, 195, 200

Joined Cases C-511/18, C-512/18 and C-520/18 *La Quadrature du Net and Others v Premier Ministre and Others* ECLI:EC:C:2020:791 .... 191–93, 195, 205, 216

European Court of Human Rights

Klass and others v Germany App no 5029/71 (ECtHR, 6 September 1978) 189

The Sunday Times v The United Kingdom App no 6538/74 (EHHR, 26 April 1979) 197–98

Airey v Ireland App no 6289/73 (EHRR, 9 October 1979) 187

Rotaru v Romania App no 28341/95 (ECtHR, 4 May 2000) 188

Z and others v UK App no 29392/95 (EHRR, 10 May 2001) 187

MM v Netherlands App no 39339/98 (EHHR, 24 September 2003) 189

S and Marper v United Kingdom App nos 30562/04 and 30566/04 (EHRR, 4 December 2008) 210

MM v United Kingdom App no 24029/07 (ECtHR, 13 November 2012) 189

MK v France App no 19522/09 (ECtHR, 18 April 2013) 189
M.N. and others v San Marino App no 28005/12 (ECtHR, 7 October 2015) 183
Affaire Brito Ferrinho Bexiga Villa-Nova v Portugal App no 69436/10 (ECtHR, 1 December 2015) 183
Roman Zakharov v Russia App no 47143/06 (ECtHR, 4 December 2015) 188
G.S.B. v Switzerland App no 28601/11 (ECtHR, 22 December 2015) 183
Sommer v Germany App no 73607/13 (ECtHR, 27 April 2017) 183
Aycaguer v France App no 8806/12 (ECtHR, 22 September 2017) 189
Centrum för Rättvisa v. Sweden App no 25252/08 (ECtHR, 25 May 2021) 188
Big Brother Watch and others v United Kingdom App nos 58170/13, 62322/14 and 24960/15 (ECtHR, 25 May 2021) 188

UK

Lloyd's Bank v Bundy [1975] QB 326 143
Parry Jones v Law Society [1969] 1 Ch. 1 143
Robertson v Canadian Imperial [1995] 1 All ER 824 143
Tournier v National Provincial Bank of England [1924] 1 KB 461 143–44
Campbell v Mirror Group Newspapers Ltd [2004] UKHL 22 172
Murray v Express Newspapers [2008] EWCA Civ 446 172
Coco v A.N. Clark (Engineers) Ltd [1968] F.S.R. 415 172

Other

US v Murgio et al, US District Court, Southern District of New York, No 15-cr-769 (AJN), 28 September 2016 35
R v Tessling, 2004 SCC 67 172
United States v Gratowski, 964 F.3d 3017 (5th Cir, 2020) 172

TABLE OF LEGISLATION

International

The United Nations Convention against Illicit Traffic in Narcotic Drugs and Psychotropic Substances (1988) 2, 51, 53, 67
Council of Europe, Convention on Laundering, Search, Seizure and Confiscation of the Proceeds from Crime (1990) 53
Convention for the Protection of Human Rights and Fundamental Freedoms (European Convention on Human Rights) 4, 175, 183, 187

EU

Charter of Fundamental Rights of the European Union (2016) OJ C202/389 .... 4, 161, 213
Consolidated version of the Treaty on European Union (2016) OJ C 202/1 .... 4, 192–193
Consolidated version of the Treaty on the Functioning of the European Union (2016) OJ C 202/1 176
Directive 2009/110/EC of the European Parliament and of the Council of 16 September 2009 on the taking up, pursuit and prudential supervision of the business of electronic money institutions amending Directives 2005/60/EC and 2006/48/EC and repealing Directive 2000/46/EC [2009] OJ L267/7 .... 25, 119, 128
Directive (EU) 2018/843 of the European Parliament and of the Council of 30 May 2018 amending Directive (EU) 2015/849 on the prevention of the use of the financial system for the purposes of money laundering or terrorist financing, and amending Directives 2009/138/EC and 2013/36/EU [2018] OJ L156/43 .... 2, 4, 6–7, 9, 11, 26, 95, 114–15, 118, 125–26, 128–29, 133, 136, 153–55, 213–14
Council Directive 2006/112/EC of 28 November 2006 on the common system of value added tax OJ L 347 35
Council Directive 91/308/ECC of 10 June 1991 on prevention of the use of the financial system for the purpose of money laundering [1991] OJ L166/77 .... 2–3, 51, 54, 98–99, 135–36, 138–41, 147–49

Directive 2001/97/EC of the European Parliament and of the Council of 4 December 2001 amending Council Directive 91/308/EEC on the prevention of the use of the financial system for the purpose of money laundering [2001] OJ L344/76............................2, 99
Directive 2005/60/EC of the European Parliament and of the Council of 26 October 2005 on the prevention of the use of the financial system for the purpose of money laundering and terrorist financing [2005] OJ L309/15............................ 2, 100
Directive (EU) 2015/849 of the European Parliament and of the Council of 20 May 2015 on the prevention of the use of the financial system for the purposes of money laundering or terrorist financing, amending Regulation (EU) No 648/2012 of the European Parliament and of the Council, and repealing Directive 2005/60/EC of the European Parliament and of the Council and Commission Directive 2006/70/EC [2015] OJ L141/73 .... 2, 100–01, 111, 137
Directive (EU) 2015/2366 of the European Parliament and of the Council of 25 November 2015 on payment services in the internal market, amending Directives 2002/65/EC, 2009/110/EC and 2013/36/EU and Regulation (EU) No 1093/2010, and repealing Directive 2007/64/EC [2015] OJ L337/35 111
Directive 2009/110/EC of the European Parliament and of the Council of 16 September 2009 on the taking up, pursuit and prudential supervision of the business of electronic money institutions amending Directives 2005/60/EC and 2006/48/EC and repealing Directive 2000/46/EC [2009] OJ L267/7 ....25, 119, 128
First Council Directive 77/780/EEC of 12 December 1977 on the coordination of laws, regulations and administrative provisions relating to the taking up and pursuit of the business of credit institutions [1977] OJ L322/30 138
Second Council Directive 89/646/EEC of 15 December 1989 on the coordination of laws, regulations and administrative provisions relating to the taking up and pursuit of the business of credit institutions and amending Directive 77/780/EEC [1989] OJ L386/1...........138
First Council Directive 79/267/EEC of 5 March 1979 on the coordination of laws, regulations and administrative provisions relating to the taking up and pursuit of the business of direct life assurance [1979] OJ L63/1 as amended by Council Directive 90/619/EEC of 8 November 1990 on the coordination of laws, regulations and administrative provisions relating to direct life assurance, laying down provisions to facilitate the effective exercise of freedom to provide services and amending Directive 79/267/EEC [1990] OJ L330/50..138

Directive 2002/83/EC of the European Parliament and of the Council of 5 November 2002 concerning life insurance [2002] OJ L345/1 and replaced by Directive 2009/138/EC of the European Parliament and of the Council of 25 November 2009 on the taking-up and pursuit of business of Insurance and Reinsurance (Solvency II) [2009] OJ L335/1 138
Directive (EU) 2016/680 of the European Parliament and of the Council of 27 April 2016 on the protection of natural persons with regard to the processing of personal data by competent authorities for the purposes of the prevention, investigation, detection or prosecution of criminal offences or the execution of criminal penalties, and on the free movement of such data, and repealing Council Framework Decision 2008/977/JHA [2016] OJ L119/89 164–65
Directive 95/46/EC of the European Parliament and of the Council of 24 October 1995 on the protection of individuals with regard to the processing of personal data and on the free movement of such data [1995] OJ L281/31 .... ??
Directive 2002/58/EC of the European Parliament and of the Council of 12 July 2002 concerning the processing of personal data and the protection of privacy in the electronic communications sector (Directive on privacy and electronic communications) [2002] OJ L201/37 192
Directive (EU) 2024/1640 of the European Parliament and of the Council of 31 May 2024 on the mechanisms to be put in place by Member States for the prevention of the use of the financial system for the purposes of money laundering or terrorist financing, amending Directive(EU) 2019/1937, and amending and repealing Directive (EU) 2015/849 [2024] OJ L, 2024/1640 .... 3, 96, 103, 163–65, 209
Regulation (EU) 1093/2010 of the European Parliament and of the Council of 24 November 2010 establishing a European Supervisory Authority (European Banking Authority), amending Decision No 716/2009/EC and repealing Commission Decision 2009/78/EC [2010] OJ L331/12 106
Regulation (EU) 2023/1113 of the European Parliament and of the Council of 31 May 2023 on information accompanying transfers of funds and certain crypto-assets and amending Directive (EU) 2015/849 (recast) [2023] OJ L150/1 .... 3, 96, 103–04, 123, 127, 132, 134, 158, 206

Regulation (EU) 2016/679 of the European Parliament and of the Council of 27 April 2016 on the protection of natural persons with regard to the processing of personal data and on the free movement of such data, and repealing Directive 95/46/EC (General Data Protection Regulation – GDPR) [2016] OJ L119/1 .... 164, 176

Regulation (EU) 2023/1114 of the European Parliament and of the Council of 31 May 2023 on markets in crypto-assets, and amending Regulations (EU) No 1093/2010 and (EU) No 1095/2010 and Directives 2013/36/EU and (EU) 2019/1937 [2023] OJ L150/40 .... 12, 115, 214

Regulation (EU) 2024/1624 of the European Parliament and of the Council of 31 May 2024 on the prevention of the use of the financial system for the purposes of money laundering or terrorist financing [2024] OJ L, 2024/1624 .... 3–4, 7, 9, 95–96, 103–04, 121–22, 126, 129, 131–32, 134, 154, 162–63, 171–72, 179, 181, 185–86, 188, 197–98, 200–01, 203–08, 213–14, 217

Regulation (EU) 2024/1620 of the European Parliament and of the Council of 31 May 2024 establishing the Authority for Anti-Money Laundering and Countering the Financing of Terrorism and amending Regulations (EU) No 1093/2010, (EU) No 1094/2010 and (EU) No 1095/2010 [2024] OJ L, 2024/1620 .... 3, 95, 103, 210

EUROPEAN UNION DOCUMENTS

European Parliament

European Parliament, 'Report on the proposal for a directive of the European Parliament and of the Council amending Directive (EU) 2015/849 on the prevention of the use of the financial system for the purposes of money laundering or terrorist financing and amending Directive 2009/101/EC' A8-0056/2017 (9 March 2017) 117

Council of the EU

Council decision 22 October 1990 concerning the conclusion on behalf of the European Economic community of the UN Convention against illicit trafficking in narcotic drugs and Psychotropic substances [1990] OJ L326/56 97–98

Council of the EU, 'Outcome of the Council Meeting 3445th Council meeting' Economic and Financial Affairs 5936/16 <https://www.consilium.europa.eu/media/22950/st05936en16v4.pdf> 108

___, 'Negotiating Mandate for Proposal for a DIRECTIVE OF THE EUROPEAN PARLIAMENT AND OF THE COUNCIL amending Directive (EU) 2015/849 on the prevention of the use of the financial system for the purposes of money laundering or terrorist financing and amending Directive 2009/101/EC' 15605/16 (19 December 2016) 117

Council of the EU, 'Initial positions of the three institutions prior to commencement of trialogues for AMLR - Proposal for a Regulation of the European Parliament and of the Council on the prevention of the use of the financial system for the purposes of money laundering or terrorist financing' 9356/23 (15 May 2023) 119

European Commission

Commission, 'Proposal for a Regulation of the European Parliament and of the Council establishing the Authority for Anti-Money

Laundering and Countering the Financing of Terrorism and amending Regulations (EU) No 1093/2010, (EU) 1094/2010, (EU) 1095/2010' COM(2021) 421 final....26, 102, 115
___ 'Proposal for a Regulation of the European Parliament and of the Council on the prevention of the use of the financial system for the purposes of money laundering or terrorist financing' COM(2021) 420 final.... 26, 102, 104, 115, 120
___ 'Proposal for a Directive of the European Parliament and of the Council on the mechanisms to be put in place by the Member States for the prevention of the use of the financial system for the purposes of money laundering or terrorist financing and repealing Directive (EU) 2015/849' COM(2021) 423 final....26, 102, 104, 115
___ 'Proposal for a Regulation of the European Parliament and of the Council on information accompanying transfers of funds and certain crypto-assets (recast) COM(2021) 422 final....26, 102, 104, 115
___ 'Blockchain Strategy' < https://digital-strategy.ec.europa .eu/en/policies/blockchain-strategy> 41
___ 'Proposal for a Council Directive on prevention of use of the financial system for the purpose of money laundering' COM (1990) 106 final OJ C106/6....98
___ 'Proposal for a European Parliament and Council Directive amending Council Directive 91/308/EEC of 10 June 1991 on prevention of the use of the financial system for the purpose of money laundering' COM (1999) 352 final....99
___ 'Report of 3 March 1995 on the implementation of Directive 91/308/EEC' COM (95) 54 final....99
___ 'Report of 1 July 1998 on the implementation of Directive 91/308/EEC' COM (98) 49 final....99
___ 'Proposal for a Directive of the European Parliament and of the Council on the prevention of the use of the financial system for the purpose of money laundering and terrorist financing' COM (2013) 45 final....100
___, 'Proposal for a Directive of the European Parliament and of the Council amending Directive (EU) 2015/849 on the prevention of the use of the financial system for the purposes of money laundering or terrorist financing and amending Directive 2009/101/EC' COM (2016) 450 final.... 5, 101, 105, 108–09, 113, 116, 125

___ 'Communication from the Commission to the European Parliament and the Council Towards better implementation of the EU's anti-money laundering and countering the financing of terrorism framework' COM(2019) 360 final 102
___ 'Communication from the Commission on an Action Plan for a comprehensive Union policy on preventing money laundering and terrorist financing' (2020/C 164/06)....102
___ 'Proposal for a Regulation of the European Parliament and of the Council on Markets in Crypto-assets, and amending Directive (EU) 2019/1937' COM(2020) 593 final 102
___ 'Proposal for a Regulation of the European Parliament and of the Council on the establishment of the digital euro' COM(2023) 369 final 26, 214
___ 'Communication from the Commission to the European Parliament, the Council, the European Economic and Social Committee and the Committee of the Regions: The European Agenda on Security' COM(2015) 185 final....106–07, 199
___ 'Communication from the Commission to the European Parliament and the Council on an Action Plan for strengthening the fight against terrorist financing' COM(2016) 50 final.... 107, 199
___ 'Commission Staff Working Document Impact Assessment Accompanying the document: Proposal for a Directive of the European Parliament and the Council amending Directive (EU) 2015/849 on the prevention of the use of the financial system for the purposes of money laundering or terrorist financing and amending Directive 2009/101/EC' SWD(2016) 223 final 108
___ 'Commission Staff Working Document Impact Assessment Accompanying the Anti-money laundering package' SWD(2021) 190 final.... 126–27
___ 'Report from the Commission to the European Parliament and the Council on the assessment of the risk of money laundering and terrorist financing affecting the internal market and relating to cross-border activities' SWD(2022)344 final 134
Commission of the European Communities, 'Recommendation for a Council Decision on Community participation in the preparatory work and the International Conference on Drug Abuse and Illicit Trafficking' COM (86) 457 final 97

Commission of the European Communities, 'First Commission's report on the implementation of the Money Laundering Directive (91/308/EEC) to be submitted to the European Parliament and to the Council' COM 95(54) final 141

Other

European Central Bank, 'Virtual Currency Schemes' (October 2012) 9, 24
___ 'Opinion of the European Central Bank on a proposal for a Directive of the European Parliament and of the Council amending Directive (EU) 2015/849 on the prevention of the use of the financial system for the purposes of money laundering or terrorist financing and amending Directive 2009/101/EC' CON/2016/49 (October 2016)................................116
Europol, 'The Internet Organised Crime Threat Assessment (IOCTA)' (2014)..24
___ 'The Internet Organised Crime Threat Assessment (IOCTA)' (2018)..45
___ 'The Internet Organised Crime Threat Assessment (IOCTA)' (2019)..45
___ 'The Internet Organised Crime Threat Assessment (IOCTA)' (2020)..62
___ 'The Internet Organised Crime Threat Assessment (IOCTA)' (2024)..62
___'European Union, Serious and Organised Crime Threat Assessment, A Corrupting Influence: The Infiltration and Undermining of Europe's Economy and Society by Organised Crime (SOCTA)' (2021) 6
___ 'Cryptocurrencies: Tracing the Evolution of Criminal Finances' (2021) Europol Report Series, Publications Office of the European Union <https://www.europol.europa.eu/cms/sites/default/files/documents/Europol%20Spotlight%20-%20Cryptocurrencies%20-%20Tracing%20the%20evolution%20of%20criminal%20finances.pdf> 6
European Banking Authority, 'EBA Opinion on virtual currencies' EBA/Op/2014/08 (July 2014)................................ 105–06, 108, 112
___ 'Guidelines on information requirements in relation to transfers of funds and certain crypto-assets transfers under Regulation (EU) 2023/1113 ('Travel Rule Guidelines')' (04 July 2024) 207

European Economic Social Committee, 'Opinion on the proposal for a Directive of the European Parliament and of the Council amending Directive (EU) 2015/849 on the prevention of the use of the financial system for the purposes of money laundering or terrorist financing and amending Directive 2009/101/EC [COM(2016) 450 final - 2016/0208 (COD)]' ECO/408 124
___ 'Opinion on the proposal for a Council Directive on prevention of the use of the financial system for the purpose of money laundering' [1990] OJ C332/86 139
European Data Protection Supervisor, 'Opinion 1/2017, EDPS Opinion on a Commission Proposal amending Directive (EU) 2015/849 and Directive 2009/101/EC' (2 February 2017) 124–25, 186–87
___ 'Assessing the necessity of measures that limit the fundamental right to the protection of personal data: A Toolkit' (11 April 2017) 194, 202–03
___ 'EDPS Guidelines on assessing the proportionality of measures that limit the fundamental rights to privacy and to the protection of personal data' (19 December 2019) 194, 200
___ 'Opinion 12/2021 on the anti-money laundering and countering the financing of terrorism (AML/CFT) package of legislative proposals' (22 September 2021) 126, 186
Article 29 Data Protection Working Party, 'Opinion 04/2007 on the concept of personal data' (WP 136) 01248/07/EN 180
Court of Justice of the European Union, 'Opinion 1/15' (26 July 2017) 196

Introduction: Anti-Money Laundering (AML) Law, Fundamental Rights and the Digital Turn

1. The Application of AML Law to Digital Currencies: A Privacy Question?

If you buy a virtual sword on an online game, should your transaction be tracked, analysed and stored as if you were a potential money launderer? And why does sending 500 Euros in cryptocurrencies to a friend require more information about your device, location and online behaviour than transferring 5,000 Euros through your bank?

These seemingly simple questions reveal a deeper tension at the heart of the EU's AML framework. As virtual asset service providers are required to collect and analyse unprecedented volumes of personal data, the privacy and data protection rights of users of digital currencies face a level of intrusion that is difficult to justify. This book makes a novel contribution by offering one of the first comprehensive assessments of the compatibility of the EU's AML framework with fundamental rights to privacy and data protection in the unexplored area of digital currencies. It advances the existing literature by combining a technological analysis of pseudonymity and decentralisation with a doctrinal examination of the shift from a risk-based AML approach, influenced by the Financial Action Task Force (FATF) Recommendations. The study also addresses an overlooked concept, namely, in-game currencies, an area largely ignored in the EU AML scholarship and demonstrates that their structure raises a distinct set of regulatory challenges. Taken together, these analyses show that digital currencies have fundamentally altered the business model of value transfer, rendering a traditional bank-centred AML framework ill-suited to the technological realities of these systems. The argument further highlights the growing fundamental rights concerns by the reliance on a criminal law instrument to shape and supervise the digital currency system, revealing the extent to which the regime risks evolving into a system of pervasive user surveillance.

To understand why this misalignment persists, it is necessary to situate the current framework within its historical development. International attention to the crime of money laundering was catalysed by the war on drugs, gaining particular momentum in the late 1980s with the adoption of the Vienna Convention against Illicit Traffic in Narcotic Drugs and Psychotropic Substances.[1] The Convention was the first international instrument to lay down rules to address money laundering. The EU subsequently aligned itself with the global effort by introducing the 1st AML Directive in 1991.[2] Fundamentally, the EU AML regime rests on two categories of measures – preventative and repressive.[3] The first category most prominently encompasses financial measures mandating specific entities to collect and retain customer information, report suspicious transactions to authorities, and monitor customer activities.[4] The second category encompasses measures imposed after the commission of the crime, such as asset freezing and confiscation.[5]

The primary objective of international (FATF) and regional (EU) AML frameworks is to prevent criminals from legitimising illicit gains with a view to addressing the threat posed by money laundering to the stability and security of financial institutions and the broader financial system.[6] The rapid technological advancements in recent decades have brought significant changes. Crucially, technology has transformed the concept of currency, giving rise to technologised payment systems. This evolution inevitably prompted a reformation of the processes employed to launder illicit funds as cash relinquished its former superiority. In response, the EU introduced a series of amendments to the 1st AML Directive.[7]

Yet, the EU legislation had seen no drastic structural shifts over the years, except for expanding the list of obliged entities and predicate offences (offences

[1] United Nations Convention against Illicit Traffic in Narcotic Drugs and Psychotropic Substances (1988) (the Vienna Convention).

[2] Council Directive 91/308/ECC of June 1991 on prevention of the use of the financial system for the purpose of money laundering [1991] OJ L166/77.

[3] Eleni Tsingou, 'Global Governance and Transnational Financial Crime: Opportunities and Tensions in the Global Anti-Money Laundering Regime' (2005 CSGR Working Paper No 161/05) 15; Guy Stessens, *Money Laundering: An International Law Enforcement Model* (Cambridge University Press, 2000) 108.

[4] ibid.

[5] ibid.

[6] Valsamis Mitsilegas, *Money Laundering Counter-Measures in the European Union: A Paradigm of Security Governance Versus Fundamental Legal Principles* (Kluwer Law International, 2003) 54–55.

[7] Council Directive 91/308/ECC of June 1991 on prevention of the use of the financial system for the purpose of money laundering [1991] OJ L166/77; Directive 2001/97/EC of the European Parliament and of the Council of 4 December 2001 amending Council Directive 91/308/EEC on the prevention of the use of the financial system for the purpose of money laundering [2001] OJ L344/76; Directive 2005/60/EC of the European Parliament and of the Council of 26 October 2005 on the prevention of the use of the financial system for the purpose of money laundering and terrorist financing [2005] OJ L309/15; Directive (EU) 2015/849 of the European Parliament and of the Council of 20 May 2015 on the prevention of the use of the financial system for the purposes of money laundering or terrorist financing, amending Regulation (EU) No 648/2012 of the European Parliament and of the Council, and repealing Directive 2005/60/EC of the European Parliament and of the Council and Commission Directive 2006/70/EC [2015] OJ L141/73; Directive (EU) 2018/843 of the European Parliament and of the Council of 30 May 2018 amending Directive (EU) 2015/849 on the prevention of the use of the financial system for the purposes of money laundering or terrorist financing, and amending Directive 2009/138/EC and 2013/36/EU [2018] OJ L156/43.

resulting in money laundering).[8] This changed when the EU, in 2024, overhauled its AML framework by adopting four new legislative instruments, with a new AML Regulation becoming the primary source of obligations for private entities specified therein.[9] Due to the fact that the 5th AML Directive remains in force at the time of writing, this compels the book to examine both the 5th AML Directive – as the first step towards the regulation of digital currencies – and the AML Regulation (along with the other newly adopted instruments), to provide a holistic understanding of the EU's AML regime in its present and future form.

The essence of the EU's (and FATF's) approach to money laundering is to delegate the responsibility for preventing criminal activity to private entities.[10] As Mitsilegas argues, 'the state acts in an indirect manner, seeking to activate non-state agencies and organisations in the fight against crime'.[11] The *raison d'être* of this privatisation is, thus, based on the limitations of state power in combating money laundering.[12] Not having access to a transaction history and client information complicates the identification and subsequent prosecution of the perpetrator by the state. Initially, the preventive measures were tailored to suit the banking system, allowing financial and credit institutions to compile necessary customer data for record-keeping.[13] With the evolution of money laundering methods, the AML framework has been substantially extended by widening both the list of

[8] According to Article 3 of Regulation (EU) 2024/1624 of the European Parliament and of the Council of 31 May 2024 on the prevention of the use of the financial system for the purposes of money laundering or terrorist financing [2024] OJ L, 2024/1624, the AML regime is applied to various entities including, but not limited to, credit and financial institutions, auditors, accountants, trust or company service providers, custodial wallet providers etc.

[9] Regulation (EU) 2024/1620 of the European Parliament and of the Council of 31 May 2024 establishing the Authority for Anti-Money Laundering and Countering the Financing of Terrorism and amending Regulations (EU) No 1093/2010, (EU) No 1094/2010 and (EU) No 1095/2010 [2024] OJ L, 2024/1620; Regulation (EU) 2024/1624 of the European Parliament and of the Council of 31 May 2024 on the prevention of the use of the financial system for the purposes of money laundering or terrorist financing [2024] OJ L, 2024/1624; Regulation (EU) 2023/1113 of the European Parliament and of the Council of 31 May 2023 on information accompanying transfers of funds and certain crypto-assets and amending Directive (EU) 2015/849 [2023] OJ L150/1; Directive (EU) 2024/1640 of the European Parliament and of the Council of 31 May 2024 on the mechanisms to be put in place by Member States for the prevention of the use of the financial system for the purposes of money laundering or terrorist financing, amending Directive (EU) 2019/1937, and amending and repealing Directive (EU) 2015/849 [2024] OJ L, 2024/1640.

[10] David Garland, 'The Limits of the Sovereign State: Strategies of Crime Control in Contemporary Society' (1996) 36 *British Journal of Criminology* 445, 452. Garland mentioned that 'the state alone is not, and cannot effectively be, responsible for preventing and controlling crime'.

[11] Mitsilegas (n 6) 12.

[12] Mitsilegas and Vavoula stated that the inclusion of private entities into the AML regime is an example of Garland's 'responsibilization strategy'. Valsamis Mitsilegas and Niovi Vavoula, 'The Evolving EU Anti-Money Laundering Regime: Challenges for Fundamental Rights and the Rule of Law' (2016) 23(2) *Maastricht Journal of European and Comparative Law* 261, 273.

[13] Council Directive 91/308/EEC of 10 June on prevention of the use of the financial system for the purposes of money laundering [1991] OJ L166/77, Art 1.

predicate offences and the list of obliged entities to cover a large part of the private sector (eg, law firms, audit companies, etc).[14]

Initially, the EU's adoption of the AML regime was met with scepticism, especially from those Member States with stringent banking secrecy laws.[15] Its critics claimed that the legislation substantially impacted bank clients' privacy.[16] Indeed, requiring obliged entities to collect and retain client information, to monitor client activity, and in some cases to transmit that information to the competent national authorities, such as Financial Intelligence Units (FIUs), constitutes an interference with the right to privacy and data protection under both the European Convention on Human Rights (ECHR),[17] as well as the Charter of Fundamental Rights of the EU. Such interferences, however, may be permissible under certain conditions. According to Article 8 of the ECHR, the right to privacy may be interfered with 'for the prevention of … crime'. Likewise, Articles 7 and 8 of the Charter, read in conjunction with Article 52(1) of the Charter, allow for restrictions on these rights, provided that they comply with the principle of proportionality.[18] While the legal framework has evolved since 1991, the privacy concerns remain prevalent to this day.

The significance of privacy as a fundamental human right is indisputable, particularly in today's societies that come under constant surveillance.[19] Nevertheless, unrestricted privacy provides an ideal environment for criminals to conceal their identities and continue illicit activities unhindered. In that sense, anonymity, a facet of privacy, has adverse implications for crime prevention, a phenomenon that the AML regime seeks to mitigate.[20] This book, therefore, examines the regulatory

[14] Nicholas Ryder, *Financial Crime in the 21st Century: Law and Policy* (Edward Elgar, 2011) 18–19; Dennis Cox, *Handbook of Anti Money Laundering* (Wiley, 2014) 60–61. Directive (EU) 2018/843 of the European Parliament and of the Council of 30 May 2018 amending Directive (EU) 2015/849 on the prevention of the use of the financial system for the purposes of money laundering or terrorist financing and amending Directive 2009/138/EC and 2013/36/EU [2018] OJ L156/43, Art 2; Regulation (EU) 2024/1624 of the European Parliament and of the Council of 31 May 2024 on the prevention of the use of the financial system for the purposes of money laundering or terrorist financing [2024] OJ L, 2024/1624, Art 3.

[15] Austria is an excellent example of bank secrecy jurisdiction in the 1990s. Barbot suggested that the secrecy regime of Austria was sheltering and protecting money launderers: Lisa A Barbot, 'Money Laundering: An International Challenge' (1995) 3 *Tul J Int'l & Compliance L* 161, 196; Michael Levi, 'Regulating Money Laundering: The Death of Bank Secrecy in the UK' (1991) 31(2) *British Journal of Criminology* 109, 111–12; Konstantinos D Magliveras, 'The European Community's Combat Against Money Laundering: Analysis and Evaluation' (1998) 5 *ILSA Journal of International & Comparative Law* 93, 112.

[16] Levi (n 15).

[17] Pursuant to Art 6(3) of the Treaty on European Union (TEU), ECHR rights constitute general principles of EU law.

[18] European Convention on Human Rights (ECHR), Art 8, www.echr.coe.int/documents/d/echr/convention_ENG; Charter of Fundamental Rights of the European Union (2012) C236/391 (the Charter), Arts 7, 8, 52(1), https://eur-lex.europa.eu/legal-content/EN/TXT/?uri=CELEX:12012P/TXT.

[19] See further David Lyon, *Surveillance Society: Monitoring Everyday Life* (Open University Press, 2005).

[20] Directive (EU) 2018/843 of the European Parliament and of the Council of 30 May 2018 amending Directive (EU) 2015/849 on the prevention of the use of the financial system for the purposes of money laundering or terrorist financing and amending Directive 2009/138/EC and 2013/36/EU [2018] OJ L156/43, recitals 8 and 9. Regulation (EU) 2024/1624 of the European Parliament and of the Council of 31 May 2024 on the prevention of the use of the financial system for the purposes of money laundering or terrorist financing [2024] OJ L, 2024/1624, recitals 58 and 160.

challenges arising from the inherent characteristics of digital currencies, especially their anonymity. It is this feature – often assumed to be absolute – that prompted international and European policymakers to view digital currencies as potential fertile ground for criminal misuse.[21] This assumption is imprecise. As explained in more detail in Chapter 1, although blockchain transactions may be pseudonymous, the transparency of most networks enables transactions to be traced, even if only to pseudonymous addresses. Criminals may employ additional obfuscation techniques, but these do not alter the underlying traceability of the system.

At the global level, the FATF responded to these anonymity-related concerns by revising its Recommendations in 2018 to bring digital currencies within the scope of the international AML regime.[22] In parallel, the EU legislature amended the then applicable 4th AML Directive to reflect the same concerns, seeking to address the perceived risks associated with the pseudonymous nature of these systems.[23]

The arrival of digital currencies and the initial introduction of the Bitcoin system made the prevention of money laundering even more complex.[24] The Bitcoin system, introduced in 2008 by Satoshi Nakamoto, marked a pivotal moment for the future of money.[25] Although digital currencies existed before Bitcoin,[26] this was the first system to attract broad public attention. It is built on blockchain technology, and in its early stages, the bitcoin unit itself had no intrinsic value.[27] Nakamoto aimed to demonstrate the feasibility of a system that could operate largely outside of the traditional banking infrastructure.[28] This aspiration rests on the decentralised architecture of blockchain technology, which ensures

[21] The European Union faced the issue of anonymity in the 1990s with the case of Austria's numbered accounts. See further Barbot (n 15); Magliveras (n 15).

[22] Financial Action Task Force, 'International Standards on Combating Money Laundering and the Financing of Terrorism & Proliferation'.

[23] Commission, 'Proposal for a Directive of the European Parliament and of the Council amending Directive (EU) 2015/849 on the prevention of the use of the financial system for the purposes of money laundering or terrorist financing and amending Directive 2009/101/EC' COM(2016) 450 final.

[24] For the purposes of this study, the author uses the word Bitcoin (with uppercase B) when he refers to the system and bitcoin (with lowercase b) when he refers solely to the currency.

[25] Satoshi Nakamoto, 'Bitcoin: A Peer-to-Peer Electronic Cash System' (Bitcoin, 31 October 2008), https://bitcoin.org/bitcoin.pdf.

[26] Various developments led to the conception of the Bitcoin, including David Chaum's DigiCash, Wei Dai's b-money, Nick Szabo's bit gold, Adam Back's Hashcash and Hal Finney's reusable proof of work; David Chaum, 'Blind Signatures for Untraceable Payments' in David Chaum, Ronald L Rivest and Alan T Sherman (eds) *Advances in Cryptology: Proceedings of Crypto 82* (Springer, 1983); Wei Dai, 'B-money' (1988), www.weidai.com/bmoney.txt; Nick Szabo, 'Bit gold' (2005), https://unenumerated.blogspot.com/2005/12/bit-gold.html; Adam Back, 'A Partial Hash Collision Based Postage Scheme' (1997), http://hashcash.org/papers/announce.txt; Hal Finney, 'RPOW – Reusable Proofs of Work' (2004), https://cryptome.org/rpow.htm; Niels Vandezande, *Virtual Currencies: A Legal Framework* (Intersentia, 2018) 51–52; Nathan Reiff and Erika Rasure, 'B-Money: Overview, Goals, Differences from Bitcoin' (*Investopedia*, 1 March 2026), www.investopedia.com/terms/b/bmoney.asp.

[27] Nakamoto (n 25); Zachary Miller, 'The Right Side of the Coin: State Approaches in Regulating Virtual Currencies' (2021) 45 *Seton Hall Legis J* 809, 809–10.

[28] Nakamoto (n 25).

that no single entity controls the system and that users can transact without relying on third-party intermediaries.[29]

Digital currencies gained rapid popularity due to their speed, decentralisation and pseudonymity. Their rise was also fuelled by growing dissatisfaction with conventional banking practices, ranging from transaction fees charged by intermediaries, the increasing monitoring of financial activity and the declining trust in established institutions, all of which encouraged users to seek alternatives.[30] Digital currencies appeared to offer such an alternative, a model in which individuals could retain direct control over their funds, incur minimal fees unless they opted to use intermediaries, and, in some cases, transact at minimal costs.[31] Alongside these economic features, the increased anonymity and decentralisation of digital currencies emerged as particularly attractive characteristics.[32]

These characteristics, however, intensified regulatory concern. The advent of digital currencies prompted fears about erosion of state control over money issuance, the potential disengagement of users from the banking system and the possibility that pseudonymity could facilitate criminal activity.[33] Whether such concerns were fully warranted, however, is debatable. Yet, when the EU chose in 2018 to regulate digital currencies through the 5th AML Directive, it did so without introducing meaningful reforms to accommodate their unique attributes.[34] The Directive rested on the premise that virtual asset service providers can monitor blockchain activity and collect the data required to mitigate money laundering risks in a manner comparable to more traditional intermediaries (eg banks).

[29] Arvin Narayanan and others, *Bitcoin and Cryptocurrency Technologies: A Comprehensive Introduction* (Princeton University Press, 2016) 27–30; Primavera De Filippi and Aaron Wright, *Blockchain and the Law: The Rule of Code* (Harvard University Press, 2018) 61; Henri Arslanian, *The Book of Crypto: The Complete Guide to Understanding Bitcoin Cryptocurrencies and Digital Assets* (Palgrave Macmillan, 2022) 51.

[30] For the concepts of ethics and trust in the banking system, see Constanza A Russo, Rosa Maria Lastra and William Blair, *Research Handbook on Law and Ethics in Banking and Finance* (Edward Elgar, 2019).

[31] Nakamoto (n 25); Narayanan and others (n 29); De Filippi and Wright (n 29); Arslanian (n 29).

[32] Narayanan and others (n 29) 27, 138; De Filippi and Wright (n 29) 33–40, 61; Arslanian (n 29) 51–54, 138.

[33] Katherine Baer and others, 'Crypto Poses Significant Tax Problems – and They Could Get Worse: Tax systems need updating to cope with crypto assets, whose anonymity and decentralized nature poses challenges – not least for the value added tax' (*IMF Blog*, 5 July 2023), www.imf.org/en/Blogs/Articles/2023/07/05/crypto-poses-significant-tax-problems-and-they-could-get-worse; Europol, 'Cryptocurrencies: Tracing the Evolution of Criminal Finances' (2021) Europol Report Series, Publications Office of the European Union, www.europol.europa.eu/cms/sites/default/files/documents/Europol%20Spotlight%20-%20Cryptocurrencies%20-%20Tracing%20the%20evolution%20of%20criminal%20finances.pdf; Europol, 'European Union, Serious and Organised Crime Threat Assessment, A Corrupting Influence: The Infiltration and Undermining of Europe's Economy and Society by Organised Crime (SOCTA)' (2021), www.europol.europa.eu/cms/sites/default/files/documents/socta2021_1.pdf, 27–32.

[34] Directive (EU) 2018/843 of the European Parliament and of the Council of 30 May 2018 amending Directive (EU) 2015/849 on the prevention of the use of the financial system for the purposes of money laundering or terrorist financing and amending Directive 2009/138/EC and 2013/36/EU [2018] OJ L156/43.

This book challenges the essence of this premise underpinning the current AML framework.

Specifically, while the 5th AML Directive – and later the AML Regulation – marked a turning point in the EU's AML framework, they both fail to account for the decentralised architecture and pseudonymity of digital currencies. Recital 24 of the 5th AML Directive, replicated verbatim in recital 76 of the AML Regulation, signals a move away from the EU's well-established risk-based approach – which relies on context-specific, proportionate assessments by obliged entities – towards a more rule-based approach, characterised by predetermined requirements intended to ensure the timely detection of risks associated with 'certain intermediary structures'.[35] This shift, motivated by concerns over the perceived anonymity of digital currencies, raises important questions about the impact of such generalised measures on users' fundamental rights to privacy and data protection that have so far been neglected by scholars. Taking fundamental rights seriously, this book casts doubt on the compatibility of the 5th AML Directive and the new AML Regulation with the right to respect for private life and personal data protection.

2. Research Questions

At the centre of this study lies the question of whether the transplantation of the EU AML regime from the banking sector to regulate digital currencies can be reconciled with the fundamental rights to privacy and personal data protection, which are protected under EU law. To that end, it addresses the following sub-questions:

(1) Which characteristics differentiate digital currencies from fiat currencies?

(2) To what extent have digital currencies made the detection and prevention of money laundering more challenging?

(3) How did the EU legislature address the phenomenon of digital currencies compared to the other traditional means of money laundering?

(4) To what extent can a virtual asset service provider apply AML preventive measures compared to other financial institutions?

(5) Does the transplantation of the AML regime to regulate digital currencies constitute an interference with the rights to privacy and data protection of the user, and, if so, is it justified in light of the principle of proportionality?

(6) Is the infringement justified?

[35] Directive (EU) 2018/843 of the European Parliament and of the Council of 30 May 2018 amending Directive (EU) 2015/849 on the prevention of the use of the financial system for the purposes of money laundering or terrorist financing and amending Directive 2009/138/EC and 2013/36/EU [2018] OJ L156/43, recital 24; Regulation (EU) 2024/1624 of the European Parliament and of the Council of 31 May 2024 on the prevention of the use of the financial system for the purposes of money laundering or terrorist financing [2024] OJ L, 2024/1624, recital 76.

Overall, the book seeks to test the appropriateness of preventive measures in the virtual environment. It will not analyse the investigation or prosecution of the crime of money laundering through digital currencies or the freezing of assets. In some instances, however, throughout the book, certain cases and events have been used to support arguments made regarding the preventive measures of the AML regime.

3. Aim and Scope of the Book

3.1. The Architecture of Financial Surveillance in Digital Currency Systems

The AML framework, both at the global level (FATF) and within regional contexts such as the EU, operates through activities that fall within the broader context of processing personal data, such as collection, retention and analysis. This process is designed to identify potentially illicit transactions and mitigate money laundering risks. Following Goede's concept of the 'chain of security', the analysis begins with the role of obliged entities within the AML regime.[36] These entities are responsible for monitoring financial transactions and transmitting relevant information to public authorities to assess and address security concerns.[37] This study focuses specifically on the stage of data gathering and retention carried out by obliged entities before a suspicious activity report is submitted and before information is exchanged with public authorities, primarily Financial Intelligence Units (FIUs).

While much of the existing literature examines the economic and technological foundations of digital currencies, legal scholarship has largely focused on defining their nature and identifying ways to integrate them into the existing financial framework with minimal disruption.[38] This book adopts a different perspective by analysing how the EU's AML regime interacts with the technological features of digital currencies and assessing the resulting implications for privacy and data protection rights of the user. Regulatory scrutiny has intensified amid concerns that criminals could exploit digital currencies for money laundering purposes, a fear often grounded – as already explained – in the misconception that these systems provide complete anonymity and render transactions untraceable.[39]

[36] Marieke de Goede, 'The Chain of Security' (2017) 44 *Review of International Studies* 24.

[37] ibid.

[38] See Vandezande (n 26).

[39] The Bitcoin system and other cryptocurrencies cannot provide complete anonymity. Narayanan and others tried to determine anonymity within the Bitcoin system and concluded that digital currencies can provide only pseudonymity. It is an environment where there is transparency but the user does not use a real name but a 'pseudo-identity'; see further Narayanan and others (n 29) 138–68.

Upon clarifying the technological characteristics of digital currencies, the analysis assesses the proportionality of the AML measures imposed on users.

3.1.1. The Concept of Digital Currencies

The book explores the concept of digital currencies. Since the emergence of Bitcoin, commentators have used a range of terms – cryptocurrencies, electronic currencies, digital currencies, virtual currencies – often interchangeably and not always accurately.[40] Yet these terms are not synonymous; for example, 'cryptocurrency' refers specifically to systems that employ cryptography, of which Bitcoin is one. To avoid confusion arising from inconsistent terminology across EU legislation (including the 5th AML Directive and the AML Regulation) and the definitions provided by the FATF, this book adopts the broader term 'digital currencies'.[41] This term provides the necessary coherence for the analysis and is sufficiently expansive to encompass both centralised and decentralised systems, which is essential given that the discussion extends beyond cryptocurrencies alone.

Within this overarching category, two specific forms of digital currencies are examined – cryptocurrencies and in-game currencies – because they present distinct yet comparable challenges for AML compliance. Although their governance structures differ (as explained in Chapter 1), with cryptocurrencies operating in decentralised environments and in-game currencies embedded in centralised platforms, both exhibit forms of pseudonymity that complicate their treatment under the AML framework. As these two systems have largely been studied in isolation, this book considers both to identify the regulatory challenges arising from their structural features.

Starting with in-game currencies, they form a distinct category of digital value operating within centralised gaming environments.[42] Although some platforms enable these currencies to be exchanged for other digital currencies or fiat money, they remain entirely outside the scope of EU AML law. [43] Their exclusion highlights a regulatory gap, particularly as the EU moves towards a comprehensive governance framework for digital currencies. Despite presenting a lower money laundering risk than cryptocurrencies (as will be explained in Chapters 1 and 2),

[40] Vandezande (n 26) 29.

[41] Directive (EU) 2018/843 of the European Parliament and of the Council of 30 May 2018 amending Directive (EU) 2015/849 on the prevention of the use of the financial system for the purposes of money laundering or terrorist financing and amending Directive 2009/138/EC and 2013/36/EU [2018] OJ L156/43, Art 3(18); Regulation (EU) 2024/1624 of the European Parliament and of the Council of 31 May 2024 on the prevention of the use of the financial system for the purposes of money laundering or terrorist financing [2024] OJ L, 2024/1624, Art 2.

[42] The author does not use the term gaming currencies in order to avoid any confusion with online casinos. In-game currencies are the currencies of Massively Multiplayer Online Role-Playing Games (MMORPGs); two well-known examples are World of Warcraft and Second Life; see eg https://secondlife.com/, https://worldofwarcraft.blizzard.com/en-gb/.

[43] European Central Bank, 'Virtual Currency Schemes' (October 2012), www.ecb.europa.eu/pub/pdf/other/virtualcurrencyschemes201210en.pdf, 6.

their similarities to entities already covered under the 5th AML Directive and the new AML Regulation suggest that some in-game currency exchange services should also fall within the scope of the AML regime.[44] Following a coherent approach to digital currency regulation, it is argued that the EU should therefore address both cryptocurrencies and in-game currencies where real-world value transfer occurs.

As for cryptocurrencies, these systems hold appeal due to three key features: (a) the system's provision of anonymity, (b) the decentralised nature of blockchain technology, and (c) the speed and global reach of transactions. As demonstrated in Chapter 1, while digital currencies appear to offer strong anonymity, blockchain records render every transaction publicly traceable, meaning that these systems provide pseudonymity rather than complete anonymity.[45] This is compounded by the decentralised structure of blockchain systems, which operate without central supervision or a governing entity. Such decentralisation poses significant challenges for the AML framework, particularly regarding who is responsible for implementing preventive measures and collecting the data necessary to mitigate money laundering risks.

At the same time, the rapid and borderless nature of cryptocurrency transactions distinguishes them from in-game currencies, where exchanges into fiat money tend to be slow and restricted, underscoring the unique structural difficulties that they present for the AML regime and the need for its adaptation to this new technological reality. The argument advanced in this book, however, does not target criminal law as a tool for combating financial crime, but the EU's broader reliance on a criminal law instrument to regulate what has effectively become a new segment of the digital economy. By using the AML framework as a regulatory tool for digital currencies, the EU extends the reach of a crime-preventive regime to economic and technological governance, thereby pursuing objectives that go beyond the ambit of AML Law.

3.1.2. The International and Regional Focus

Focusing primarily on the EU, a regional organisation, and its AML framework, this book also aims to demonstrate its interaction with the FATF, which was among the first international bodies to draw attention to the money laundering risks associated with digital currencies.[46]

As the global standard-setter for AML, the FATF Recommendations are closely followed by many jurisdictions.[47] In 2018, the FATF formally incorporated digital

[44] For example, Second Life can be seen as an exchanger as it provides the possibility for the user to exchange in-game currencies for fiat currencies (and vice versa) through the game's platform; see eg https://community.secondlife.com/knowledgebase/english/buying-and-selling-linden-dollars-r46/.

[45] Narayanan and others (n 29) 138–41

[46] See www.fatf-gafi.org/en/topics/virtual-assets.html.

[47] Financial Action Task Force, 'International Standards on Combating Money Laundering and the Financing of Terrorism & Proliferation'.

currencies into the international AML regime and required virtual asset service providers to apply preventive measures such as Know Your Customer (KYC), Customer Due Diligence (CDD), record keeping and transaction monitoring.[48] The definition of virtual asset service providers adopted by the FATF is deliberately broad, covering a wide range of entities offering services for digital currencies.[49] Rather than redesigning the framework, the FATF retained a risk-based approach in principle, aiming both to ensure a secure regulatory environment without undermining the technological systems and to maintain adaptable terminology capable of responding to future innovations. Nonetheless, recognising the distinct characteristics of digital currencies, the FATF concluded that risk assessment in this context requires providers to collect additional information from clients, including geo-location data, IP addresses, device identifiers, and other details.[50] As Chapter 3 will reveal, the collection of this additional information from all clients appears contradictory to the risk-based approach.

In response to the FATF's approach, the EU decided to regulate digital currencies accordingly. Faced with the dilemma of whether to regulate digital currencies from a financial perspective – that is, as part of the broader financial system, focusing on market stability, consumer protection, and financial innovation – or from a criminal law perspective aimed at preventing the misuse of these systems for money laundering,[51] the EU opted for the criminal law perspective, integrating digital currencies into the AML regime. While this is the focus of Chapter 4, it is important to underline here the two significant consequences stemming from this policy choice: (a) digital currencies are to some extent regulated for criminal law purposes and lack legal tender status under EU law; and (b) by using the AML regime as the initial step for regulation, the EU stigmatises digital currencies, emphasising their potential danger.

By bringing digital currencies within the scope of its AML regime, the EU encountered the same challenge as the FATF concerning the implementation of AML measures in a decentralised and pseudonymous environment. In response, the EU initially focused on the gatekeepers of the real-world economy, specifically virtual asset service providers connected to the physical world.[52] Consequently, only exchanges between fiat currencies and digital currencies and custodial wallet providers fall under the obligations of the 5th AML Directive. The newly adopted

[48] The FATF decided in 2018 (Outcomes of FATF plenary 17–19 October) to revise Recommendation 15 and add the definition of 'virtual asset' and 'virtual asset service provider' in the AML regime, in order to cover the phenomenon of digital currencies: www.fatf-gafi.org/en/publications/Fatfgeneral/Outcomes-plenary-october-2018.html.

[49] Financial Action Task Force, 'International Standards on Combating Money Laundering and the Financing of Terrorism & Proliferation', 137.

[50] Financial Action Task Force, 'Updated Guidance for a Risk-Based Approach: Virtual Assets and Virtual Asset Service Providers' (October 2021) 79–80.

[51] See, Chapter 4.

[52] Directive (EU) 2018/843 of the European Parliament and of the Council of 30 May 2018 amending Directive (EU) 2015/849 on the prevention of the use of the financial system for the purposes of money laundering or terrorist financing and amending Directive 2009/138/EC and 2013/36/EU [2018] OJ L156/43, Art 1(1)(c).

AML Regulation significantly expands this approach by extending obligations to a broader range of actors within the digital currency ecosystem.

A core argument developed in Chapter 4 is that the 5th AML Directive departs from the well-established risk-based approach, a shift that is particularly evident in the context of digital currencies. Faced with the speed of transactions and the technological challenges of monitoring clients, the Directive moves towards a more rule-based model. This evolution raises proportionality concerns, as a rule-based approach may lead to broader measures, increased surveillance, and profiling of all digital currency users, potentially having a disproportionate impact on privacy and data protection rights. The new AML Regulation consolidates this development by extending monitoring requirements to a wider range of actors across the digital currency ecosystem and favouring standardised compliance over contextual risk assessment. These measures reinforce the move towards generalised scrutiny of users, amplifying concerns about systematic and intrusive interference with fundamental rights.

3.1.3. Limitations of the Research

A key limitation of this book pertains to in-game currencies. As they are expressly excluded from the EU's AML regime, the proportionality and necessity test, which relates to the impact on the right to privacy and data protection, would be hypothetical. Although it is argued that, under the definitions set out in the 5th AML Directive, certain in-game currencies could fall within the notion of digital currencies, the revision of the AML framework (primarily the AML Regulation) and the Markets in Crypto-Assets (MiCA) Regulation explicitly exclude them from the definitions.[53]

Another limitation concerns the choice to focus on the Bitcoin system as the most extensively researched cryptocurrency in terms of its technological limits and capabilities. Given that many cryptocurrencies share similar structural features, the core analysis can be applied across a range of systems. Particular attention is paid to the most challenging environments – such as permissionless blockchain and privacy-oriented currencies – where decentralisation and enhanced anonymity pose heightened difficulties for AML compliance.

4. The Book's Contribution

Digital currencies have attracted growing scholarly attention, spanning multiple disciplines such as law, economics, technology and sociology. While economic and technological research mainly explores the capabilities of digital currencies and

[53] Regulation (EU) 2023/1114 of the European Parliament and of the Council of 31 May 2023 on markets in crypto-assets, and amending Regulations (EU) No 1093/2010 and (EU) No 1095/2010 and Directives 2013/36/EU and (EU) 2019/1937 [2024] OJ L150/40, Art 3 (MiCA).

blockchain technology, legal studies have predominantly grappled with the (now outdated) question of whether digital currencies should be regulated under EU law. There has also been limited analysis of the implications of digital currencies within the current EU AML regime.[54] Indeed, previous works have examined the shortcomings of the AML regime only sporadically, paying particular attention to the legal definitions of digital currencies and virtual asset service providers.[55]

Contributing to this ongoing debate, this book extends beyond the mere evaluation of definitions to assess the proportionality and the necessity of KYC and CDD measures and their impact on the fundamental rights to privacy and data protection of the end user. Taking into account the most recent development of the EU's AML regime, it seeks to alert policy-makers that any unjustified interference with users' fundamental rights of privacy and data protection would render the regime inappropriate.

This book distinguishes itself by framing the scope around surveillance and data retention from the perspective of obliged entities. As Quintel highlighted in 2022, a comprehensive examination of the prolonged storage of financial information remains lacking.[56] Indeed, research concerning privacy and the intersection of the AML regime is limited to date, with the main focus being on FIUs, access to retained data, the processing of such data, and cooperation among FIUs.[57] Relevant studies, such as Pavlidis' work, discuss the access of law enforcement agencies to centralised bank account registries and the exchange of information between FIUs and law enforcement bodies.[58] Nonetheless, while Pavlidis acknowledges the need for safeguards, he does not conduct a detailed analysis of the interference with privacy and data protection rights.[59] Mouzakiti's thesis provides another

[54] Henri Arsalian and Fabrice Fischer, 'The Future of Finance: The Impact of FinTech, AI and Crypto on Financial Services' (2019); Arsalian (n 29); Narayanan and others (n 29), De Filippi and Wright (n 29).

[55] Valentina Covolo, 'The EU Response to Criminal Misuse of Cryptocurrencies: The Young, Already Outdated 5th Anti-Money Laundering Directive' (2019) University of Luxembourg Law Working Paper No 2019-015; Lars Haffke, Mathias Fromberger and Patrick Zimmermann, 'Virtual Currencies and Anti-Money Laundering – The Shortcomings of the 5th AML Directive (EU) and How to Address Them' (2020) 21(2) *Journal of Banking Regulation* 125.

[56] Teresa Quintel, 'Data protection rules applicable to Financial Intelligence Units: still no clarity in sight' (2022) 23 ERA Forum, Springer 20.

[57] Valsamis Mitsilegas, 'New Forms of Transnational Policing: The Emergence of Financial Intelligence Units in the European Union and the Challenges for Human Rights: Part 1' (1999) 3(2) *Journal of Money Laundering Control* 147; Valsamis Mitsilegas 'New Forms of Transnational Policing: The Emergence of Financial Intelligence Units in the European Union and the Challenges for Human Rights: Part 2' (2000) 3(3) *Journal of Money Laundering Control* 250; Foivi Mouzakiti, 'Financial Surveillance, Money Laundering and Terrorist Financing in the EU: The Case of the Financial Intelligence Units' (PhD Thesis, Queen Mary University of London, 2020); Foivi Mouzakiti, 'Cooperation between Financial Intelligence Units in the European Union: Stuck in the middle between the General Data Protection Regulation and the Police Data Protection Directive' (2020) 11(3) *New Journal of European Criminal Law* 351; Foivi Mouzakiti, 'Cooperation between financial intelligence units in the EU: Challenges for the rights to privacy and data protection' in Katie Benson, Colin King and Clive Walker (eds), *Asset, Crimes and the State* (Routledge, 2020); Quintel (n 56) 53; George Pavlidis, 'Financial information in the context of anti-money laundering: Broadening the access of law enforcement and facilitating information exchanges'(2020) 23(2) *Journal of Money Laundering Control* 369.

[58] Pavlidis (n 57).

[59] ibid 374.

notable example, examining FIUs from a human rights perspective by focusing on different organisational structures and their implications on privacy and data protection.[60] Additionally, Quintel and Mouzakiti have contributed to the literature on the cooperation of FIUs and the applicable data protection framework, specifically addressing the clash between the General Data Protection Regulation (GDPR) and the Law Enforcement Directive (LED).[61] Considering also that the Court of Justice of the European Union (CJEU) has not yet assessed the limits of data retention for financial information, there is a notable gap in the literature regarding the AML regime's conformity within the blockchain environment with the rights of privacy and data protection that this book aims to cover.

A distinct contribution of this book is that it provides a novel understanding of the nature of the data stored on the blockchain. To accomplish this, it draws on Finck's work to discern the nature of such data, specifically examining whether it qualifies as personal information.[62] The investigation builds upon Finck's classification of 'transactional data' and public keys. It is noteworthy, however, that said classification is limited to the overarching question of whether the GDPR can effectively adapt to blockchain technology. This study stands out in that it evaluates the application of AML measures within the blockchain environment in a comprehensive manner.

5. Methodology

To address the complex regulatory questions raised by digital currencies, this book employs an interdisciplinary, doctrinal, and comparative methodology, integrating technological analysis, legal reasoning and cross-framework (FATF and EU) evaluation to assess the alignment of the AML regime with the rights to privacy and data protection.

Given the interdisciplinary nature of the subject matter, the book places at its centre the capabilities of the technology and the feasibility of the commission of money laundering through digital currencies. The rationale behind this is to highlight the challenges in regulating digital currencies and to shed light on the capabilities and limitations of virtual asset service providers. In doing so, it maps the technological environment, scrutinising blockchain technology and digital currency characteristics (Chapter 1), as well as assesses the feasibility of money laundering through cryptocurrencies and in-game currencies (Chapter 2). This inquiry clarifies both the operational powers and the structural constraints of virtual asset service providers in the decentralised blockchain environment.

[60] Mouzakiti (n 57).
[61] ibid; Quintel (n 56).
[62] Michèle Finck, 'Blockchain and the General Data Protection Regulation: Can Distributed Ledgers be Squared with European Data Protection Law?' (2019) Study for the European Parliament, Panel for the Future of Science and Technology, PE 634.445.

Once we establish the technological 'bedrock' of the research, the study transitions to the FATF's approach. In Chapter 3, we examine the governance of digital currencies from the international AML regime in order to determine and evaluate the influence of the FATF's 'soft law' on the EU's AML framework. The examination uses both textual and teleological interpretations. As the AML regime is based on the objective of mitigating risks, this particular *telos* of the Recommendations is the focal point, which is important when considering whether the FATF remains loyal to the risk-based approach.

Chapter 5 adopts a comparative perspective by looking at one of the oldest obliged entities of the regime (ie banks) and the newest (ie virtual asset service providers). Through this comparative approach, we determine, from a practical perspective, how the technology changes the relationship between provider and client and the actual limitations of applying AML preventive measures in the blockchain environment. Once we establish that the technological characteristics necessitate more intrusive surveillance of users by the providers, Chapter 6 moves on to the proportionality assessment of the AML measures.

The book's doctrinal aspect is particularly evident in the final part, where we assess the compatibility of AML measures with privacy and data protection rights. In this context, the case law of the ECtHR has been relied upon mainly to determine that financial information is personal data. Furthermore, the analysis considers EU policy documents (eg European Parliament committee reports, European Commission legislative proposals and impact assessments), trialogue documents from the EU legislative process, as well as the FATF's reports, methodology documents and guidelines. Of particular importance are the opinions and reports delivered by the European Central Bank (ECB), the European Banking Authority (EBA), the European Data Protection Supervisor (EDPS) and the European Data Protection Board (EDPB).

Due to the lack of transparency and the limited information publicly available concerning the FATF's decision-making process, it was a challenge to determine the reasons behind the decisions taken for the inclusion of digital currencies in the international AML regime. The research concludes at a time when there is a regulatory fever around the phenomenon of blockchain technology and digital currencies. It is unfortunate that there are no judgments as yet at the EU level concerning the intersection of digital currencies, surveillance and privacy. As a result, it was necessary to apply existing case law by analogy.

6. Structure of the Book: Chapter Outline

The book is divided into three parts. Part I comprises two chapters, focusing on the concept of digital currencies and the crime of money laundering. **Chapter 1** provides an overview of the technology, outlining key technological characteristics for later legal analysis. It defines digital currencies and categorises the analysis into cryptocurrencies and in-game currencies/virtual worlds. **Chapter 2** depicts the process of the crime of money laundering through the two different systems (ie blockchain technology and virtual worlds) using some schematics.

Part II consists of two chapters, examining the international (FATF) and EU frameworks for digital currencies. This part maps the approaches of the FATF and the EU and evaluates their policy options for the current framework. **Chapter 3** analyses the evolution of the phenomenon of digital currencies within the development of the international AML regime. The discussion shows that the FATF uses technologically neutral language when defining digital currencies and virtual asset service providers. However, these catch-all definitions might result in over-regulation. Despite the nature of the technology and the difficulties that digital currencies pose, the FATF insists on the risk-based approach. Nevertheless, the guidance provided by the FATF for the risk-based approach is deemed to be generic and insufficient.

Chapter 4 transitions from the international to the regional regime to examine the EU's AML regime and its evolution. To this end, the chapter analyses the policy background of the 5th AML Directive concerning digital currencies and the adoption of the new AML Regulation. The chapter comes to the conclusion that the AML Regulation (following the 5th AML Directive) departs from the well-established risk-based approach and shifts to a rule-based approach, failing on proportionality grounds.

In Part III, **Chapter 5** compares two different types of providers, ie banks and virtual asset service providers and the relationship with their clients. The aim of this comparison is to test whether the EU's AML regime, tailored to traditional intermediary structures such as banks, is ill-suited to address the difficulties faced by virtual asset service providers. The chapter's key conclusion is that, on the blockchain, the virtual asset service providers need a combination of data to be able to de-anonymise and monitor transactions, and the only way to gather this information is to search for it proactively. Therefore, considering the requirements on the virtual asset service providers under the rule-based approach, the AML measures imposed by the EU can be considered as surveillance.

Building on the previous chapter, **Chapter 6** assesses whether the intrusive measures applied by virtual asset service providers to their clients interfere with the rights to privacy and data protection, as they are guaranteed under EU law. Having determined that the interference exists, the chapter analyses the nature of the financial information on the blockchain to establish if it falls within the notion of 'personal data'. Relying on the jurisprudence of the CJEU and ECtHR, the analysis applies the multilayer proportionality test to expose whether such interference is justified.

1

Digital Currencies: An Analysis of the Technological Characteristics

Introduction

Technological evolution has rendered the regulation of new payment systems necessary. Digital currencies and blockchain technology have significantly changed everyday transactions, creating many legal concerns. This chapter analyses the evolution of payment systems and the characteristics of digital currencies and blockchain technology. A brief overview of digital currencies is necessary as a preliminary step. Considering that this book focuses on the transplantation of the European Union's (EU's) anti-money laundering (AML) regime to digital currencies and its impact on end users, such an evaluation requires an in-depth understanding of how the technology operates and what the challenges are.

The main objectives of this chapter are twofold. The first is to set out the background of the research and to frame its scope. To achieve this, the chapter explores the terminology debate around these currencies and provides the terminology used in this book. The second objective is to illustrate the different categories of digital currencies that currently exist. Consequently, the aim is to explain these currencies to inform the analysis. To this end, the chapter is loosely divided into three parts: (a) the evolution of money (fiat currencies), (b) the introduction of cryptocurrencies, and (c) in-game currencies and virtual worlds. Using this structure, the chapter compares the three currencies to determine whether digital currencies can be understood as 'money'.

The chapter is structured as follows: the first section provides an overview of the concept of money. It depicts the evolution of money until the invention of Bitcoin and other digital currencies. The second section explains and typifies the types of digital currencies. The chapter analysis outlines three general categories: (a) closed virtual currencies (eg in-game currencies); (b) unidirectional virtual currencies (eg Amazon coins); and (c) bidirectional virtual currencies (eg cryptocurrencies). In conclusion, the section determines that the scope of the research includes only the categories of in-game currencies and cryptocurrencies.

The third section explains the technology of digital currencies. The most well-known cryptocurrency is Bitcoin. For this reason, Bitcoin is used as an example to describe the characteristics of cryptocurrencies, including (a) cryptography,

(b) decentralisation, (c) immutability, and (d) pseudonymity/anonymity. These characteristics are crucial for the book because they are the main characteristics that render the regulation of cryptocurrencies challenging. Nevertheless, Bitcoin is not the only cryptocurrency, and cryptocurrencies are not the only digital currencies. This section additionally analyses two other categories of 'coins', namely privacy-oriented cryptocurrencies and in-game currencies.

To complete the analysis of the technology, the fourth section turns the emphasis towards the underlying technology of cryptocurrencies, ie blockchain technology. Blockchain technology facilitates the functioning of cryptocurrencies, and each cryptocurrency is associated with a blockchain. The technology is similar to all cryptocurrencies. However, this section explains the different types of blockchain technology and how these different types impact the end user. The last section of the chapter attempts a novel analysis of the actors in cryptocurrencies (industry/stakeholders) using the pseudonymity/anonymity of the end user as a standard parameter. To this end, the research analyses service providers and evaluates how different structures impact the pseudonymity/anonymity of the end user.

This chapter serves as the basis for evaluating the EU's AML regime in relation to digital currencies. Both the international and EU regimes treat these currencies as equals to fiat currencies and the virtual asset service providers as financial intermediaries. Digital currencies might satisfy some of the conditions to be considered as money, but the technology, as analysed in the chapter, manifests certain characteristics that render the regulation of digital currencies challenging and the transplantation of a regime tailored to the traditional form of money highly problematic.

1. The Evolution of the Concept of Money through Time

New methods and different techniques to enable money laundering do not necessarily alter the nature of the crime. Digital currencies, especially cryptocurrencies, operate in a digital environment separate from the real-world economy. Yet they can still be used to facilitate money laundering in fundamentally the same way. Therefore, the first step is to analyse and understand what money is, to juxtapose it with digital currencies. The following subsection is an overview of the concept of money, the development of digital currencies and their connection with the financial system.

1.1. History of Money: Barter and First Forms of Money

The concept of money is one that has evolved through the years. The classification of 'money' entails three characteristics: (a) store of value, (b) medium of exchange, and (c) unit of account.[1] The first characteristic implies that people can use money for more extended periods of time, as it can store value.[2] The second one promotes money as a means to buy products.[3] The last characteristic dictates a common basis for prices.[4] At a certain point in history, humans started assigning value to objects to develop commerce. Whether these objects are money depends on the definition of the concept of 'money'. In ancient times and in a multicultural world, money took various forms,[5] most prominently that of cash. Technically, though, cash is still a group of objects, ie metal and paper.[6] These objects are practically worthless, but they are money because they encompass the three characteristics outlined above.

The interconnection between money and value is linked to the human need for commerce and trade. The initial form of trade was barter. In this form, people exchanged one object for another.[7] These objects do not have fixed values; therefore, it depends on the traders to assign the ratio between two objects. The barter best operates in a particular area and precisely when the traders live close to each other.[8] Lastly, barter is coincidental, ie in order for the exchange to take place, one trader must be willing to accept what the other trader offers.[9]

Eventually, barter was deemed inadequate for the evolution of trade. In different parts of the world, people began to use commodities.[10] Some products that were used as commodities included salt, tobacco, almonds, barley, butter, dried cod, etc.[11] Tellingly, Weatherford points out that, etymologically, the English word *salary* is derived from the Latin word *salrius*, which means 'of salt'.[12] The use of commodities resolved some problems associated with barter because commodities had a dual purpose. These products served as means of payment and units of

[1] Simon Gleeson, *The Legal Concept of Money* (Oxford University Press, 2018) 7; Irena Asmundson and Ceyda Oner, 'Back to Basics: What is Money?' (International Monetary Fund, September 2012), www.imf.org/external/pubs/ft/fandd/2012/09/basics.htm; Nishibe points out that there are four characteristics, adding to the list the 'Money as a means of payment' function in Makoto Nishibe, *The Enigma of Money: Gold, Central Banknotes, and Bitcoin* (Springer, 2016) 38; however, it can be argued that the characteristic of 'medium of exchange' includes the characteristic added by Nishibe. See further on the history of money, Jack Weatherford, *The History of Money* (Crown Publishers, 1997).

[2] Asmundson and Oner (n 1).

[3] ibid.

[4] ibid.

[5] John Madinger, *Money Laundering: A Guide for Criminal Investigators*, 3rd edn (CRC Press, Taylor & Francis Group, 2012) 1.

[6] ibid.

[7] ibid.

[8] ibid 2.

[9] Also known as the 'double coincidence of wants' mentioned by Henri Arslanian, *The Book of Crypto: The Complete Guide to Understand Bitcoin, Cryptocurrencies and Digital Assets* (Palgrave Macmillan, 2022) 2.

[10] Weatherford (n 1) 20; The Oxford online dictionary explains commodity as 'a product or a raw material that can be bought and sold', www.oxfordlearnersdictionaries.com/definition/english/commodity?q=commodity.

[11] Weatherford (n 1) 20–21.

[12] Weatherford (n 1) 21; Also, based on the Oxford online dictionary, the origin of the word *salary* is the Latin word *sal* (salt), www.oxfordlearnersdictionaries.com/definition/english/commodity?q=commodity.

account.[13] Therefore, certain products served as a benchmark value to calculate the value of other products.[14] To this end, Einzig described such units or objects as 'primitive money'.[15]

These forms of 'consumable commodities' failed to satisfy the last characteristic of money, ie the store of value.[16] Only strong materials that can last over time can store value, therefore generating the opportunity to exchange them after more extended periods.[17] However, these forms of money have value because of their functionality within a culture.[18] Cowrie shells, for example, were at some point a commodity in Africa, although these objects were of no value for the rest of the world.[19] Eventually, societies moved on to use precious metals.[20] There is evidence that in Mesopotamia, in 2500 BC, silver was used as a means of exchange, although, due to its value, it was limited only to trades with a high number of products.[21]

1.2. The Invention of Coins and the New Era of Money

There is a debate regarding the invention of coins derived from metal. It is generally accepted that China was the first region (around the 2nd millennium BC) to use objects similar to coins produced from metal.[22] The materials of the coins were base metals (bronze and copper). Therefore, the coins as objects did not have the value of precious metals like gold or silver.[23] However, these coins had two main weaknesses. First, it was relatively easy to imitate the unsophisticated process and produce counterfeit coins due to the fact that the base materials were not very expensive and easily accessible.[24] Second, these coins held low value; therefore, it was still necessary to weigh precious metals to calculate value.[25] Consequently, China was the first to introduce this method of payment, but due to the disadvantages of the system, other parts of the world found a different path.[26]

China may have used a method of payment similar to what we understand today as 'coins'; however, the first minted coins can be traced back to the kingdom

[13] Benjamin Geva, 'Cryptocurrencies and the Evolution of Banking, Money and Payments' in Chris Brummer (ed), *Cryptoassets: Legal, Regulatory and Monetary Perspectives* (Oxford University Press, 2019) 15.

[14] ibid.

[15] Paul Einzig, *Primitive Money: In its ethnological, Historical and Economic Aspects*, 2nd edn (Pergamon Press, 1966) 317.

[16] Weatherford (n 1) 23; Asmundson and Oner (n 1).

[17] Weatherford (n 1) 23.

[18] Einzig (n 15) 15; Einzig argues that these objects are 'social institution'; Nishibe (n 1) 35.

[19] Weatherford (n 1) 24; Arslanian (n 9) 6–7.

[20] William Ridgeway, *The Origin of Metallic Currency and Weight Standards* (Cambridge University Press, 1892) 114.

[21] Weatherford (n 1) 27; Arslanian (n 9) 11; Geva (n 13).

[22] Glyn Davies, *A History of Money*, 4th edn (University of Wales Press, 2016) 58. According to Weatherford (n 1) 30, Lydia was the first one (640–630 BC) to mint coins.

[23] ibid.

[24] Arslanian (n 9) 12.

[25] Arslanian (n 9) 12.

[26] Davies (n 22) 58.

of Lydia.[27] Lydian coins were made of precious metals, namely electrum, a natural alloy of gold and silver.[28] The coins were stamped with the symbol of the lion, guaranteeing their authenticity.[29] This way, Lydians managed to resolve the issue of fake coins, and they also abolished the need to weigh the gold (the coins had the same weight).[30] As a consequence, this system made the transactions faster. Weatherford argues that the establishment of this payment system created the first shops, namely, commercial brothels and gambling establishments.[31]

Until the invention of coins, many civilisations worldwide had their own systems. However, one particular civilisation saw a rapid development, namely the Greeks. A lesser known element is that scholars like Plato and Aristotle had interesting opinions about money.[32] Plato disagreed with the value of the coins and argued that money should be valueless; he also advocated outlawing gold and silver.[33] Aristotle was not an opponent of money *per se*, but established theories about the market, taking the view that the centre of the transaction was the parties and not the object.[34]

The Greeks saw the importance of money and became the first civilisation to be transformed by this invention.[35] The Greeks incorporated 'money' into society and created a financial system.[36] This new system helped transform Greece into a powerful state, which managed to defeat the Persians during the Greco-Persian Wars.[37] Soon after, in ancient Greece, Alexander the Great was born. In 336 BC, Alexander took the throne. After every conquest, he established a new mint in each land so that the empire would have the same system.[38] Alexander minted coins with his image, took all the decisions about the system and successfully used the money to influence conquered civilisations.[39]

1.3. From Metal to Paper and from Paper to Plastic

China was the first country to incorporate paper money.[40] Each paper (bill) had the same value as a certain amount of gold or silver. Like Alexander the Great, Kublai Khan (the Mongol emperor of China) saw the importance of control over

[27] James DiBiasio, *Cowries to Crypto: The History of Money, Currency and Wealth* (OANDA, 2020) 18; Weatherford (n 1) 30; Lydia was a kingdom during the Iron Age (1200–546 BC), located between the Hellenic and the Persian worlds. The Kingdom was later conquered (546 BC) by the Persian Empire.
[28] DiBiasio (n 27) 18; Weatherford (n 1) 30–31.
[29] DiBiasio (n 27) 18; Weatherford (n 1) 30–31.
[30] Weatherford (n 1) 30–31.
[31] Weatherford (n 1) 30–32; DiBiasio (n 27) 21.
[32] Weatherford (n 1) 41.
[33] Weatherford (n 1) 41.
[34] Weatherford (n 1) 42.
[35] Weatherford (n 1) 43.
[36] Geva (n 13).
[37] DiBiasio (n 27) 29.
[38] DiBiasio (n 27) 34.
[39] DiBiasio (n 27) 34.
[40] Weatherford (n 1) 126.

money. To ensure the use of these bills by the people, Kublai confiscated all the gold and silver.[41] The emperor used paper money to control the system and to gather precious metals. The main difficulty was in convincing people that a piece of paper had a value greater than the paper itself.

The Dutch, the British and the Americans incorporated paper money into their societies and began to build on the financial and banking systems from 1600 onwards.[42] After the end of the First World War, the world faced a global depression, and by the end of the Second World War, nations were determined not to repeat past mistakes. Even before the end of the war, the United States met with 44 other countries in New Hampshire to decide on the new international monetary system.[43] In this new system, everything was comparable to the dollar, and it was agreed that the dollar would be tied to gold ($35 per ounce of gold).[44] This system was called Bretton Woods, taking its name from the area where the meeting was held.[45] The Bretton Woods system collapsed in 1971 after the failure of the United States to redeem dollars for gold at the agreed rate.[46]

A series of events led to an expansion of international trade. In 1991, the Soviet Union collapsed, and the newly independent countries began to fall in line with the Western system, along with the resurfacing of China.[47]

While the international monetary system was developing, the world was introduced to various financial innovations. Beginning in the 1950s, Diners Club released a plastic card for payments, with 10,000 members.[48] After the first 'plastic cards', many companies decided to introduce this payment method, including American Express and Barclays.[49] The purpose of this financial innovation was twofold: first, to make trade more accessible and bring purchasers and vendors closer together, and, second, to improve the everyday lives of people globally.

Despite these developments, the system was and still is susceptible to crisis. The two most recent examples are the financial crisis in Asia in 1997 and the global financial crisis in 2008.[50] There were many reasons that led to the last crisis, including severe miscalculations from financial institutions.[51] The start of the global crisis came with the collapse of a colossal financial institution, Lehman Brothers. It continued with the near-collapse of the American International Group, the largest

[41] Weatherford (n 1) 127.
[42] Arslanian (n 9) 28–35.
[43] Weatherford (n 1) 183.
[44] 'Creation of the Bretton Woods System' (*Federal Reserve History*, 22 November 2013), www.federalreservehistory.org/essays/bretton-woods-created.
[45] Weatherford (n 1) 184.
[46] 'Creation of the Bretton Woods System' (n 44).
[47] DiBiasio (n 27) 128.
[48] Diners Club International, 'The Story Behind the Card', www.dinersclubus.com/home/about/dinersclub/story#:~:text=February%201950.,world's%20first%20multipurpose%20charge%20card.
[49] Barclaycard, https://home.barclaycard/about-us/; '1963: BBC Home, 'American Express comes to Britain', http://news.bbc.co.uk/onthisday/hi/dates/stories/september/10/newsid_3031000/3031968.stm.
[50] Arslanian (n 9) 38–39.
[51] Luca De Paoli and Jeremy Hill, 'The Last of Lehman Brothers' (*Bloomberg UK*, 18 May 2022), www.bloomberg.com/features/2022-lehman-brothers-collapse-plan-repay-after-bankruptcy/?leadSource=uverify%20wall.

insurer in America.[52] The 2008 crisis was catastrophic, leaving many homeless and unemployed worldwide. However, the crisis marked the starting point of something extraordinary: the Bitcoin system. While the timing has led some to link the two, the foundations for Bitcoin and decentralised finance were laid long before the crisis.[53]

1.4. Fiat Currency and the Banking System

Before moving to the virtualisation of money, it is beneficial to outline some information about the banking system. Banks can be considered financial intermediaries. They provide a link between an individual and the economy.[54] However, there is no clear definition of a bank because it provides a wide range of services to customers as an institution.[55] Banks receive money from individuals and subsequently use those funds for other activities, eg lending and investing.[56] The bank is obliged to return the equivalent amount – after its activities – on demand.[57] Arora argues that the nature of the bank depends on the following: 'A broader approach to banking business, would define the bankers' business as a means of safeguarding and facilitating the exchange of chattels (money) for goods and services, and the accumulation of financial wealth.'[58]

In law, the definition of the term 'bank' is primarily based on the purpose to be achieved.[59] There are specific requirements in order to recognise a legal person as a bank, although the definition may vary due to the multiplicity of services. For this book, the important element is the services banks offer customers. Particularly, for money laundering purposes, the Financial Action Task Force (FATF) does not even use the term 'bank'. In the AML standards, the FATF framed the banking industry broadly using the term 'financial institutions'.[60] The definition is wide enough to capture the services provided by banks, and it is not limited to accepting deposits and transferring funds.[61] This mirrors the purpose of the standards to regulate the totality of services provided by banks to mitigate money laundering risks.

[52] ibid; Andrew Clark, 'AIG's $61.7bn crash sends markets plunging' (*The Guardian*, 3 March 2009), www.theguardian.com/business/2009/mar/02/aig-insurance-loss.

[53] Noelle Acheson, 'Opinion, Crypto Long & Short: No, Bitcoin was not a Response to the Financial Crisis' (*CoinDesk*, 14 September 2021), www.coindesk.com/markets/2021/01/24/crypto-long-short-no-bitcoin-was-not-a-response-to-the-financial-crisis/.

[54] Mathias Dewatripont and Jean Tirole, *The Prudential Regulation of Banks* (The MIT Press, 1994) 1–7.

[55] Anu Arora, *Cases and Materials in Banking Law* (Pitman Publishing, 1993) 1.

[56] Anu Arora, *Banking Law* (Pearson, 2014) 6.

[57] ibid.

[58] ibid.

[59] Eliahu Ellinger, Eva Lomnicka and Christopher Hare, *Ellinger's Modern Banking Law*, 5th edn (Oxford University Press, 2011) 80.

[60] Financial Action Task Force, 'International Standards on Combating Money Laundering and the Financing of Terrorism & Proliferation', 126–27.

[61] ibid.

1.5. From Plastic to Virtual

On 31 October 2008 (the start of the financial crisis), Satoshi Nakamoto published the Bitcoin whitepaper entitled 'Bitcoin: A Peer-to-Peer Electronic Cash System', introducing the world to the Bitcoin network.[62] Satoshi built an electronic cash system that operates perpetually without the need for any third party.[63] The system is based on an independent network that validates and executes the transactions.[64] In particular, it is 'based on cryptographic proof instead of trust, allowing any two willing parties to transact directly . . . without the need for a trusted third party'.[65] In theory, Satoshi deemed the whole banking system obsolete. This preliminary system was designed to demonstrate that: (a) technology can replace financial institutions (no need for trusted third parties), and (b) technology can improve transparency and simultaneously guarantee privacy for the end user.

Sixteen years after the publication of the whitepaper, thousands of new cryptocurrencies have been issued, and Bitcoin is one of the largest payment systems.[66] However, cryptocurrencies were initially met with scepticism. In 2012, the European Central Bank published a report outlining the essential characteristics of digital currencies and highlighting that they have the 'potential to become an alternative currency for drug dealing and money laundering as a result of [their] high degree of anonymity'.[67] Along similar lines, Europol warned that digital currencies are risky due to anonymity and decentralisation.[68]

Bitcoin was portrayed as an evil development for two main reasons, namely its criminal potential and because it privatises money.[69] Both reasons are significantly important in understanding the impact of digital currencies. As illustrated by Alexander the Great's approach towards money, those who control money also have some influence over people.[70] From the economic and legal perspectives, the question of whether cryptocurrencies qualify as money is highly debatable. To this end, countries worldwide are reluctant to give legal tender to cryptocurrencies in order to maintain their ability to control the issuance and supply of money. On 7 September 2021, El Salvador caused shockwaves with a decision to give legal

[62] Satoshi Nakamoto, 'Bitcoin: A Peer-to-Peer Electronic Cash System' (*Bitcoin*, 31 October 2008), https://bitcoin.org/bitcoin.pdf; Primavera De Filippi and Aaron Wright, *Blockchain and the Law: The Rule of Code* (Harvard University Press, 2018) 20.

[63] Nakamoto (n 62); The name 'Satoshi Nakamoto' is a pseudonym; to this day it is not clear whether Satoshi is one or more persons.

[64] Nakamoto (n 62); De Filippi and Wright (n 62).

[65] Nakamoto (n 62)

[66] De Filippi and Wright (n 62); Fabio Duarte, 'How many Cryptocurrencies are there in 2025?' (*Exploding Topics*, 1 April 2025), https://explodingtopics.com/blog/number-of-cryptocurrencies.

[67] European Central Bank, 'Virtual Currency Schemes' (October 2012), www.ecb.europa.eu/pub/pdf/other/virtualcurrencyschemes201210en.pdf, 6.

[68] Europol, 'The Internet Organised Crime Threat Assessment (iOCTA)' (2014), www.europol.europa.eu/cms/sites/default/files/documents/europol_iocta_web.pdf, 41.

[69] Richard Partington, 'Digital currencies pose threat to economy, warns Bank of England' (*The Guardian*, 7 June 2021), www.theguardian.com/business/2021/jun/07/digital-currencies-pose-threat-to-economy-warns-bank-of-england.

[70] DiBiasio (n 27) 34.

tender to Bitcoin, promoting it as a currency.[71] The results might appear mixed, with some adoption in certain sectors but limited overall use and ongoing debate about its economic impact. For now, digital currencies are on the rise, people have progressively become more positive towards their use, and some companies accept them as a means of payment. As digital currencies progressively become mainstream, regulations should adapt to protect users.

2. An Umbrella Concept for Digital Currencies

2.1. Terminology: Virtual, Digital or Electronic

Virtual, Digital or *Electronic* currencies? These terms have been used interchangeably to describe the concept of currencies covered in this book. Nevertheless, there are different standpoints concerning the most appropriate term with which to refer to these currencies. That said, the term 'e-money' will not be used to avoid misconceptions; under the EU, it has a specific meaning. In particular, pursuant to the Electronic Money Directive, 'e-money':

> means electronically, including magnetically, stored monetary value as represented by a claim on the issuer which is issued on receipt of funds for the purpose of making payment transactions as defined in point 5 of Article 4 of Directive 2007/64/EC, and which is accepted by a natural or legal person other than the electronic money issuer.[72]

Based on this definition, digital currencies should not be confused with e-money since e-money is, essentially, the digital representation of fiat money, ie paper money and currencies issued by banks, eg the Euro, the British pound, etc.

The term 'virtual' denotes something close to reality but not precisely real.[73] 'Digital' relates *inter alia* to computer technology; it involves digital data and/or the use of a computer or other devices.[74] According to Andrew Wagner, the term 'digital' constitutes an umbrella definition in the sense that it encompasses the term 'virtual'.[75] On that premise, all virtual currencies are digital currencies, but not all digital currencies are virtual currencies.[76] According to the *Oxford English*

[71] Fernado E. Alvarez, David Argente and Diana Van Patten, 'Are Cryptocurrencies Currencies? Bitcoin as Legal Tender in El Salvador' (2022) National Bureau of Economic Research Working Paper 29968, 1, www.nber.org/system/files/working_papers/w29968/w29968.pdf.

[72] Directive 2009/110/EC of the European Parliament and of the Council of 16 September 2009 on the taking up, pursuit and prudential supervision of the business of electronic money institutions amending Directives 2005/60/EC and 2006/48/EC and repealing Directive 2000/46/EC [2009] OJ L267/7, Art 2(2).

[73] David Lee, *Handbook of digital currency: bitcoin, innovation, financial instruments, and big data* (Elsevier/AP, 2015) 6.

[74] *Oxford English Dictionary* (OED Online, Oxford University Press); 'digital' (2014).

[75] Andrew Wagner, 'Digital Vs Virtual Currencies', (*BITCOIN Magazine*, 22 August 2014), https://bitcoinmagazine.com/articles/digital-vs-virtual-currencies-1408735507.

[76] ibid.

Dictionary, 'virtual' can also mean 'a computerized or digitized simulation of something; spec. (esp. in earlier use) simulated in virtual reality' and 'established or conducted using computer technology rather than more traditional means'.[77]

There are some differences regarding the terminology of digital currencies.[78] Many entities and organisations have used these terms almost interchangeably in the past years. The European Union used the term 'virtual currencies' in the 5th AML Directive and the term 'crypto-assets' in the newly adopted AML framework, which aligns with the Regulation on Markets in Crypto-assets, while the FATF uses the term 'virtual assets'.[79] For some, the term 'digital' is broader; for others, the term 'virtual' is better suited for these currencies.[80] As noted above, Andrew Wagner argues that 'digital' is a general term for currencies that are stored and exchanged electronically.[81] Moreover, 'virtual' is a more appropriate term for currencies that are only used in a distinct virtual community.[82] Another argument is that the term must be defined by the nature of the coins, ie 'virtual' encompasses decentralised currencies, and 'digital' covers centralised currencies.[83] However, in light of the recent proposal of the European Commission for a Regulation on the establishment of the digital euro, an important distinction should be made between public digital money, eg Central Bank Digital Currencies, and private, eg unbacked cryptocurrencies.[84]

[77] Oxford English Dictionary (OED Online, Oxford University Press); 'virtual' (2014).

[78] Niels Vandezande, *Virtual Currencies: A Legal Framework* (KU Leuven Centre for IT & IP Law Series, Intersentia, 2018) 30.

[79] Directive (EU) 2018/843 of the European Parliament and of the Council of 30 May 2018 amending Directive (EU) 2015/849 on the prevention of the use of the financial system for the purposes of money laundering or terrorist financing, and amending Directives 2009/138/EC and 2013/36/EU [2018] OJ L156/43; Commission, 'Proposal for a Regulation of the European Parliament and of the Council establishing the Authority for Anti-Money Laundering and Countering the Financing of Terrorism and amending Regulations (EU) No 1093/2010, (EU) 1094/2010, (EU) 1095/2010' COM(2021) 421 final; Commission, 'Proposal for a Regulation of the European Parliament and of the Council on the prevention of the use of the financial system for the purposes of money laundering or terrorist financing' COM(2021) 420 final; Commission, 'Proposal for a Directive of the European Parliament and of the Council on the mechanisms to be put in place by the Member States for the prevention of the use of the financial system for the purposes of money laundering or terrorist financing and repealing Directive (EU) 2015/849' COM(2021) 423 final; Commission, 'Proposal for a Regulation of the European Parliament and of the Council on information accompanying transfers of funds and certain crypto-assets (recast) COM(2021) 422 final; Financial Action Task Force, 'International Standards on Combating Money Laundering and the Financing of Terrorism & Proliferation', 135.

[80] Wagner (n 75).

[81] ibid.

[82] ibid.

[83] Jens Münzer, 'Bitcoins: Supervisory assessment and risks to users' (*BaFin: Federal Financial Supervisory Authority*, 17 February 2014), www.bafin.de/SharedDocs/Veroeffentlichungen/EN/Fachartikel/2014/fa_bj_1401_bitcoins_en.html.

[84] Commission, 'Proposal for a Regulation of the European Parliament and of the Council on the establishment of the digital euro' COM(2023) 369 final; Rosa María Lastra and Jason Grant Allen, 'Virtual Currencies in the Eurosystem: Challenges Ahead' (2018) Study requested by the ECON committee of the European Parliament, PE 619.020, 6; The International Institute for the Unification of Private Law (UNIDROIT) uses the term 'digital asset' to cover different types of these currencies. In a recent publication, UNIDROIT drew a distinction between virtual currencies operating on public blockchains and Central Bank Digital Currencies. However, both categories were encompassed within the concept of digital currencies; International Institute for the Unification of Private Law (UNIDROIT), 'Principles on Digital Assets and Private Law' (April 2023) 18.

Unavoidably, the constant developments of these systems deem the hunt for the proper term impossible. Based on the analysis, the author will use the term 'digital' as this term is better fitted for the scope of this book, which covers in-game currencies that operate in virtual worlds and cryptocurrencies. However, since various bodies and organisations use different terms to describe these currencies, some overlap in terminology is unavoidable.

2.2. A Typology of Digital Currencies

Digital currencies include various types of digitalised 'money'.[85] In 2012, the ECB attempted to divide digital currencies into three broad categories.[86] The first category is *closed virtual currencies,* which are not connected to the real world and are used by a closed community, like multiplayer online games, to conduct transactions within the virtual world's environment.[87] They are also known as *in-game currencies* due to the fact that users of such games use them to buy and sell virtual objects or services within a particular game.[88] Two of the most recognised in-game currencies are 'gold' from the game World of Warcraft and the 'Linden Dollar' from the game Second Life.[89]

A second type of digital currency that the ECB recognises are *virtual currencies with unidirectional flow.* In short, individuals can exchange fiat money for these currencies, but not the reverse.[90] As a third type, the ECB lists *bidirectional virtual currencies,* which are used for transactions of real and/or virtual objects.[91] Cryptocurrencies, eg Bitcoins, altcoins, etc, fall under this category.[92] These currencies can be exchanged for fiat money and *vice versa.*[93] However, this is not the only characteristic differentiating them from other digital currencies. Cryptocurrencies are the only ones to use a 'peer-to-peer electronic cash system'.[94] Peer-to-peer is a system in which an individual can interact with another individual without the need for an intermediary third party.[95]

The Bitcoin system is a decentralised network allowing parties to make transactions amongst themselves using the bitcoin currency, while peer-to-peer technology verifies and executes all the transactions.[96] This currency operates

[85] Vandezande (n 78).
[86] The ECB is the central bank for the euro and the organisation which has oversight of the monetary policy of the Eurozone.
[87] European Central Bank (n 67) 3.
[88] ibid.
[89] See eg https://worldofwarcraft.com.
[90] European Central Bank (n 67) 14.
[91] ibid 14.
[92] Niels Vandezande, 'Virtual currencies under EU anti-money laundering law' (2017) 33(3) *Computer Law & Security Review* 341.
[93] ibid.
[94] Lee (n 73) 8.
[95] Nakamoto (n 62) 1.
[96] Lee (n 73) 14.

on the basis of blockchain technology. In general, cryptocurrencies are based on cryptography, and thus, in this system, individuals have an account and two keys, namely a private key and a public key.[97] When a user transfers bitcoins to another user, the transaction is concluded with the private key, and then members of the system validate this transaction.[98] The confirmation of the transaction is called 'mining', which is a distributed consensus system.[99] In order for the confirmation to take place, the transactions are arranged into 'blocks' with high-level cryptographic rules.[100] In effect, those rules prohibit the modification of past transactions.[101]

In this process, users have 'wallets', which help them operate their accounts.[102] Due to the fact that bitcoins have no physical appearance, they have to be stored

Figure 1.1 The Bitcoin Transaction (Blockchain)

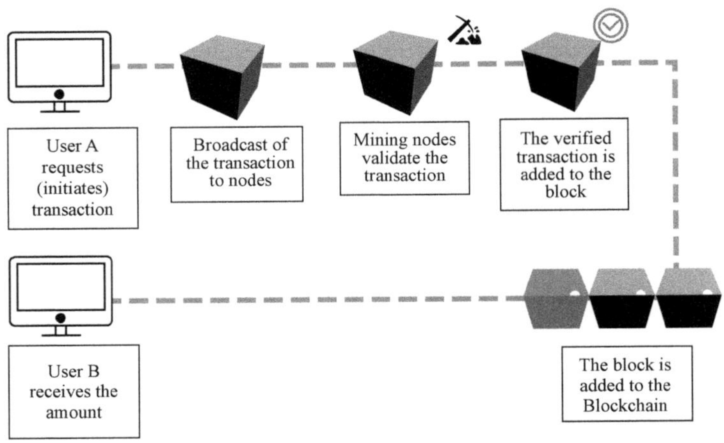

Figure 1.2 The Bitcoin Transaction (Keys)

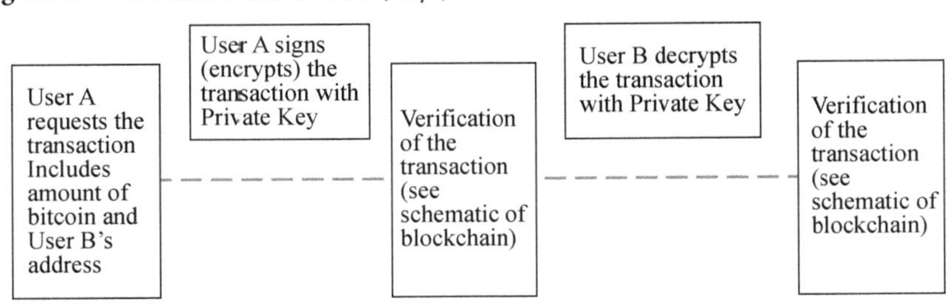

[97] De Filippi and Wright (n 62) 21; the recipient's public key and the sender's private key combined conclude the transaction.

[98] ibid.

[99] See, eg, 'How does Bitcoin work?' (bitcoin), https://bitcoin.org/en/how-it-works.

[100] ibid.

[101] ibid.

[102] De Filippi and Wright (n 62) 21.

somewhere. The wallet can be used to store a user's private key.[103] Data concerning the transactions is stored on the blockchain, which is open to the public due to its nature as a type of distributed ledger.[104] Blockchain might be transparent, but individuals are masked behind pseudonymity.[105] The following section will analyse the main characteristics of digital currencies. The book inevitably uses Bitcoin as a general example for two main reasons: (a) the number of cryptocurrencies is very high, and it is impossible to analyse each one separately; and (b) Bitcoin is one of the most well-known cryptocurrencies, and it has specific characteristics which are common to the majority of coins.

The author also chooses the term 'digital currencies' as an umbrella term because the research encompasses different categories of coins. The first category contains *bidirectional virtual currencies* (ie cryptocurrencies). The second category covers *closed virtual currencies* (ie in-game currencies). Both categories have come under scrutiny for their potential use in, or compatibility with, financial crimes. Even though both types of currencies fall under the same umbrella, they do not share the same characteristics. The following section analyses the characteristics of digital currencies in more depth.

3. Digital Currencies: Types and Characteristics

To understand how digital currencies can be used in various contexts and for different purposes, it is necessary first to comprehend the nature of the coins and their characteristics. This section explains the characteristics of digital currencies, focusing on cryptocurrencies and in-game currencies. Emphasis is placed on three key characteristics of cryptocurrencies, namely decentralisation, immutability and anonymity/pseudonymity.

3.1. The Characteristics of Cryptocurrencies (Bitcoin)

3.1.1. Cryptography

Cryptocurrencies are based on cryptography – which is also one of the main differences between cryptocurrencies and other digital currencies.[106] The word has its origin in the Greek language based on the words '*κρυπτός*' (hidden) and '*γράφω*' (write). Cryptography does not conceal the user's identity; however, it is a technique to secure communications.[107] It has many forms, and one of the most

[103] See, eg, 'What is a Bitcoin Wallet? A beginner's guide to storing BTC' (Cointelegraph), https://cointelegraph.com/learn/articles/bitcoin-wallets-a-beginners-guide-to-storing-btc .

[104] Arvind Narayanan and others, *Bitcoin and cryptocurrency technologies: a comprehensive introduction* (Princeton University Press, 2016) 138.

[105] ibid.

[106] De Filippi and Wright (n 62) 21; the main reason why these coins are named cryptocurrencies.

[107] Arslanian (n 9) 45.

well-known is encryption; but cryptography has a much more sophisticated role in the Bitcoin system. In cryptocurrencies, cryptography is used to protect the system.[108] This is achieved by encoding the rules of Bitcoin in its system.[109] For cryptocurrencies, cryptography can also be used for an additional purpose, which is to create new units of currencies.[110] Cryptography is grounded in mathematical protocols and processes that draw on knowledge from multiple research fields. However, the technical details are not germane to the core argument of this book and therefore will not be elaborated upon here.

3.1.2. Decentralisation

In 2014, the FATF published a report with key definitions for the phenomenon of digital currencies. The FATF understood the decentralised digital currencies as '... distributed, open-source, math-based peer-to-peer virtual currencies that have no central administrating authority and no central monitoring or oversight ...'. Some examples include Bitcoin, LiteCoin, and Ripple.[111] With this definition, FATF intended to depict the decentralised nature of these currencies, which is connected to the fact that the Bitcoin system is not governed by any central authority.

The element of decentralisation is not unique to cryptocurrencies. The Internet and email are also decentralised, despite the fact that some prefer to use certain companies that provide the service from a central point.[112] As an illustrative example, an individual can use a virtual asset service provider for the exchange of cryptocurrencies, although this does not alter the decentralised nature of the system. Bitcoin achieves decentralisation through a series of elements. Comparing the Bitcoin system to a bank, it is evident that the bank exists to regulate the environment of payments, execute transactions, and prevent individuals from spending more than they have.[113] If the Bitcoin system had such an intermediary, then the system would have been centralised.[114] The innovation of Bitcoin is that it allows everyone to become the 'bank' of the system.[115] As there is no central authority, the information on the transactions is recorded on the blockchain (the public ledger).[116] The blockchain of the Bitcoin system is public; therefore, anyone can

[108] Narayanan and others (n 104) 1.
[109] ibid.
[110] ibid.
[111] Financial Action Task Force, 'Virtual Currencies: Key Definitions and Potential AML/CFT Risks' (June 2014) 5; Lexis® PSL TMT Team (eds), *An Introduction to Technology Law* (LexisNexis, 2018) 635.
[112] Narayanan and others (n 104) 27.
[113] Tobias Andrian and Tommaso Mancini-Griffoli, 'The Rise of Digital Money' (2021) 13 *Annual Review of Financial Economics* 57, 60.
[114] Raghava Rao Mukkamala and Ravi Vatrapu, 'Distributed Ledger Technologies and Blockchain for Fintech' in K Thomas Liaw (ed), *The Routledge Handbook of Fintech* (Routledge, Taylor & Francis Group, 2021) 79.
[115] Arslanian (n 9) 51.
[116] Joseph Bonneau and others, 'SoK: Research Perspectives and Challenges for Bitcoin and Cryptocurrencies' (*IEEE Symposium on Security and Privacy*, 2015) 104.

download it.[117] Satoshi described a space where there are no trusted third parties and only the system members are responsible for its function: 'To accomplish this without a trusted party, transactions must be publicly announced, and we need a system for participants to agree on a single history.'[118] The lack of a central authority makes the regulation of digital currencies challenging.

3.1.3. *Immutability*

Once all the participants agree, the new information is added to the blockchain. If we consider the blockchain as a giant ledger with pages, each page is a separate block. To move forward, you need to fill out each page.[119] The blockchain is based on the data that is recorded on the blocks. This data can only be added to the blockchain if there is a consensus in the network regarding the validity of the information.[120] Therefore, it is essential to safeguard the integrity of the system. This importance is justified by the fact that the information on the blocks depicts the order of the transactions.[121]

The lack of a trusted third party creates a series of problems for the integrity of the blockchain. These problems are successfully resolved by technology. There is no need to trust the participants within the system because the technology will protect the information on the blockchain. Satoshi designed a system where information (once recorded) is almost impossible to be altered.[122] Each block on the chain consists of a header which is unique for each block, and each header includes a hash (information about all the transactions in a specific block along with a timestamp and the hash of the previous block).[123] The immutability of the system is structured on the hashes. In order to change one block, you need to change every block before it.[124]

3.1.4. *Pseudonymity/Anonymity*

The Bitcoin system is not completely anonymous. Nevertheless, the fear around cryptocurrencies was based on the fact that the system conceals the user's identity.[125] The truth is quite different. The system is not entirely anonymous.[126] Before Bitcoin and other cryptocurrencies, the world was introduced to new payment systems, such as PayPal, which is not anonymous, given that the transactions pass

[117] De Filippi and Wright (n 62) 22; Narayanan and others (n 104) 28; Lee (n 73) 15.
[118] Nakamoto (n 62) 2.
[119] De Filippi and Wright (n 62) 22.
[120] ibid 24.
[121] Arslanian (n 9) 51–53.
[122] De Filippi and Wright (n 62) 23.
[123] Narayanan and others (n 104) 10–12; In De Filippi and Wright (n 62) 22–23, the authors describe the hash as a unique fingerprint.
[124] Arslanian (n 9) 54.
[125] Nishibe (n 1) 50.
[126] Jerry Brito and Andrea Castillo, 'Bitcoin: A primer for policymakers' (2013) 29(4) *Policy* 3, 5

through third-party intermediaries. Those third parties collect data concerning the identities of both the sender and the recipient. Using a simplified example, if X wants to transfer money to Z using PayPal, then the system will have a record of this transaction and also gather information about the parties' identities. This is probably because PayPal accounts are linked with credit card numbers or bank accounts. However, if the transaction takes place in the real world with cash, and both X and Z do not know each other, then the transaction is completely anonymous.[127]

Bitcoin transactions are undertaken somewhere in between the two examples above. A Bitcoin transaction occurs online using two addresses, ie that of the sender and that of the recipient. However, given that this transaction is conducted within the Bitcoin system, no third-party intermediaries can gather the necessary information.[128] This concerns only the user's data because the information regarding the transaction is recorded on the blockchain itself.[129]

To understand the anonymity of Bitcoin, we must first understand anonymity as a concept. Narayanan and others propose a dual interpretation for anonymity in Bitcoin:

> interacting without using your real name, or interacting without using any name at all. These two interpretations lead to very different conclusions as to whether Bitcoin is anonymous. . . . You do not need to use your real name to interact with the system, but you do use your public key hash as your identity . . . by the second interpretation . . . the address that you use is pseudo-identity.[130]

Pseudo-identity is another term to describe pseudonymity.[131] An example of pseudonymity is online gaming. When entering a game's virtual world, you create an avatar. This avatar conceals the player's real identity; however, the individual is not entirely anonymous because there are ways to link the pseudo-identity with a real-world identity. This linkability is the core element of understanding anonymity in Bitcoin. To this end, the two terms contain different attributes. Pseudonymity is relevant when the discussion is around the identity of the user. Anonymity within Bitcoin indicates the user's pseudonymity and the transaction's unlinkability to a specific user.[132]

Notwithstanding the true nature of the technology, the panic around cryptocurrencies is based on this alleged anonymity. The legal issue regarding anonymity is, basically, the use of this technology to commit a crime in a manner that will offer the perpetrator the necessary non-traceability. Specifically, some underline that the technology's complete anonymity will increase the crime risk.[133] In the

[127] Lee (n 73) 21.
[128] Fulya Teomete Yalabık and İsmet Yalabık, 'Anonymous Bitcoin v enforcement law' (2019) 33 *International Review of Law, Computers & Technology* 34, 37
[129] Bonneau and others (n 116).
[130] Narayanan and others (n 104) 138–39.
[131] ibid.
[132] ibid 139–41; Malcom Campbell-Verduyn, 'Bitcoin, crypto-coins, and global anti-money laundering governance' (2018) 69(1) *Crime Law and Social Change* 283, 286.
[133] Rajesh R, 'Bitcoin – Genesis, Opportunities, Risk and Possibilities' (2018) 7(5) *Global Journal for Research Analysis*.

event of a crime, it will thus be impossible for law enforcement agencies to locate the funds and subsequently link the sender and recipient with their real-world identities.[134] As reported, in 2019, about 46% of Bitcoin transactions per year were rooted in illegal activities.[135]

3.2. Beyond Bitcoin: Crypto-assets and Other Coins

In the last 10 years, the crypto field has seen remarkable developments and expanded beyond Bitcoin's borders. Not everything in this field is a cryptocurrency, and not all cryptocurrencies are the same. Arslanian categorises and divides different crypto-assets using a simple structure.[136] According to Arslanian, crypto-assets have two major categories.[137] The first category includes three subcategories of fungible tokens: (1) payment tokens, eg cryptocurrencies, stablecoins, central bank digital currencies, (2) utility tokens, and (3) security tokens. The second category encompasses two further subcategories of non-fungible tokens: (1) non-transferable, and (2) transferable.[138] The scope of the book covers only the subcategory of payment tokens.[139]

3.2.1. Cryptocurrencies and Other Payment Tokens

In general, payment tokens are cryptocurrencies with the necessary characteristics to be considered money. But are cryptocurrencies money? [140] Most users perceive cryptocurrencies only as a store of value and acquire them as investments. To achieve all the characteristics of money, cryptocurrencies need to reach mass adoption.[141] However, even then, the state must give legal tender to these coins (the difference between national currencies and cryptocurrencies).[142] Under such circumstances, cryptocurrencies might serve as a medium of exchange (payment) only if the two parties to the transaction agree on this.[143]

[134] Eric Engle, 'Is Bitcoin rat poison? Cryptocurrency, crime, and counterfeiting' (2015) 16 *Journal of High Technology Law* 365.

[135] Sean Foley, Jonathan R Karlsen and Tālis J Putniņš, 'Sex, Drugs, and Bitcoin: How Much Illegal Activity Is Financed through Cryptocurrencies?' (2019) 32 *Review of Financial Studies* 1798.

[136] Arslanian (n 9) 133–34.

[137] ibid.

[138] ibid.

[139] The reason is that payment tokens are closer to what we understand as money. A utility token is a cryptocurrency on smart contracts and is not designed as a medium of exchange. Lastly, the security token is similar to traditional investment assets, eg bonds and stocks.

[140] Gleeson (n 1) 7; Asmundson and Oner (n 1); Nishibe (n 1) 38.

[141] Arslanian (n 9) 138–40.

[142] Charles Proctor, *Mann on the Legal Aspect of Money*, 7th edn (Oxford University Press, 2012) 1.17–1.29.

[143] Charles Proctor, 'Cryptocurrencies in International and Public Law Conceptions of Money' in David Fox and Sarah Green (eds), *Cryptocurrencies in Public and Private Law* (Oxford University Press, 2019) 36.

To answer the question of whether cryptocurrencies are money, it is necessary to consider the prevailing theories. First, the state theory of money encompasses the three characteristics analysed in subsection 1.1.[144] Proctor argues: 'If one adheres to the State theory of money in its fullest rigour, then cryptocurrencies can never be "money" because they lack the necessary origins within legislation and the machinery of the State.'[145] However, Ludwig von Mises criticised the state theory, arguing that 'To ascribe to the state the power of dictating the laws of exchange is to ignore the fundamental principles of money-using society.'[146] This theory mainly concentrates on the state's power to determine what can be considered money, which ignores, to some extent, market practice. Second, the Societary theory focuses on society and market practice.[147] Based on this theory, everything that can be used as a medium of exchange can be considered money even if the other requirements (such as origins within legislation and the machinery of the state) are not satisfied.[148] The two theories present different viewpoints, but only the state theory has certainty and clarity, both of which are necessary for a modern society.[149] Based on this argument, cryptocurrencies cannot be perceived as money because they do not satisfy the legal requirements (state theory).

Nevertheless, the Court of Justice of the European Union (CJEU), in Case C-264/14 *Skatteverket v Hedqvist* regarding VAT on cryptocurrencies, defined the purpose of Bitcoin as 'to be a means of payment'.[150] The Court underlines that even without legal tender, cryptocurrencies qualify as a means of payment if the two parties to the transaction agree on that.[151] Commenting on the decision, Proctor finds it flawed because 'the judgment considers the acceptance of Bitcoin, it does not discuss whether Bitcoin is generally accepted for these purposes'.[152] The comment has its merits from the legal/state perspective. Proctor dismissed digital currencies as money even with Societary theory, arguing that digital currencies must reach a satisfactory level of acceptance.[153] Therefore, according to this argument, digital currencies will be considered money only if they become mainstream.

Contrary to Proctor's view, Athanassiou states that 'to the extent that a VC [Virtual Currency] operates as a medium of exchange for those willing to accept it, as a store of value, and as a unit of account, it is apt to qualify as "money", at least in

[144] Gleeson (n 1) 7; Asmundson and Oner (n 1); Nishibe (n 1) 38; Georg Knapp, *Staatliche Theorie des Geldes*, 4th edn (Duncker & Humbolt, 1923) as cited in Charles Proctor, 'Cryptocurrencies in International and Public Law Conceptions of Money' in David Fox and Sarah Green (eds), *Cryptocurrencies in Public and Private Law* (OUP, 2019) 33.
[145] ibid.
[146] Ludwig von Mises, *The Theory of Money and Credit* (Liberty Fund Incorporated, 1981) 84.
[147] Proctor (n 143) 34.
[148] Proctor (n 142) 1.29.
[149] This is because, based on the Societary theory, everything can be considered money, including future technological developments.
[150] Case C-264/14 *Skatteverket v Hedqvist* [2015] ECLI:EU:C:2015:718, paras 49–52.
[151] ibid.
[152] Proctor (n 143) 37.
[153] ibid.

conceptual and functional terms'.[154] Athanassiou based the argument on the decision of the CJEU mentioned above. This decision's importance lies in the Court's recognition that exchanges between bitcoin and fiat currency were exempt from VAT based on the VAT Directive.[155] According to Article 135(1)(e):

> transactions, including negotiation, concerning currency, bank notes and coins used as legal tender, with the exception of collectors' items, that is to say, gold, silver or other metal coins or bank notes which are not normally used as legal tender or coins of numismatic interest

are exempt from VAT.[156] The CJEU clearly includes bitcoin under the concept of 'money' as the analysis depicts bitcoin as equivalent to currency, bank notes and coins used as legal tender.

The concept of digital currencies has catalysed a heated debate among academics and courts worldwide. In 2014, a court in the Netherlands decided that bitcoin could not be considered money but could be recognised as a medium of exchange.[157] To the contrary, another important decision for the purposes of this book comes from the US. On 19 September 2016, the Judge of a US District Court in New York decided that 'it is clear that bitcoins are funds within the plain meaning of that term'.[158] The criminal case was linked to the operation of Coin.mx, an underground bitcoin exchange.[159] The defendant argued that bitcoins were not 'funds'; therefore, it was not necessary to acquire a licence for the operation of Coin.mx.[160] The argument was met by the Judge's decision that bitcoin falls within the definition. Among others, the defendant was sentenced to five-and-a-half years in prison for operating the exchange, which was used to launder more than $10 million.[161] This case's importance lies in the connection between the concept of money and the crime of money laundering. For criminal law purposes, the Judge saw digital currencies as equivalent to money.

Based on the analysis of this subsection, it can be argued that digital currencies might satisfy, to a certain extent, the conditions of 'money'. Despite Proctor's view concerning the level of acceptance, the CJEU determined that bitcoin is a means of payment because it can be accepted as such. Therefore, it can be argued that the

[154] Phoebus Athanassiou, 'Impact of Digital Innovation on the Processing of Electronic Payments and Contracting: An Overview of Legal Risks' (2017) European Central Bank Legal Working Paper Services 16/2017, 19.

[155] Council Directive 2006/112/EC of 28 November 2006 on the common system of value added tax [2006] OJ L347/1.

[156] ibid, Art 135(1)(e).

[157] Case C/08/140456/HA ZA 13-25 *Rechtbank Overijssell* (14 May 2014) as cited by Athanassiou (n 154).

[158] *US v Murgio et al*, US District Court, Southern District of New York, No 15-cr-769 (AJN), 28 September 2016, 6.

[159] The operators of Coin.mx – an underground bitcoin exchange – were arrested for operating an unlicensed exchange. Among others, they were also charged with money laundering.

[160] A question of whether bitcoin is money.

[161] Bitcoin Magazine, 'Operator of Illegal Bitcoin Exchange Coin.mx Sentenced to Prison' (*Nasdaq*, 30 June 2017), www.nasdaq.com/articles/operator-of-illegal-bitcoin-exchange-coin.mx-sentenced-to-prison-2017-06-30.

issue is not whether digital currencies satisfy all the conditions to be 'money'; the common denominator (from the cases mentioned above and the literature) is that digital currencies can be considered a medium of exchange.

3.2.2. Privacy Coins

Privacy coins are cryptocurrencies with enhanced privacy. They are included in the general category of payment tokens.[162] As analysed in subsection 3.1.4., the concept of anonymity in the Bitcoin system includes the pseudonymity of the user and the unlinkability of the transactions. Narayanan and others argue that if a user seeks privacy, then pseudonymity is not enough.[163] The user has to make sure that the transactions (recorded on the blockchain) cannot be linked with their real-world identity.[164] To achieve this in the Bitcoin system, the user needs to take active steps. However, there are cryptocurrencies that provide higher levels of anonymity. On the one hand, increased anonymity is beneficial for the privacy of the end user. On the other hand, increased anonymity can facilitate crime. The latter brought privacy coins under the spotlight.[165] These privacy coins are also known as 'shadow' cryptocurrencies.[166] This subsection will briefly examine the three most well-known cases of privacy-oriented cryptocurrencies, namely Monero, Zcash and Dash.

By way of a general remark, these privacy coins operate on blockchain technology, and the difference lies in the way in which the transaction information is handled. One of the key features is that privacy coins hide information concerning users' wallets.[167] Monero uses cryptography in order to conceal the addresses of the users and also the amount of the transaction; interestingly, in the Bitcoin system, this information is publicly available on the blockchain.[168] Monero appeared in 2014 and is governed virtually away from any centralised authority.[169] If Monero can provide complete anonymity, it follows naturally that it can be used by criminals.

Dash[170] was also launched in 2014, and its creators claim that they created this coin because Bitcoin was not anonymous enough.[171] When a user conducts

[162] Arslanian (n 9) 133–34.

[163] Narayanan and others (n 104) 138–39.

[164] ibid.

[165] John Harvey and Ines Branco-Illodo, 'Why Cryptocurrencies Want Privacy: A Review of Political Motivations and Branding Expressed in "Privacy Coin" Whitepapers' (2020) 19 *Journal of Political Marketing* 107, 110.

[166] Foley, Karlsen and Putniņš (n 135) 1801.

[167] See, eg, Tiffany Madison, 'Privacy Coins: How Monero, Dash, and ZCash Will Enable True Privacy' (*Medium*, 28 March 2019), https://blog.goodaudience.com/privacy-coins-what-you-need-to-know-975a3460d944.

[168] See, eg, 'What is Monero (XMR)?', https://web.getmonero.org/get-started/what-is-monero/.

[169] Tom Wilson, 'Explainer: "Privacy coin" Monero offers near total anonymity' (*Reuters*, 15 May 2019), www.reuters.com/article/us-crypto-currencies-altcoins-explainer/explainer-privacy-coin-monero-offers-near-total-anonymity-idUSKCN1SL0F0.

[170] See, eg, www.dash.org/.

[171] Evan Duffield and Daniel Diaz, 'Dash: A Privacy-Centric Crypto-Currency' (2015), www.exodus.com/assets/docs/dash-whitepaper.pdf.

a transaction, the Dash system uses a process called mixing to disguise the origin of the coins. Thus, when one performs a transaction, the system mixes the coins with the coins of at least two other users. First, the system breaks down the inputs, and then the wallet sends a message to software nodes called 'masternodes'.[172] When the masternode receives at least two other similar messages, it mixes the inputs and sends the mixed inputs back to the users' wallets.[173] Second, the wallet will pay each break-down input back to itself, although in a different address.[174] The user may choose up to 16 rounds of mixing.

Finally, Zcash[175] allows people to transact with each other without revealing the information of the sender, the receiver or the amount of coins. Nevertheless, Zcash offers the user the ability to disclose any information that the user deems necessary.[176] Allegedly, the transactions within the Zcash system are completely untraceable due to the fact that this system uses encryption called 'zk-SNARK'.[177] The fundamental role of privacy in the cryptocurrency environment is also apparent from the Bitcoin whitepaper.[178]

3.2.3. Virtual Worlds and In-game Currencies

The concept of digital currencies does not encompass only cryptocurrencies. In-game currencies or *closed virtual currencies* (an ECB classification) are currencies that do not have any connection with the real world and are used only inside a closed community.[179] These currencies also belong to the concept of digital currencies, even though they are only used within the borders of a virtual world. The fact that these currencies are only utilised to buy virtual goods or services in the game's environment explains why their existence is governed only by the company which owns the game through the terms of service agreements.[180]

Generally, the virtual world of a game can be considered an integral part of these systems, which explains the argument not to strictly regulate. However, games like World of Warcraft[181] are not just 'games'.[182] Virtual worlds have three classifications. The first is the Massively Multiplayer Online Role-Playing Game (MMORPG), a virtual world in which users can create a character, an 'avatar', and wander in the fictional terrain.[183] The second classification is a virtual world based on the virtual objects that are created by the players. An example of this

[172] See, eg, https://docs.dash.org/en/stable/introduction/features.html#privatesend.
[173] ibid.
[174] ibid.
[175] See, eg, https://z.cash/the-basics/.
[176] ibid.
[177] ibid.
[178] Nakamoto (n 62).
[179] European Central Bank (n 67) 3.
[180] See, eg, www.blizzard.com/en-gb/legal/fba4d00f-c7e4-4883-b8b9-1b4500a402ea/blizzard-end-user-license-agreement.
[181] See, eg, https://worldofwarcraft.com/en-gb/.
[182] Daniel Adeoyé Leslie, *Legal Principles for Combatting Cyberlaundering* (Springer, 2014) 86.
[183] Christoph Klimmt, 'Virtual Worlds as a Regulatory Challenge: A User Perspective' in Kai Cornelius and Dieter Hermann (eds), *Virtual Worlds and Criminality* (Springer, 2011) 3.

type is the game Second Life.[184] The third and final classification is social media, eg Facebook, due to the audio and visual representation of individuals together with the interactive environment which they create.[185]

Despite the various worlds, this research focuses only on those with in-game currencies. This is because only virtual worlds with more complex internal economies can facilitate the crime of money laundering.[186] Two examples will be analysed more thoroughly in this respect. The games World of Warcraft and Second Life are examined on account of their internal economy and previous accusations that users took advantage of the 'anonymity' to commit crimes.[187] Specifically, in World of Warcraft, a player can navigate through the world and gain 'gold' in order to buy virtual objects and boost the power of the avatar; there is also the ability to trade through an auction house.[188] In Second Life, 'residents' can exchange fiat money for the game's currency (Linden Dollars (L$)). At the same time, it is also possible to trade virtual property and services within the game.

The selection of these two virtual worlds is based on their popularity. In 2024, it was estimated that the revenue of the gaming industry was US$187.7 billion, representing a 2.1% rise annually.[189] One of the main elements of these economies is that they operate inside the game's environment.[190] The characteristics of the online environment amalgamated with limited self-regulation and the fact that the laws are not extended to the game can create a fortress of anonymity.[191] Cryptocurrencies and in-game currencies share some common features, eg lack of regulation, anonymity, and absence of face-to-face transactions. Nevertheless, there is an exception to this. In-game currencies are governed by entities (the companies that own the games), they are centrally controlled, and the rules covers any conflict according to the terms of the service agreement (ie in-game currencies are not decentralised).

From a critical perspective, these games pose three main challenges. First, there is no strict regulation for the games as the primary purpose is to provide entertainment, and regulation might be a hurdle for the gaming industry. Hence, the self-regulated environment provided by gaming companies cannot efficiently

[184] See, eg, http://secondlife.com.

[185] Leslie (n 182) 87.

[186] For the importance of the virtual economy of games, see Andreas Karapatakis, 'Virtual Worlds and Money Laundering under the EU Law: The Inadequacy of the Existing Legal Framework and the Challenges of Regulation' (2019) 10 *New Journal of European Criminal Law* 128, 132.

[187] Stephen Adams, 'Online Communities Face Money-Laundering' (*The Telegraph,* May 2007), www.telegraph.co.uk/news/uknews/1551482/Online-communities-face-money-laundering.html.

[188] Angela SM Irwin and Jill Slay, 'Detecting Money Laundering and Terrorism Financing Activity in Second Life and World of Warcraft' (International Cyber Resilience Conference, Perth Western Australia, August 2010) 41, 42–43, http://ro.ecu.edu.au/icr/5/.

[189] See 'Global Games Market Report' (2024), https://best-of-gaming.be/wp-content/uploads/2024/09/2024_Newzoo_Global_Games_Market_Report.pdf, 19; Tom Wijman, 'The Games Market in 2022: The Year in Numbers' (*newzoo*, 21 December 2022), https://newzoo.com/insights/articles/the-games-market-in-2022-the-year-in-numbers.

[190] European Central Bank (n 67) 330.

[191] Clare Chambers, 'Can You Ever Regulate the Virtual World Against Economic Crime?' (2012) 7(4) *Journal of International Commercial Law and Technology* 339.

prevent the commission of crimes.[192] Second, there is no governmental oversight for either the games or their internal economies. Even though in-game currencies are centralised, the companies are not bound by the same regulations as financial and credit institutions. Third, anonymity facilitates the operation of the game's virtual environment because it is not necessary to provide identification details to become a player of the game.[193]

Drawing from the analysis of the concept of anonymity from subsection 3.1.4., it is concluded that, like cryptocurrencies, anonymity in the game is derived from the user's pseudonymity and the transactions' unlinkability. However, in-game currencies and cryptocurrencies have a significant distinction. The distinction is the acceptability of the coins and their connection with the concept of 'money'. Are in-game currencies 'money'? To be 'money', in-game currencies must have three characteristics, namely store of value, medium of exchange, and unit of account.[194]

Beginning with the medium of exchange requirement, in-game currencies are generally accepted within the game. Nonetheless, the requirement implies that the coins must be used as a medium of exchange in the real world. Also, they cannot be units of account as they cannot provide a base for prices outside the game.[195] Lastly, in-game currencies can be perceived as a store of value. The issue with the last requirement is how to agree on the value of in-game currencies.

It can be argued that, similar to cryptocurrencies, in-game currencies must reach mass adoption to hold all three characteristics.[196] Two parties can agree to make a transaction with in-game currencies, though they also have to decide the value of the coins. The general misconception among regulators is that virtual objects of the game have no value, which is the heart of the problem. In-game currencies and other virtual objects have real value outside the game.[197] The question of who sets the value of these objects remains. The answer is that the object owner sets the value outside the game in black markets.

In a report issued in 2014, the FATF explicitly refers to MMORPGs and the fact that the existing rules set by the gaming companies are not adequate to tackle the 'black markets' that operate outside of the virtual world where users can exchange fiat money with in-game currencies.[198] These black markets are not inherently illegal due to the lack of regulation of in-game currencies. On the contrary, they are only illegal from the perspective of the gaming industry because they harm the games.[199] The user can buy 'gold' (World of Warcraft's currency) from another user

[192] Ashley S Lipson and Robert D Brain, *Computer and Video Game Law: cases, statutes, forms, problems & materials* (Carolina Academic Press, 2009) 513.

[193] Leslie (n 182) 55.

[194] Gleeson (n 1) 7; Asmundson and Oner (n 1); Nishibe (n 1) 38.

[195] Asmundson and Oner (n 1).

[196] Arslanian (n 9) 138–40.

[197] Antoine Moiseienko and Kayla Izenman, 'Gaming the System: Money Laundering Through Online Games' (2019) 39(9) Rusi Newsbrief, https://static.rusi.org/20191011_newsbrief_vol39_no9_moiseienko_and_izenman_web.pdf.

[198] Financial Action Task Force (n 111) 4.

[199] See, eg, www.g2g.com/wow-eu/gold-2522-19248.

in a black market (with fiat money), who then transfers the 'gold' to the first user's avatar in the game. Therefore, the first transaction occurs in the real world and the second in the virtual world.

Games must be distinguished, however. In those such as Second Life, a user can exchange in-game currencies or virtual items straight from the website for fiat money.[200] In games like World of Warcraft, a user cannot exchange fiat money for in-game currencies from the game's webpage.[201] Therefore, a player who needs more 'gold' for World of Warcraft can visit specific websites, add a credit card and exchange fiat money for in-game currencies.[202] Interestingly, in the past, the site eBay traded annually over $30 million in virtual objects.[203] However, from the point of view of a company which controls a game, an out-of-the-game market that trades its products, making a profit, can be considered problematic. These black markets gave rise to several court battles in the United States for breaching the terms of service agreements.[204] As a result, in 2007, eBay announced the termination of the trading of in-game currencies/virtual objects through its website.[205]

Thus, objects from virtual worlds, including in-game currencies, have a particular value and can therefore be used for many purposes, including the commission of criminal offences. Notably, on 28 October 2019, Valve Corporation[206] admitted that the majority of the trades of 'container keys'[207] were 'believed to be fraud-sourced'.[208] Allegedly, these keys were bought with stolen credit card details, and the perpetrators were reselling them.[209] But since they cannot receive fiat money from in-game trades, the perpetrators can cash out from the aforementioned black market websites.[210] Additionally, a study by the cybersecurity firm Sixgill found that the popular game Fortnite had been used by criminals.[211] In the same way, perpetrators were exchanging fiat money for V-bucks (the currency of Fortnite) with stolen credit card details, and afterwards reselling them to launder their proceeds.[212]

From the analysis above, it is clear that cryptocurrencies and in-game currencies share specific characteristics but also have significant differences. Both

[200] See, eg, http://secondlife.com.

[201] See, eg, https://worldofwarcraft.com/en-gb/.

[202] See, eg, www.g2g.com/wow-eu/gold-2522-19248.

[203] Edward Castronova, *Synthetic Worlds: The Business and Culture of Online Games* (The University of Chicago Press, 2005) 149.

[204] Moiseienko and Izenman (n 197).

[205] Nate Anderson, 'eBay bans the auction of in-games items' (*arstechnica*, 30 January 2007), https://arstechnica.com/gaming/2007/01/8731/.

[206] The company which developed the game in question, Counter-Strike.

[207] A virtual object within the game that was tradeable; players can buy these keys (with fiat money) to win several rewards.

[208] 'Counter-terrorists win: Financial crime through video games is on the rise' (*The Economist*, 9 November 2019), www.economist.com/finance-and-economics/2019/11/07/financial-crime-through-video-games-is-on-the-rise.

[209] ibid.

[210] ibid.

[211] Anthony Cuthbertson, 'How children playing Fortnite are helping to fuel organised crime' (*The Independent*, 13 January 2019), www.independent.co.uk/news/fortnite-v-bucks-discount-price-money-dark-web-money-laundering-crime-a8717941.html.

[212] ibid.

currencies share the characteristic of pseudonymity, but only cryptocurrencies are decentralised. These differences and similarities underscore both the importance and originality of the research, thereby justifying the choice of coins under study. A comprehensive examination of their characteristics can provide valuable insights into the measures necessary for regulation and how regulation affects the user. Cryptocurrencies have their own economy, which has ties to the real-world economy. In-game currencies operate solely within a game, completely separate from the real economy. Three different forms of 'money', three different economies, and one end user. Can one regulation bind everything?

4. The Technology behind Cryptocurrencies

Although Nakamoto developed the technology underlying cryptocurrencies, the term 'blockchain' does not appear in the Bitcoin whitepaper.[213] While this technology is most commonly associated with payment services, it has a wide range of other applications.[214] The European Commission defines blockchain technology as the technology that 'allows people and organisations who may not know or trust each other to collectively agree on and permanently record information without a third-party authority'.[215]

Admittedly, there is more than one blockchain.[216] There is a large number of blockchains with different functions and characteristics. Two of the best-known blockchains are Bitcoin and Ethereum.[217] To describe the differences among blockchains, Arslanian uses as an example the operating systems of Apple iOS vs Google Android.[218] However, most blockchains share specific characteristics. These characteristics have already been covered during the abovementioned analysis of Bitcoin and cryptocurrencies.

(1) *Decentralisation*: Data can be stored in different locations; there is not a single/central database nor a central authority in the blockchain. However, each blockchain can have a different degree of decentralisation.[219]

(2) *Consensus protocol*: Data are updated on the ledger after the participants reach a consensus.[220]

(3) *Immutability*: Data on the blockchain cannot be altered.[221]

[213] Arslanian (n 9) 121.

[214] Arnold Verbeek and Maria Lundqvist, 'Artificial intelligence, blockchain and the future of Europe: How disruptive technologies create opportunities for a green and digital economy' (2021) Report for DG Connect of the European Commission 32.

[215] Commission 'Blockchain Strategy', https://digital-strategy.ec.europa.eu/en/policies/blockchain-strategy.

[216] Arslanian (n 9) 122; Michèle Finck, 'Blockchain and the General Data Protection Regulation: Can distributed ledgers be squared with European data protection law?' (2019) Study for the European Parliamentary Research Service, PE 634.445, 4.

[217] ibid.

[218] ibid.

[219] Arslanian (n 9) 122–23; Verbeek and Lundqvist (n 214).

[220] ibid; Finck (n 216).

[221] ibid.

Usually, authors refer to blockchain technology as distributed ledger technology (DLT). The two terms are not synonymous. Based on Rauchs and others, DLT 'has established itself as an umbrella term to designate multi-party systems that operate in an environment with no central operator of authority'.[222] Blockchain technology is a type of DLT.[223] Moreover, not all blockchains are the same. The most well-known division is private (permissioned) vs public (permissionless) blockchain.

4.1. Permissioned vs Permissionless Blockchain

The difference between permissioned (private) and permissionless (public) relates to who can participate in the blockchain.[224] The former is a blockchain that does not allow everyone to become a participant and has certain restrictions.[225] The latter is a type of blockchain in which anyone can join without restrictions.[226] For example, Bitcoin and Ethereum are permissionless blockchains, but Ripple is permissioned.[227] Primarily, permissioned blockchains are designed for business purposes. Consequently, these types are not consensus-driven, as the decisions are taken by the blockchain owners. Similarly, most of the private blockchains are centralised or partially decentralised. Lastly, these blockchains are not as transparent as permissionless blockchains due to security reasons.[228] For crime prevention purposes, permissioned blockchains are governed by central authorities having the ability to know the identity of individuals before providing access to the blockchain.

There is no need to analyse the technological characteristics of blockchain technology further. The scope of the book solely encompasses those blockchains that are used as payment services. Notably, due to the criminal aspect of the research, the focus is on blockchains that create challenges for regulation, ie permissionless (public) blockchains.

[222] Michel Rauchs and others, 'Distributed Ledger Technology Systems: A Conceptual Framework' (University of Cambridge Centre for Alternative Finance, August 2018) 15, www.jbs.cam.ac.uk/wp-content/uploads/2020/08/2018-10-26-conceptualising-dlt-systems.pdf.

[223] Mukkamala and Vatrapu (n 114) 80.

[224] Arslanian (n 9) 123.

[225] Zenu Sharma and Yun Zhu, 'Platform Development in Blockchains, Risks, and Regulation' in Maurizio Pompella and Roman Matousek (eds), *The Palgrave Handbook of FinTech and Blockchain* (Palgrave Macmillan, 2021) 308.

[226] ibid.

[227] Developer Resource Center, 'Permissioned Blockchain' (*Oracle*, 18 August 2022), https://developer.oracle.com/learn/technical-articles/permissioned-blockchain; Heikki Marjosola, 'Security Tokens and the Future of EU Securities Law: Rethinking the Harmonisation Project' in Emilios Avguleas and Heikki Marjosola (eds), *Digital Finance in Europe: Law, Regulation and Governance* (De Gruyter, 2022) 364.

[228] 'Permissioned blockchain vs. permissionless blockchain: Key differences' (*Cointelegraph*), https://cointelegraph.com/blockchain-for-beginners/permissioned-blockchain-vs-permissionless-blockchain-key-differences.

5. The Actors in Cryptocurrencies

Within the cryptocurrency system, some actors can provide services to users. From the broad spectrum of the financial system, intermediaries, such as banks, hold clients' funds, facilitate transactions and gather identification information of clients in order to comply with laws and regulations. Banks are the central intermediaries in the financial system, and they acquire complete knowledge of the transactions and the clients, ie the system is not decentralised, and the client cannot hide behind pseudonymity. Who then are the main actors within the systems of cryptocurrencies? The concept of 'intermediary' is entirely null in the decentralised nature of blockchain technology (especially permissionless) since the whole structure of the cryptocurrency payment system is that there are no third-party intermediaries.

Different cryptocurrency systems operate in different manners. The Bitcoin network, for example, is transparent, rendering the transactions publicly visible on the blockchain. By contrast, privacy-oriented coins (eg Zcash) do not reveal the history of transactions, thereby providing an environment with higher levels of anonymity. Therefore, to find a way to regulate these currencies, it is crucial to comprehend how these actors operate. As the focus of the research is the illegal use of these coins, this section will analyse the actors in cryptocurrencies to evaluate their ability to tackle crime and how certain actors can facilitate crime.

According to the FATF, the entities involved with the cryptocurrency payment systems are called virtual asset service providers. These providers include (i) exchanges between fiat currencies and cryptocurrencies, (ii) exchanges between different cryptocurrencies, (iii) transfer of virtual assets, (iv) safekeeping and/or administration of virtual assets or instruments enabling control over virtual assets, and (v) participation in and provision of financial services related to an issuer's offer and/or sale of a virtual asset.[229] From a criminal law perspective, anonymity and decentralisation create opportunities for crime and pose significant risks for law enforcement and regulatory authorities. Therefore, if these entities were at some point obliged to implement identification regimes for their customers, it would be possible to monitor the transactions and link real identities with accounts. This section analyses five important virtual asset service providers. The selection is based on the position that some providers hold as gatekeepers between the real and virtual economy (eg exchanges and wallet providers), but also on their services that can be abused for criminal purposes (eg mixing services, wallet providers, peer-to-peer platforms).

[229] Financial Action Task Force, 'International Standards on Combating Money Laundering and the Financing of Terrorism & Proliferation', 135.

5.1. Exchanges Between Fiat Currencies and Cryptocurrencies

The exchanges through which an individual can purchase cryptocurrencies will be the first step for identification. Obviously, the entities from which someone can acquire cryptocurrencies are obliged to keep records of their clients, even though some of these cryptocurrencies promote privacy. Coinbase, for example, requires its customers' identification details before the exchange of fiat money for crypto-currencies.[230] That is the norm, with some exceptions. Moreover, privacy-oriented currencies, eg Zcash, have as an asset the high level of privacy they provide. Based on this, someone could infer that the designers of these cryptocurrencies are unwilling to de-anonymise their clients. However, this is not exactly the case. Specifically, the Zcash team released a statement in September 2019 describing how the cryptocurrency fully complies with AML and terrorist financing regimes.[231]

Nevertheless, this is debatable. Zcash is determined to keep the transactions of users free of record keeping, which implies that when two users make a transaction with cryptocurrencies and fiat money, there will be no record. On the website of Zcash, under the compliance section, it is implied that, although Zcash will not keep a record of identities (with the option to have shielded transactions), this does not mean that the cryptocurrency does not comply with customer due diligence because the virtual asset service providers can keep records of identities.[232] Zcash announces to users that they will have a high level of anonymity. However, when a user exchanges the Zcash coins back to fiat money and sends this money electronically to an account, the providers will ask for identification details.

To this end, exchanges between cryptocurrencies and fiat currencies will require identification details of their customers for de-anonymisation processes. However, there is a limited number of exchanges that do not require any identification (with a withdrawal limit). Thus, if one combines a privacy-oriented cryptocurrency with an exchange that does not require identification details, the level of anonymity will rise.

5.2. Exchanges Between Different Cryptocurrencies and Swappers

Users who can exchange one type of cryptocurrency for another, eg, buy Zcash with bitcoins, are required to provide limited identification information.[233] In general, regulators were focused on the entities that transact with fiat money (the gatekeepers

[230] See, eg, https://www.coinbase.com/legal/user_agreement.
[231] See, eg, https://z.cash/compliance/.
[232] ibid.
[233] Robby Houben and Alexander Snyers, 'Cryptocurrencies and blockchain: Legal context and implications for financial crime, money laundering and tax evasion' (2018) Study requested by the TAX3 committee of the European Parliament, PE 619.024, 26.

of the real-world economy).[234] Consequently, a user who conducts transactions between cryptocurrencies will enjoy higher levels of anonymity. Technological developments can render regulations inadequate quickly. To this end, these types of exchanges have evolved into what is known as swappers.[235] These systems have automation, do not require any identification details to access them, and allow users to exchange both fiat money and cryptocurrencies.[236] The critical aspect of these systems is that they do not use intermediaries, ie the transaction does not require a centralised exchange. Transactions occur between the blockchains of different cryptocurrencies and, in some swaps, even outside the blockchain.[237] As a result, again, when a user conducts a transaction with these decentralised systems, there will not be any authority to collect identification details.

5.3. Trading Platforms – Peer-to-peer Exchanges

The rise of trading platforms from where someone can transact through a peer-to-peer system raises many concerns, mainly due to their decentralised nature and the fact that they do not require any identification details.[238] These platforms are markets where users meet in order to buy or sell cryptocurrencies and communicate directly with one another.[239] The major difference between these platforms and the exchanges is that the platforms do not transact cryptocurrencies. Instead, they just bring together users who want to buy or sell.[240] Fundamentally, peer-to-peer platforms cannot identify users because of decentralisation and the fact that identification of users remains at the discretion of the party with which they transact. Specifically, in order for X to buy bitcoins from Z through a trading platform, X asks for an identity in order to keep a record in case the transaction was a scam.

5.4. Wallet Providers

There are different types of wallet providers for a user to choose from. Primarily, wallet providers are divided into two categories: (a) custodial wallet providers, and (b) non-custodial wallet providers.[241] The former are third parties that keep the private keys of the users, which means that users do not have complete control over

[234] Europol, 'Internet Organised Crime Threat Assessment (IOCTA)' (2019) 59.
[235] Europol, 'Internet Organised Crime Threat Assessment (IOCTA)' (2018) 59.
[236] ibid
[237] See Jake Frankenfield, Somer Andrerson and Jared Ecker, 'Atomic Swap: Definition, How it Works With Cryptocurrency Trade' (*Investopedia*, 19 July 2024), www.investopedia.com/terms/a/atomic-swaps.asp.
[238] Europol (n 235) 59.
[239] Houben and Snyers (n 233) 77.
[240] ibid 27.
[241] See 'Custodial vs Non-Custodial Wallets: What's The Difference?' (*Medium*, 28 February 2023), https://medium.com/@HaloDotSocial/custodial-vs-non-custodial-wallets-whats-the-difference-kucoin-wallet-web3-academy-3f09818c702a.

their funds.[242] Also, the custodial wallet provider is centrally controlled, and therefore it has complete records of users' identification details. Despite the decentralised and pseudonymous nature of cryptocurrencies, if the user has a custodial wallet provider for the transaction, then the level of anonymity is considerably lower.

Non-custodial wallet providers usually offer software or hardware wallets, which allow users to have full control of their funds.[243] Here the position shifts towards anonymity.[244] A hardware wallet, which can be bought online, maintains the decentralisation and anonymity of the system.[245] This is similar to a software wallet, although in the latter case the user downloads the software on a device.[246] Despite the fact that an entity or a person has developed the software, this does not make them a third party, and they do not have any power over who downloads the software. The important element for these wallets is that the users have full control over their funds and accounts.[247]

Similar to privacy-oriented cryptocurrencies, there are also privacy-oriented wallets, and the combination of these two alongside other anonymisation tools can raise the anonymity of the user to very high levels.[248] Dark Wallet was one of the first privacy-oriented wallets. It was a platform that a user could download and install in either Chrome or Firefox.[249] This wallet provided users with stealth addresses (for every transaction, a new address is generated) and mixing services, thereby providing a higher level of anonymity.[250] However, this whole idea became troubling in 2014 when the Dark Wallet was mentioned in an article by Ali Shukri Amin, an Islamic State supporter, entitled 'Bitcoin wa Sadaqat al-Jihad' (Bitcoin and the Charity of Violent Physical Struggle).[251] The article informed its audience that this wallet would provide complete anonymity.[252]

Dark Wallet is currently non-operational, but it inspired one of the most well-known privacy-oriented wallets, the Samurai Mobile Wallet. Samurai was a Bitcoin wallet which was commonly referred to as 'a bitcoin wallet for the street'. Moreover, its developers – who called themselves privacy activists – advertised that with this wallet a user could circumvent financial surveillance, and they announced that they would not comply with any regulation for the de-anonymisation of cryptocurrency users. To support this statement, when asked whether

[242] ibid.
[243] ibid.
[244] Houben and Snyers (n 233) 78.
[245] 'Secure Your Bitcoin: Top Safe Storage Methods' (*Investopedia*), www.investopedia.com/news/bitcoin-safe-storage-cold-wallet/.
[246] ibid
[247] Houben and Snyers (n 233) 78.
[248] Eimantas Žemaitis, 'Top 5 Privacy-Oriented Crypto Wallets' (*Cryptonews*, 26 June 2023), https://cryptonews.com/exclusives/top-5-privacy-oriented-crypto-wallets-3490.htm.
[249] See Jake Frankenfield, Erika Rasure and Michael Logan, 'Dark Wallet: What It Was, Concerns, Future' (*Investopedia*, 6 July 2024), www.investopedia.com/terms/d/dark-wallet.asp.
[250] ibid.
[251] See Ahmad Helmi Bin Mohamad Hasbi, 'Cryptocurrencies: Potential for Terror Financing?' (CSS ETH Zurich, 23 May 2018), https://isnblog.ethz.ch/technology/cryptocurrencies-potential-for-terror-financing.
[252] ibid.

they would comply with the 5th AML Directive of the European Union, under which certain wallet providers are obliged to gather identification information of their customers, they answered through Twitter: 'The plan? To not be in any EU member state . . . We will not and cannot comply with AML5D.'[253] According to the website, the wallet has been seized by US authorities.[254]

5.5. Mixing Services

Mixing services are designed to provide a certain degree of privacy. In fact, the design of these services is strongly oriented against the de-anonymisation of users. In other words, the service might not even require the creation of an account, given that its role is to obfuscate the origin of the cryptocurrencies.[255] In May 2019, the Dutch Fiscal Information and Investigation Service, cooperating with Europol and the authorities in Luxembourg, shut down one cryptocurrency mixing service called 'Bestmixer.io'. In that respect, Europol stated that the services offered were designed to mix potentially tainted cryptocurrencies.[256] In the press release, Europol underlines that transactions of a criminal origin were detected, and Dutch authorities collected information on all the transactions of the last year (including IP addresses, transaction details and bitcoin addresses).[257] Despite the information gathered, it is unclear how the Dutch authorities proceeded.[258]

Another example is situated outside the European Union. Larry Harmon, the CEO of Coin Ninja, was arrested in the USA for allegedly laundering $311 million.[259] In its statement, the US Department of Justice underlined that these services are actually a crime.[260] This is a rather dangerous statement that could potentially create a precedent on mixing services, meaning that someone who creates a mixing service, eg a developer, may be considered a criminal. Both these incidents have shown that mixing services can increase the user's anonymity.

[253] Žemaitis (n 248).

[254] See, eg, https://samouraiwallet.com; see further www.justice.gov/usao-sdny/pr/founders-and-ceo-cryptocurrency-mixing-service-arrested-and-charged-money-laundering; Landon Manning, 'Dutch Authorities Shut Down Bestmixer' (*Bitcoin Magazine,* 22 May 2019), https://bitcoinmagazine.com/culture/dutch-authorities-shut-down-bestmixer?utm_source=chatgpt.com.

[255] Malte Möser, Rainer Böhme and Dominic Breuker, 'An Inquiry into Money Laundering Tools in the Bitcoin Ecosystem' (2013) APWG eCrime researchers summit, 3.

[256] Europol press release, www.europol.europa.eu/newsroom/news/multi-million-euro-cryptocurrency-laundering-service-bestmixerio-taken-down.

[257] ibid.

[258] Rahman Ravelli, 'Arrest of Alleged Bitcoin Fog Operator Signals Continued DOJ Focus on Crypto "Mixers"' (*Lexology,* 18 May 2021), www.lexology.com/library/detail.aspx?g=b46073d7-0731-42d2-b319-270bd0c17c6e.

[259] Leigh Cuen, 'Interview: US DOJ Calls Bitcoin Mixing "a Crime" in Arrest of Software Developer' (CoinDesk, 13 February 2020), www.coindesk.com/podcasts/coindesk-podcast-network/interview-us-doj-calls-bitcoin-mixing-a-crime-in-arrest-of-software-developer.

[260] United States Department of Justice, 'Ohio Resident Charged with Operating Darknet-Based Bitcoin "Mixer," which Laundered Over $300 Million', www.justice.gov/opa/pr/ohio-resident-charged-operating-darknet-based-bitcoin-mixer-which-laundered-over-300-million.

Conclusion

This chapter was dedicated to the evolution of 'money' and the technology of digital currencies. The evaluation of the impact of the AML regime on the end user will only be successful if the research establishes a basic knowledge of the technology. The conclusion for the analysis of the concept of 'money' is that digital currencies (cryptocurrencies and in-game currencies) hold value and can be used as a medium of exchange, even though states do not provide them with legal tender.

Moreover, two characteristics of cryptocurrencies are crucial for the following parts of the research. First, decentralisation is a novel characteristic of cryptocurrencies, which poses significant challenges. The decentralised nature of the technology renders cryptocurrencies difficult to control. There is no single authority to apply rules, to govern and oversee the system. Therefore, in the case of a crime, the authorities will have to gather information from several entities. The second novel characteristic is the anonymity/pseudonymity of the user during the execution of transactions in the system. Despite the transparent nature of the blockchain, the identity of the user is not known. The analysis determined that the user possesses only pseudonymity, and in order to reach higher levels of anonymity, it is necessary to achieve unlinkability of the transactions. To this end, the user will have to choose the appropriate service providers in order to augment the levels of anonymity, achieve unlinkability and, therefore, protect privacy.

The chapter also covered the case of in-game currencies. The characteristics of in-game currencies are different. Virtual worlds are not decentralised. The company that owns the game has the ability to apply rules and oversee the game centrally. However, the pseudonymity of the end user is, once more, a significant part of the system. Legislators usually overlook in-game currencies and virtual worlds. But setting aside their similarities and differences, in-game currencies and cryptocurrencies pose a major challenge, ie legal uncertainty. The existing European framework, especially regulations regarding the financial industry (eg the AML regime), is designed for traditional systems (eg the banking system) and is not tailored to blockchain technology.

Despite recent reform, the existing European AML regime fails – to a certain extent – to contemplate these developments. The current framework is based on following the money through the traditional path, mainly the banking system, where centrally controlled entities collect data about their customers. The effort to oblige certain entities in the digital currencies' system to apply due diligence and know your customer rules might not bring the desired results. These regulations might even have a negative impact on the end user. The technological characteristics have already demonstrated the problem and the legal gap.

The analysis in this first chapter sets the basis for structuring the research. Due to the difficulty of the subject matter, ie the technological aspect, it is deemed necessary to analyse the technology of these digital currencies in order for this research to be relatable to a broader audience. The following chapters proceed to the legal analysis of the existing AML regime and address the issue of money laundering through digital currencies. Before moving to the more specified framework of the European Union, it is crucial to consider the broader international framework.

2

The Crime of Money Laundering and Digital Currencies

Introduction

The previous chapter provides a basic understanding of the underlying technology of digital currencies and serves as a comparison between fiat currencies, crypto-currencies and in-game currencies. The technology is essential for understanding the analysis of this second chapter. Money laundering is a sophisticated crime with several steps.[1] The ultimate goal of this process is to conceal the criminal origin of the funds.[2] To achieve this goal, it is necessary to go through a number of intermediary levels.[3] The process of the commission of the offence is influenced by the degree of complexity of the organisational structure of the criminal organisation; the type of criminal activities in the illegal market and their infiltration into legitimate industries; the illegal gains produced and the vulnerabilities within the relationships between criminal organisations, banks and financial institutions.[4] In general, money laundering has three distinct stages: placement, layering and integration.[5] Nevertheless, it is debatable whether the three stages are always identifiable (especially in more technologised processes).[6]

Money laundering is a chameleon crime that can be committed through various techniques. Given the technological developments of the last 20 years, criminals now have a new playing field for laundering the proceeds of crime. Technology can be seen as the vehicle for a more efficient process, but the technique of the commission is specified based on technological tools. To this end, digital currencies pose a significant challenge for regulation. The technical characteristics of

[1] William C Gilmore, *Dirty Money: The Evolution of Money Laundering Counter-Measures*, 2nd edn (Council of Europe Publishing, 1999) 29; Jeffrey Robinson, *The Laundrymen: Inside Money Laundering, the World's Third-Largest Business* (Pocketbooks, 1995).

[2] Ernesto U Savona and Michael A De Feo, 'International Money Laundering Trends and Prevention /Control Policies' in Ernesto U Savona (ed), *Responding to Money Laundering: International Perspectives* (Routledge, 1997) 10.

[3] Guy Stessens, *Money Laundering: A New International Law Enforcement Model* (Cambridge University Press, 2000) 83.

[4] Ernesto U Savona, 'Mafia Money Laundering versus Italian Legislation' (1993) 1 *European Journal of Criminal Policy and Research* 31, 35.

[5] Valsamis Mitsilegas, *Money Laundering Counter-Measures in the European Union: A New Paradigm of Security Governance Versus Fundamental Legal Principles* (Kluwer Law International, 2003) 27.

[6] Doug Hopton, *Money laundering: a concise guide for all business* (Gower Publishing Ltd, 2009) 3.

these currencies, and especially decentralisation (for cryptocurrencies) and pseudonymity (for both cryptocurrencies and in-game currencies), attract criminals.[7] However, as the technology becomes faster, the boundaries between the three stages of money laundering are becoming blurred.

This chapter focuses on the commission of money laundering through cryptocurrencies and in-game currencies. At this point, the analysis in the chapter is based on schematics to depict how the three-stage process applies to digital currencies. The purpose of the analysis is to establish whether the problem of money laundering through digital currencies is real, in which case it will be necessary to analyse the policy choices to regulate the digital economy. While money laundering through digital currencies has been subject to some academic scrutiny, the involvement of in-game currencies in this process has hardly attracted the attention of scholars. Mainly, in-game currencies have been characterised as 'unsuitable' for money laundering due to the fact that there is no apparent connection to the real economy.[8] This chapter illustrates that it is not the connection of the two economies that determines the suitability of in-game currencies but rather their convertibility into fiat currencies.

Even though the process of money laundering can be applied (in theory) to both digital currencies, in order to determine whether the problem is real, it is necessary to analyse the available data. The analysis applies a quantification exercise based on existing literature. The purpose is to illustrate if the value of such currencies is substantial enough to be considered a noteworthy money laundering technique and to determine the difficulty of such process, ie if it is feasible to convert such currencies back to fiat currencies. Quantification is a difficult task, but the literature provides relevant data to safely reach the conclusion that the amount of money laundered through cryptocurrencies is enough to warrant action. The problem again lies with the category of in-game currencies, the value of which is unconfirmed; hence, there is no available data regarding the amounts being laundered. To reach a valid conclusion, the analysis turns to research on black markets in in-game currencies, where users can sell these currencies for fiat currencies.

The first section discusses money laundering as a crime and delves into a more theoretical framework regarding the separate harm between money laundering and predicate offences. The second section analyses the three-stage process and its application to cryptocurrencies and in-game currencies, considering opposing arguments, especially concerning the latter. The third section moves on to the criminal abuse of available technology, which aids the criminal's efforts to launder the proceeds of crime to illustrate the complexity of the process. Lastly, the chapter analyses the available data to determine the size of the money laundering problem in digital currency systems. The purpose of the chapter is to evaluate whether the traditional money laundering process is applicable to digital currencies and

[7] Niels Vandezande, *Virtual Currencies: A Legal Framework* (Intersentia, 2018) 278; Jacek Czarnecki, 'Digital Currencies and the Anti-Money Laundering/Counter-Terrorism Financing Regulation in the EU: Imaginary Risk or Real Challenge?' in Katalin Ligeti and Michele Simonato (eds), *Chasing Criminal Money: Challenges and Perspectives on Asset Recovery in the EU* (Hart Publishing, 2017) 287.

[8] Vandezande (n 7) 279.

to determine whether this problem is real. The latter is important, especially for in-game currencies, because they are currently unregulated. The former sets the path for the argument of the book. If the process of traditional money laundering is the same in digital currencies, then the transplantation of the existing regime can, to some extent, be justified. However, if the available technology alters the essence of the process, then there is a need for a more sophisticated approach.

1. Money Laundering

Money laundering is a crime, which can be committed with many techniques and can include many perpetrators.[9] The concept of money laundering was first used to describe the mafia's practices to obscure the origin of funds illegally acquired.[10] Al Capone and his operation dominated the scene of organised crime during the 1920s and early 1930s and are inextricably linked with the dawn of money laundering. Al Capone's 'enterprise' managed to launder approximately $100 million of the proceeds of crime.[11] However, the first international action against the crime of money laundering came much later, especially in 1988 when the United Nations adopted the Convention against Illicit Traffic in Narcotic Drugs and Psychotropic Substances (the Vienna Convention).[12] At a European level, the issue was addressed in 1991 when the European Union (EU) adopted the 1st Anti-Money Laundering Directive (AML).[13]

The process of money laundering is deemed complex as it encompasses several steps to obscure the origins of the funds.[14] It is designed to encompass any property or gains derived from criminal activity, and the objective is to present their source as legitimate. Cox divides the process into two categories: professional and amateur.[15] Based on this division, the former occurs when the perpetrator identifies the weaknesses of the financial system and launders funds in a structured way.[16] The latter is when a perpetrator launders funds more profoundly without covering the incriminating steps properly.[17] Nevertheless, money laundering is an artificial crime conditional upon completing a primary offence. This main crime is

[9] Madelyn J Daley, 'Effectiveness of United States and International Efforts to Combat International Money Laundering' [2000] *St Louis-Warsaw Transatlantic Law Journal* 175; Svenja Berg and Killian J McCarthy, 'An introduction to the challenges of money laundering' in Killian J McCarthy (ed), *The Money Laundering Market: Regulating the Criminal Economy* (Agenda Publishing, 2018) 14.

[10] ibid.

[11] ibid.

[12] The United Nations Convention against Illicit Traffic in Narcotic Drugs and Psychotropic Substances (1988) (hereinafter Vienna Convention).

[13] Council Directive 91/308/ECC of 10 June 1991 on prevention of the use of the financial system for the purpose of money laundering [1991] OJ L166/77.

[14] Gilmore (n 1) 29; Savona and De Feo (n 2) 10; Brigitte Unger 'Money Laundering Regulation: From Al Capone to Al Qaeda' in Brigitte Unger and Daan van der Linde (eds), *Research Handbook on Money Laundering* (Edward Elgar, 2013) 19.

[15] Dennis Cox, *Handbook of Anti-Money Laundering* (Wiley, 2014) 6.

[16] ibid.

[17] ibid.

called a predicate offence.[18] International and European instruments have enlarged the list of predicate offences, leading to a broad list of crimes and many activities that may be considered laundering.[19]

1.1. The Ancillary Crime of Money Laundering and Predicate Offences

An essential element of the fight against money laundering is the criminalisation of the offence. Nevertheless, the offence of money laundering has fundamental differences from the traditional model of crimes. Abrams classifies traditional crimes as conduct 'when a person, acting with the requisite mental state, causes an identifiable harm either to a person or to a property'.[20] If there is an identifiable harm, then the crimes can be considered as 'primary harm, or substantive'.[21] Money laundering is a crime without 'primary harm', and due to its association with a predicate offence, it can be classified as an 'ancillary' crime.[22] Based on the detailed analysis of Abrams, money laundering is categorised as a derivative, 'after-the-fact' crime because it involves conduct occurring after the substantive offence.[23]

Such criminalisation created a separate criminal offence, and liability in this offence is similar to 'accomplice liability'.[24] For both liabilities, the conduct upon which the liability is based does not fall within the sphere of the primary harm.[25] However, there is a significant difference between the two categories. On the one hand, the traditional form of complicity includes aid before or at the time of the primary criminal harm.[26] On the other hand, the liability of money laundering encompasses conduct (aid) after the commission of the primary criminal harm.[27] Ultimately, Abrams reaches the conclusion that the offence of money laundering is best described as 'a special form of accessory-after-the-fact offense, but with heavier penalties'.[28]

'After-the-fact' money laundering resembles the commission of the offence of receiving stolen goods, which is based on past conduct (theft).[29] Abrams identifies

[18] This term is used in Article 2(h) of the United Nations Convention against Transnational Organized Crime, to indicate the crime that generates the proceeds.

[19] Peter Alldridge, 'Money Laundering and Globalization' (2008) 35(4) *Journal of Law and Society* 437, 441.

[20] Norman Abrams, 'The New Ancillary Offenses' (1989) 1 *Criminal Law Forum* 1, 1.

[21] ibid 2.

[22] ibid 2; this is because the crime has a direct or indirect relationship to the primary harm offence; Mitsilegas (n 5) 103–04; Abrams underlines that ancillary-type crimes are 'characterized by group activity or conduct leading up to [. . .] the commission of substantive offenses, or they define as criminal, conduct practised in the aftermath of a primary harm crime.'

[23] ibid 5–6.

[24] ibid 7.

[25] ibid; the criminality of the offence is based on the relationship with the primary criminal harm.

[26] ibid.

[27] ibid.

[28] ibid.

[29] ibid 10; Abrams argues that the creation of the crime (receiving stolen goods) is justified in order to fight a specific target, the professional fence, which is an essential actor of the crime of theft. The crime itself is based on past knowledge rather than on future conduct.

three main similarities between the two crimes: 'both categories require knowledge of past crime(s); both involve the possession of things that are the product of the prior crime; and both often involve activity by professionals in that sort of business'.[30] Nonetheless, money laundering acquires a broader scope of applicability. The receiving of stolen goods is focused on the product of theft, but money laundering encompasses the placement of the proceeds of primary harm offences (not limited only to theft).[31] As a result, money laundering is flexible and adaptable to any primary harm offence which produces illegal gains.

Money laundering is an artificial crime which raises concerns with regard to the determination of scope. Prior to the criminalisation of money laundering, the crime of robbery (for example) was focused on the conduct itself, and as a primary harm offence, the after-the-fact conduct (transactions) was not a separate offence.[32] The artificiality of money laundering is based on the decision of the regulator to carve that after-the-fact (non-punishable) conduct into a new offence.[33] The link between 'primary harm offences' and 'after-the-fact' money laundering generates the question of whether the latter creates a separate harm.[34] Mitsilegas argues that the 'answer to this question is linked with the necessity of this new offence to protect a specific legal interest, and whether the latter is identical to the one of the primary harm offence'.[35]

To criminalise money laundering, it is necessary to determine what 'primary harm offences' can lead to money laundering. Initially, the regulation covered only specific offences. In 1988, under Article 3(1)(a) of the Vienna Convention, the prohibition was limited to the money laundering of proceeds from drug trafficking only.[36] However, in 1990, the Convention on Laundering, Search, Seizure and Confiscation of the Proceeds from Crime (Council of Europe) introduced a new term for the 'primary harm offences'.[37] Under Article 1(a), the Convention used the term 'predicate offence' to describe any 'criminal offence as a result of which proceeds were generated that may become the subject of money laundering'.[38] Nevertheless, legislators worldwide struggled to decide which offences should be

[30] ibid 10.

[31] ibid; the crime of money laundering is primarily focused on the obscuration of the origin of the proceeds.

[32] ibid 8.

[33] ibid 8; Abrams does not speak about an artificial crime; however, he argues that 'These new offenses were created by breaking into subparts the total transaction involved in the commission of a traditional primary harm offense and creating new, separate crimes out of a part of the transaction that was not heretofore generally punishable as a separate crime.'

[34] ibid 8; Abrams argues that there is a distinct harm due to the enormity of the funds involved and the fact that money laundering became regularised. As a result, the commission of money laundering does not seem anymore part of the primary harm. Moreover, the sophistication of the process indicates that it is a separate activity.

[35] Mitsilegas (n 5) 104; Mitsilegas' argument (based on Abrams' observations) can also lead to the conclusion that money laundering is a separate activity (due to the distinction between the legal interest to be protected).

[36] Vienna Convention, Art 3(1)(a).

[37] Council of Europe, Convention on Laundering, Search, Seizure and Confiscation of the Proceeds from Crime (1990).

[38] ibid Art 1(a); Alldridge (n 19) 442.

covered by the concept of 'predicate offence'. Under the 1st AML Directive (1991), the EU chose to follow the Vienna Convention, using as a clear predicate offence the crime of drug trafficking.[39] However, at the same time, the Directive allowed the Member States to define as predicate offences any other criminal activity.[40] One relatively convenient solution is to determine that all 'serious crimes' can be predicate offences that result in money laundering.[41] This solution has been followed by the Financial Action Task Force (FATF). The FATF supported the opinion that the 'serious offence' solution will lead to the widest range of predicate offences,[42] and it maintains the same line in its guidelines. Nevertheless, the EU departed from the approach of the Vienna Convention and started the enlargement of the list of predicate offences in the subsequent Directives.

2. The Process of Money Laundering: The Traditional Form

The classical process of money laundering encompasses three different stages.[43] These stages are as follows:

(1) *Placement*: First, the funds are introduced into the financial system. This can be achieved by placing the 'dirty' money in financial institutions (eg banks) or by purchasing a non-monetary asset.[44] Generally, this is a process of removing the funds from the source (the predicate offence) and converting them into another form.

(2) *Layering*: In the second stage, the criminal makes an effort to distance the money from its origin, trying to obscure the source. This can be accomplished by several financial transactions in order to confuse the trail of the money.[45]

[39] Council Directive 91/308/ECC of 10 June 1991 on prevention of the use of the financial system for the purpose of money laundering [1991] OJ L166/77, Art 1.

[40] Mitsilegas (n 5) 117.

[41] Michael Levi and Peter Reuter, 'Money Laundering' (2006) 34 *Crime and Justice* 289, 332; a solution chosen by the United Kingdom at the time.

[42] Financial Action Task Force, 'International Standards on Combatting Money Laundering and the Financing of Terrorism & Proliferation' (2003) Recommendation 1; the FATF underlines, though, that predicate offences 'may be described by reference to all offences, or to a threshold linked either to a category of serious offences or to the penalty of imprisonment applicable to the predicate offence (threshold approach), or to a list of predicate offences, or a combination of these approaches'. The FATF sets out that the international community should, at a minimum, categorise as predicate any offences 'that are punishable by a maximum penalty of more than one year's imprisonment, or, for those countries that have a minimum threshold for offences . . . , predicate offences should comprise all offences that are punished by a minimum penalty of more than six months imprisonment'.

[43] Mitsilegas (n 5) 27.

[44] ibid.

[45] Karen Harrison and Nicholas Ryder, *The Law Relating to Financial Crime in the United Kingdom*, 2nd edn (Routledge, 2017) 11.

(3) *Integration*: Lastly, the money re-enters the financial system to be joined with other legitimate funds.[46]

Money laundering can be committed through various techniques. A traditional example is cash smuggling when the perpetrator moves money across borders.[47] Other techniques are real estate transactions, transactions with high-value assets, and the use of shell companies, etc.

While money laundering can be conceptualised within these three stages, it is not certain that all three stages have to occur every time.[48] As Hopton argues, the traditional three-stage crime is a convenient way to understand the process but does not always mirror reality.[49] This is usually the case in a more structured and complex money laundering process, where the lines between the stages are blurred. To this end, the process of this crime should not be understood merely in this oversimplified depiction, as it involves a series of actions taking place within the three stages.[50]

2.1. The Case of Cryptocurrencies

The pseudonymity of cryptocurrencies provides a level of disguise, resulting in them being elevated to a choice for launderers.[51] The extent to which the three-stage process is identifiable in the environment of cryptocurrencies merits further exploration. With regard to the placement stage, the funds will be introduced into the financial system by acquiring cryptocurrencies (not necessarily the same type of coin). By doing this, the perpetrators will enjoy the higher level of anonymity offered by these systems.[52] At the layering stage, numerous transactions will occur within the cryptocurrency system, or the funds will be transferred to multiple crypto accounts. This stage can encompass the exchange between different digital currencies and the movement of funds amongst different perpetrators who may reside in multiple countries.[53] As for the integration stage, cryptocurrencies will exit the system and be exchanged back to fiat money.[54] It is not necessary for the funds to exit the crypto environment;

[46] ibid.

[47] For methods of cash smuggling, see Michele Riccardi and Michael Levi, 'Cash, Crime and Anti-Money Laundering' in Colin King, Clive Walker and Jimmy Gurulé (eds), *The Palgrave Handbook of Criminal and Terrorism Financing Law*, Vol 1 (Palgrave Macmillan, 2018) 135.

[48] Mitsilegas (n 5) 29.

[49] Hopton (n 6) 3.

[50] Angela Itzikowitz, and others, 'Nature of Money Laundering' in *Anti Money Laundering Guide* (Sweet & Maxwell, 2017) 250.

[51] Vandezande (n 7) 278.

[52] David Lee, *Handbook of digital currency: bitcoin, innovation, financial instruments, and big data* (Elsevier/AP 2015) 303.

[53] ibid.

[54] ibid.

Figure 2.1 Placement

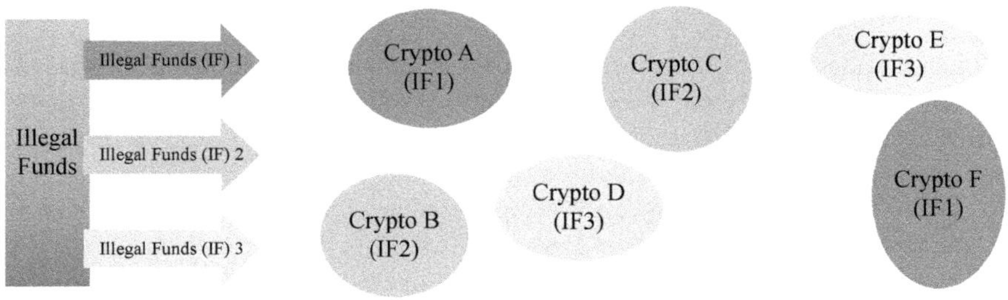

Figure 2.2 Layering

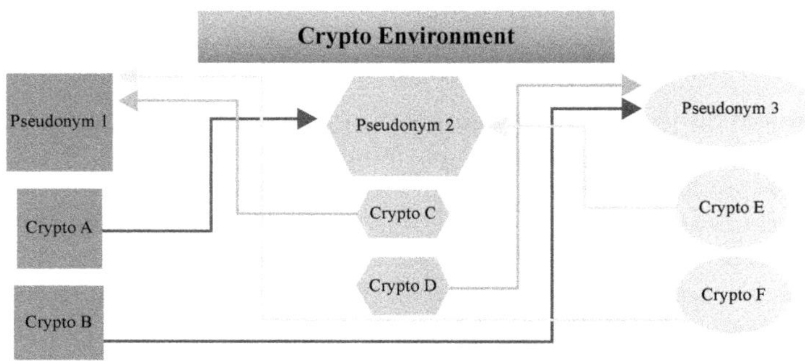

Figure 2.3 Integration

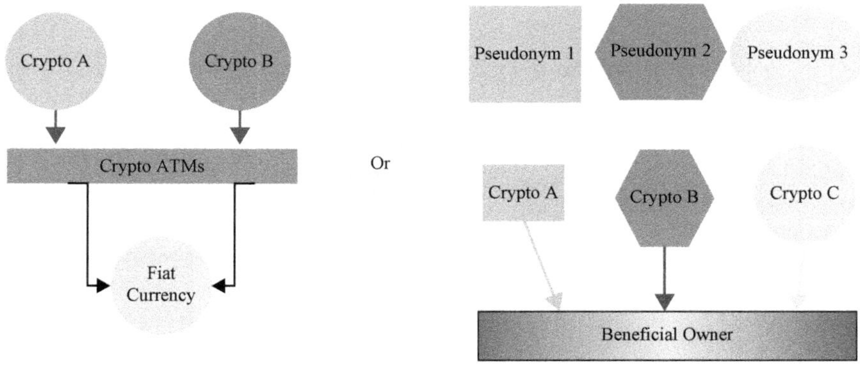

they can also be used for purchases. Even though the stages can overlap, the process can be completed through cryptocurrencies, as indicated in the figures above.

2.2. The Case of In-Game Currencies and Virtual Worlds

The application of the three-stage process of money laundering to virtual worlds and in-game currencies builds upon the overview of these systems from subsection 3.2.3. in Chapter 1. As mentioned, in-game currencies can be perceived as closed scheme currencies because they operate only within a closed community (the virtual world).[55] However, there is a debate concerning virtual worlds that also provide exchange services. For example, the online game Second Life provides the ability to exchange fiat currency for in-game currency and *vice versa*.[56] Those currencies can fit into the category of bidirectional currencies.[57] Even though the Linden Dollar (the currency of Second Life) can be perceived as a bidirectional currency, it does not change the fact that it can only be used within the closed environment of the virtual world.

To this end, Vandezande argues that closed scheme virtual currencies are inherently unsuited for money laundering purposes.[58] The argument is based on the fact that in-game currencies cannot 'leave' the barriers of the virtual world, ie there is no interconnection with the real economy. Nevertheless, the fact that in-game currencies are not connected with the real economy does not necessarily mean they cannot be traded for fiat currencies. For example, in the game World of Warcraft, Blizzard (the owner company) does not allow users to exchange in-game currencies for fiat currencies and *vice versa* through the game's servers (thus, not included in the bidirectional category). This was a breeding ground for third-party platforms that systematise the exchange of in-game currencies. These platforms are known as black markets but are not illegal from a criminal law perspective.[59]

As underlined by Jean-Loup Richer, online games can be an easy way for criminals to launder money due to their anonymity.[60] A user can create accounts in the game and transfer the currencies through them, converting the money to a black market without leaving any trace.[61] The three-stage process of the crime is not formed as clearly as in the case of cryptocurrencies, and the reason is the connection between a virtual world and a black market. Concerning games like World of

[55] Vandezande (n 7) 278–79.

[56] Second Life, https://secondlife.com/.

[57] See section 2.2. in Chapter 1.

[58] Vandezande (n 7) 279.

[59] Robert Purchese, 'World of Warcraft and the battle against black market gold' (*Eurogamer.net*, April 2015), www.eurogamer.net/articles/2015-04-29-world-of-warcraft-and-the-battle-against-black-market-gold; 'black markets' for in-game currencies are not illegal from a criminal law perspective, but they carry that name because they usually violate the game's terms of services agreement.

[60] Jean-Loup Richet, 'Laundering Money Online: a review of cybercriminals' methods' (2013), arXiv:1310.2368; see subsection 3.2.3. of Chapter 1 for the issue of anonymity/pseudonymity in virtual worlds.

[61] ibid.

Warcraft, the most critical stage of the process is the transfer of in-game currencies between accounts within the game. The perpetrator can buy in-game currencies from a user (not a criminal) in a black market, who then transfers the funds to the perpetrator's avatar. Next, the perpetrator transfers the in-game currencies to another account (different avatar), and, ultimately, the currencies are sold again on the black market. Therefore, the last transaction connects the utilisation of the virtual world to cash out in the real economy.[62] The anonymity can mask the transaction at two different points: (i) the real-world purchase to the transfer in the game, and (ii) the virtual transfer between different gaming accounts.[63]

Vandezande's argument concerning the unsuitability of in-game currencies has its merits. The process requires several associates and time to be completed, as the above figure shows. However, this unsuitability is not attached to the fact that in-game currencies have no interconnection with the real economy. It is essential to take into consideration the value of the currency. As in-game currencies do not have legal tender, the market forms the actual value of in-game currencies.[64] There is a large number of offers for the World of Warcraft's in-game currency on a single platform.[65] At the time of writing, according to a platform (G2G: Gamer to Gamer), the lowest price is 0.02226013GDP/K gold.[66] This is markedly low for money laundering purposes; however, a single user can offer from thousands to millions of 'gold'. The calculation shows that a user has to pay 2,226.78 GBP to buy 100,000K (22,267.76 GBP for 1,000,000K). As mentioned above, based only on one platform, there are thousands of offers.[67] Considering the offers and demand for

Figure 2.4 The Intersection of Virtual Worlds and the Real Economy

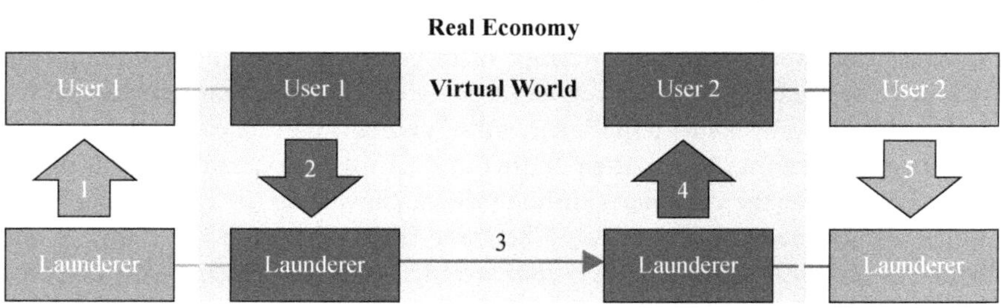

[62] Despite the fact that closed scheme virtual currencies do not have a profound connection with the real-world economy, this stage shows that black markets can operate as brokers to connect the two economies.

[63] Angela SM Irwin and Jill Slay, 'Detecting Money Laundering and Terrorism Financing Activity in Second Life and World of Warcraft' (International Cyber Resilience conference, Perth, Western Australia, August 2010) 41, 42–43, http://ro.ecu.edu.au/icr/5/; these two fundamental points can be perceived as the placement and integration stages of money laundering which overlap.

[64] In particular, the game users will attach a value when they try to sell in-game currencies in black markets.

[65] See www.g2g.com/categories/wow-gold?page=1.

[66] ibid; 'gold' is the in-game currency of World of Warcraft.

[67] Considering that there are a lot of online platforms providing such services, the amount of funds is not marginal.

these currencies, the perpetrator (and associates) can sell the gold afterwards on the same platforms to cash out. Lastly, not necessarily included in the strict category of in-game currencies, a perpetrator can apply the same process using virtual objects (eg a virtual sword in the game). These objects hold value and have similar features to in-game currencies.[68] At the time of writing, a single platform had more than 5,000 virtual objects (for World of Warcraft) at the highest price of around 9,000 GBP.[69]

3. Criminal Abuse of Technology During the Money Laundering Process: Covering the Tracks in the Blockchain Environment

While blockchain technology offers an advanced payment system, it is evident that its international, decentralised and pseudonymous nature makes it vulnerable to money laundering. First and foremost, the Bitcoin website provides several guidelines on protecting privacy.[70] To increase anonymity, creating a different address for each transaction is desirable.[71] To this end, multiple addresses cannot easily be linked to a specific user when a transaction occurs. Additionally, it is advisable to conceal the IP address when interacting with the blockchain, thereby facilitating the Onion Router (TOR) software. [72] In simple terms, TOR is a group of servers allowing an improved privacy status. As the name indicates, the onion has many layers, and users connect in the network via several spots called 'tunnels'.[73] Similar to cryptocurrencies and other privacy-oriented subjects, TOR is questionable as it can provide higher levels of anonymity. One of those reasons is that TOR can be facilitated to mask online activity, ie cover the digital footprint during the money laundering process.[74] Even though there are ways to circumvent TOR – mainly used by law enforcement agencies during investigations – this process is not entirely efficient as the user will be able to reconnect to TOR.[75]

To further disguise the origin of cryptocurrencies, the so-called mixing services can be used during the layering stage.[76] At the time of writing, mixing services for cryptocurrencies include 'Mixero' and 'Bitcoin Fog' (now defunct),[77] which are

[68] This case is similar to cryptocurrencies and non-fungible tokens (NFTs). NFTs are crypto-assets, which is a general category encompassing also cryptocurrencies.

[69] See, eg, www.g2g.com/categories/wow-Item?sort=highest_price.

[70] See, eg, https://bitcoin.org/en/protect-your-privacy.

[71] ibid; the address can be perceived as an account.

[72] An IP (internet protocol) address is a label assigned to devices connected to a computer network.

[73] See, eg, https://2019.www.torproject.org/about/overview.html.en.

[74] ibid.

[75] Perri Reynolds and Angela SM Irwin, 'Tracking digital footprints: Anonymity within the bitcoin system' (2017) 20(2) *Journal of Money Laundering Control* 172, 7; Arvind Narayanan et al, *Bitcoin and cryptocurrency technologies: a comprehensive introduction* (Princeton University Press, 2016) 143.

[76] See, eg, https://bitcoin.org/en/protect-your-privacy.

[77] See, eg, https://mixero.io; https://bitcoinfog.info; interestingly to use Bitcoin Fog, the user had to have TOR software.

anonymity tools to tangle the flow of cryptocurrencies. These platforms return the cryptocurrencies to the owner after keeping an amount as a fee.[78]

Mixing services render the fight against money laundering considerably more challenging when it comes to blockchain-based transactions.[79] These platforms amalgamate different transactions on blockchain technology, which can be identified as the layering stage of the money laundering process. As a result, the mixer conceals the identities of the sender and receiver of the cryptocurrencies.[80] Such services are also known as bitcoin laundering, an unfortunate characterisation, though, because it gives the impression that only criminals use them. However, a user can easily enter the website and then send the cryptocurrencies to the service's address, informing them who the recipient is. The latter will receive different cryptocurrencies from the ones of the sender because the service has mixed them with other transactions.[81]

An additional way to obscure the origins of funds within the cryptocurrency system is the use of certain wallet providers (privacy-oriented wallets) which facilitate the concealment of transactional links and enhance the pseudonymity of the user.[82] As explained, wallets are the services where private keys are saved.[83] Different types of wallets offer varying degrees of privacy depending on their design and functionalities. Similar to mixing services, wallet providers may therefore play a significant role during the layering stage of money laundering.

4. The Dark Side of Digital Currencies: A Quantification Exercise

Despite the theoretical analysis regarding the commission of money laundering through different systems (ie virtual worlds and blockchain), it is crucial to demonstrate that this is a problem worth investigating. The quantification of money laundering is a relatively new concern.[84] In 1998, Michel Camdessus (the managing director of the International Monetary Fund (IMF)) claimed during a meeting of the FATF that 'the estimates of the present scale of money laundering transactions are almost beyond imagination – 2 to 5 per cent of global GDP'.[85]

[78] Malte Möser, Rainer Böhme and Dominic Breuker, 'An inquiry into money laundering tools in the Bitcoin ecosystem' (2013) APWG eCrime researchers summit 3.

[79] Primavera De Filippi and Aaron Wright, *Blockchain and the law: the rule of code* (Harvard University Press, 2018) 66.

[80] ibid.

[81] Narayanan et al (n 75) 153.

[82] See section 5.4. of Chapter 1.

[83] ibid.

[84] See further Donato Manciandaro and others, *Black Finance: The Economics of Money Laundering* (Edward Elgar Publishing, 2007); Brigitte Unger, *The Scale and Impact of Money Laundering* (Edward Elgar, 2007).

[85] Michel Camdessus, 'Money Laundering: the Importance of International Countermeasures' (International Monetary Fund, 10 February 1998), www.imf.org/en/News/Articles/2015/09/28/04/53/sp021098.

Even though Camdessus confessed that 'we cannot guarantee the accuracy of our figures', his statement was criticised due to the lack of sources and evidence.[86] The first notable attempt to estimate the extent of the money laundering problem took place in 1995 when John R Walker, using the 'Walker model', argued that the global problem had risen to $2.8 trillion.[87] Estimations of global money laundering are based strongly on the methodology used.[88]

With regard to in-game currencies, there is no reliable and concrete data concerning the gaming industry at the time of writing. EU regulators largely overlooked in-game currencies in the last two amendments to the AML regime, which allows crime to flourish. Nevertheless, the gaming industry raises considerable amounts. In 2025, it generated $188.8 billion globally, which amounts to more than double the industry's revenue of $91.8 billion in 2015.[89] Evidently, this industry has been rising steadily over the past decade, indicating a need to regulate it to some extent.

Regarding cryptocurrencies, there is some data depicting the money laundering problem through blockchain technology. In 2022, it was estimated that the total cryptocurrency laundered was $23.8 billion, and, in 2024, it was recorded that more than $40 billion was received by illicit addresses.[90] Moreover, in the report of Chainalysis from 2020, it is stated that 1.1% of $1 trillion worth of cryptocurrency

[86] See Peter Reuter and Edwin M Truman, *Chasing Dirty Money: The Fight Against Money Laundering* (Institute for International Economics, 2004).

[87] John Walker and Brigitte Unger, 'Measuring global money laundering: the "Walker Gravity Model"' in Brigitte Unger and Daan van der Linde (eds), *Research Handbook on Money Laundering* (Edward Elgar, 2013); the 'Walker model' has been developed over time, see further John Walker, 'Estimates of the extent of money laundering in and through Australia' (1995) Study for the Australian Transaction Reports and Analysis Centre, Queanbeyan: John Walker Consulting Services; John Walker, 'How Big is Global Money Laundering' (1999) 3(1) *Journal of Money Laundering Control* 25; John Walker, 'Money Laundering: Quantifying International Patterns' (2000) 2(6) *Australian Social Monitor* 139; John Walker and Brigitte Unger, 'Measuring Global Money Laundering: "The Walker Gravity Model"' (2009) 5(2) *Review of Law & Economics* 821.

[88] United Nations Office on Drugs and Crime (UNDOC), 'Estimating Illicit Financial Flows Resulting from Drug Trafficking and Transnational Organized Crimes', Research report (October 2011) UNDOC 9, www.unodc.org/documents/data-and-analysis/Studies/Illicit_financial_flows_2011_web.pdf.

[89] See 'Global Games Market Report' (2025), https://resources.newzoo.com/hubfs/Free%20Reports/Games%20Market%20Report%20and%20Forecasts/2025_Newzoo_Free_Global_Games_Market_Report.pdf?utm_campaign=15407504-2025%20GMRF&utm_medium=email&_hsenc=p2ANqtz--fR95582yZhdfU5t_why0YhbXriKmu7Z93LOLfem93Pz8OQUi-w8E4zsly1DfZrXbsq1gD7jIld9Vz7iAZnEPwBJdgVw&_hsmi=377586429&utm_content=377586429&utm_source=hs_automation; Tom Wijman, 'The Games Market in 2022: The Year in Number' (*newzoo*, 21 December 2022), https://newzoo.com/insights/articles/the-games-market-in-2022-the-year-in-numbers; Trend Micro Forward-Looking Threat Research (FTR) Team, 'The Cybercriminal Roots of Selling Online Gaming Currency' (2016) A TrendLabs Research Paper, www.trendmicro.com/vinfo/us/security/news/cybercrime-and-digital-threats/cybercriminal-roots-selling-online-gaming-currency.

[90] Chainalysis, 'The 2023 Crypto Crime Report: Everything you need to know about cryptocurrency-based crime' (February 2023), https://go.chainalysis.com/rs/503-FAP-074/images/Crypto_Crime_Report_2023.pdf; Chainalysis, 'The 2025 Crypto Crime Report: The rising role of cryptocurrency in all forms of crime and how its transparency is creating unique opportunities for investigation' (February 2025), www.chainalysis.com/wp-content/uploads/2025/03/the-2025-crypto-crime-report-release.pdf; see also Sean Foley, Jonathan R Karlsen and Tālis J Putniņš, 'Sex, Drugs, and Bitcoin: How Much Illegal Activity Is Financed through Cryptocurrencies?' (2019) 32(5) *Review of Financial Studies* 1798.

transactions originated in illicit activities.[91] However, the reports do not specify the methodologies used for such estimations. In the 2022 Crypto Crime Report, Chainalysis underlines that:

> We also need to note that these numbers only account for funds derived from 'cryptocurrency-native' crime, meaning cybercriminal activity such as darknet market sales or ransomware attacks in which profits are virtually always derived in cryptocurrency rather than fiat currency. It's more difficult to measure how much fiat currency derived from offline crime.[92]

Even if we take these numbers with a grain of salt, it can be established that money laundering through digital currencies is a current and growing problem. Europol has also found that the number of criminal abuses of digital currencies has grown and that privacy-oriented coins (which provide a higher level of anonymity) are a major concern for investigators.[93]

The crimes within digital currency systems can be divided into three categories. First, as identified by Europol, digital currencies are the target of criminal activities.[94] This category encompasses the crimes of hacking, ransomware attacks, etc.[95] Second, digital currencies can become part of a criminal offence, eg tax evasion.[96] Third, digital currencies are used to facilitate traditional crimes in a technologised way, eg money laundering and extortion.[97]

This is an interesting categorisation of virtual environment crimes involving digital currencies. When the spotlight turns towards the virtual environment, it is necessary to consider the overall proportion of crime conducted through these systems because, at some point, these funds will be converted to fiat money and reintroduced into the financial system. Interestingly, Chainalysis in its 2020 report referred to the crime of money laundering as the 'common denominator between all forms of crypto crimes'.[98] This solidifies that every crime involving

[91] Michael Kapilkov, 'Chainalysis: Only 1% of $1 Trillion Transacted in Crypto in 2019 was Illicit' (*Cointelegraph*, 5 March 2020), https://cointelegraph.com/news/chainalysis-only-1-of-1-trillion-transacted-in-crypto-in-2019-was-illicit; Chainalysis is a blockchain data platform that provides services, data and research to government agencies, exchanges, financial institutions and insurance and cybersecurity companies in over 70 countries, according to the website www.chainalysis.com/company/.

[92] Chainalysis, 'The 2022 Crypto Crime Report: Original data and research into cryptocurrency-based crime' (February 2022) 11, https://go.chainalysis.com/rs/503-FAP-074/images/Crypto-Crime-Report-2022.pdf.

[93] Europol, 'The Internet Organised Crime Threat Assessment (IOCTA)' (2020) 17; Europol, 'Internet Organised Crime Threat Assessment (IOCTA)' (2024) 13; for an analysis of privacy-oriented coins, see subsection 3.2.2. of Chapter 1.

[94] ibid.

[95] ibid.

[96] Valentina Covolo, 'The EU response to criminal misuse of cryptocurrencies: the young, already outdated 5th anti-money laundering directive' (2020) 28(3) *European Journal of Crime, Criminal Law and Criminal Justice* 217, 224.

[97] Europol, 'The Internet Organised Crime Threat Assessment (IOCTA)' (2020) 17.

[98] Chainalysis, 'The 2020 Crypto Crime Report: Everything you need to know about cryptocurrency-based crime' (January 2020) 7, https://ag-pssg-sharedservices-ex.objectstore.gov.bc.ca/ag-pssg-cc-exh-prod-bkt-ex/257%20-%20001%20Appendix%20A%20-%202020-Crypto-Crime-Report%20Chainanalysis.pdf.

cryptocurrencies (and, in general, digital currencies) will inevitably result in money laundering.

Conclusion

As discussed, money laundering is highly sophisticated and a chameleon crime that can be committed with various techniques. This chapter has focused on the process of money laundering through cryptocurrencies and in-game currencies in order to examine the influence of technology on the essence of the crime. It has illustrated that despite the strict boundaries of the traditional three-stage process, money laundering can be committed with the use of digital currencies. The application of the process is straightforward in the case of cryptocurrencies (see Figures 2.1–2.3). However, for in-game currencies, the analysis is challenging. The research overcomes an argument of the literature that in-game currencies are inherently unsuited for money laundering purposes.[99] The argument is based on the fact that in-game currencies (closed scheme category) have no interconnection with the real-world economy and, therefore, cannot be used in money laundering.[100] This might be correct; however, in-game currencies can be exchanged for fiat currencies and *vice versa* through black markets, which are platforms dedicated to in-game currencies.[101] The argument concludes that the facilitation of in-game currencies for the crime of money laundering is arduous because it is a process that demands time and not because there is no connection to the real economy.

The analysis determines that substantial amounts of money are being laundered every year through cryptocurrencies. The lack of data regarding the amounts being laundered through in-game currencies forced the research to turn to the black markets for a comparison of value. This does not reveal the quantity of money laundering in virtual worlds. Still, the high number of offers of in-game currencies for exchange reinforces the argument that these currencies can serve as a medium for money laundering purposes. Even if money laundering through digital currencies is considered a drop in the bucket compared to overall laundered funds, this does not exclude this phenomenon from the AML regime. The critical point is that both currencies can facilitate crime, which is enough.

In this respect, it is important to make two observations. First, the three-stage process has been used to illustrate that money laundering can be committed through digital currencies and that the lines between separate steps are not completely identifiable in the technologised process of digital currencies. Jan van Koningsveld argues that using a five-stage depiction of the crime is more accurate,

[99] Vandezande (n 7) 279.
[100] ibid.
[101] Irwin and Slay (n 63).

including the justification and investment stages.[102] However, the conclusion remains that technology distorts the stages.[103] The common denominator is that digital currencies cannot be described in general by the term 'technology'. The systems and tools of digital currencies are numerous, which leads to an even more sophisticated crime.[104] The combination of the pseudonymity (and decentralisation) of digital currencies with TOR and mixing services does not alter the harm or the core of the crime;[105] however, it alters elements of the process. The levels of anonymity are considerably higher than those of other traditional techniques of money laundering, and the interaction with intermediaries is lower.

Second, the problem is no longer just a hypothesis. In 2015, Reid argued that, 'The lack of fungibility of crypto-currencies, the limited opportunities and avenues to transfer value and tendency for these currencies to be used for micro-payments . . . mean that . . . crypto-currencies are not a viable vehicle for wide-spread, concerted money laundering.'[106] However, many things have changed since 2015, and based on the available data, funds laundered through cryptocurrencies have increased. The data shows that laundered funds can be noteworthy for a single transaction, even for in-game currencies. The scepticism behind the problem of money laundering through in-game currencies is based on the misconception that there is no connection with the real economy. Nevertheless, in-game currencies can be transferred to fiat currencies and *vice versa*. This research establishes that the problem is real and that elements of the money laundering process have been altered due to various technological characteristics. Therefore, the question is now whether the existing AML regime is adapted to this new technique of money laundering. For this reason, the next chapter will delve into an analysis of the FATF's international AML regime.

[102] See Jan van Koningsveld, 'Money Laundering – "You don't see it, until you understand it": rethinking the stages of the money laundering process to make enforcement more effective' in Brigitte Unger and Daan van der Linde (eds), *Research Handbook on Money Laundering* (Edward Elgar, 2013) 435.

[103] Koningsveld based the argument for a five-stage process on the conclusion that the enforcement of AML is more effective. However, in the technologised environment of digital currencies, things are not as clear as usual, eg the trade between different currencies can be seen as the layering stage (as per the analysis in section 2.1.) or as the investment stage (suggested by Koningsveld).

[104] It is obvious that the process of money laundering through digital currencies and the use of anonymising tools to conceal the steps cannot be executed by someone who has a basic understanding of technology.

[105] See section 3.

[106] Alan S Reid, 'Virtual currency in a virtual world: Virtually unstoppable?' in Nicholas Ryder, Umut Turksen and Sabine Hassler (eds), *Fighting Financial Crime in the Global Economic Crisis* (Routledge, 2015) 185; it is essential to underline at this point that the argument dates back to 2015, and Reid clarified that the threat of crypto-currencies will increase as they become more widespread and mainstream.

3

The International Anti-Money Laundering (AML) Regime of the Financial Action Task Force (FATF)

Introduction

The transnational character of the crime of money laundering compelled the international community to cooperate in the development of a comprehensive regime.[1] Ryder describes money laundering as 'a cancer that undermines the financial integrity of jurisdictions', thus showing the dire need for coordinated international action.[2] On the development of the AML regime, Tsingou argues that there are 'two fronts, prevention and enforcement, and three levels: national, regional and international'.[3] A fundamental step towards the development of the international AML regime was the establishment of the FATF.[4] The 40-member intergovernmental body is the global money laundering and terrorist financing watchdog that sets international standards for action against these crimes.[5] The main contribution of the FATF is its 40 Recommendations, which are 'a complete set of AML procedures which covers the relevant laws and their enforcement, the activities and regulation of the financial system and matters relating to international co-operation'.[6]

As we have seen in Chapter 2, money laundering in digital currencies is a current and real problem. Nevertheless, due to the technological characteristics

[1] United Nations, 'The Impact of Organized Criminal Activities Upon Society at Large: Report of the Secretary General', UN Doc E/CN.15/1993/3 (11 January 1993) 4 as cited in William C Gilmore, *Dirty Money: The evolution of money laundering counter-measures* (Council of Europe Press, 1995) 14; Leonardo Borlini and Franee Jelske Anema, 'Money Laundering Regulation in the European Union' in Killian J McCarthy (ed), *The Money Laundering Market: Regulating the Criminal Economy* (Agenda Publishing, 2018) 55; Guy Stessens, *Money Laundering: A New International Law Enforcement Model* (Cambridge University Press, 2000) 18; Nicholas Ryder, *Financial Crime in the 21st Century: Law and Policy* (Edward Elgar, 2011) 13.

[2] Nicholas Ryder, *Money Laundering – An Endless Cycle? A Comparative Analysis of the Anti-Money Laundering Policies in the United Kingdom, Australia and Canada* (Routledge, 2012) 8.

[3] Eleni Tsingou, 'Global Governance and Transnational Financial Crime: Opportunities and Tensions in the Global Anti-Money Laundering Regime' (2005) CSGR Working Paper No 161/05, 15.

[4] Ryder (n 2) 16–17.

[5] See www.fatf-gafi.org/en/the-fatf/what-we-do.html.

[6] Jackie Johnson, 'Is the Global Financial System AML/CFT Prepared?' (2008) 15 *Journal of Financial Crime* 7, 8.

of these systems, the AML regime must adapt appropriately. A regime aimed at preventing money laundering from a centralised point might not be suitable for the decentralised nature of digital currencies (mainly cryptocurrencies). This chapter focuses on the Recommendations of the FATF to evaluate the current international AML regime in relation to digital currencies. The scope is limited to the prevention measures of the Recommendations and the guidelines for the private sector (virtual asset service providers). The purpose of the analysis is twofold: (i) to determine whether the international regime covers both cryptocurrencies and in-game currencies, and (ii) to evaluate the response of the FATF and establish in what ways the regime has been adapted to the systems of digital currencies.

To achieve this, the analysis examines the evolution of the Recommendations (chronologically) to determine how the FATF decided to regulate digital currencies. Bearing in mind that the Recommendations are standards for domestic legislation, the analysis turns to the definitions of 'virtual assets' and 'virtual asset service providers' to assess the level of discretion left to individual countries to determine what type of currencies fall within the definitions. The influence of the FATF and its Recommendations is significant in the development of the European Union's (EU's) AML Directives.[7] Thus, it is imperative to analyse the international regime first before moving on to the regional (EU) regime. Due to the character of the FATF as an intergovernmental body, the decisions of the regime are taken based only on the parameter of tackling the crime without any consideration of the fundamental rights of the end user. The chapter's analysis, ultimately, aims to discover whether the FATF deviates from the well-established approach of the AML regime for digital currencies to determine any new obligations with regard to virtual asset service providers.

The first section is divided into three parts to set the scene for the chapter. First, there is an overview of the FATF as a body (its purpose and structure). Second, the analysis turns to the main product of the FATF, the Recommendations, focusing on the preventive measures and the obligations of the private sector. Third, the section discusses the legal status of the Recommendations to determine how an informal body like the FATF can produce 'binding' measures. The second section moves on to the phenomenon of digital currencies. The analysis is based on the chronological order of the amendments to the Recommendations to depict the FATF's developing strategy towards digital currencies. However, the analysis begins with the Recommendations of 2003 because there were no provisions concerning technology before the 2003 amendments. The third section focuses on the definitions of virtual assets and virtual asset service providers to establish what tokens are covered by the regime and which private entities are obliged to prevent money laundering. The fourth section continues the analysis of the international regime by investigating the guidelines provided by the FATF to the private sector with regard to the regulation of digital currencies. It is important that the analysis of the FATF's

[7] Borlini and Anema (n 1) 55.

publications comprises a separate section. The FATF produces such guidelines in order to explain to the private sector how to comply with the Recommendations. Therefore, it is essential first to understand the measures and then to analyse how they are applied. The fifth and last section briefly criticises FATF's approach towards virtual asset service providers. The significance and the novelty of this chapter lie in its analytical examination of the FATF Recommendations across different periods, focusing on technology and, by extension, digital currencies, in order to cohesively trace their evolution and highlight how regulatory approaches have adapted over time.

1. The International Response to the Crime of Money Laundering: The FATF

Money laundering was brought into the spotlight in 1988 by the United Nations Convention against Illicit Traffic in Narcotics Drugs and Psychotropic Substances (hereinafter the Vienna Convention).[8] The Vienna Convention prohibits the laundering of the proceeds of drug trafficking, but does not explicitly refer to the phenomenon of money laundering. In July 1989, following a US initiative, the FATF was established in Paris by the G7 Summit,[9] which included the seven major industrial nations and the President of the Commission of the European Communities (ie United States, Japan, Germany, France, United Kingdom, Italy, Canada, and the Commission of the European Communities).[10]

The Summit discussed the major issues of the period's economic setting, with drug trafficking as the epicentre.[11] The focus on the deprivation of the proceeds of drug trafficking became prominent after the unsuccessful US war on drugs.[12] The Summit committed to continuing the fight not only against drug trafficking but also against the connected crime of money laundering.[13] In particular, the declaration highlighted the need for measures to dismantle the operations of drug

[8] The United Nations Convention against Illicit Traffic in Narcotic Drugs and Psychotropic Substances (1988) (hereinafter Vienna Convention).

[9] Maria Bergström, 'The Global AML Regime and the EU AML Directives: Prevention and Control' in Colin King, Clive Walker and Jimmy Gurulé (eds), *The Palgrave Handbook of Criminal and Terrorism Financing Law*, Vol 1 (Palgrave Macmillan, 2018) 35; Valsamis Mitsilegas and Niovi Vavoula, 'The Evolving EU Anti-Money Laundering Regime' (2016) 23(2) *Maastricht Journal of European and Comparative Law* 261, 263.

[10] Financial Action Task Force, 'Report 1990' (1990) 3, www.fatf-gafi.org/media/fatf/documents/reports/1990%20ENG.pdf.

[11] G7 Summit, 'The declaration of 1989' (Paris, 16 July 1989), www.g8.utoronto.ca/summit/1989paris/communique/index.html.

[12] Brigitte Unger, 'Money Laundering Regulation: From Al Capone to Al Qaeda' in Brigitte Unger and Daan van der Linde (eds), *Research Handbook of Money Laundering* (Cheltenham Edward Elgar, 2013) 19.

[13] G7 Summit, 'The declaration of 1989' (Paris, 16 July 1989), www.g8.utoronto.ca/summit/1989paris/communique/index.html; Bruce Zagaris and Elizabeth Kingma, 'Asset Forfeiture International and Foreign Law: An Emerging Regime' (1991) 5 *Emory International Law Review* 445, 460.

traffickers, one of which was the establishment of a Financial Action Task Force.[14] The latter aimed to assess the measures dedicated to preventing criminals from using the financial system and strategically develop new preventive measures.[15]

The first meeting of the FATF was held by France, and it released its first report in 1990.[16] This report outlined that the task force first had to research the extent and nature of the money laundering process (extent and methods). Second, the FATF needed to research and evaluate the existing (for that period) weaponry against the crime of money laundering.[17] Lastly, it was decided that the measures against this crime were quite inadequate, and there was an urgent need for stricter standards. Based on this, the FATF issued a set of recommendations that explicitly addressed money laundering.[18] The recommendations aimed at improving the national systems, cooperating with financial systems and supporting an international wave against money laundering.[19]

1.1. The Purpose and Structure of the FATF

The FATF is an intergovernmental body that sets the standards to prevent money laundering and terrorist financing.[20] As a body, it is not based on a treaty.[21] Its informal nature was highlighted by the 1992 report, which also stated that the FATF needed consensus for the decision-making process.[22] The purpose of the FATF primarily took the form of goals which the organisation had to fulfil to be successful or at least to justify its *raison d'être*. Therefore, the mandate was laid down in the 1991 report.[23] In the report, four tasks were clearly stated. These tasks included:

(1) self-reporting and mutual assessment (monitoring and surveillance) on the adoption and implementation of FATF recommendations by all members;

[14] ibid.

[15] ibid.

[16] Financial Action Task Force, 'Report 1990' (n 10); William Gilmore, *International Efforts to Combat Money Laundering* (Cambridge University Press, 1992) 3.

[17] Financial Action Task Force, 'Report 1990' (n 10).

[18] ibid 15.

[19] ibid; John Drage, 'Countering Money Laundering: The Response of the Financial Sector' in Hector L MacQueen (ed), *Money Laundering: Hume Papers on Public Policy*, Vol 1(2) (Edinburgh University Press, 1993) 65.

[20] See www.fatf-gafi.org/about/whoweare/; Tom Sherman, ' International Efforts to Combat Money Laundering: The Role of Financial Action Task Force' in Hector L MacQueen (ed) *Money Laundering: Hume Papers on Public Policy*, Vol 1(2) (Edinburgh University Press, 1993) 20; Petrus C Van Duyne, Jackie H Harvey and Liliya Y Gelemerova, *The Critical Handbook of Money Laundering: Policy, Analysis and Myths* (Palgrave Macmillan, 2018) 123.

[21] Bergström (n 9) 36.

[22] Financial Action Task Force, 'Annual Report 1991-1992' (25 June 1992) 18; due to the fact that consensus can be reached easier with fewer members, the FATF did not accept any new members at that stage.

[23] Financial Action Task Force, 'Report 1990-1991' (1991) 3.

(2) coordination and oversight of efforts to encourage non-members to adopt and implement the recommendations;

(3) making further recommendations and evaluations of the counter-measures while serving as a forum for considering developments in money laundering techniques domestically and worldwide, and for the exchange of information on enforcement techniques to combat money laundering; and

(4) standing ready to facilitate cooperation between organisations concerned with combating money laundering and between individual countries or territories.[24]

During the review of the FATF's operation and the expansion process between 1997–1998, the FATF did not change the mandate; however, it prioritised its tasks.[25] To this end, the FATF highlighted the importance of establishing a global network 'to spread the FATF's message to all continents'.[26] Two additional tasks followed by the FATF were monitoring the implementation of the recommendations and conducting constant research and review of money laundering trends.[27] Shortly after stabilising the FATF's mandate, specifically on 11 September 2001, the events in the USA altered the whole focus for the organisation.[28] On 30 October 2001, just after the attacks, the FATF held an extraordinary plenary to discuss the financing of terrorism.[29] The plenary report was entitled 'FATF Cracks down on Terrorist Financing', which enlarged the FATF's scope to include measures against terrorist financing.[30] The amendment of the regime continued with a fundamental revision in 2012 when the FATF included in the recommendations the financing of weapons of mass destruction.[31]

Today, the FATF has 40 members (38 countries and two regional organisations).[32] Among those members, there are 15 European Union Member States

[24] ibid.

[25] William C Gilmore, *Dirty Money: The Evolution of International Measures to Counter Money Laundering and the Financing of Terrorism*, 3rd edn (Council of Europe Publishing, 2004) 91. The expansion process sought to address the lack of members from Latin America. In 2000, Argentina, Brazil and Mexico became members of the FATF, and in 2003 the Russian Federation and South Africa were admitted to the group. Gilmore highlights that the minimum criteria for admission to the FATF were: (a) to be fully committed at the political level; (b) to be fully active or be prepared to participate in the work of the FATF; (c) to be a strategically important country; (d) to have already criminalised money laundering; and (e) to have already obliged financial institutions to apply preventive measures.

[26] Financial Action Task Force, 'Annual Report 1997-1998' (June 1998) paras 16–17.

[27] ibid para 17.

[28] Gilmore (n 25) 120.

[29] Financial Action Task Force, 'FATF Cracks down on Terrorist Financing' (31 October 2001).

[30] ibid; Gilmore (n 25) 119–20; Valsamis Mitsilegas, 'Countering the Chameleon Threat of Dirty Money: "Hard" and "Soft" Law in the Emergence of a Global Regime against Money Laundering and Terrorist Finance' in Adam Edwards and Peter Gill (eds), *Transnational Organised Crime: Perspectives on Global Security* (Routledge, 2003) 195–211.

[31] See www.fatf-gafi.org/en/the-fatf/history-of-the-fatf.html.

[32] See www.fatf-gafi.org/about/membersandobservers/.

that acceded to the EU prior to 2004.[33] None of the EU Member States that joined the EU after 2004 is a full member of the FATF.[34] But they are members of MONEYVAL – the Committee of Experts on the Evaluation of Anti-Money Laundering Measures – a regional body of FATF.[35] The FATF-style regional bodies are associate members involved in the FATF's work.[36] This translates to the regionalisation strategy of the FATF. Based on this strategy, the FATF can expand its global AML plans by including countries which are not its members. FATF-style regional bodies participate and support the FATF in its work and monitor their members' compliance with the AML regime.[37]

1.2. The Recommendations

In 1990, the FATF laid down 40 standards (the Recommendations).[38] From that moment, the FATF highlighted that these Recommendations are 'a minimal standard in the fight against money laundering for the countries participating in this Task Force, as well as for other countries'.[39] This statement illustrates two significant points. First, the members must have measures to meet these minimum standards. Second, the FATF stressed the issue of money laundering measures with regard to non-members in mobilising a global fight against money laundering. The Recommendations are broad and flexible, even on a brief examination. Overall, the FATF provides guidance and an aim; how the countries will achieve this is at their discretion.

The FATF Recommendations are constantly under rigorous review and are updated to follow money laundering trends and methods. Notably, research on money laundering techniques is one of the FATF's priorities, and the FATF alters the Recommendations when it has been established that they are outdated.[40] The Recommendations are divided into seven parts.[41] To begin with, there are recommendations for AML and CFT ('countering the financing of terrorism')

[33] Mitsilegas and Vavoula (n 9) 263; Valsamis Mitsilegas, 'Regional Organisations and Suppression of Transnational Crime' in Neil Boister and Robert J Currie (eds), *Routledge Handbook on Transnational Criminal Law* (Routledge, 2014) 73–84.

[34] ibid.

[35] ibid.

[36] Michele Riccardi and Michael Levi, 'Cash, Crime and Anti-Money Laundering' in Colin King, Clive Walker and Jimmy Gurulé (eds), *The Palgrave Handbook of Criminal and Terrorism Financing Law*, Vol 1 (Palgrave Macmillan, 2018) 157.

[37] ibid 158.

[38] Financial Action Task Force, 'Report 1990' (n 10); Mitsilegas and Vavoula call the publication of the Recommendations the 'main normative output of the FATF': Mitsilegas and Vavoula (n 9) 263.

[39] Financial Action Task Force, 'Report 1990' (n 10).

[40] ibid.

[41] Financial Action Task Force, 'International Standards on Combating Money Laundering and the Financing of Terrorism & Proliferation' 5–6 (hereinafter FATF Recommendations).

policies and coordination (R1, R2);[42] recommendations concerning the offence of money laundering and confiscation (R3, R4);[43] terrorist financing and financing of proliferation recommendations (R5–R8);[44] preventive measures (R9–R23);[45] recommendations regarding transparency and beneficial ownership of legal persons and arrangements (R24, R25);[46] the powers and responsibilities of competent authorities (R26–R35);[47] and lastly international cooperation (R36–R40).[48]

The Recommendations have been amended in 1996, 2003, 2012 and 2019.[49] In October 2001 (after September 11), the FATF issued eight special Recommendations to include terrorist financing in the regime.[50] Additionally, in 2004, the FATF published one more Recommendation to reinforce the fight against terrorism.[51] Thus, in 2004, the FATF concluded an action plan – the 40 plus nine Recommendations – which was and still is the most comprehensive and critical set of international standards against money laundering and terrorist financing.

The review that brought the Recommendations into the technological era, improving their effectiveness against modern (particularly with new technologies) money laundering techniques, came in 2012.[52] In February 2012, after a detailed review of the AML regime, the FATF published a revised set of Recommendations.[53] Amongst other changes, the FATF added to the regime Recommendation 15 (entitled 'new technologies') to address technologised money laundering techniques. The first impression was that the new set of Recommendations had been produced to strengthen the regime against money laundering and terrorist financing in the modern era.

Mitsilegas identifies three objectives of the international AML regime: 'the improvement of national legal AML systems, most notably in the field of criminal law; the strengthening of international co-operation; and the enhancement of the role of the financial system'.[54] The third objective is linked to the preventive measures of the regime, and it is the most elaborated area of AML (covering Recommendations 9–23). The preventive element of the regime outlines the

[42] FATF Recommendations 10–11.
[43] FATF Recommendation 12.
[44] FATF Recommendation 13.
[45] FATF Recommendations 14–21.
[46] FATF Recommendation 22.
[47] FATF Recommendations 23–26.
[48] FATF Recommendations 27–30; see also Richard Sansonnetti, 'Money Laundering – An International Perspective from Switzerland' in Barry Rider and Michael Ashe (eds), *Money Laundering Control* (Round Hall, Sweet & Maxwell, 1996) 263–64.
[49] Mitsilegas (n 30) 195–211.
[50] See, eg, www.fatf-gafi.org/about/historyofthefatf/.
[51] ibid.
[52] ibid.
[53] ibid.
[54] Mitsilegas (n 30) 199.

obligations of private sector actors towards their customers. These obligations can largely be divided into two categories:[55]

(1) Customer identification and record keeping – private actors, especially financial and credit institutions, are obliged to identify their customers and verify their identity based on documentation; these entities should maintain, for at least five years, the necessary records on transactions.[56]

(2) Reporting of suspicious transactions – private entities are obliged to file a suspicious transaction report (to the domestic Financial Intelligence Unit) when there is a suspicion or reasonable grounds to suspect that funds are the proceeds of criminal activity or are linked to terrorist financing.[57]

The international AML regime signalled a new era for policing.[58] Private entities (not limited to credit and financial institutions) are taking a central and proactive role in the fight against money laundering and terrorist financing.[59] Garland characterises this approach as the 'responsibilisation strategy', where the responsibility to prevent the crime is passed on from the state to the private sector.[60]

1.3. Norm-Making and not Law-Making Body

Ryder notes that the FATF should not be perceived as a law-making body.[61] The FATF Recommendations are guidelines and not a legally binding instrument, providing minimum standards for countries.[62] Therefore, it is more accurate to state that the FATF is a norm-making body. The debate around the issue of norms

[55] ibid.

[56] FATF Recommendation 11; along with the identification of the customer, the obliged entity has to identify the beneficial owner, obtain information on the purpose and intended nature of the relationship with the customer and conduct ongoing due diligence on the business relationship and scrutiny of the transactions.

[57] FATF Recommendation 20.

[58] See, Michael Levi, 'Evaluating the "New Policing": Attacking the money trail of organized crime' (1997) 30 *Australian & New Zealand Journal of Criminology*.

[59] Mitsilegas (n 30) 200; Mitsilegas notes that private entities 'cannot afford to follow the "amoral" laws of business any more, as even their negligent association with the "dirty" money from drugs makes the morally stigmatised and, thus, criminal'.

[60] David Garland, 'The Limits of the Sovereign State: Strategies of Crime Control in Contemporary Society' (1996) 36 *British Journal of Criminology* 445; Garland notes that this responsibility covers also citizens as it 'must be made to recognize that they too have a responsibility in this regard, and must be persuaded to change their practices in order to reduce criminal opportunities and increase informal controls'. However, the regime of FATF does not oblige citizens in a general manner and the opinion of Garland is debatable from a legal perspective. Only from a moral perspective can citizens have a 'responsibility' to increase informal controls which still can be opposed on philosophical grounds.

[61] Ryder (n 2) 15; see also Dionysios S Demetis, *Technology and Anti-Money Laundering: A Systems Theory and Risk-Based Approach* (Edward Elgar, 2010) 45; even though the FATF is not a law-making body, Demetis notes that 'it does make recommendations that have a global reach'.

[62] Mitsilegas (n 30) 199.

is connected to the legal status of norms.[63] Often, the FATF Recommendations are recognised as 'soft law' because they are not legally binding but exert significant influence on countries and their legislation.[64] However, as a phenomenon, the norms produced by FATF-like bodies can be covered under the theoretical framework of global administrative law.[65]

To this end, Mouzakiti suggests that the FATF falls within the 'informal international lawmaking' concept.[66] The concept was put forward by Pauwelyn in a project to assess the accountability of activity due to the fact that informal international lawmaking falls outside the boundaries of domestic and international law.[67] According to Pauwelyn's research, the concept of 'informal international lawmaking' encompasses three elements. First, output informality refers to the activity itself, depicting that it does not lead to a formal treaty (the traditional source of international law) but rather to a guideline or a standard.[68] Second, process informality refers to informal international cooperation occurring in an informal setting (international network or body).[69] Third, actor informality concerns the actors involved in the process, such as domestic regulators, independent or semi-independent agencies, etc, rather than diplomats.[70]

Thus, the FATF can clearly fit within this concept. It is not a formal international organisation; the main product of the body is the Recommendations, which are guidelines (not legally binding), and it does not involve diplomatic actors. This, however, does not establish whether the Recommendations are law. The norms produced by the FATF have a significant influence over the domestic legislation of its members.[71] The question is why countries follow the FATF's norms. One

[63] See Gunnar Folke Schuppert, 'New Modes of Governance and the Rule of Law' in Michael Zurn, Andre Nolkaemper and Randall Peerenboom (eds), *Rule of Law Dynamics: In an Era of International and Transnational Governance* (Cambridge University Press, 2012), 92.

[64] Stessens (n 1) 15–17; Stessens characterises the FATF Recommendations as the 'crown jewel of soft law'.

[65] See further Sabino Cassese, 'Administrative Law without the State – the Challenge of Global Regulation' (2005) 37 *NYU Journal of International Law and Politics* 663; Nico Krisch and Benedict Kingsbury, 'Introduction: Global Governance and Global Administrative Law in the International Legal Order' (2006) 17(1) *European Journal of International Law*; Karl-Heinz Ladeur, 'The Emergence of Global Administrative Law and Transnational Regulation' (2012) 3(3) *Transnational legal theory* 243; James Thuo Gathii, 'The Financial Action Task Force and Global Administrative Law' (2010) *Journal of the Professional Lawyer* 197; Valsamis Mitsilegas, 'Legal Responses to Transnational Crime: a Global Perspective' in Valsamis Mitsilegas, Saskia Hufnagel and Anton Moiseienko (eds), *Research Handbook on Transnational Crime* (Edward Elgar Publishing, 2019).

[66] Foivi Mouzakiti, 'Financial Surveillance, Money Laundering and Terrorist Financing in the EU: The Case of Financial Intelligence Units' (PhD Thesis, Queen Mary University of London, 2021) 39–40.

[67] Joost Pauwelyn, 'Informal International Lawmaking: Framing the Concept and Research Questions' in Joost Pauwelyn, Ramses Wessel and Jan Wouters (eds), *Informal International Lawmaking* (Oxford University Press, 2012) 14; See also B Kingsbury and R Stewart, 'Legitimacy and Accountability in Global Regulatory Governance: The Emerging Global Administrative Law and the Design and Operation of Administrative Tribunals of International Organizations' in S Flogaitis (ed), *International Administrative Tribunals in a Changing World* (Esperia Publications, 2008).

[68] Pauwelyn (n 67) 15.

[69] ibid; Pauwelyn compares the G-20 Basel Committee and the FATF with the UN and the WTO to explain the nature of the informal process.

[70] ibid.

[71] Including the regional bodies (eg MONEYVAL).

answer might be that FATF-like bodies are authorities in specific fields.[72] In order to resolve this conundrum, Mouzakiti uses the definition of Bogdandy, Dann and Goldmann that 'any kind of governance activity by international institutions, be it administrative or intergovernmental, should be considered as an exercise of public authority if it determines individuals, private associations, enterprises, states or other public institutions'.[73] Therefore, even though the Recommendations are not legally binding, they do have domestic legal significance due to the authority of the FATF being defined as 'the legal capacity to determine others and to reduce their freedom, i.e. to unilaterally shape their legal or factual situation'.[74]

Mouzakiti's argument has its merits, but when it comes specifically to the FATF, there is another component to the fact that its norms produce 'binding' outputs. Even though it can be argued that the FATF exercises authority, the organisation has other means to 'gently' push countries to follow its guidelines via a 'black list' or 'grey list'.[75] Due to the negative connotation of the term 'black list', the FATF divides countries that do not abide by its guidelines into two categories: (1) high-risk jurisdictions subject to a call for action (ie black list), and (2) jurisdictions under increased monitoring (ie grey list).[76] According to the FATF, this process is effective in coercing jurisdictions to adopt legislation based on its guidelines. In February 2023, 98 jurisdictions were publicly identified as having weak regimes, 72 of whom 'have since made the necessary reforms to address their AML/CFT weaknesses'.[77] As a result, the FATF removed those jurisdictions from the lists. Based on this, it can be argued that the FATF exercises authority through its accountability function in relation to money laundering; however, countries are also concerned about the consequences of being publicly identified as jurisdictions which facilitate money laundering.

2. 'Digital' Money Laundering and the FATF Recommendations: The Timeline

As the world progresses and technology develops, criminals tend to find more innovative ways to launder their proceeds of crime. The FATF Recommendations covered, in a general manner, the use of technology for the commission of money laundering. However, the development of digital currencies and their widespread

[72] Armin Von Bogdandy and others, *The Exercise of Public Authority by International Institutions: Advancing International Institutional Law* (Springer Science & Business Media, 2010); Nico Krisch, 'Global Governance as Public Authority: An Introduction' (2012) 10(4) *International Journal of Constitutional Law* 976.

[73] Mouzakiti (n 66) 41; Armin von Bogdandy, Philipp Dann and Matthias Goldmann, 'Developing the Publicness of Public International Law: Towards a Legal Framework for Global Governance Activities' (2008) 9(11) *German Law Journal* 1375.

[74] ibid 1382.

[75] See Guy Stessens, 'The FATF "Black List" of Non-Cooperative Countries or Territories' (2001) 14 *Leiden Journal of International Law* 199.

[76] See www.fatf-gafi.org/en/countries/black-and-grey-lists.html.

[77] ibid.

use call for a more sophisticated international regime. This section implements an analytical exercise for each recommendation (concerning technology and, by extension, digital currencies) from different periods to cohesively illustrate the phenomenon's evolution. The purpose of the chronological order is twofold. First, the order of the amendments provides a ground for analysis with regard to the extent of regulation (ie what currencies and virtual asset service providers are covered). Second, the chronological order helps map out the regulatory steps of the EU in line with the FATF Recommendations.

2.1. The 2003 Recommendations: General Advice

In the early days, the FATF was not preoccupied with the commission of money laundering with the use of technology.[78] In 2003, Recommendation 8 (hereinafter R8) stated that:

> Financial institutions should pay special attention to any money laundering threats that may arise from new or developing technologies that might favour anonymity and take measures, if needed, to prevent their use in money laundering schemes. In particular, financial institutions should have policies and procedures in place to address any specific risks associated with non-face to face business relationships or transactions.[79]

It refers only to financial institutions, ie the banking system, which results in the exclusion of other non-financial-related professions. Ostensibly, the definition of a financial institution reveals that R8 obliges only banking systems or any other institutions that offer services connected to fiat currency (ie exchanges, commodities, securities, and financial guarantees).[80] Interestingly, the only point relatively close to this research's scope (digital currencies) is point four of the definition concerning financial institutions, ie 'the transfer of money or value'.[81]

The concept of value can connect digital currencies to the services above, with the justification that digital currencies may not conventionally be money, but they hold a certain value.[82] An example given by the FATF is alternative remittance activity.[83] This encompasses services outside the financial sector, transferring value or money among different locations.[84] The hawala system and the black market peso exchange are well-known examples.[85] These services have been accused of

[78] Financial Action Task Force, 'The Forty Recommendations' (1990); Financial Action Task Force, 'The Forty Recommendations' (1996).

[79] Financial Action Task Force, 'The Forty Recommendations' (2003) R8.

[80] FATF Recommendations 2003, 16, See the glossary to the Recommendations for the definition of the term 'Financial Institutions'.

[81] ibid.

[82] See eg https://coinmarketcap.com/ for the value of digital currencies.

[83] FATF Recommendations 2003, 16.

[84] See www.fatf-gafi.org/en/publications/Methodsandtrends/Moneylaunderingthroughmoneyremittanceandcurrencyexchangeproviders.html.

[85] Financial Action Task Force, 'Combating the Abuse of Alternative Remittance Systems' (20 June 2003) 2.

terrorist financing.[86] Nevertheless, these systems were used for the commission of these crimes, primarily because they were inherently anonymous and could transfer money to regions where the banking system did not.[87]

Furthermore, the FATF merely recognised that the technology might be a threat; the wording of R8 is too generic, and the phrase 'new or developing technologies' can include anything.[88] Notably, in the glossary to the FATF Recommendations of 2003, there is no mention of what these technologies might be. R8 also stresses that these technologies 'might favour anonymity'.[89] The concept of anonymity is extremely important to money laundering and is one of the features that makes digital currencies attractive to criminals. One of the main tools of AML law is customer due diligence and record-keeping, which are obligations of the private sector to eliminate anonymity.[90] Lastly, R8 highlights the risks posed by 'non-face to face transactions'.[91] Understandably, the FATF urges measures to mitigate the risks from non-face to face transactions. When a money laundering technique is based on technology, the transaction is mostly non-face to face.

The FATF continued improving its international standards by making minor changes to its text or altering the interpretive notes.[92] In February 2012, after a detailed review of the AML regime, the FATF published a revised set of Recommendations.[93] The analysis of the evolution of the Recommendations illustrates an interesting shift towards the use of technology to facilitate money laundering.

2.2. The 2012 Recommendations: Minor Changes for a Developing Phenomenon

Since 2003, there have been many technological developments, in particular the development of digital currencies, eg cryptocurrencies and in-game currencies. The phenomenon of in-game currencies is not new, as it existed before Bitcoin. Bitcoin was released on 3 January 2009; it was not convertible initially and did not have value.[94] Therefore, it was not deemed sufficient to explicitly include the phenomenon of digital currencies in R8, covering, in a general manner, the use of technology for the facilitation of money laundering. Nevertheless, in 2010, a programmer exchanged 10,000 bitcoin for 2 Papa John's pizzas (US $25), and from this first real transaction, the bitcoin gained value.[95] By that, it is implied that the

[86] ibid.
[87] ibid; these systems had been used to send money to the terrorists connected with the 2001 attacks.
[88] FATF Recommendations 2003, R8.
[89] FATF Recommendations 2003, R8.
[90] See section B of the FATF Recommendations 2003.
[91] FATF Recommendations 2003, R8.
[92] See www.fatf-gafi.org/publications/fatfrecommendations/documents/fatf-recommendations.html.
[93] ibid.
[94] Lexis® PSL TMT Team (eds), *An Introduction to Technology Law* (LexisNexis, 2018) 636.
[95] ibid.

FATF was aware of cryptocurrencies and their convertibility and value before revising the Recommendations in 2012.

The revision of the Recommendations in 2012 was significant.[96] The most relevant Recommendation is Recommendation 15 (hereinafter R15), dedicated to technologised money laundering techniques, which reads as follows:

> 15. New technologies
>
> Countries and financial institutions should identify and assess the money laundering or terrorist financing risks that may arise in relation to (a) the development of new products and new business practices, including new delivery mechanisms, and (b) the use of new or developing technologies for both new and pre-existing products. In the case of financial institutions, such a risk assessment should take place prior to the launch of the new products, business practices or the use of new or developing technologies. They should take appropriate measures to manage and mitigate those risks.[97]

By referring to 'countries', the FATF deemed it necessary to alert the states when it comes to technological developments.[98] It is also possible that the organisation considered cryptocurrencies, particularly Bitcoin, to require closer cooperation between the countries and the private sector. R15 uses the same generic phrase by referring to the use of new or developing technologies.[99] Even though R15 is slightly more precise than its predecessor (R8), it still remains too vague considering the removal of the parts concerning 'anonymity' and 'non-face to face business relationships or transactions'.[100] Nevertheless, from a critical perspective, R15 is an open-ended guideline structured to generally encompass every technological development that exists or will be developed in the future. This is also evidenced by the fact that in the 2012 version, R15 does not have an interpretative note. Moreover, the glossary does not contain any definition or at least an indication of what new or developing technologies might constitute. Therefore, it is implied that R15 also refers to digital currencies.

Whereas the 2012 revision improved the AML framework regarding the utilisation of the technology concerning digital currencies, R15 did not provide clear and precise guidelines.[101] Since 2012, the FATF has continued the development of the international AML regime. In 2018, the FATF amended the Recommendations to include a specific reference to digital currencies and their technology. The 2018 revision was vital for the international (and EU's) regulatory wave, as this was the first time digital currencies had been recognised as an explicit technique of money laundering.

[96] See www.fatf-gafi.org/about/historyofthefatf/.

[97] Financial Action Task Force, 'International Standards on Combating Money Laundering and the Financing of Terrorism & Proliferation' (2012) R15.

[98] FATF Recommendations 2012, R15.

[99] FATF Recommendations 2012, R15.

[100] FATF Recommendations 2003, R8.

[101] FATF Recommendations 2012.

2.3. The 2018 Amendment and the Introduction of Digital Currencies to the International AML Regime

R15 of 2012 did not specifically identify digital currencies, although based on the open-ended nature of that provision, these currencies can be included in the regime.[102] The rise of digital currencies provided an incentive for minor changes to R15. Therefore, in October 2018, the FATF revised R15 and added two more definitions for the terms 'virtual asset' and 'virtual asset service provider' to the glossary.[103] In June 2019, the FATF added an interpretive note for R15.[104] These can be perceived as minor changes but are significant in nature. Based on these alterations, the FATF clarified how the AML requirements apply to digital currencies.[105]

Therefore, R15 today explicitly refers to the phenomenon of digital currencies as a potential vehicle for the crime of money laundering. The latest version of R15 adds:

> 15. New technologies
>
> [. . .] To manage and mitigate the risks emerging from virtual assets, countries should ensure that virtual asset service providers are regulated for AML/CFT purposes, licensed or registered and subject to effective systems for monitoring and ensuring compliance with the relevant measures called for in the FATF Recommendations.'[106]

The main body of R15 remains the same, with the addition of the second paragraph (above) that unambiguously refers to digital currencies. R15 was the first international guideline determining the need to regulate the crypto industry. Based on their decentralised nature, digital currencies exist outside the banking system.[107] This is why the FATF bluntly states in R15 that 'countries should ensure that virtual asset service providers are regulated for AML/CFT purposes'. This latest version, alongside the insertion of two definitions in the FATF's glossary and an interpretive note, tries to clear the nebulous environment that had existed before. Digital currencies or, as the FATF defines them, virtual assets are deemed vulnerable to the crime of money laundering, or at least are considered by the FATF to entail risks.

[102] Financial Action Task Force, 'International Standards on Combating Money Laundering and the Financing of Terrorism & Proliferation' (2023) R15 (FATF Recommendations).

[103] See www.fatf-gafi.org/publications/fatfgeneral/documents/outcomes-plenary-october-2018.html; FATF Recommendations, 135.

[104] FATF Recommendations, 135.

[105] FATF Recommendations, 135.

[106] FATF Recommendations, R15.

[107] See subsection 3.1.2. in Chapter 1.

3. The International AML Framework to Protect Digital Currencies from Criminals

This section analyses R15, particularly its second paragraph, which explicitly refers to digital currencies. The analysis continues to the definition of virtual assets to determine what types of currencies are covered by this (also bearing in mind that this research is dedicated to cryptocurrencies and in-game currencies). Lastly, the focus shifts to the definition of virtual asset service providers to comprehend what entities are obligated under the international AML regime.

3.1. Recommendation 15: A New Playing Field

The Recommendation is primarily concerned with the entities involved in the digital currency industry rather than with different types of virtual assets. The novelty of R15 is based on the fact that the FATF acknowledges that digital currencies are outside the banking system. The underlying technology, ie blockchain, is a decentralised system that can execute transactions without the need for traditional third parties (eg banks).[108]

The Recommendation introduces the notion of virtual asset service providers and essentially adds them to the list of obliged entities.[109] However, because digital currencies are not overseen by any central authority, the FATF deemed it necessary for the states to impose AML obligations on these services.[110] Additionally, countries are responsible for having a register for virtual asset service providers or requiring those providers to acquire a licence to provide their services.[111] The difficulty with regulating digital currencies is that these currencies are not tangible and are not issued or governed by any bank or state.[112] Therefore, the FATF is trying, in R15, to cover every entity involved in the digital currency industry. Lastly, R15 also obliges states to monitor that all the virtual asset service providers registered in their territory have in place measures to mitigate the risks of money laundering and terrorist financing.[113]

3.2. Defining Virtual Assets

In October 2018, the FATF added two new definitions of the terms 'virtual asset' and 'virtual asset service provider' to the glossary to the Recommendations.[114]

[108] Primavera De Filippi and Aaron Wright, *Blockchain and the Law: The Rule of Code* (Harvard University Press, 2018) 63.
[109] FATF Recommendation R15.
[110] De Filippi and Wright (n 108) 70.
[111] FATF Recommendation R15.
[112] De Filippi and Wright (n 108) 70.
[113] FATF Recommendation R15.
[114] FATF Recommendations, 120 (Glossary).

These definitions were added to clarify how the regime can be applied to virtual assets, and this is because, even today, there is uncertainty about what a virtual asset or currency is.

According to the definition given by the FATF:

> A virtual asset is a digital representation of value that can be digitally traded, or transferred, and can be used for payment or investment purposes. Virtual assets do not include digital representations of fiat currencies, securities and other financial assets that are already covered elsewhere in the FATF Recommendations.[115]

The definition uses technologically neutral language: 'a digital representation of value'; this means that the FATF is not concerned with the type of technology. The FATF is also preoccupied with which currencies are not included in its scope. In light of this, the definition's wording indicates that any digital representation of value issued by a country or an authority of the country is not a virtual asset. This includes the concept of electronic money, eg the digital representation of the Euro or the US dollar. The exclusion of digital representations of fiat currencies does not encompass digital representations of value attached to a currency with legal status, eg so-called stablecoins.[116] Therefore, a digital currency attached to (not a representation of) a currency with legal status is a virtual asset based on the FATF definition.

With regard to the conditions for a virtual asset, the first condition is that the digital representation of value can be digitally traded or transferred. Arguably, this means that it is not necessary that digital currencies are traded or transferred because the definition uses the word 'can'. The essential point is that the technology underlying the digital currencies must have the capability to trade or transfer, and if it does, then it is included in the definition, which is the case for both cryptocurrencies and in-game currencies.

The second condition – that a virtual asset can be used for payment or investment purposes – might raise a problem with in-game currencies, which are used only in a closed environment. Again, the use of the word 'can' means that it is not necessary that the currencies are used for these purposes; only that there is the capability. Furthermore, the FATF did not use other phrases to define it more strictly; for example, it does not mention that these currencies must be means of exchange or be accepted by natural or legal persons. Therefore, based on interpretation, there is no obstacle which excludes in-game currencies from this scope because they can be used as a payment in the virtual world, and, obviously, they can be used as an investment. Thus, there is no specificity regarding the environment in which they can be used.

The general observation from this analysis of the FATF definition of virtual assets is that it includes both cryptocurrencies, which operate with blockchain technology, and in-game currencies. With this definition, the FATF aimed to

[115] FATF Recommendations, 135
[116] Stablecoin is a virtual currency whose value is attached to a currency with a legal status, eg Euro.

include every category of digital currency existing today. It is a broad definition with a generic essence, not strict wording and technologically neutral language. This is quite understandable because a narrow definition would require constant revision based on technological development.

3.3. Defining Virtual Asset Service Providers

The FATF defines a virtual asset service provider as follows:

> Virtual asset service provider means any natural or legal person who is not covered elsewhere under the Recommendations, and as a business conducts one or more of the following activities or operations for or on behalf of another natural or legal person:
>
> i. exchange between virtual assets and fiat currencies;
> ii. exchange between one or more forms of virtual assets;
> iii. transfer of virtual assets;
> iv. safekeeping and/or administration of virtual assets or instruments enabling control over virtual assets; and
> v. participation in and provision of financial services related to an issuer's offer and/or sale of a virtual asset.[117]

The definition encompasses natural and legal persons who must conduct one or more of the above activities or operations. The important condition of the first paragraph is that an entity (or person) does not need to commit all of these activities in order to be presumed as a virtual asset service provider.[118] Therefore, the question is whether service providers of in-game currencies and cryptocurrencies provide at least one of the services outlined in the definition.[119] The analysis begins with the in-game currencies. The reason is that in-game currencies are centrally controlled by the entity which owns the game or the virtual world; therefore, there are fewer entities to analyse. For example, the online game and virtual world, Second Life, which was launched in 2003, uses as an in-game currency something called Linden Dollars.[120] The entity that owns the game allows users to exchange fiat currency for Linden Dollars directly from its website.[121] Consequently, Liden Lab is involved in the first activity listed by the FATF in the definition, ie the exchange between fiat and virtual currency.[122]

The Linden Lab also provides transfer, safekeeping and administration services for its digital currency because the user has an account in the game, and from that account can save the currencies or send them to another user.[123] But it is necessary to extend the analysis to another example. The online game World of Warcraft,

[117] FATF Recommendations, 130.
[118] FATF Recommendation R15.
[119] FATF Recommendations, 135.
[120] See https://secondlife.com.
[121] ibid.
[122] FATF Recommendations, 135.
[123] FATF Recommendations, 135.

launched in 2004 by Blizzard Entertainment Inc, uses 'gold' as a currency.[124] The difference is that Blizzard does not provide the possibility to exchange fiat currency for gold through its website. However, users can exchange fiat currency for something called a 'wow token', an item of value because, after the exchange, users can sell it in the game in exchange for gold or redeem it for game time.[125] Even if one could claim that the wow token is not a virtual asset, and therefore Blizzard does not provide exchange services, it does not necessarily mean that this entity is not a virtual asset service provider. Through the virtual world of World of Warcraft, similar to Second Life, the user can transfer their currencies to another user, and all the in-game currencies reside in the game's servers; thus, the company provides transfer services, safekeeping and administration of virtual assets.[126] Consequently, it is an entity which falls under the FATF's definition. These two online games have been used here because they are big virtual worlds with many customers, but there are a lot of games and virtual worlds that have similar functions.

The following example considers the concept of cryptocurrencies (eg bitcoin), which operate using blockchain technology. Blockchain technology is decentralised and not governed by any entity.[127] Based on this, the FATF deemed that it must include all the blockchain technology intermediaries in the Recommendations. The intermediaries of digital currencies will be divided into four categories to assist the analysis in this section.

The primary entities to be included in the list of obliged entities under the AML regime are the issuers of cryptocurrencies. So, like Bitcoin, an individual can design a cryptocurrency, and the blockchain will start providing the digital currency. The FATF's definition includes: 'participation in and provision of financial services related to an issuer's offer and/or sale of a virtual asset'. As described by the FATF, this activity can be considered puzzling because the issuer might not be involved in the sale. However, it might be argued that an issuer has participated in the offer, so, along with the entities that sell a newly issued cryptocurrency, it can be considered a virtual asset service provider.

Second, there are the cryptocurrency exchangers, which have a crucial role in these systems as they exchange fiat currencies for cryptocurrencies.[128] These entities are also called secondary markets.[129] They are clearly included in the definition and particularly in the first activity listed within it: 'i. exchange between virtual assets and fiat currencies'.[130] It makes sense that the FATF recommends these entities to be obliged because, compared to other entities, exchanges between fiat currency and cryptocurrency are closer to the heavily regulated banking system.

[124] See https://worldofwarcraft.com/en-gb/.

[125] See https://eu.shop.battle.net/en-gb/product/world-of-warcraft-token.

[126] FATF Recommendations, 135.

[127] See section 4 in Chapter 1.

[128] De Filippi and Wright (n 108) 27.

[129] Lars Haffke, Mathias Fromberger and Patrick Zimmermann, 'Virtual Currencies and Anti-Money Laundering – The Shortcomings of the 5th AML Directive (EU) and How to Address Them' (2020) 21 *Journal of Banking Regulation* 125.

[130] FATF Recommendations, 135.

In order to buy cryptocurrencies from an online exchange with fiat money, an individual will use the banking system to transfer the money.

The third category includes exchanges between digital currencies and other digital currencies, ie an individual wants to buy bitcoin using Ethereum (both are cryptocurrencies). This activity is also covered by the definition of virtual asset service providers given by the FATF.[131] Therefore, all exchangers are encompassed in the definition irrespective of the services, ie exchange between fiat currency and digital currency or between digital currencies.

Lastly, there are the wallet providers. Wallets are used to save the user's private key.[132] The private key is needed for the completion of a cryptocurrency transaction.[133] This category is tricky because an individual does not use a wallet to save the digital currencies; it only saves the private key. Although activity 'iv' of the definition covers 'safekeeping and/or administration of virtual assets or instruments enabling control over virtual assets',[134] it is established that wallets do not serve for the safekeeping or administration of virtual assets; however, they do provide services, eg safekeeping of instruments which enable control over virtual assets. The private key can be considered such an instrument because, without it, the user cannot complete transactions.

In conclusion, the FATF's definition of virtual asset service providers aims to include many entities. The entities encompassed in that definition are bound by R15, meaning they must get a licence or register in their respective jurisdictions to provide their services.[135] Moreover, these entities need to follow all the measures laid down by the FATF in the Recommendations to 'protect' digital currencies from criminal abuse. From the analysis, it has been determined that the four categories of entities that provide services for cryptocurrencies and those that provide services for in-game currencies can and should be considered virtual asset service providers based on the FATF's definition.

4. FATF Guidelines for Virtual Asset Service Providers

Digital currencies are an emerging phenomenon. Today, there are thousands of different cryptocurrencies.[136] However, their evolution took time. In October 2010, the FATF issued a key typology study entitled 'Money Laundering Using New Payment Methods'.[137] This research focused on prepaid cards, internet payment, and mobile payment services,[138] and assessed the risks from these methods, indicating

[131] FATF Recommendations, 135.
[132] See subsection 5.4. in Chapter 1.
[133] ibid.
[134] FATF Recommendations, 135.
[135] FATF Recommendation R15.
[136] See https://currency.com/how-many-cryptocurrencies-are-there.
[137] Financial Action Task Force, 'Money Laundering Using New Payment Methods' (October 2010).
[138] ibid 14–20.

a series of suspicious activities through these systems.[139] The report concluded that the greatest hurdle for legislation on these new payment methods was the different national approaches.[140] Interestingly, the report acknowledges (since 2010) that internet payment methods also include digital currencies.[141] However, in the glossary to the report, there is only a definition of a digital currency provider: 'A type of internet payment service. Digital currency providers (DCP) keep and administer accounts for their customers, but typically do not directly issue "digital currency" to their customers/account holders.'[142]

In the same section, the report links the category of internet payment methods to virtual worlds.[143] Virtual worlds are, according to the report, 'simulated world[s] ... within a virtual environment. This ... refers to computer games which are based on the internet such as Second Life. Often the economy is based upon a digital currency which can be bought and/or converted into real money.'[144] The FATF highlights the connection between the real economy and the virtual one: '... the emergence of electronic currencies linked to virtual worlds, where users convert real currencies into virtual currencies in order to complete purchases within the virtual world environment.'[145]

The fact that the FATF has referred to digital currencies since 2010 is important. Notably, this report was published two years before the fundamental revision of the FATF Recommendations. In a plenary FATF meeting held in Paris from 12–14 February 2014 under the Russian presidency, it was agreed that it was necessary to conduct further research on the AML implications of digital currencies.[146] Consequently, in a meeting of the FATF in Paris from 25–27 June 2014, the organisation adopted and published the first explicit guidelines for digital currencies entitled 'Virtual Currencies: Key Definitions and Potential AML/CFT Risks'.[147]

The report encompasses both digital currencies covered by this book.[148] As a first step, the study defines these currencies, presenting at the same time their different types of systems, and it exposes the potential risks of digital currencies. [149] More precisely, the study highlights that these systems do not require any identification details, allowing greater anonymity than the traditional financial system.[150] Another risk is the decentralised nature of digital currencies. As a result, these systems rely on many entities, making pinpointing the responsible entity difficult. Additionally, all these characteristics constitute

[139] ibid 47.
[140] ibid 66.
[141] ibid 17.
[142] ibid 112.
[143] ibid 17.
[144] ibid 116.
[145] ibid 17.
[146] See www.fatf-gafi.org/publications/fatfgeneral/documents/plenary-outcomes-feb-2014.html.
[147] Financial Action Task Force, 'Virtual Currencies: Key Definitions and Potential AML/CFT Risks' (June 2014).
[148] ibid 5.
[149] ibid 4.
[150] ibid 9.

a hurdle for law enforcement agencies to find and access customer and transaction records.[151]

Even though the study defines the concept of digital currencies, it does not analyse the underlying technology. Therefore, the alleged risks are not based on any concrete data. Although the FATF considers the issue of anonymity within digital currencies, it does not accompany its paper with an evaluation of this anonymity. The continuation of the research around digital currencies was a priority for the Australian presidency of the FATF (2014-2015).[152] In a plenary meeting in Paris from 25–27 February 2015, the FATF discussed the need to build upon the 2014 report on digital currencies.[153] Eventually, the FATF adopted, in a meeting from 24–26 June 2015, a report entitled 'Guidance for a risk-based approach to virtual currencies'.[154]

The guidance report of 2015 regarding digital currencies built on the typologies report published a year earlier. Despite the general definitions and identification of potential risks provided by the FATF in its 2014 report, the application of the Recommendations within this emerging context created uncertainty for the industry, as the Recommendations at that time made no explicit reference to digital currencies. Therefore, the purpose of the 2015 guidance report was twofold: to explain how to apply the Recommendations to the virtual asset service providers, and to discover any obstacles towards the compliance of this technology with AML measures.[155] The scope of the guidance report of 2015 was primarily the convertible digital currency exchanges, ie the exchanges where a user can convert fiat money to digital currencies.[156] Oddly, the report addressed the issue of suspicious activity reporting without identifying any specific red flags to help the providers understand what is meant by 'suspicion' in these systems.[157] Lastly, the scope of the report was limited to a single entity, namely, exchangers, and it failed to provide guidance for law enforcement agencies.

Eight years after the report on new payment methods and the first considerations on digital currencies, the FATF decided in a plenary meeting held from 17–19 October 2018 to amend the FATF Recommendations to regulate virtual assets.[158] These amendments came after the request of the G20 Ministers, and it was an effort to clarify to what activities the Recommendations apply and what businesses are obliged to take measures to mitigate the risks from digital currencies.[159] In particular, the FATF revised R15 and added two new definitions in

[151] ibid 10.

[152] See www.fatf-gafi.org/publications/fatfgeneral/documents/objectives-2014-2015.html.

[153] Financial Action Task Force, 'Virtual Currencies: Key Definitions and Potential AML/CFT Risks' (June 2014); see www.fatf-gafi.org/publications/fatfgeneral/documents/plenary-outcomes-february-2015.html.

[154] See www.fatf-gafi.org/publications/fatfgeneral/documents/outcomes-plenary-june2015.html#RBA-VC; Financial Action Task Force, 'Guidance for a Risk-Based Approach: Virtual Currencies' (June 2015).

[155] Financial Action Task Force, 'Guidance for a Risk-Based Approach: Virtual Currencies' (June 2015) 4.

[156] ibid 6.

[157] ibid 13.

[158] Financial Action Task Force, 'Money Laundering Using New Payment Methods' (October 2010); see www.fatf-gafi.org/publications/fatfgeneral/documents/objectives-2018-2019.html.

[159] See www.fatf-gafi.org/publications/fatfgeneral/documents/objectives-2018-2019.html.

the framework, defining the concept of virtual assets for the first time under the international regime.

Shortly after these amendments, the FATF moved on to further improvements. More precisely, in a plenary meeting between 16–21 June 2019, the FATF introduced the interpretive note to R15 to clarify its requirements towards activities and businesses involved with virtual assets.[160] In the same plenary meeting, the FATF adopted a report entitled 'Guidance for a Risk-Based Approach: Virtual Assets and Virtual Asset Service Providers'.[161] This was an updated version for guidance to clarify the application of the risk-based approach to the concept of virtual assets.[162]

In the introduction to the FATF's updated version of the guidance (2019), the report underlines the real reason for this continuing revision of the framework, which is the constant development of technology.[163] Having as a basis the publications from 2014 and 2015, namely, 'Virtual Currencies: Key Definitions and Potential AML/CFT Risks' and 'Guidance for a Risk-Based Approach to Virtual Currencies', the FATF realised that a lot of new products had emerged, a fact that rendered these reports obsolete.[164] The updated guidance states that improvements were necessary because new currencies and services can significantly improve anonymity, a desired element for criminals.[165]

The FATF's journey to regulate digital currencies continues today. In October 2021, the FATF further updated the guidance to virtual asset service providers and published a report concerning the red flag indicators in the systems of digital currencies to aid providers in complying with reporting obligations. The FATF continues to publish updates on the implementation of its standards regarding virtual assets and the service providers, with the most recent report issued in June 2025 monitoring international progress in combating money laundering. However, the focus of this chapter is limited to the guidance provided by the FATF, rather than the statistics on compliance or the difficulties faced by jurisdictions during implementation.

4.1. Risk-Based Approach Tailored to Virtual Assets and Virtual Asset Service Providers

The FATF's risk-based approach appeared in the Recommendations of 2003, but the application of the approach was narrow in scope. It was only with the revision

[160] See www.fatf-gafi.org/publications/fatfgeneral/documents/outcomes-plenary-june-2019.html.

[161] ibid.

[162] Financial Action Task Force, 'Guidance for a Risk-Based Approach: Virtual Assets and Virtual Asset Service Providers' (June 2019).

[163] ibid 6.

[164] Financial Action Task Force, 'Virtual Currencies: Key Definitions and Potential AML/CFT Risks' (June 2014); Financial Action Task Force, 'Guidance for a Risk-Based Approach: Virtual Currencies' (June 2015).

[165] Financial Action Task Force, 'Guidance for a Risk-Based Approach: Virtual Assets and Virtual Asset Service Providers' (June 2019) 6.

of the Recommendations in 2012 that the risk-based approach took a central role in the application of the international framework.[166] The FATF published the updated public and private sector guidance in October 2021. The publication has six parameters: (a) clarification of the definition of virtual assets; to underline that this definition is open-ended and there should not be a case where a relevant asset is not covered by the standards; (b) to provide guidance for the application of the standards to stablecoins; (c) to provide guidance to address risks associated with peer-to-peer transactions; (d) to provide guidance on the licensing and registration of the providers; (e) to provide guidance on the implementation of the 'travel rule'; and (f) to present principles of information-sharing and cooperation.[167]

The report aims to help virtual asset service providers apply the Recommendations to a decentralised environment. The novelty of the phenomenon is that providers need to apply the standards even when only one of the parties to a transaction uses an intermediary. To begin with, the guidance states that the providers must first identify the customer when establishing business relations.[168] For this process, the provider should collect the necessary data. Such data include the customer's name, physical address, date of birth and national identity number or passport number.[169] However, due to the nature of these transactions (pseudonymity and decentralisation), the FATF urges providers to collect further data necessary to determine the risk. This additional information encompasses IP addresses with time stamps, geo-location data, device identifiers, wallet addresses, and transaction hashes.[170] These categories of information exceed that which applies to the banking system framework. Based on these guidelines, virtual asset service providers must conduct deep proactive research on all customers. This results from the decentralised environment and has significant consequences. To begin with, it is an additional burden for providers, which endangers the provider–customer relationship.[171] Furthermore, customers have to provide sensitive information (geo-location data, device identifiers, IP addresses), which might be considered, from the end user perspective, as an invasion of their privacy.

A peculiar statement by the FATF in the report is that providers 'must therefore increase the amount or type of information obtained or the extent to which they verify such information where the risks associated with the business relationship

[166] See www.coe.int/en/web/moneyval/implementation/risk-based-approach.

[167] Financial Action Task Force, 'Updated Guidance for a Risk-Based Approach: Virtual Assets and Virtual Asset Service Providers' (October 2021) 5–6.

[168] ibid 79; this corresponds to Recommendation 10 (customer due diligence)

[169] ibid.

[170] ibid 79–80.

[171] A reminder for the reader is that virtual currency transactions are executed based on blockchain technology. The role of the intermediary is marginal compared to the bank–customer relation. Individuals choose to use intermediaries, such as virtual asset service providers; therefore, the relationship is based on trust. The collection of geo-location data and device identifiers might make individuals lose faith in providers.

or VA [(virtual asset)] activities is higher'.[172] Providers have to collect additional information if they have already determined that the risk is higher. The problem is that providers need to collect additional information in order to determine the risk, as per the guidance of the FATF. However, the FATF does not specify how far the provider should go. An argument here is that, for the phenomenon of digital currencies, the collection of additional information is the default, ie, it occurs before the assessment of the risk. Then, when the risk is higher, the provider should proceed to ongoing customer monitoring.[173] Ongoing monitoring of customers is a situation where the providers monitor the customers' transactions regularly.[174] The FATF underlines that this monitoring is 'an essential component in identifying transactions that are potentially suspicious'.[175] This results in a further impact on the end user. The ongoing monitoring is based on an arbitrary risk decision rather than on suspicion of a crime. The last argument concerning the effect on the end user is reinforced by the fact that the FATF suggests using automated systems to analyse the transactions.[176]

Moving forward, the report highlights the importance of the application of the 'travel rule' to transactions in digital currencies. The 'travel rule' is codified in Recommendation 16, which 'includes the obligation to obtain, hold, and submit required originator and beneficiary information associated with VA transfers in order to identify and report suspicious transactions, take freezing actions, and prohibit transactions with designated persons and entities'.[177] This process can only be achieved using technology, usually built into the underlying distributed ledger technology.[178] After applying the 'travel rule', the receiving provider has to implement mechanisms to scrutinise the information.[179] The FATF suggests that '[t]his could be done by combining other customer information, transaction history, and additional transaction data that it or its counterparty VASP [(virtual asset service provider)] obtained from its customer'.[180]

Nevertheless, not all providers have the same structure, and not all users have a provider. This creates a problem with the application of the 'travel rule'. This is evident in the case of unhosted wallets and peer-to-peer platforms.[181] In this

[172] Financial Action Task Force, 'Updated Guidance for a Risk-Based Approach: Virtual Assets and Virtual Asset Service Providers' (October 2021) 80.

[173] As the FATF does not specify what additional information should be collected when the risk is established, it is logical to conclude that this mirrors the concept of enhanced customer due diligence and ongoing monitoring of customers.

[174] Financial Action Task Force, 'Updated Guidance for a Risk-Based Approach: Virtual Assets and Virtual Asset Service Providers' (October 2021) 81.

[175] ibid 81.

[176] ibid.

[177] ibid 82.

[178] ibid; the FATF does not specify the technology to be used.

[179] ibid.

[180] ibid.

[181] For the analysis of wallets, see subsection 5.4. in Chapter 1; for the analysis of peer-to-peer platforms, see subsection 5.3. in Chapter 1. An unhosted wallet is a cold wallet. Usually, a hardware wallet or a mobile phone software wallet allows the user to maintain cryptocurrencies without any intermediary.

situation, there is only one intermediary, meaning that one of the parties to the transaction (sender/recipient) is not using a provider. The FATF states that when there is one provider, it 'should obtain the required originator and beneficiary information from their customer, because they cannot obtain the relevant information from another VASP'.[182] However, this is wildly impractical and not feasible. The argument is that the provider cannot transfer the obligation to the end user. The FATF establishes standards for states and the private sector; therefore, the end user cannot be obliged by any means to provide information concerning another user, and this is because the end user might not be aware of such information.

4.2. Red Flag Indicators in Digital Currencies

In September 2020, the FATF issued a report to help providers identify red flags concerning digital currencies. The findings of this report should be taken with a grain of salt, as there is no way to evaluate the methodology used by the FATF. The basis of the report is the findings of the 'Confidential FATF Report on Financial Investigations Involving Virtual Assets'.[183] The report is divided into six categories: red flags indicators related to (a) transactions, (b) transaction patterns, (c) anonymity, (d) senders and recipients, (e) source of funds or wealth, and (f) geographical risks.[184]

The analysis will not go into detail regarding each category because the research aims to investigate the impact on the end user and not to frame the suspicion in the virtual environment. First, concerning transactions (for all users), the FATF states that it is a red flag when there are frequent transactions in a certain period to the same virtual asset account by more than one person, from the same IP address by one or more persons, or concerning large amounts.[185] Second, regarding anonymity, the FATF establishes that it is a red flag when the transaction involves privacy-oriented coins; the customer is using peer-to-peer platforms or unhosted wallets; the customer is using mixing services, the wallet is linked with suspicious sources such as darknet marketplaces, mixing services, questionable gambling services and/or illegal activities. Moreover, suspicion is raised if the user transacts with a provider using an IP address associated with the darknet or similar software that allows anonymous communication (eg encrypted email and virtual private networks (VPNs).[186] Lastly, it could constitute a red flag if the transaction is initiated from a non-trusted IP address, IP addresses from sanctioned jurisdictions, or those previously flagged as suspicious, but also when there are discrepancies

[182] Financial Action Task Force, 'Updated Guidance for a Risk-Based Approach: Virtual Assets and Virtual Asset Service Providers' (October 2021) 86.

[183] Financial Action Task Force, 'Virtual Assets: Red Flag Indicators of Money Laundering and Terrorist Financing' (September 2020) 4.

[184] ibid 1.

[185] ibid 8.

[186] ibid 9–12.

between IP addresses associated with the customer's profile and the IP addresses from which transactions are being initiated.[187]

From the examples mentioned above, two main arguments emerge. First, virtual asset service providers must conduct proactive research on customers to collect such data (the list encompasses information regarding the criminal profile of customers, IP addresses, and association with the darknet). This implies that providers must collect substantial amounts of data to establish the risk, which somewhat negates the purpose of the risk-based approach if the totality of customers is affected. Second, the report states at the beginning that it also aims to help law enforcement authorities, which is evident in the list of red flags.[188] The FATF has confused, to some extent, the powers of the providers with police powers. Some of the suggestions in the report are impractical from the provider's perspective, especially concerning the connection of IP addresses or the user's connection with darknet marketplaces and anonymous communications.[189] To reach this point, the provider must have access to a substantial amount of data regarding the totality of customers, which results in extensive profiling from a private actor. These suggestions exceed what is feasible based on the powers of providers and mirror the investigative powers of the police.

5. Money Laundering and Digital Currencies: How the FATF Tries to Kill Two Birds with One Large Stone

The FATF was created to prevent criminals from using the banking system and other financial institutions to launder their crime proceeds and to establish new preventive measures.[190] Therefore, initially, its scope was the crime of money laundering. However, around a decade later, this changed. In September 2001, the events in the USA reshaped the mandate of the FATF. Shortly after the attacks, the FATF announced eight new Recommendations to address the problem of terrorist financing.[191] However, as it turned out, the FATF just added to its scope the crime of terrorist financing without altering its prior regime too much. Money laundering and terrorist financing have rather opposite meanings. The regime to fight the crime of money laundering is based on the premise that there is a need to deprive the criminal of the proceeds of the crime.[192] However, terrorist financing indicates

[187] ibid 12–15.
[188] ibid 3.
[189] ibid 9–12.
[190] G7 Summit, 'The declaration of 1989' (Paris, 16 July 1989), www.g8.utoronto.ca/summit/1989paris/communique/index.html.
[191] Financial Action Task Force, 'FATF Cracks down on Terrorist Financing' (31 October 2001).
[192] Leonardo Borlini and Francesco Montanaro, 'The Evolution of the EU Law Against Criminal Finance: The "Hardening" of FATF Standards within the EU' (2016) 48 *Georgetown Journal of International Law* 1009, 1017.

the funnelling of clean money for the commission of unlawful activities.[193] On the one hand, the essence of the crime of money laundering is to obscure the origin of the money; on the other hand, terrorist financing is concerned with the result, ie the terrorist activity.[194]

The rationale that both crimes might use the same financial institutions and/or techniques does not change the fact that the FATF uses the same strategy to tackle different problems. In the case of digital currencies, the FATF treated this phenomenon as another vehicle for the commission of money laundering or terrorist financing. The first warning regarding digital currencies came in 2010.[195] Back then, the FATF categorised these currencies as a new payment method.[196] However, sooner or later, the FATF realised that this fast-developing phenomenon needed a closer look. After almost a decade of research, reports, and a whole gamut of definitions and guidelines, the FATF made the decision in 2018 to promote digital currencies as a distinct part of its Recommendations. Therefore, the research states that there is no comparison between digital currencies and the crime of money laundering or terrorist financing because this phenomenon is merely another technique in these crimes. However, the problem requires a more sophisticated approach as it involves a technological aspect that necessitates expertise.

From an initial perspective, the FATF has undertaken very comprehensive research on digital currencies, and indeed has published a number of reports regarding this phenomenon. The subject focus of the FATF was selected during the plenary.[197] Apparently, the members of the plenary decided to put digital currencies under the spotlight, although for no precise reason. After choosing the subjects, the 'experts' of the FATF begin their research. The first study on the issue of digital currencies was published by the FATF in 2014.[198] This study does not contain any data analysis to illustrate why the FATF considers digital currencies to be a money laundering trend.[199] In one of its reports (Guidance for a Risk-Based Approach: Virtual Assets and Virtual Asset Service Providers (2019)), the FATF uses a number of jurisdictions (Italy, Norway, Sweden, Finland, Mexico, Japan, United States) to show examples of approaches; however, there is no in-depth analysis of data.[200] This analysis is particularly crucial when the research is conducted by a group of experts and the regime will affect many countries.[201]

[193] Unger (n 12) 21.

[194] Leonardo Borlini, 'Regulating Criminal Finance in the EU in the Light of the International Instruments' (2017) 36 *Yearbook of European Law* 553, 557.

[195] Financial Action Task Force, 'Money Laundering Using New Payment Methods' (October 2010).

[196] ibid.

[197] Van Duyne, Harvey and Gelemerova (n 20) 148.

[198] Financial Action Task Force, 'Virtual Currencies: Key Definitions and Potential AML/CFT Risks' (June 2014).

[199] Van Duyne, Harvey and Gelemerova (n 20) 150.

[200] Financial Action Task Force, 'Guidance for a Risk-Based Approach: Virtual Assets and Virtual Asset Service Providers' (June 2019).

[201] Van Duyne, Harvey and Gelemerova (n 20) 150.

As regards the Recommendations of the FATF, particularly R15 and the definitions of virtual assets and virtual asset service providers, there is not much to analyse further. The wide definitions show that the FATF wanted a catch-all, future-proof regime. The research indicates that the definitions encompass all the types of digital currencies and extend obligations to all entities operating within these systems. This approach is straightforward; since cryptocurrencies are founded on pseudonymous and decentralised technologies, the FATF opted to impose stringent obligations on the entities engaged in the virtual currency environment.

These obligations are similar to the ones imposed on the banking system, although there is a major difference. Most of the entities involved in digital currencies are smaller than banks, and the burden from these obligations is significantly heavier.[202] Evidently, the phenomenon of digital currencies needs a more sophisticated approach. The analysis indicates that the FATF did not present any significant data to support the inclusion of digital currencies in the existing AML regime. However, digital currencies can potentially be used to commit the crime of money laundering. This chapter does not support the statement that digital currencies should remain unregulated. Nevertheless, given that these systems are outside of the traditional banking system, it is deemed that there is a need for a different approach.

Conclusion

The analysis of the international AML regime of the FATF exposes the problems concerning the application of the Recommendations to virtual asset service providers. As a first step, it is determined that both in-game currencies and cryptocurrencies fall within the definition of virtual assets. Similarly, intermediaries of cryptocurrencies and virtual worlds are considered virtual asset service providers based on the FATF's regime. However, the regime is tailored to the banking system, and its application to virtual asset service providers is problematic. The analysis is focused on cryptocurrencies because the characteristics of the technology are considerably different from the banking system. However, the arguments concern both in-game currencies and cryptocurrencies.[203]

Based on the Recommendations, the virtual asset service providers must apply customer due diligence measures to their customers.[204] However, the information collected is insufficient to conduct a risk assessment. To this end, the FATF suggests that providers collect additional data (including geo-location data, IP addresses

[202] Tsingou (n 3) 15.

[203] A fundamental difference between cryptocurrencies and the banking system is that cryptocurrencies are usually decentralised. Therefore, virtual asset service providers face difficulties collecting the necessary information. The arguments can be applicable to both in-game currencies and cryptocurrencies because the pseudonymity of both systems creates the same effect.

[204] FATF Recommendation R10.

etc).[205] The problem is that the provider must do proactive research, which is an extra burden on the provider and constitutes an impact on the end user. This burden has a similar effect as the ongoing monitoring obligation for high-risk customers. The issue becomes confusing when the FATF concludes that ongoing monitoring (ie enhanced due diligence) should be conducted to determine suspicious transactions.[206] The suggestion that providers must collect additional information before establishing the risk, to a certain extent, nullifies the risk-based approach. The FATF provides certain standards and not rules. The difference is that standards are not as precise as rules.[207] If we follow the analysis of Unger and van Waarden, 'a risk-based approach gives private actors more discretion as to what to report'.[208] The argument focuses on the reporting obligations of private entities; however, it can still be applied to other measures, eg due diligence. The important element is the discretion left to private actors. Based on the analysis of this chapter, the FATF guidelines to virtual asset service providers concerning due diligence are becoming more precise. Even if the FATF insists that the guidelines for virtual asset service providers remain in the realm of the risk-based approach, it is obvious that they leave less discretion to private entities.

Lastly, the application of the 'travel rule' to virtual assets is alarming from the end user's perspective. The FATF's guidance concerning red flag indicators confuses the powers of the providers with the investigative powers of the police. The list of red flag indicators is largely based on the capability of the provider to collect IP addresses and establish a link with the criminal behaviour of customers.[209] To reach this point, the provider must have access to a substantial amount of data regarding the totality of customers, which results in extensive profiling from a private actor. The arguments in this chapter illustrate a contradiction between the international regime and the well-established risk-based approach, resulting in an impact on the end user. The next chapter evaluates the regional European AML regime to determine whether this contradiction is crystallised further in the EU's regime.

[205] Financial Action Task Force, 'Updated Guidance for a Risk-Based Approach: Virtual Assets and Virtual Asset Service Providers' (October 2021) 79–80.

[206] ibid 81.

[207] Brigitte Unger and Frans van Waarden, 'How to dodge drowning in data? Rule- and Risk-Based Anti-Money Laundering Policies Compared' in Brigitte Unger and Daan van der Linde (eds) *Research Handbook on Money Laundering* (Edward Elgar, 2013) 401. See further Ehrlich Isaac and Richard Allen Posner, 'An Economic Analysis of Legal Rule Making' (1974) 3 *Journal of Legal Studies* 257; Carol S Diver, 'The Optimal Precision of Administrative Rules' (1983) 93 *Yale Law Journal* 65.

[208] Unger and van Waarden (n 207) 400.

[209] Financial Action Task Force, 'Virtual Assets: Red Flag Indicators of Money Laundering and Terrorist Financing' (September 2020) 9–12.

4

The Evolution of the European Anti-Money Laundering (AML) Regime and the Policy Choice to Regulate Digital Currencies

Introduction

The European Union (EU) consistently follows the developments of the Financial Action Task Force (FATF), as the Recommendations act as a global incentive to combat money laundering and terrorist financing.[1] These Recommendations are considered flexible guidelines, allowing for quick adaptation to the ever-changing nature of money laundering. Nonetheless, they are not legally binding, which means that the EU Member States can utilise them as guiding principles. Building upon the international framework provided by the FATF, the EU has developed an extensive and far-reaching regime spanning over three decades, aimed at harmonising the efforts of its Member States in the fight against money laundering and terrorist financing.[2] Recently, the AML regime has undergone a complete transformation.[3]

After examining the international regime's approach to money laundering, the focus shifts to the main research scope, the regional level of the EU. This chapter critically evaluates the initial inclusion of digital currencies in the 5th AML Directive as well as the implications under the new AML regime.[4] Following an overview of

[1] Leonardo Borlini and Fransenco Montanaro, 'The Evolution of the EU Law Against Criminal Finance: The "Hardening" of FATF Standards within the EU' (2017) *Georgetown Journal of International Law* 1009.

[2] Valsamis Mitsilegas and Niovi Vavoula, 'The Evolving EU Anti-Money Laundering Regime: Challenges for Fundamental Rights and the Rule of Law' (2016) 23(2) *Maastricht Journal of European and Comparative Law* 261, 262.

[3] See https://finance.ec.europa.eu/publications/anti-money-laundering-and-countering-financing-terrorism-legislative-package_en.

[4] Directive (EU) 2018/843 of the European Parliament and of the Council of 30 May 2018 amending Directive (EU) 2015/849 on the prevention of the use of the financial system for the purposes of money laundering or terrorist financing, and amending Directive 2009/138/EC and 2013/36/EU [2018] OJ L156/43; The new AML regime contains four new instruments namely: (a) Regulation (EU) 2024/1620 of the European Parliament and of the Council of 31 May 2024 establishing the Authority for Anti-Money Laundering and Countering the Financing of Terrorism and amending Regulations (EU) No 1093/2010, (EU) No 1094/2010 and (EU) No 1095/2010 [2024] OJ L, 2024/1620; (b) Regulation (EU) 2024/1624 of

the evolution of the EU's AML regime, the chapter details the 5th AML Directive as well as the new amendments in a comprehensive three-part structure: the negotiations for the regime, the assessment of adopted amendments pertaining to digital currencies, and the new developments and their impact on the central argument.

Chapter 3 concluded by asserting that despite the well-established risk-based approach of the AML regime, certain FATF guidelines regarding digital currencies exhibit characteristics of a more stringent rule-based approach.[5] This chapter offers a novel exposition of the hitherto unexplored relationship between the FATF Recommendations and the EU's AML framework in relation to digital currencies. It seeks to determine whether the EU's approach mirrors the FATF's departure from the traditional risk-based model, and, in doing so, whether the EU remains normatively aligned with the FATF's standards. Building on this inquiry, the chapter critically assesses how such a deviation may recalibrate the balance between financial integrity objectives and the protection of fundamental rights, particularly those of customers of virtual asset service providers. By situating this analysis within the broader discourse on the accountability and legitimacy of transnational financial regulation, the chapter contributes original insight into how international soft law norms are internalised within the EU legal order and the human rights implications that follow.

1. The EU's AML Regime: History, Content and Evolution

The analysis of the evolution of the EU's AML framework reveals a consistently close relationship between the EU and the FATF. All EU AML instruments have been established with reference to FATF developments, indicating that the EU's regulatory trajectory is largely shaped by the FATF's standards. This finding forms the basis for the argument that such alignment is constitutive of a deeper normative tension. The emerging human rights concerns stem from this dependency, as the EU must simultaneously maintain financial integrity and uphold fundamental rights, thereby creating a persistent conflict at the core of its AML regime.

In September 1985, the European Parliament took action by adopting five resolutions aimed at addressing the escalating concerns surrounding drug abuse.[6] The Parliament's apprehensions echoed the subsequent findings of the European Council

the European Parliament and of the Council of 31 May 2024 on the prevention of the use of the financial system for the purposes of money laundering or terrorist financing [2024] OJ L, 2024/1624; (c) Regulation (EU) 2023/1113 of the European Parliament and of the Council of 31 May 2023 on information accompanying transfers of funds and certain crypto-assets and amending Directive (EU) 2015/849 [2023] OJ L150/1; (d) Directive (EU) 2024/1640 of the European Parliament and of the Council of 31 May 2024 on the mechanisms to be put in place by Member States for the prevention of the use of the financial system for the purposes of money laundering or terrorist financing, amending Directive(EU) 2019/1937, and amending and repealing Directive (EU) 2015/849 [2024] OJ L, 2024/1640.

[5] See Conclusion in Chapter 3.

[6] 'on action to combat drug abuse', combating drug abuse', 'measures to combat drugs-taking', 'measures to combat the spread of drug abuse', 'measures to combat the spread of drugs' – OJ C 262, 14.10.1985, 119–23.

in The Hague, 1986.[7] In the conclusions, the European Council reiterated the dangers of the drug abuse issue and advised to 'organize ad hoc collaboration between the Member States and the European Commission to examine what initiatives could be taken'.[8] As a result, the European Commission put forth a recommendation for a Council decision regarding the active involvement of the European Community in the United Nations conference.[9] The Commission's recommendation document explicitly alluded to the illicit economy of drugs and how it

> could imperil the structures and very survival of the states in question to the advantage of other interest groups, which have been multiplying their gains not only in the developed consumer countries but also, albeit to a much lesser extent (10%), in the most speculative sectors of the domestic economies of the producer countries, thanks to the 'laundering' of illicit trafficking revenue, with numerous financial institutions – having the most respectable credentials – collaborating, and sharing in the profits.[10]

Based on the International Conference on Drug Abuse and Illicit Trafficking of the United Nations, the Commission explained that the Community would be involved in several ways. These included stepping up of intra-Community and intra-European cooperation in accordance with the responsibilities vested in the Community in this area, cooperation at bilateral and regional levels with developing countries that produce drugs, and participation in conventional international instruments, with a particular view to contributing to the drafting of the new International Convention.[11]

With this objective in mind, the significance of the drug abuse issue affecting Europe was highlighted, necessitating the proactive engagement of the European Community in the 1987 International Conference.[12] This recommendation led to the Community's participation in the Conference, enabling an active role in the finalisation of the Vienna Convention.[13]

1.1. The Influence of the FATF on the Evolution of the EU's AML Regime

The analysis, in Chapter 3, concluded that the FATF operates as a non-legislative entity, rendering its Recommendations a form of 'soft law' lacking binding

[7] As reproduced (annex IV) in Commission of the European Communities, 'Recommendation for a Council Decision on Community participation in the preparatory work and the International Conference on Drug Abuse and Illicit Trafficking' COM (86) 457 final, 5 August 1986.

[8] ibid.

[9] ibid.

[10] ibid 3–4; Mitsilegas notes that this was the first time that the crime of money laundering was mentioned in an official document of the European Community, in Valsamis Mitsilegas, *Money Laundering Counter-Measures in the European Union: A New Paradigm of Security Governance Versus Fundamental Legal Principles* (Kluwer Law International, 2003) 53.

[11] ibid 6.

[12] ibid.

[13] Council Decision of 22 October 1990 concerning the conclusion on behalf of the European Economic Community of the UN Convention against illicit trafficking in narcotic drugs and Psychotropic substances [1990] OJ L326/56.

legal effect.[14] Nonetheless, the influence exerted by the FATF on the development of the European regulatory framework is of considerable degree. Almost all the European Directives and Regulations were adopted based on advancements within the FATF's international regime. Initially, the EU lacked competence in criminal matters as stipulated by the treaties. Consequently, the Union based the conclusion of the Vienna Convention on its competence in the area of commercial policy (Article 113 of the EEC Treaty).[15] The endorsement of the Vienna Convention marked the introduction of the AML regime into Community law. In April 1990, the Commission made the decision to propose a Council Directive on prevention of use of the financial system for the purposes of money laundering.[16] Notably, the Commission explicitly referred to the FATF and emphasised the imperative of maintaining consistency with the FATF's framework in the preamble of the proposed Directive.[17]

The proposed Directive rested upon two key arguments. First, it emphasised the necessity of safeguarding the financial system, as money laundering posed potential risks for financial institutions.[18] Second, the dire societal consequences associated with drug abuse warranted the implementation of measures by the Community to mitigate such outcomes.[19] The protection of financial institutions and the broader financial system has served as a primary and uncritically adopted justification for supporting the European AML regime, notwithstanding the arguments that money laundering does not inherently pose a threat to financial institutions.[20]

In 1991, the Council officially adopted the 1st AML Directive.[21] The adoption of this Directive was grounded in the principles of the internal market and the freedom of movement.[22] Notably, this Directive effectively incorporated the preventive framework outlined in the FATF Recommendations into Community law.[23] Gilmore notes that the 1991 Directive, 'in contrast to the 1988 and 1990 convention precedents, fully embraces the preventive approach to money laundering'.[24]

[14] Mitsilegas and Vavoula (n 2) 264; see also Alan Boyle, 'Some Reflections on the Relationship of Treaties and Soft Law' (1999) 48 *International and Comparative Law Quarterly* 901.

[15] Council Decision of 22 October 1990 concerning the conclusion on behalf of the European Economic community of the UN Convention against illicit trafficking in narcotic drugs and Psychotropic substances [1990] OJ L326/56.

[16] Commission, 'Proposal for a Council Directive on prevention of use of the financial system for the purpose of money laundering' COM (1990) 106 final, OJ C106/6.

[17] ibid.

[18] Mitsilegas (n 10) 54; see also Ernesto U Savona, *European Money Trails* (Harwood Academic Publishers, 1999) 25.

[19] ibid.

[20] For further discussion, see Peter Alldridge, *What Went Wrong With Money Laundering Law?* (Palgrave, 2015) 13.

[21] Council Directive 91/308/EEC of 10 June 1991 on prevention of the use of the financial system for the purpose of money laundering [1991] OJ L166/56.

[22] EEC Treaty, Arts 57(2) and 100a; for further discussion regarding the legal basis of the 1st AML Directive, see Mitsilegas (n 10) 56.

[23] Mitsilegas and Vavoula (n 2) 264.

[24] William C Gilmore, *Dirty Money: The Evolution of International Measures to Counter Money Laundering and the Financing of Terrorism*, 3rd edn (Council of Europe Publishing, 2004) 194.

The Directive primarily concentrated on credit and financial institutions, outlining the measures they could employ to address money laundering risks rather than just focusing on the investigatory stage.[25]

The 1st AML Directive introduced a comprehensive framework encompassing a definition of the crime of money laundering. It also contained various preventive measures and mandated Member States to combat money laundering. The European Commission assumed the role of a vigilant guardian, ensuring that Member States undertook necessary actions to adhere to this new framework.[26]

In a relatively short period following the adoption of the 1st Directive in 1991, the FATF revised its Recommendations (1996).[27] Consequently, in 1999, the Commission issued a proposal for the 2nd Directive, justifying its necessity to align with the evolving nature of the crime and to implement the revised FATF Recommendations.[28] The 2nd Directive was officially adopted in 2001.[29] The process of amending the Directive entailed extensive deliberations, given that the proposal for the Directive was published in July 1998, and its adoption occurred on 4 December 2001. The two most significant amendments to the Directive were as follows. First, the EU deemed it imperative to expand the scope of the predicate offences, resulting in the definition of 'criminal activity' being broadened to encompass 'any kind of criminal involvement in the commission of a serious crime'.[30] Second, the Commission determined that the Directive should cover additional professions and non-financial businesses, leading to an extension of the list of obliged entities.[31] Gilmore highlights that the Commission's stance on obliged entities was heavily influenced by the content of the annual reports on money laundering typologies produced by the FATF.[32]

[25] Peter Cullen, 'The European Community Directive' in Hector L MacQueen, *Money Laundering: Hume Papers on Public Policy*, Vol 1(2) (Edinburgh University Press, 1993) 34–36.

[26] Commission, 'Report of 3 March 1995 on the implementation of Directive 91/308/EEC' COM (95) 54 final; Commission, 'Report of 1 July 1998 on the implementation of Directive 91/308/EEC' COM (98) 49 final.

[27] Mitsilegas and Vavoula (n 2) 263.

[28] Commission, 'Proposal for a European Parliament and Council Directive amending Council Directive 91/308/EEC of 10 June 1991 on prevention of the use of the financial system for the purpose of money laundering' COM (1999) 352 final, 3.

[29] Directive 2001/97/EC of the European Parliament and of the Council of 4 December 2001 amending Council Directive 91/308/EEC on the prevention of the use of the financial system for the purpose of money laundering [2001] OJ L344/76.

[30] ibid Art 1E.

[31] Recital 13 of the 2nd AML Directive highlights that: 'There is evidence that the tightening of controls in the financial sector has prompted money launderers to seek alternative methods for concealing the origin of the proceeds of crime.'

[32] Gilmore (n 24) 202; recital 14 of the 2nd AML Directive highlights that: 'There is a trend towards the increased use by money launderers of non-financial businesses. This is confirmed by the work of the FATF on money laundering techniques and typologies.' The inclusion of the legal profession in the list of obliged entities was an issue of disagreement during the negotiations. Mitsilegas notes that '[d]isagreement on this issue threatened to derail the proposal altogether, with the European Parliament advocating a broader exemption of the legal profession by the Directive Duties than it could be accepted by the Council and the Commission' in Mitsilegas (n 10) 96.

During the same year, 2001, the global community was shaken by the terrorist attacks in the United States on September 11. In response, the FATF made significant amendments to its regime by introducing eight special Recommendations specifically targeting the fight against terrorist financing.[33] The aftermath of these attacks elevated the priority of combating terrorist financing on the political agenda of the EU.[34] Consequently, in 2005, the EU adopted the 3rd AML Directive to align with international standards.[35] This Directive broadened the framework's scope to encompass the prevention of terrorist financing and introduced a risk-based approach to address both money laundering and terrorist financing.[36]

Similarly, the impetus for the discussion surrounding the 4th Directive within the EU stemmed primarily from the need to align again with the FATF's international framework. Following a thorough evaluation, the FATF published a revised set of Recommendations in February 2012.[37] In a prompt response, the Commission issued a proposal for the 4th Directive in February 2013.[38] In the explanatory note accompanying the proposal, the Commission notes:

> A revision of the Directive at this time is complementary to the revised FATF Recommendations, which in themselves represent a substantial strengthening of the AML and combating terrorist financing framework. The Directive itself further strengthens elements of the revised Recommendations.[39]

The adoption of the 4th Directive took place in May 2015, encompassing several key provisions.[40] Notably, the Directive expanded the list of predicate offences to include tax crimes, emphasised the importance of identifying ultimate beneficial ownership, enhanced customer due diligence measures, and introduced

[33] See www.fatf-gafi.org/about/historyofthefatf/.

[34] Valsamis Mitsilegas, 'The European Union and the Rest of the World: Criminal Law and Policy Interconnections' in Malcolm Evans and Panos Koutrakos (eds), *Beyond the Established Legal Orders: Policy Interconnections Between the EU and the Rest of the World* (Bloomsbury Publishing, 2011) 175.

[35] Directive 2005/60/EC of the European Parliament and of the Council of 26 October 2005 on the prevention of the use of the financial system for the purpose of money laundering and terrorist financing [2005] OJ L309/15.

[36] Maria Bergström, 'The Many Uses of Anti-Money Laundering Regulation – Over Time and into the Future' (2018) 19(5) *German Law Journal* 1149, 1159; 3rd AML Directive, recital 8; for further discussion, see Valsamis Mitsilegas and Bill Gilmore, 'The EU Legislative Framework Against Money Laundering and Terrorist Finance: A Critical Analysis in the Light of Evolving Global Standards' (2007) 56 *International and Comparative Law Quarterly* 119.

[37] See www.fatf-gafi.org/about/historyofthefatf/.

[38] Commission, 'Proposal for a Directive of the European Parliament and of the Council on the prevention of the use of the financial system for the purpose of money laundering and terrorist financing' COM (2013) 45 final.

[39] ibid 3.

[40] Directive (EU) 2015/849 of the European Parliament and of the Council of 20 May 2015 on the prevention of the use of the financial system for the purposes of money laundering or terrorist financing, amending Regulation (EU) No 648/2012 of the European Parliament and of the Council, and repealing Directive 2005/60/EC of the European Parliament and of the Council and Commission Directive 2006/70/EC [2015] OJ L141/73.

requirements for screening Politically Exposed Persons (PEPs).[41] According to the Directive, Member States were required to adopt the necessary measures by June 2017.[42]

However, the Commission decided to introduce further amendments even before the deadline for the transposition of the Directive by the Member States.[43] In July 2016, the Commission issued a proposal for a new Directive.[44] The amendment of the 4th Directive aimed to cover deficiencies of the framework.[45] The new act was adopted on 30 May 2018.[46] The primary objective was to tackle emerging trends in money laundering and terrorist financing, including the use of digital currencies (the Directive used the term 'virtual currencies').[47] Key aspects addressed in the 5th Directive include the identification of high-risk third countries and the reinforcement of the Financial Intelligence Units' (FIUs') powers in terms of accessing information.[48] It is evident from this analysis that the EU's AML regime closely aligns with the international framework set by the FATF. The Commission consistently issues proposals to amend the European regime based on developments within the FATF.[49] This alignment is further strengthened by the fact that the Commission and several EU Member States are permanent members of the FATF.[50]

Hence, the primary mechanism driving the advancement of the EU's AML regime lies in the adaptation of the international framework to the needs of the European region.[51] The table below demonstrates a clear pattern wherein each revision of the FATF Recommendations, or the identification of new trends through other publications, triggers corresponding amendments proposed by the European Commission to the AML regime. Notably, there is only one occasion on which the EU regulated a specific sector prior to the revision of FATF Recommendations. According to the table, the EU adopted the 5th Directive, incorporating provisions

[41] Patrícia Godinho Silva, 'Recent developments in EU legislation on anti-money laundering and terrorist financing' (2019) 10 *New Journal of European Criminal Law* 57, 61.

[42] Directive (EU) 2015/849 of the European Parliament and of the Council of 20 May 2015 on the prevention of the use of the financial system for the purposes of money laundering or terrorist financing, amending Regulation (EU) No 648/2012 of the European Parliament and of the Council, and repealing Directive 2005/60/EC of the European Parliament and of the Council and Commission Directive 2006/70/EC [2015] OJ L141/73, Art 67.

[43] ibid.

[44] Commission, 'Proposal for a Directive of the European Parliament and of the Council amending Directive (EU) 2015/849 on the prevention of the use of the financial system for the purposes of money laundering or terrorist financing and amending Directive 2009/101/EC' COM(2016) 450 final.

[45] Silva (n 41).

[46] Directive (EU) 2018/843 of the European Parliament and of the Council of 30 May 2018 amending Directive (EU) 2015/849 on the prevention of the use of the financial system for the purposes of money laundering or terrorist financing, and amending Directive 2009/138/EC and 2013/36/EU [2018] OJ L156/43.

[47] Bergström (n 36) 1165.

[48] ibid.

[49] Eleni Tsingou, 'Money Laundering' in Daniel Mügge, *Europe and the Governance of Global Finance* (Oxford University Press, 2014) 352.

[50] Mitsilegas and Gilmore (n 36) 123.

[51] Tsingou (n 49) 358.

pertaining to digital currencies, before the revision of the Recommendations. However, this does not imply that the EU established rules blindly or without guidance. While the Recommendations at that time encompassed a broad category of 'new technologies', the FATF had raised concerns regarding the risks associated with digital currencies since 2014 and provided guidance on implementing a risk-based approach towards digital currencies since 2015.[52]

Drawing upon the efforts undertaken by the FATF to address the issue of money laundering involving digital currencies, the European Commission responded by introducing a series of proposals aimed at improving the AML framework and regulating the phenomenon of digital currencies, particularly cryptocurrencies. In July 2019, the Commission issued a communication outlining strategies for enhancing the implementation of the existing AML regime.[53] To further bolster the regime, the Commission adopted an action plan on 7 May 2020, which aimed to ensure its effective implementation. This comprehensive plan sought to establish an EU single rule book on AML, strengthen AML supervision, enforce criminal law provisions, enhance information exchange, and reinforce the international dimension of the EU framework.[54]

Building upon the action plan, the Commission presented a legislative package encompassing a significant overhaul of the EU AML regime. The package contained four legislative proposals: (a) a Regulation introducing the new EU AML Authority (AMLA), intending to enhance AML supervision and promote cooperation among FIUs; (b) a new Regulation on AML/CFT, providing directly applicable rules for obliged entities; (c) a 6th AML Directive, replacing the existing regime, containing and incorporating more detailed rules pertaining to FIUs; and (d) revision of the 2015 Regulation on transfer of funds, aiming to enable tracing of transfers involving virtual assets, commonly known as the 'travel rule'.[55] The EU also proposed a Regulation on the market of crypto-assets, signalling the beginning of a European harmonised framework for digital currencies.[56]

[52] See further section 4 in Chapter 3.

[53] Commission, 'Communication from the Commission to the European Parliament and the Council Towards better implementation of the EU's anti-money laundering and countering the financing of terrorism framework' COM(2019) 360 final.

[54] Commission, 'Communication from the Commission on an Action Plan for a comprehensive Union policy on preventing money laundering and terrorist financing' (2020/C 164/06), 2.

[55] Commission, 'Proposal for a Regulation of the European Parliament and of the Council establishing the Authority for Anti-Money Laundering and Countering the Financing of Terrorism and amending Regulations (EU) No 1093/2010, (EU) 1094/2010, (EU) 1095/2010' COM(2021) 421 final; Commission, 'Proposal for a Regulation of the European Parliament and of the Council on the prevention of the use of the financial system for the purposes of money laundering or terrorist financing' COM(2021) 420 final; Commission, 'Proposal for a Directive of the European Parliament and of the Council on the mechanisms to be put in place by the Member States for the prevention of the use of the financial system for the purposes of money laundering or terrorist financing and repealing Directive (EU) 2015/849' COM(2021) 423 final; Commission, 'Proposal for a Regulation of the European Parliament and of the Council on information accompanying transfers of funds and certain crypto-assets (recast)' COM(2021) 422 final.

[56] Commission, 'Proposal for a Regulation of the European Parliament and of the Council on Markets in Crypto-assets, and amending Directive (EU) 2019/1937' COM(2020) 593 final (MiCA).

Table 4.1 Chronological Overview of FATF Developments and EU AML Legislation

Year	FATF Recommendations (and other publications)	Proposals by the European Commission for amendments	Adoption of new EU Directive
1990	Publication of the Recommendations (40)	1990	In 1991 the EU adopted the 1st AML Directive
1996	Revision of the Recommendations	1999	In 2001 the EC adopted the 2nd AML Directive
2001	The FATF added to its regime the crime of Terrorist Financing (40 Recommendations + 8 special for Terrorist Financing)	–	–
2003	Revision of the Recommendations (40 + 8)	–	–
2004	The FATF adds a Recommendation for Terrorist Financing (40 + 9)	2004	In 2005 the EU adopted the 3rd AML Directive
2012	Revision of the Recommendations	2013	In 2015 the EU adopted the 4th AML Directive
2018	Addition of two new definitions concerning 'virtual assets' and 'virtual asset service providers' and revision of Recommendation 15	2016	In May 2018 the EU adopted the 5th AML Directive
		2021	In May 2023 the EU adopted a Regulation for the implementation of the FATF's travel rule (Regulation (EU) 2023/1113). In May 2024 the EU adopted three new instruments to align the regime with the FATF's guidelines (Directive (EU) 2024/1640; Regulation (EU) 2024/1624; and Regulation (EU) 2024/1620)

Concerning the proposals above, the Commission emphasises in their preambles that amendments are necessary to implement the revised framework of the FATF.[57] All the proposals have been adopted, with those that have significant impact on the phenomenon of digital currencies being the new AML Regulation and the 'travel rule' Regulation.[58] While the FATF has played a decisive role in shaping the EU's AML framework, its nature raises fundamental questions regarding the rule of law.[59] The FATF operates with minimal transparency and accountability, consisting of experts who aim to combat money laundering effectively but often prioritise expanding state power over ensuring a balanced approach to human rights.[60] As demonstrated in this section, the EU's decision-making institutions tend to follow the FATF's approach unquestioningly, as further evidenced by the table above, which illustrates the extent of the FATF's influence on EU policymaking.

2. The Path Towards the Introduction of Digital Currencies in the EU's AML Regime

Recognising the vulnerabilities and potential criminal exploitation within the realm of digital currencies, the FATF undertook extensive research on this phenomenon. Following a series of deliberations and reports, the FATF ultimately decided to amend its framework to include digital currencies within the scope.[61] Consequently, it became imperative for the EU to adopt corresponding measures to mitigate the risks associated with digital currencies. In line with the FATF's revised guidance, the EU amended its regime to incorporate provisions addressing the use of digital currencies. This harmonised response underscores the close relationship between the two regimes, with the EU actively implementing the FATF's Recommendations.

In light of these developments, the EU introduced further changes in 2018 through the amendment of the 4th AML Directive, incorporating the phenomenon of digital currencies into the AML framework without further regulation from a financial perspective. This decision was based on an approach to protect the existing financial system from the 'negative' influence and the alleged 'criminal' nature of digital currencies. However, the research unveils that the initial inclusion of digital currencies in the AML framework, even though a step in the right direction, was solely focused on interaction between the real-world economy and the crypto environment, leaving the latter mostly unregulated.

[57] Proposal COM(2021) 420 final, recital 6; Proposal COM(2021) 423 final, recital 5; Proposal COM(2021) 422 final, 6.

[58] Regulation (EU) 2024/1624 of the European Parliament and of the Council of 31 May 2024 on the prevention of the use of the financial system for the purposes of money laundering or terrorist financing [2024] OJ L, 2024/1624; Regulation (EU) 2023/1113 of the European Parliament and of the Council of 31 May 2023 on information accompanying transfers of funds and certain crypto-assets and amending Directive (EU) 2015/849 [2023] OJ L150/1.

[59] Mitsilegs and Vavoula (n 2) 266.

[60] Joshua Cohen and Charles F Sabel, 'Global Democracy?' (2004) 37 *NYU Journal of International Law and Policy* 763, 764.

[61] Financial Action Task Force, 'International Standards on Combating Money Laundering and the Financing of Terrorism & Proliferation' (FATF Recommendations), Recommendation 15.

2.1. The Warning by the European Banking Authority (EBA)

On 4 July 2014, two years prior to the European Commission's proposal to amend the 4th AML Directive, the EBA released an opinion specifically addressing digital currencies.[62] The objective of this opinion was to comprehensively examine the phenomenon of digital currencies, including their definitions and proposed regulatory measures, with the aim of informing and alerting the EU to the risks associated with this emerging technology. In its analysis, the EBA identified a total of 70 distinct risks.[63] These risks are divided into five categories:[64] risks for individuals, market participants, financial integrity, payment systems and regulatory authorities.[65] Furthermore, these risks were further classified based on their severity, categorised as high, medium or low risk.[66]

Of particular relevance to this study are the risks falling within the categories of financial integrity (eg money laundering, terrorist financing and financial crime) and risks to regulatory authorities.[67] The risks associated with financial integrity are considered the most significant, as they directly relate to one of the key justifications for the existence of the AML regime. As highlighted by the EBA, the utilisation of digital currencies for the purposes of money laundering, terrorist financing or other financial crimes poses a significant threat to financial integrity.[68]

The EBA identified several risks associated with digital currencies, stemming from their inherent anonymity and the potential for criminals to exploit them for money laundering purposes.[69] The utilisation of peer-to-peer networks further enhances the anonymity of these transactions, as there are no intermediary parties involved in requesting or recording identification details.[70] This alarming reality highlights the seriousness of the risk associated with digital currencies.[71] One of the risks identified by the EBA is the fast and irreversible transfer and deposit of digital currencies, which is facilitated by the absence of intermediaries and solely requires internet access.[72] This characteristic makes these systems attractive to criminals and terrorists seeking to finance their illicit activities.[73]

[62] European Banking Authority, 'EBA Opinion on virtual currencies', EBA/Op/2014/08 (July 2014) ('EBA Opinion'); Commission, 'Proposal for a Directive of the European Parliament and of the Council amending Directive (EU) 2015/849 on the prevention of the use of the financial system for the purposes of money laundering or terrorist financing and amending Directive 2009/101/EC' COM(2016) 450 final.

[63] EBA Opinion 21–22.

[64] ibid 2.

[65] ibid 8.

[66] ibid 22.

[67] ibid.

[68] ibid 32.

[69] ibid.

[70] Peer-to-peer is a network where two individuals can trade digital currencies between them without the need for an intermediary party and without any identification details.

[71] EBA Opinion 22.

[72] ibid 32.

[73] ibid.

Law enforcement agencies face significant challenges when investigating crimes involving digital currencies due to the anonymity they provide and their global reach.[74] Collecting data and linking digital currency transactions to individuals pose major obstacles for authorities.[75] Moreover, criminals may attempt to manipulate system participants to facilitate the commission of crimes.[76] The EBA categorises all of these risks as high, mainly due to their association with criminal activity.[77]

In addition, the EBA raised concerns about the ease with which anyone can create their own digital currency scheme, enabling criminals to develop these currencies while maintaining anonymity.[78] This is exemplified by the fact that the identity of Bitcoin's creator, Satoshi Nakamoto, remains unknown since its creation in 2009.[79] Limited information exists regarding Satoshi's true identity, leaving uncertainty as to whether they are an individual or a group.[80]

The EBA's opinion aimed to inform both the EU and national authorities about the risks associated with digital currency systems.[81] As the authority responsible for monitoring financial activities and issuing guidelines, the EBA underscored the need for effective measures to mitigate these risks.[82] Ultimately, the EBA emphasised that an inadequate framework could undermine the ability to address the risks posed by digital currencies effectively. As Lastra and Allen pointed out, 'the [EBA] recommended a shielding approach until such time as a comprehensive European regime is established for regulating VCs'.[83] This approach can only tackle risks that occur where digital currencies interact with the regulated financial system, since it does not address the workings of the digital currency economy itself.[84]

2.2. The Realisation by the European Commission

On 28 April 2015, approximately one year after the EBA's opinion,[85] the European Commission released the European Agenda on Security for the period 2015–2020.[86] The main objective of the Commission was to introduce new measures to

[74] ibid 33.
[75] ibid.
[76] ibid.
[77] ibid 22.
[78] ibid 35.
[79] Primavera De Filippi and Aaron Wright, *Blockchain and the Law: The Rule of Code* (Harvard University Press, 2018) 20.
[80] ibid.
[81] EBA Opinion 45.
[82] Regulation (EU) 1093/2010 of the European Parliament and of the Council of 24 November 2010 establishing a European Supervisory Authority (European Banking Authority), amending Decision No 716/2009/EC and repealing Commission Decision 2009/78/EC [2010] OJ L331/12, Art 9.
[83] Rosa María Lastra and Jason Grant Allen, 'Virtual Currencies in the Eurosystem: Challenges Ahead' (2018) Study requested by the ECON committee of the European Parliament, PE 619.020, 14.
[84] ibid.
[85] EBA's opinion.
[86] Commission, 'Communication from the Commission to the European Parliament, the Council, the European Economic and Social Committee and the Committee of the Regions: The European Agenda on Security' COM(2015) 185 final ('2015 Security Agenda').

combat money laundering and terrorist financing.[87] In detail, the agenda emphasised the necessity of closer cooperation on various issues due to the emergence of new threats.[88] Member States could no longer tackle specific types of crimes independently, highlighting the need for collaboration.[89] The agenda's key priorities were terrorism, organised crime and cybercrime, stressing the importance of an effective framework to identify transactions.[90] Specifically, the agenda established a link between organised crime and money laundering, stressing the importance of an effective framework to identify transactions.[91] Regarding digital currencies, the Commission recognised the need for regulatory measures to mitigate the associated risks.[92] Building on this, the Commission published on 2 February 2016 an 'Action Plan for strengthening the fight against terrorist financing'.[93] The primary focus of the action plan was combating terrorist financing and ensuring the framework could adapt to developments in this field.[94] Concerning digital currencies, the Commission acknowledged these systems as 'new financial tools' that could be exploited by criminals to fund terrorism, capitalising on their anonymity.[95]

In 2016, recognising the absence of regulation for digital currencies at the EU level, the European Commission proposed the amendment of the AML regime to include digital currency exchange platforms.[96] The significance of digital currency exchange platforms stems from their pivotal position as gatekeepers within the digital currency market. The FATF specifically emphasised that these platforms serve as an entry point where users initially exchange fiat currencies for digital currencies.[97] Therefore, it becomes imperative for these platforms to be obliged to gather the necessary information from their users. However, considering the diverse range of participants involved in this digital market, it can be contended that imposing obligations solely on these platforms may not sufficiently address the challenges posed by money laundering and terrorist financing. Consequently, the Commission chose to keep the matter open for debate, contemplating the inclusion of other actors within the AML regime.[98]

[87] Bergström (n 36) 1150.
[88] 2015 Security Agenda 2.
[89] ibid.
[90] ibid.
[91] ibid 17.
[92] ibid 17.
[93] Commission, 'Communication from the Commission to the European Parliament and the Council on an Action Plan for strengthening the fight against terrorist financing' COM(2016) 50 final ('2016 Action Plan').
[94] Silva (n 41).
[95] 2016 Action Plan 3.
[96] ibid 5.
[97] Financial Action Task Force, 'Second 12-Month Review of the Revised FATF Standards on Virtual Assets and Virtual Asset Service Providers' (July 2021) 34.
[98] 2016 Action Plan 5.

2.3. The Proposal for the Amendment of the 4th AML Directive

Following the release of the Action Plan, the Economic and Financial Affairs Council, on 12 February 2016, urged the Commission to present a proposal for amending the 4th AML Directive.[99] The Council's meeting outcomes emphasised the need for significant and immediate progress in various areas, including digital currencies, enhanced access to information for FIUs, such as bank and payment account data, appropriate measures concerning prepaid payment instruments, and measures addressing illicit cash movements.[100]

Given the numerous warnings and publications by the FATF regarding the risks associated with digital currencies, as well as the opinion expressed by the EBA, it was inevitable for the Commission to acknowledge the challenges posed by this emerging phenomenon.[101] The exponential growth of digital currencies within the EU, coupled with the absence of sufficient regulatory measures at the EU level, fostered an environment where it became challenging to effectively address risks associated with crimes such as money laundering and terrorist financing.

Furthermore, in the absence of legislation at the EU level, some Member States took it upon themselves to establish their own regulatory frameworks governing digital currencies. These frameworks encompassed various aspects, including definitions, licensing requirements and obligations for entities operating within the digital currency market. However, in the impact assessment of the proposal for the 5th AML Directive, the European Commission emphasised that these divergent approaches by Member States could result in regulatory arbitrage.[102] As a result, the adoption of a harmonised framework across the EU was deemed the most suitable course of action to effectively address the challenges associated with digital currencies. This decision was influenced by careful consideration of the warnings issued and the call from the Economic and Financial Affairs Council.

On 5 July 2016, in response to these concerns, the European Commission issued a proposal to amend the AML regime.[103] The explanatory note accompanying the proposal outlined the rationale behind the new Directive. One of the key concerns highlighted was the emergence of new and innovative methods used by terrorists

[99] Commission, 'Proposal for a Directive of the European Parliament and of the Council amending Directive (EU) 2015/849 on the prevention of the use of the financial system for the purposes of money laundering or terrorist financing and amending Directive 2009/101/EC' COM(2016) 450 final.

[100] Council of the EU, 'Outcome of the Council Meeting, 3445th Council meeting, Economic and Financial Affairs' 5936/16, 8, www.consilium.europa.eu/media/22950/st05936en16v4.pdf.

[101] EBA Opinion; see section 4 in Chapter 3.

[102] Commission, 'Commission Staff Working Document Impact Assessment Accompanying the document: Proposal for a Directive of the European Parliament and the Council amending Directive (EU) 2015/849 on the prevention of the use of the financial system for the purposes of money laundering or terrorist financing and amending Directive 2009/101/EC' SWD(2016) 223 final, 25 ('Impact Assessment').

[103] Commission, 'Proposal for a Directive of the European Parliament and of the Council amending Directive (EU) 2015/849 on the prevention of the use of the financial system for the purposes of money laundering or terrorist financing and amending Directive 2009/101/EC' COM(2016) 450 final.

to finance their activities, necessitating the implementation of measures to mitigate such risks.[104] Additionally, the Commission acknowledged that technological advancements had facilitated the rapid global transfer and concealment of funds by criminals, with digital currencies being one of the notable developments in this regard. [105]

The influence of the FATF's regime on the EU's AML framework was once again emphasised. The Commission assured that the proposed measures would align with the guidance provided by the FATF.[106] The inclusion of digital currencies in the Directive goes beyond the mere definition of these currencies and the obligations imposed on the private sector. Given the perceived anonymity associated with digital currencies, the identification of beneficial owners becomes challenging.[107] Consequently, the careful integration of this phenomenon within the AML regime is crucial, as it intersects with measures pertaining to customer due diligence, beneficial ownership, FIUs and information gathering, among others.[108]

An important consideration regarding fundamental rights is the potential compatibility of these amendments, particularly the incorporation of new private entities into a comprehensive regulatory framework, with the principle of proportionality. The explanatory note accompanying the proposal asserts that the amendments adhere to the principle of proportionality.[109] The Commission justifies the inclusion of digital currency exchange platforms as a necessary measure, deeming these entities as the gatekeepers of the digital currency market, responsible for facilitating exchanges between fiat currencies and digital currencies.[110] However, it is crucial to note that this is not the exclusive method of acquiring digital currencies. On this point, it is important to highlight that the Commission chose to mandate regulations solely for exchanges between digital currencies and fiat currencies, excluding platforms facilitating exchanges between different types of digital currencies. This development created a regulatory lacuna, leaving the digital currency market largely outside the scope of oversight.

The absence of regulation surrounding digital currencies restricted the ability of FIUs and national authorities to access identification and transaction information maintained by virtual asset service providers. Considering all relevant factors, the Commission had to determine appropriate measures, striking a balance between regulation (AML measures) and technological innovation.[111] The explanatory note to the proposal emphasises that the regulatory framework

[104] ibid 2.

[105] ibid.

[106] ibid 18.

[107] Fabian Maximilian Johannes Teichmann, 'Financing terrorism through cryptocurrencies – a danger for Europe?' (2018) 21(4) *Journal of Money Laundering Control* 513.

[108] Bergström (n 36) 1165.

[109] Commission, 'Proposal for a Directive of the European Parliament and of the Council amending Directive (EU) 2015/849 on the prevention of the use of the financial system for the purposes of money laundering or terrorist financing and amending Directive 2009/101/EC' COM(2016) 450 final, 7.

[110] ibid.

[111] ibid.

should not impede the development of these systems.[112] Despite recognising that the obligations for customer due diligence may pose an additional burden on these new entities, the Commission assured that such obligations would not hinder their ability to provide services. Nevertheless, this assertion remains open to debate.

The impact assessment identifies anonymity within digital currency systems as the primary concern.[113] To substantiate this point, the Commission cited the example of Ali Shukri Amin and his Twitter guidelines on using Bitcoin to transfer funds to Daesh.[114] The impact assessment highlights three key issues resulting from this problem: (a) the perceived anonymity (although these currencies are not entirely anonymous), (b) the mass adoption and acceptance of digital currencies by individuals and companies globally, and (c) the ease of exchanging fiat currencies for digital currencies and *vice versa*.[115]

2.4. The Available Policy Choices

The primary objective of the inclusion of digital currencies in the AML regime was to identify the participants in the digital currency market and impose obligations on entities capable of collecting essential identification information. Based on this, the Commission reached the conclusion that in order to address the issue of anonymity effectively, the key participants would be exchanging platforms, custodial wallet providers and users.[116] As previously mentioned, the Commission's Action Plan, presented in February 2016, left room for including wallet providers within the AML regime. This inclusion can be considered crucial, as it enhances the feasibility of addressing the problem of anonymity by encompassing multiple categories of entities. However, the Commission did not, at that point, consider incorporating the issuers of digital currencies into the regulatory framework.

Overall, six options were examined by the Commission, divided into three categories of targets. First, regarding users, the Commission proposed mandatory registration to combat anonymity (Option A). This option entailed the normalisation of the use of Legal Entity Identifiers (LEI) for digital currency transactions. The alternative (Option B) was the voluntary self-registration of users. This option would have provided users with a channel to self-register (eg to the national FIU, the European Banking Authority, etc). Under Option B, the Commission argued that anonymity could be upheld, but law enforcement authorities could rapidly identify the registered users.[117] Regulating users of digital currencies can

[112] ibid.

[113] Impact Assessment 8.

[114] ibid 15; see Yessi Bello Perez, 'US Arms Dealer Allegedly Used Bitcoin for Purchases' (*Coindesk*, 12 August 2015), www.coindesk.com/markets/2015/08/12/us-arms-dealer-allegedly-used-bitcoin-for-purchases.

[115] Impact Assessment 17.

[116] ibid 31.

[117] ibid 32.

be a challenging task, as anticipated. Option B, in particular, raises controversy. Anonymity represents a highly appealing characteristic of digital currencies, and suggesting self-registration as a means to address anonymity for users who specifically utilise digital currencies for this purpose raises significant doubts and concerns.

Second, in relation to the exchange platforms, the Commission proposed introducing digital currencies in the 4th AML Directive (Option C). This required the inclusion of specific private entities (service providers) in the list of obliged entities of the AML regime, requiring them to apply customer due diligence measures and essentially to verify the identity of their customers and report suspicious transactions that may be linked to money laundering. The alternative (Option D) was to fight anonymity by regulating digital currency exchange platforms under the Directive on Payment Services (PSD2). This approach would have the benefit of automatically bringing exchange platforms within the 4th AML Directive, while submitting them to broader consumer protection rules, minimum capital requirements and other safeguarding requirements.[118]

This category was the subject of extensive discussion within the Commission's action plan in February 2016. It should be noted that the impact assessment does not provide clarification on whether this includes all exchange platforms, such as those facilitating exchanges between fiat currencies and digital currencies, as well as exchanges between different types of digital currencies. Option C represents a straightforward approach, wherein these platforms would be classified as obliged entities under the AML Directive.[119] However, Option D presents a particularly intriguing perspective. This option would allow the potential of regulating digital currencies through an alternative instrument (PSD2).[120] This signified the existence of a viable choice for a comprehensive approach to regulating digital currencies as a whole phenomenon. It should be emphasised that through the implementation of PSD2, digital currencies would appear to be legitimate and safe due to more complete regulation, while still operating within the purview of the AML framework.

The third category encompassed the custodial wallet providers. Similar to the approach for exchange platforms, it was suggested that custodial wallet providers could be regulated under the AML Directive (Option E) or PSD2 (Option F).[121] The analysis and the comments regarding custodial wallet providers remain consistent with those for exchange platforms. However, there is an additional

[118] ibid 32–33.

[119] Directive (EU) 2015/849 of the European Parliament and of the Council of 20 May 2015 on the prevention of the use of the financial system for the purposes of money laundering or terrorist financing, amending Regulation (EU) No 648/2012 of the European Parliament and of the Council, and repealing Directive 2005/60/EC of the European Parliament and of the Council and Commission Directive 2006/70/EC [2015] OJ L141/73, Art 2.

[120] Directive (EU) 2015/2366 of the European Parliament and of the Council of 25 November 2015 on payment services in the internal market, amending Directives 2002/65/EC, 2009/110/EC and 2013/36/EU and Regulation (EU) No 1093/2010, and repealing Directive 2007/64/EC [2015] OJ L337/35 (PSD2).

[121] Impact Assessment 33.

concern specifically pertaining to custodial wallet providers. It is worth noting that a user does not necessarily require a custodial wallet provider to engage in transactions involving digital currencies.[122] As elaborated further in Chapter 1, there are various categories of wallets, some of which may not be subject to regulation. For instance, software wallet providers do not possess or control the private key in the same manner as custodial wallet providers.[123] This is the primary reason why custodial wallet providers receive particular attention, as they have greater ease in collecting the identification details of users.

Furthermore, valuable input was gathered from stakeholders' observations on the proposal.[124] As anticipated, consumers expressed concerns regarding the objective of reducing anonymity in digital currencies. However, they accepted the imposition of obligations on the gatekeepers of these systems, namely exchangers and wallet providers (options C, D, E, F).[125] Following consultations with the Member States (28 Members prior to the United Kingdom's exit), option C, which involves regulating digital currency exchange platforms under the AML regime, emerged as the most preferred course of action.[126] Only one Member State supported option D, which entails regulating digital currency exchange platforms under PSD2 rather than the AML regime.[127]

The approach of the Member States was anticipated, considering the concerns surrounding the potential criminality associated with digital currencies. However, the widespread acceptance of these currencies and the continuous development of the underlying technology suggest the need for a more comprehensive approach to establish an overall secure digital environment. The decision made by the Member States aligns with the opinion of the EBA, which emphasises the high-priority risks of digital currencies, particularly regarding the crime of money laundering.[128] The EBA's opinion advocated for the inclusion of digital currencies in the AML regime as a crucial step in mitigating risks associated with their anonymity.[129]

Nevertheless, the Member States' choice was not solely based on this factor. The majority of Member States underlined their lack of support for the inclusion of digital currencies in PSD2 (options D and F).[130] Their main reasoning was that PSD2 would provide digital currency systems with the necessary legitimacy to present them as secure for European consumers.[131] This perspective is somewhat

[122] See subsection 5.4. in Chapter 1.
[123] See subsection 5.4. in Chapter 1.
[124] Impact Assessment 33.
[125] ibid.
[126] ibid.
[127] ibid.
[128] EBA Opinion 22.
[129] ibid.
[130] Impact Assessment 33–34.
[131] Impact Assessment 33.

peculiar, as including digital currencies in PSD2 to primarily protect consumers does not necessarily exclude their regulation under the AML regime.[132]

The nature of digital currencies, which can operate without the involvement of third parties and can be issued by anyone rather than centrally by the EU or Member States, diverges significantly from that of the well-established banking system. The idea that the EU and the Member States would lose control over the issuance and provision of money poses evident challenges. However, even from a financial standpoint, it can be argued that a holistic regulatory approach encompassing the digital currency market is the most appropriate way to mitigate a wide range of risks, including financial, consumer and criminal exploitation. This perspective was also shared by the stakeholders in the crypto industry, who sought to establish a safe environment for consumers while simultaneously addressing the risks.[133] The crypto industry envisioned a framework focused on the digital currency market to enhance safety for businesses and consumers.[134]

The policy options of the proposal for the 5th AML Directive, analysed above, were mainly based on the 'shielding' approach of the EBA at that point in time. The purpose was to regulate the risks from the interaction between digital currencies and regulated sectors. This is also evident from the fact that the Directive covered only the gatekeepers of the real economy (ie intermediaries which are located between digital currencies and the regulated financial services sector).[135]

At that point, the EU made the decision to incorporate digital currency exchange platforms and custodial wallet providers in the AML regime.[136] However, the Commission kept options open concerning the regulation of users.[137] A critical assessment of the option to regulate digital currencies through the AML regime reveals that the concern over the anonymity of these systems, while ostensibly valid, conceals a deeper institutional fear, namely, the potential loss of state control over money and the mass adoption of decentralised forms of money. Arguably, the true regulatory anxiety may lie in the broader systemic implications of digital currency adoption. Such currencies challenge the monopoly of states and central banks over money creation and monetary policy. To this end, the AML framework can operate as an instrument to reassert state authority and maintain control over the financial system rather than just a tool against money laundering. Troublingly, the Commission assured in the explanatory note to the proposal that the obligations imposed on entities would not hinder their ability to provide services.[138] However, in the 'Analysis of the impact of the policy options proposed' section

[132] See Option D.

[133] Impact Assessment 34.

[134] Evidently, this came years later with the adoption of MiCA.

[135] Lastra and Allen (n 83).

[136] Commission, 'Proposal for a Directive of the European Parliament and of the Council amending Directive (EU) 2015/849 on the prevention of the use of the financial system for the purposes of money laundering or terrorist financing and amending Directive 2009/101/EC' COM(2016) 450 final, 9.

[137] ibid.

[138] ibid.

of the proposal, specifically analysing option C (the most favoured option), the Commission stated:

> More generally, the VC industry will undoubtedly suffer from the reduced anonymity that such an initiative would bring as anonymity has been a key component of their success. Platforms and custodians that are not able to comply would have to disappear (at least from the EU market and other regulated markets such as the US), and a consolidation phase could take place, leaving a few major exchange platforms and custodians on the market, where the transactions would be concentrated, thus making their business more profitable.[139]

The wording of this statement, openly acknowledging that only a limited number of prominent exchange platforms and custodial wallet providers would remain following the integration of digital currencies into the AML regime, raises concerns regarding the proportionality of the chosen policy. It creates an imbalanced situation for smaller and medium-sized enterprises, placing them at a distinct disadvantage.

3. The Newly Adopted AML Regime and the Evolving Reality for Virtual Asset Service Providers

After undergoing consultations with Member States, considering various opinions, and progressing through the specific stages of the European legislative process, the 5th AML Directive was finally adopted on 30 May 2018.[140] The deadline for transposing this Directive into national legal systems was 10 January 2020.[141] Currently, all Member States have the necessary laws and regulations to implement the measures outlined in the 5th AML Directive.[142]

In the 5th Directive, the EU decided to incorporate policy options C and E, as discussed above. Consequently, the Directive includes in its scope only those platforms engaged in providing exchange services between fiat currencies (such as the Euro) and digital currencies, as well as custodial wallet providers.[143] As a result, these entities are obliged to request and collect identification details from

[139] Impact Assessment 52.

[140] Directive (EU) 2018/843 of the European Parliament and of the Council of 30 May 2018 amending Directive (EU) 2015/849 on the prevention of the use of the financial system for the purposes of money laundering or terrorist financing, and amending Directive 2009/138/EC and 2013/36/EU [2018] OJ L156/43.

[141] ibid Art 4.

[142] See https://eur-lex.europa.eu/legal-content/EN/NIM/?uri=celex:32018L0843.

[143] Directive (EU) 2018/843 of the European Parliament and of the Council of 30 May 2018 amending Directive (EU) 2015/849 on the prevention of the use of the financial system for the purposes of money laundering or terrorist financing, and amending Directive 2009/138/EC and 2013/36/EU [2018] OJ L156/43, recital 8.

their customers and report any suspicious transactions. Through this process, Member States will be able to oversee transactions conducted with the use of digital currencies. This initiative aims to minimise the anonymity associated with such currencies by enabling FIUs to link digital currency transactions with bank accounts, thereby enhancing the ability to identify individuals involved.

However, the adoption of the 5th AML Directive can be described as premature. The EU sought to regulate digital currencies by incorporating them into the existing regulatory framework without adequately considering the distinct features of this technology. The Directive's primary emphasis lies in safeguarding the traditional financial system against the potential risks associated with digital currencies.[144] Furthermore, this Directive provides limited, if any, meaningful contribution to the combat against money laundering and terrorist financing. Even the Directive itself acknowledges this limitation by obliging only two specific categories of entities, leaving the majority of this digital economy unregulated.[145]

In light of these considerations, the European Commission recognised the presence of numerous risks that consumers and investors encounter within the unregulated realm of digital currencies. Simultaneously, Member States began implementing their own rules and regulations pertaining to this technology, resulting in a fragmented approach to the digital economy. To prevent regulatory competition and establish harmonised standards across the EU, the European Commission took the initiative by proposing a Regulation on Markets in Crypto-Assets on 24 September 2020 (MiCA).[146] This ground-breaking proposal represented the world's inaugural endeavour to adopt a comprehensive regulatory framework specifically tailored to digital currencies.

To bolster AML efforts, the European Commission introduced four new legislative proposals on 20 July 2021. These proposals encompass: (a) the establishment of a new EU AML Authority (AMLA) through a Regulation; (b) the implementation of an AML Regulation; (c) the introduction of a 6th AML Directive; and (d) the revision of the 2015 Regulation on transfers of funds (the travel rule Regulation).[147]

[144] The Directive obliges only the gatekeepers to the real economy, ie exchange platforms and custodian wallet providers.

[145] Directive (EU) 2018/843 of the European Parliament and of the Council of 30 May 2018 amending Directive (EU) 2015/849 on the prevention of the use of the financial system for the purposes of money laundering or terrorist financing, and amending Directive 2009/138/EC and 2013/36/EU [2018] OJ L156/43, recital 9.

[146] Regulation (EU) 2023/1114 of the European Parliament and of the Council of 31 May 2023 on markets in crypto-assets, and amending Regulations (EU) No 1093/2010 and (EU) No 1095/2010 and Directives 2013/36/EU and (EU) 2019/1937 [2024] OJ L150/40 (MiCA).

[147] Commission, 'Proposal for a Regulation of the European Parliament and of the Council establishing the Authority for Anti-Money Laundering and Countering the Financing of Terrorism and amending Regulations (EU) No 1093/2010, (EU) 1094/2010, (EU) 1095/2010' COM(2021) 421 final; Commission, 'Proposal for a Regulation of the European Parliament and of the Council on the prevention of the use of the financial system for the purposes of money laundering or terrorist financing' COM(2021) 420 final; Commission, 'Proposal for a Directive of the European Parliament and of the Council on the mechanisms to be put in place by the Member States for the prevention of the use of the financial system for the purposes of money laundering or terrorist financing and repealing Directive (EU) 2015/849' COM(2021) 423 final; Commission, 'Proposal for a Regulation of the European Parliament and of the Council on information accompanying transfers of funds and certain crypto-assets (recast)' COM(2021) 422 final.

It is important to note that the 6th AML Directive primarily addresses provisions related to national supervisors and FIUs of the Member States, while the AML Regulation focuses on the obligations of the private sector. This includes obligations imposed on obliged entities, customer due diligence requirements, and rules on beneficial ownership. Consequently, the discussion concentrates exclusively on the AML Regulation and the revised Regulation on transfers of funds (travel rule), as these two instruments specifically involve obligations related to virtual asset service providers, which is the focal point of this research. This section presents a novel exposition of the previously unexplored implications of these Regulations, arguing that the new regime continues the trajectory established by the 5th AML Directive in moving away from the risk-based approach.

3.1. Defining the Phenomenon of Digital Currencies: from the 5th AML Directive to the Regulation on Markets in Crypto-Assets (MiCA): A New Playing Field

In relation to digital currencies, the text of the 5th Directive differs from the Commission's proposal (using the term 'virtual currencies'). The officially adopted text defines digital currencies as:

> a digital representation of value that is not issued or guaranteed by a central bank or a public authority, is not necessarily attached to a legally established currency and does not possess a legal status of currency or money, but is accepted by natural or legal persons as a means of exchange and which can be transferred, stored and traded electronically.[148]

Although the wording of the definition resembles the Commission's proposal, it is more precise in its scope. In the Commission's proposed definition, digital currencies 'means a digital representation of value that is neither issued by a central bank or a public authority, nor necessarily attached to a fiat currency, but is accepted by natural or legal persons as a means of payment and can be transferred, stored or traded electronically'.[149]

The significant difference lies in the inclusion of the term 'payment' in the proposed definition, making it narrower than the term 'exchange', which encompasses the concept of payment. The European Central Bank (ECB) supported the broader term 'exchange' in its 2016 opinion.[150] The ECB argued that the term

[148] ibid; the 5th AML Directive used the term 'virtual currencies'.

[149] Commission, 'Proposal for a Directive of the European Parliament and of the Council amending Directive (EU) 2015/849 on the prevention of the use of the financial system for the purposes of money laundering or terrorist financing and amending Directive 2009/101/EC' COM(2016) 450 final, 30.

[150] European Central Bank, 'Opinion of the European Central Bank on a proposal for a Directive of the European Parliament and of the Council amending Directive (EU) 2015/849 on the prevention of the use of the financial system for the purposes of money laundering or terrorist financing and amending Directive 2009/101/EC' CON/2016/49 (October 2016), 3–4 ('ECB Opinion').

'payment' could misrepresent digital currencies as actual money, whereas the term 'exchange' was more appropriate.[151] The ECB further recommended the addition of the phrase 'and possibly also for other purposes' to broaden the definition's scope.[152]

During negotiations, debates arose over the nature of digital currencies reflected in the definition. As a result, the Senate of the Czech Republic, in a resolution in November 2016, called for a more precise definition.[153] On this matter, the ECB strongly advocated for the Commission to establish a precise definition of digital currencies that clearly distinguishes them from legal currencies or traditional money.[154] The ECB emphasised the importance of avoiding undue legitimisation of digital currencies within the EU.[155]

The Council of the EU also supported this argument, as evidenced by its decision on 19 December 2016 to adopt a negotiating mandate for the trilogue process, which aligned with the ECB's approach.[156] The Council's definition was primarily focused on differentiating digital currencies from fiat currencies by emphasising that digital currencies do not possess legal tender status and do not fall under the category of funds as defined in PSD2.[157] Similarly, in its negotiating report, adopted in March 2017, the European Parliament maintained an identical approach, albeit without specifically referring to PSD2.[158]

The definition of digital currencies in the adopted text aligned closely with the approaches of the ECB and the European Parliament.[159] This demonstrates that the concerns regarding the legitimacy of digital currencies were taken into account by the EU. The adopted text explicitly clarifies that digital currencies are not considered money and lack the legal status of a currency. The substitution of the word 'payment' with 'exchange' in the definition further supports the objective of preventing the normalisation of digital currencies (primarily cryptocurrencies).

[151] ECB Opinion 3.

[152] ibid 4.

[153] The Senate of the Parliament of the Czech Republic, '38th Resolution of the Senate on anti-money laundering package' (30 November 2016).

[154] ECB Opinion 3.

[155] ibid 2.

[156] Council of the EU, 'Negotiating Mandate for Proposal for a Directive of the European Parliament and of the Council amending Directive (EU) 2015/849 on the prevention of the use of the financial system for the purposes of money laundering or terrorist financing and amending Directive 2009/101/EC' 15605/16 (19 December 2016) 21.

[157] ibid; PSD2.

[158] European Parliament, 'Report on the proposal for a directive of the European Parliament and of the Council amending Directive (EU) 2015/849 on the prevention of the use of the financial system for the purposes of money laundering or terrorist financing and amending Directive 2009/101/EC' A8-0056/2017 (9 March 2017) 22. The proposed definition by the European Parliament is the same as the ECB's definition.

[159] ECB Opinion 3–4; European Parliament, 'Report on the proposal for a directive of the European Parliament and of the Council amending Directive (EU) 2015/849 on the prevention of the use of the financial system for the purposes of money laundering or terrorist financing and amending Directive 2009/101/EC' A8-0056/2017 (9 March 2017) 22.

Another notable comment raised during the discussion on the proposed amendments was the absence of a definition for custodial wallet providers.[160] Given the relatively new nature of digital currency technology and entities like wallet providers, there are several questions regarding their operations. Specifically, different categories of wallet providers exist, each with distinct functions.

The adopted text addresses this concern by including a definition for custodial wallet providers. Thus, Article 3 was amended to include: '(19) "custodian wallet provider" means an entity that provides services to safeguard private cryptographic keys on behalf of its customers, to hold, store and transfer virtual currencies.'[161] According to this definition, entities that safeguard the private keys of users and handle the storage and transfer of digital currencies fall under the category of obliged entities. However, this definition might be considered too narrow, as some wallet providers may solely offer storage services without safeguarding the private keys. Consequently, such non-custodial wallet providers would not be subject to the obligations outlined in the Directive. Additionally, it can be argued that custodial wallet providers could potentially evade the obligations of the Directive if they require customers to manually input their private keys for each transaction.

On closer analysis of the legislative framework at hand, it becomes evident that the 5th AML Directive, particularly the inclusion of digital currencies in the regime, raises significant concerns. The analysis of the definitions of digital currencies and custodial wallet providers reveals that while this was an important step towards regulating these currencies, the amendments were not sufficient to address the underlying issues.

This changed, to a certain extent, in June 2023, when the EU successfully concluded negotiations and adopted the MiCA Regulation.[162] MiCA represents a landmark legislative achievement as it is the first comprehensive regulatory framework specifically addressing digital currencies (the Regulation is focused primarily on crypto-assets). Its introduction highlights the growing importance of the digital economy and the urgent need for a tailored approach to its regulation. The focus is shifted to MiCA, as it is intricately connected to the AML regime. It is worth noting that to avoid any redundancy or overlap between the new AML regime and MiCA, the Commission deliberately excludes AML obligations from MiCA. Nonetheless, MiCA does provide updated versions of essential definitions for crypto-assets and crypto-asset service providers, laying the foundation for effective regulation in this domain.[163]

[160] See subsection 2.5.

[161] Directive (EU) 2018/843 of the European Parliament and of the Council of 30 May 2018 amending Directive (EU) 2015/849 on the prevention of the use of the financial system for the purposes of money laundering or terrorist financing, and amending Directive 2009/138/EC and 2013/36/EU [2018] OJ L156/43, Art 1(2)(d).

[162] MiCA.

[163] MiCA uses the terms crypto-asset and crypto-asset service provider, rather than 'virtual' in order to focus solely on cryptography-based currencies.

The process of defining digital currencies has proven to be a complex challenge, with differing perspectives among European institutions. The chosen approach in the AML regime aimed to provide a strict definition by emphasising that digital currencies lack the legal status of traditional money. However, MiCA's definition has significant differences from its predecessor under the 5th AML Directive. MiCA takes a distinct approach by focusing on the technological characteristics of these currencies. According to the Regulation, crypto-assets are defined as 'a digital representation of a value or of a right that is able to be transferred and stored electronically using distributed ledger technology or similar technology'.[164] This definition strikes a balance, encompassing a wide range of existing crypto-assets while excluding digital currencies that do not rely on distributed ledger technology, such as blockchain.[165] The Regulation clarifies that '"distributed ledger technology" or "DLT" means a technology that enables the operation and use of distributed ledgers', and '"distributed ledger" means an information repository that keeps records of transactions and that is shared across, and synchronised between, a set of DLT network nodes using a consensus mechanism'.[166]

Based on this focused approach, MiCA further clarifies the scope by defining three distinct categories, namely asset-referenced tokens, electronic money tokens and utility tokens. The first category includes crypto-assets that are not electronic money tokens and that purport to maintain a stable value by referencing another value or right or a combination thereof, including one or more official currencies.[167] Electronic money tokens, by contrast, maintain a stable value by referencing the value of one official currency.[168] Utility tokens differ from both, as they are only intended to provide access to a good or a service supplied by their issuers.[169] Therefore, based on this, the scope encompasses asset-referenced tokens, e-money tokens, and a catch-all category (under Title II) which covers mainly utility tokens.[170] However, the EU with MiCA clearly illustrates the incompatibility of legal regulation with the decentralised nature of some digital currencies (eg bitcoin). At the trilogue stage of the legislative process, the Council's mandate included a declaration that MiCA is only applicable when at least 'part of such activity or services is performed in a decentralized way'.[171] The European Parliament, during the negotiations, accepted this inclusion which was later transformed into recital 22 in the adopted text. According to the recital, 'Where crypto-asset services are

[164] MiCA, Art 3(5).

[165] MiCA covers unbacked crypto-assets, stablecoins, asset-referenced tokens, e-money tokens and utility tokens. However, the Regulation does not encompass non-fungible tokens and decentralised finance.

[166] MiCA, Art 3(1)(2).

[167] MiCA, Art 3(1)(6).

[168] MiCA, Art 3(1)(7); e-money tokens are not to be confused with 'e-money', as per Art 2 of MiCA which does not apply to e-money as defined in Article 2 of Directive 2009/110/EC, except where they qualify as electronic money tokens under MiCA.

[169] MiCA, Art 3(1)(9).

[170] MiCA, Title II.

[171] Council of the European Union, 'Initial positions of the three Institutions prior to commencement of trilogues' (15 May 2023) 9356/23, , recital 12(a) ('Trilogue Table').

provided in a fully decentralised manner without any intermediary, they should not fall within the scope of this Regulation.'[172] Consequently, even if a crypto-asset falls into the third 'catch-all' category under Title II, the MiCA Regulation will not apply in the case of complete decentralisation. This is due to the argument that has already been stated in this book: that in a completely decentralised environment, there are no intermediaries to be obliged.

Moreover, another difference is that under the MiCA Regulation, the vast majority of services and virtual asset service providers are regulated. According to Article 3(1)(15) and (16):

> 'crypto-asset service provider' means a legal person or other undertaking whose occupation or business is the provision of one or more crypto-asset services to clients on a professional basis . . .;[173]
>
> 'crypto-asset service' means any of the following services and activities relating to any crypto-asset: (a) providing custody and administration of crypto-assets on behalf of clients; (b) operation of a trading platform for crypto-assets; (c) exchange of crypto-assets for funds; (d) exchange of crypto-assets for other crypto-assets; (e) execution of orders for crypto-assets on behalf of clients; (f) placing of crypto-assets; (g) reception and transmission of orders for crypto-assets on behalf of clients; (h) providing advice on crypto-assets; (i) providing portfolio management on crypto-assets; (j) providing transfer services for crypto-assets on behalf of clients;[174]

In contrast to the 5thth AML Directive, the MiCA Regulation takes a broader approach by extending the regulatory scope beyond the gatekeepers of the traditional economy to encompass the entire digital economy. It should be noted, however, that the MiCA Regulation is designed to align closely with the newly adopted AML Regulation, which will be discussed in the following subsections.

3.2. The Proposal and the Newly Adopted AML Regulation

The European Commission's proposal for an AML Regulation, issued on 20 July 2021, was eventually adopted on 31 May 2024.[175] The objective of this new act is multi-fold: (a) addressing emerging risks by introducing new definitions for crypto-assets and virtual asset service providers; (b) ensuring consistent application of rules, including customer due diligence measures; (c) establishing requirements for due diligence measures concerning third countries, politically exposed persons, and beneficial ownership; (d) providing clear guidelines for reporting

[172] MiCA, recital 22.
[173] MiCA, Art 3(15).
[174] MiCA, Art 3(16).
[175] Commission, 'Proposal for a Regulation of the European Parliament and of the Council on the prevention of the use of the financial system for the purposes of money laundering or terrorist financing' COM(2021) 420 final.

suspicious transactions, including the identification of red flags; (e) ensuring compliance with data protection rules; and (f) imposing limitations on the use of cash.[176] This Regulation primarily focuses on the obligations imposed on the private sector, specifically pertaining to the preventive regime. The transformation of relevant provisions from the 5th AML Directive into a Regulation results in a directly applicable framework, limiting the discretion of Member States in determining the method of implementation.

The European Commission justifies the proposal for the Regulation based on recent developments within the FATF.[177] It recognises the inadequacy of the 5th AML Directive in addressing the complexities surrounding digital currencies and consequently calls for the inclusion of additional providers within the regulatory framework.[178] Notably, the European Parliament is the sole institution advocating for the incorporation of non-fungible tokens (NFTs) and decentralised finance (DeFi) into the AML framework.[179] However, it should be noted that such phenomena are excluded from the scope of MiCA as discussed above.

The AML Regulation addresses the issue of anonymity associated with digital currencies, recognising the use of technological tools that enhance anonymity.[180] To tackle this, the Regulation prohibits service providers from offering and storing 'anonymous crypto-asset accounts or accounts allowing for the anonymisation or the increased obfuscation of transactions by crypto-asset service providers, including through anonymity-enhancing coins'.[181] It is important to note that this prohibition does not entail a complete ban on the use of such wallets, but, rather, regulated providers are restricted from providing anonymising services. Furthermore, the European Parliament advocated unsuccessfully, during the negotiations, for an amendment to expand this prohibition to include mixing service providers, whose main objective is to obscure the origin of funds.[182]

In terms of definitions, Article 2 of the AML Regulation refers to MiCA regarding the concepts of crypto-assets and crypto-asset service providers.[183] This indicates that the obliged entities of the crypto industry are defined in the MiCA Regulation for the purposes of the new AML Regulation. However, there appeared to be differing approaches regarding the classification of these providers. The European Parliament and the Council, as indicated in their negotiating mandates,

[176] ibid 3.

[177] ibid 11; it is essential to remind the reader that the 5th AML Directive was adopted before the amendment of FATF Recommendations.

[178] ibid 18–19.

[179] ibid 11–12; this might be exactly the reason why the European Parliament is pushing for their inclusion in the new Regulation.

[180] Regulation (EU) 2024/1624 of the European Parliament and of the Council of 31 May 2024 on the prevention of the use of the financial system for the purposes of money laundering or terrorist financing [2024] OJ L, 2024/1624, recital 160.

[181] ibid; see subsection 5.4. in Chapter 1.

[182] Trilogue Table 124; see subsection 5.5. in Chapter 1.

[183] Regulation (EU) 2024/1624 of the European Parliament and of the Council of 31 May 2024 on the prevention of the use of the financial system for the purposes of money laundering or terrorist financing [2024] OJ L, 2024/1624, Art 2(1)(7), (8), (9).

aimed to categorise crypto-asset service providers as 'financial institutions' by adding these services under the respective definition.[184] This agreement between the two institutions was eventually reflected in Article 2(6)(i), where crypto-asset service providers were introduced under the general umbrella definition of 'financial institution'.[185]

Article 19 of the Regulation establishes the circumstances under which obliged entities are required to implement customer due diligence measures (CDD).[186] During the negotiation, the Council's mandate included a more stringent stance concerning crypto-asset service providers and crypto-transactions, proposing an amendment that mandates the application of basic CDD even for occasional transactions below the threshold of 1,000 Euros.[187] This essentially frames cryptocurrencies as a high risk phenomenon, a view that is reinforced through the wording of the adopted text. Therefore, it can be argued that the new AML regime of the EU (including the 5th AML Directive onwards) clearly departs from the well-established risk-based approach. Article 19(3)(a) illustrates that by way of derogation from the general provision, crypto-asset service providers should apply CDD measures for occasional transactions of at least 1,000 Euros.[188] This is a decrease from the general threshold of EUR 10,000 in Article 19(1)(b).[189] Nevertheless the text goes further in paragraph (3)(b) to establish that crypto-asset service providers are obliged to apply 'at least customer due diligence measures referred to in Article 20(1), point (a), when carrying out an occasional transaction where the value is below EUR 1 000'.[190] This is a considerable development as it applies a blanket measure affecting all users with transactions executed by the regulated digital economy.

Furthermore, both the European Parliament and the Council advocated for an additional Article that would emphasise the necessity of applying enhanced due diligence measures to correspondent cross-border relationships involving crypto-asset service providers[191] The European Parliament's suggestion is specifically focused on relationships with non-Union entities.[192] Additionally, both the European Parliament and the Council proposed the application of more intrusive measures (enhanced due diligence) for crypto-asset transactions involving a self-hosted address.[193]

[184] ibid 141–42.

[185] ibid Art 2(1)(6)(i).

[186] ibid Art 19.

[187] Trilogue Table 242.

[188] Regulation (EU) 2024/1624 of the European Parliament and of the Council of 31 May 2024 on the prevention of the use of the financial system for the purposes of money laundering or terrorist financing [2024] OJ L, 2024/1624, Art 19 (3)(a).

[189] ibid Art 19(1)(b)

[190] ibid Art 19(3)(b); the CDD measures referred to in Article 20(1)(a) of the Regulation encompass the identification of the customer and verification of the customer's identity.

[191] Trilogue Table 328–32.

[192] ibid.

[193] ibid 334–36.

3.3. The New Regulation on the Transfer of Funds and the Application of the 'Travel Rule' to Digital Currencies

The FATF's Recommendation 16 mandates financial institutions to incorporate precise details regarding the originator and beneficiary of wire transfers, commonly referred to as the 'travel rule'.[194] According to the FATF's guidelines, virtual asset service providers are also obliged to acquire, retain and transmit relevant information when engaging in transactions involving digital currencies.[195] However, the transfer of funds Regulation did not extend the travel rule to providers operating within the cryptocurrency industry. Consequently, there was the need to amend the Regulation governing fund transfers to include digital currencies within its framework.

On 31 May 2023, the new travel rule Regulation was adopted and subsequently published in the *Official Journal* in June 2023. The Regulation specifies that, generally, the travel rule applies to transactions exceeding the threshold of 1,000 Euros.[196] However, for crypto-asset transactions, the travel rule applies to all transactions regardless of their amount or whether they are domestic or cross-border.[197]

Nevertheless, there exists a flaw in this approach. Not all users of crypto-assets utilise a service provider. For instance, the Regulation acknowledges that some users possess self-hosted wallets, as defined in Article 3(20): '"self-hosted address" means a distributed ledger address not linked to either of the following: (a) a crypto-asset service provider; (b) an entity not established in the Union and providing services similar to those of a crypto-asset service provider.'[198] In order to address this issue, the Regulation stipulates that, 'In the case of a transfer to or from a self-hosted address, the crypto-asset service provider should collect the information on both the originator and the beneficiary, usually from its client.'[199] However, this solution enshrined in the Regulation is controversial and questionable, as it places the obligation on the end user rather than the service provider. This is a substantial development as it can be viewed as a dangerous expansion of the 'responsibilisation strategy' to include the clients of the already 'responsible' providers.

By eliminating the threshold of 1,000 Euros, the Regulation moves on to impose blanket measures on the service providers. According to the Regulation, crypto-asset service providers will be obliged to collect and exchange the necessary information for all transactions conducted by the provider, irrespective of the

[194] FATF Recommendations, Recommendation 16.
[195] Financial Action Task Force, 'Targeted Update on Implementation of the FATF Standards on Virtual Asset and Virtual Asset Service Providers' (June 2020) 10.
[196] Regulation (EU) 2023/1113 of the European Parliament and of the Council of 31 May 2023 on information accompanying transfers of funds and certain crypto-assets and amending Directive (EU) 2015/849 (recast) [2023] OJ L150/1, recital 29.
[197] ibid recitals 30 and 38.
[198] ibid Art 3(20).
[199] ibid recital 39.

transaction amount, which inevitably raises concerns about the proportionality of these measures.

3.4. Fundamental Rights Concerns Arising from the Inclusion of Digital Currencies in the AML regime and the Subsequent Expansion

Initially, the amendments put forth by the 5th AML Directive gave rise to various issues and raised concerns regarding the potential impact on the fundamental rights of end users. Of particular concern is the strict adherence of the EU to the guidelines set forth by the FATF. While the objective of the FATF is to combat money laundering and terrorist financing, it does not adequately consider the evaluation of the impact on fundamental rights when adopting appropriate measures. However, in the EU, it is crucial that the proposed measures do not result in severe interference with fundamental rights.

Significant concerns arise from the potential impact of the AML measures on the processing of personal data and the right to privacy of customers. These concerns hold particular relevance in relation to digital currency systems and the obligations imposed on entities within the digital currency industry. The use of blockchain technology entails the recording of sensitive transaction information, including details such as time and date, location, public key, and fund amounts. However, as multiple entities and national authorities have access to this information, there exists an increased risk of potential interference with the fundamental rights of end users.[200]

The utilisation of the risk-based approach within the AML regime would have addressed most of these concerns, as it is considered the most suitable method to ensure proportionality. However, with regard to digital currencies, the regime appears to have additional policy objectives beyond the primary goal of combating money laundering and terrorist financing.[201] The inclusion of digital currencies in the 5th AML Directive and the subsequent expansion of the newly adopted AML Regulation appear to serve as a multifaceted tool aimed

[200] European Economic Social Committee, 'Opinion on the proposal for a Directive of the European Parliament and of the Council amending Directive (EU) 2015/849 on the prevention of the use of the financial system for the purposes of money laundering or terrorist financing and amending Directive 2009/101/EC [COM(2016) 450 final - 2016/0208 (COD)]' ECO/408, 7 (EESC's opinion); Regarding the issue of Blockchain technology, the European Economic and Social Committee (EESC) believes that 'it would be useful to set up a European tool for surveillance, coordination and anticipating technological change'. In the last few years, technology has progressed at an unforeseen pace, rendering the legislative process a slow-moving machine that cannot keep up. However, the Committee fails to elaborate further on this issue; therefore, there are no recommendations as to what powers this tool will have or how it will operate.

[201] European Data Protection Supervisor, 'Opinion 1/2017, EDPS Opinion on a Commission Proposal amending Directive (EU) 2015/849 and Directive 2009/101/EC' (2 February 2017), 12 ('EDPS Opinion 2017').

at combating these crimes, reducing anonymity, and protecting customers. The presence of these diverse objectives, however, complicates the application of the principle of proportionality, making it challenging to conduct a thorough risk assessment of customers and potentially resulting in the implementation of generalised measures.[202]

The first concern revolves around the departure of the AML regime from the well-established risk-based approach, which raises questions about the principle of proportionality.[203] Recital 24 of the 5th AML Directive suggests the elimination of the risk-based approach due to the higher risk associated with certain intermediary structures, which closely resemble the structure of virtual asset service providers and the unique characteristics of digital currencies that may hinder timely risk detection and assessment.[204] The Commission argued that a departure from the risk-based approach is necessary when the risk is elevated and time constraints exist for detection and assessment.[205] However, the European Data Protection Supervisor (EDPS) found this worrisome as it interferes with the principle of proportionality.[206]

The issue stems from the implication in recital 24 that the EU deviates from the established risk-based approach when dealing with digital currencies. The text of the 5th AML Directive mentions the need to monitor certain clearly specified categories of existing customers on a regular basis without providing any details about these customer categories.[207] The EDPS raised concerns about the lack of clarity in determining these categories, particularly when the risk-based approach is not considered appropriate.[208] During the negotiations for the adoption of the 5th Directive, the EDPS asserted that such measures can only be justified in life-or-death situations, citing the example of terrorist financing but not tax evasion.[209] Therefore, it is debatable whether the inherent anonymity and fast global fund transfers of digital currencies can serve as a sufficient basis for general customer monitoring without assessing the associated risks.

[202] EDPS Opinion 2017, 12.
[203] ibid.
[204] Directive (EU) 2018/843 of the European Parliament and of the Council of 30 May 2018 amending Directive (EU) 2015/849 on the prevention of the use of the financial system for the purposes of money laundering or terrorist financing, and amending Directive 2009/138/EC and 2013/36/EU [2018] OJ L156/43, recital 24.
[205] Commission, 'Proposal for a Directive of the European Parliament and of the Council amending Directive (EU) 2015/849 on the prevention of the use of the financial system for the purposes of money laundering or terrorist financing and amending Directive 2009/101/EC' COM(2016) 450 final, recital 19.
[206] EDPS Opinion 2017, 12.
[207] Directive (EU) 2018/843 of the European Parliament and of the Council of 30 May 2018 amending Directive (EU) 2015/849 on the prevention of the use of the financial system for the purposes of money laundering or terrorist financing, and amending Directive 2009/138/EC and 2013/36/EU [2018] OJ L156/43, recital 19.
[208] EDPS Opinion 2017, 12.
[209] ibid.

The content of recital 24 in the 5th Directive remained unchanged during the negotiations for the new AML Regulation and was adopted as it was.[210] This recital mirrors virtual asset service providers and essentially brands digital currencies as a high-risk phenomenon. This observation reaffirms the concern that the AML regime deviates from a risk-based approach, particularly with regard to digital currencies. Consequently, transactions involving digital currencies are automatically categorised as high risk, necessitating the implementation of enhanced due diligence measures.[211] The new AML Regulation strengthens this tendency by obliging entities to apply CDD measures even for occasional crypto-asset transactions below 1,000 Euros.

The impact assessment accompanying the proposal reinforces the argument concerning the departure from the risk-based approach by stating that the new Regulation 'would also better cover transactions involving crypto-assets. Such rules, however, could still be sufficiently flexible for the specific purpose of accommodating a risk-based approach at national level, leaving some scope for national rules going further.'[212] The impact assessment, though, fails to elaborate further on how this will enhance harmonisation and legal certainty and why these rules are clearer and more consistent.[213] Additionally, the EDPS repeated in the opinion concerning the new AML Regulation, in 2021, the same concern highlighted in the previous opinion for the 5th AML Directive that '(notably the Proposal for a Regulation) should identify the categories of personal data to be processed'.[214] The opinion underlines that the Regulation should provide clear indications on conditions and limits for the processing of special categories of personal data.[215] Despite the repeated warnings from the EDPS, the new AML Regulation still fails to provide specific categories of data or specific categories of customers to be monitored, in order to satisfy the specificity requirement to be in line with the principle of proportionality.[216]

Generally, the European Commission acknowledged that obligations from the new Regulation will raise various technical challenges, especially for virtual asset

[210] Regulation (EU) 2024/1624 of the European Parliament and of the Council of 31 May 2024 on the prevention of the use of the financial system for the purposes of money laundering or terrorist financing [2024] OJ L, 2024/1624, recital 76; Directive (EU) 2018/843 of the European Parliament and of the Council of 30 May 2018 amending Directive (EU) 2015/849 on the prevention of the use of the financial system for the purposes of money laundering or terrorist financing, and amending Directive 2009/138/EC and 2013/36/EU [2018] OJ L156/43, recital 24. During the trilogue, both the European Parliament and the Council made no revisions to this recital.

[211] Regulation (EU) 2024/1624 of the European Parliament and of the Council of 31 May 2024 on the prevention of the use of the financial system for the purposes of money laundering or terrorist financing [2024] OJ L, 2024/1624, Art 20(2).

[212] Commission, 'Commission Staff Working Document Impact Assessment Accompanying the Anti-money laundering package' SWD(2021) 190 final, 37 ('Impact Assessment 2021').

[213] ibid.

[214] European Data Protection Supervisor, 'Opinion 12/2021, on the anti-money laundering and countering the financing of terrorism (AML/CFT) package of legislative proposals' (22 September 2021) 16 (EDPS Opinion 2021).

[215] ibid.

[216] ibid 13, 16.

service providers that were not already obliged under the 5th AML Directive.[217] As a response, the industry (ie service providers' representatives) put forward the claim that, due to the lack of global standardisation, these obligations will eventually lead to the exclusion of small and medium-sized businesses, a claim that was also underlined during the legislative process for the 5th AML Directive.[218] Even though this is a valid concern from the industry, the Commission swiftly dismissed it by stating that these obligations stem from the FATF, which is the global standard-setter, and therefore will be implemented worldwide.[219] This is a relatively unsubstantiated argument by the Commission, because despite the fact that the FATF has a global reach, it does not change the fact that the Recommendations are not legally binding.

A notable concern arises from the regime's apparent confusion between Know Your Customer (KYC) obligations and CDD. The existing AML regime solely focuses on CDD measures, whereas KYC measures pertain to the mandatory process preceding the provision of financial products and services, entailing the collection and verification of information.[220] CDD, on the other hand, involves the processing of information to evaluate risks.[221] This ambiguity obstructs the effective alignment of CDD measures with the risk-based approach, as it fails to provide clear guidance on the specific categories and extent of data required.[222]

Lastly, taking into consideration the elimination of the minimum threshold for cryptocurrency transactions under the travel rule Regulation, the argument concerning the principle of proportionality and the risk-based approach is strengthened further. Recital 27 emphasises, in particular, that due to the specific characteristics of crypto-asset technology, there should be no exemption from the Regulation's scope for domestic low-value transfers of such currencies.[223]

3.5. Critical Evaluation of the Limitations of the New Regulatory Framework

The decision under the 5th AML Directive to impose obligations on only two categories of entities raises concerns about the effectiveness of the Directive in reducing the anonymity associated with these systems. By obliging only exchange platforms facilitating transactions between fiat currencies and digital currencies, as well as custodial wallet providers, the majority of the digital environment remained unregulated. The European Commission acknowledged

[217] Impact Assessment 2021, 40–41.
[218] ibid.
[219] ibid.
[220] EDPS Opinion 2021, 13
[221] ibid.
[222] ibid.
[223] Regulation (EU) 2023/1113 of the European Parliament and of the Council of 31 May 2023 on information accompanying transfers of funds and certain crypto-assets and amending Directive (EU) 2015/849 (recast) [2023] OJ L150/1, recital 27.

this significant disadvantage of the Directive by underlining that the inclusion of only two entities in the AML regime 'will not entirely address the issue of anonymity . . . as a large part of the virtual currency environment will remain anonymous because users can also transact without such providers'.[224] The EU's rationale behind this initial approach was to target entities acting as gatekeepers to the real economy. However, it failed to consider that users can engage in digital currency transactions without relying on these obliged entities. For instance, peer-to-peer platforms enable users to exchange fiat currencies with digital currencies without the involvement of exchange platforms.[225] This limitation remains in the new AML regime (including the MiCA Regulation) – despite the fact that the majority of service providers are now obliged, the Regulation does not engage with the issue of decentralisation.

The EU highlights in recital 19 of MiCA that crypto-assets and particularly e-money tokens should not be confused with electronic money, which is explicitly defined in Article 2 of Directive 2009/110/EC (this declaration was also included in the 5th AML Directive in recital 10).[226] Additionally, the MiCA Regulation explicitly excludes in-game currencies from its scope, and as a result, excludes them from the AML regime as well. This exclusion is based on the fact that the definition of crypto-assets clearly states that such currencies must be operating on distributed ledger technology or similar technology.[227] This follows the same direction as the 5th AML Directive which clearly excluded in-game currencies by stating that 'Virtual currencies should not to be confused with . . . in-games currencies, that can be used exclusively within a specific game environment'.[228] This distinction is crucial as in-game currencies, although classified as digital currencies, differ from cryptocurrencies. In-game currencies are centralised and governed by a single entity, making them more amenable to regulation.

The EU has been diligent in adhering to the guidelines and Recommendations of the FATF. However, there is a discrepancy regarding the treatment of in-game currencies. While the FATF's definition of virtual assets includes in-game currencies, the EU has chosen to exclude them from the scope of the MiCA Regulation and subsequently from the scope of the AML regime.[229] This decision raises questions, particularly considering that certain virtual worlds, such as Second Life,

[224] Directive (EU) 2018/843 of the European Parliament and of the Council of 30 May 2018 amending Directive (EU) 2015/849 on the prevention of the use of the financial system for the purposes of money laundering or terrorist financing, and amending Directive 2009/138/EC and 2013/36/EU [2018] OJ L156/43, recital 9.

[225] ibid recital 9.

[226] ibid recital 10; Directive 2009/110/EC of the European Parliament and of the Council of 16 September 2009 on the taking up, pursuit and prudential supervision of the business of electronic money institutions amending Directives 2005/60/EC and 2006/48/EC and repealing Directive 2000/46/EC [2009] OJ L267/7.

[227] MiCA.

[228] Directive (EU) 2018/843 of the European Parliament and of the Council of 30 May 2018 amending Directive (EU) 2015/849 on the prevention of the use of the financial system for the purposes of money laundering or terrorist financing, and amending Directive 2009/138/EC and 2013/36/EU [2018] OJ L156/43, recital 10.

[229] FATF Recommendations, 135; see subsection 3.2. in Chapter 3.

allow users to exchange fiat currencies for digital currencies and *vice versa*.[230] As a platform facilitating currency exchanges, Second Life would fall under the EU's AML regime. However, since in-game currencies are excluded, Second Life is not obliged to collect customer identification details.

The exact reasons behind the EU's decision to exclude in-game currencies from the concept of digital currencies remain unclear. It is possible that the EU determined that in-game currencies do not pose a significant risk of money laundering and terrorist financing compared to other categories of currencies. Alternatively, the EU may have relied on the self-regulation of these games, considering that in-game currencies are centralised.

Furthermore, the concerns raised by the EDPS regarding the departure from the risk-based approach were not taken into account by the EU.[231] The EDPS expressed worries about the Commission's approach, which leaned towards a rule-based regime rather than the more appropriate risk-based approach for addressing money laundering and terrorist financing crimes. Recital 24 of the 5th AML Directive, which retained the exact wording in recital 76 of the new AML Regulation, grants powers to monitor customers on a regular basis.[232] This has clear implications for the implementation of the principle of proportionality.

The reasons behind the EU's shift in approach towards money laundering and terrorist financing are not explicitly provided. In the context of digital currencies, one could argue that the regime departs from the risk-based approach due to the challenges of conducting risk assessments within these systems. However, one counter-argument is that the public and irreversible nature of blockchain technology allows for risk assessments to be performed. Even if this approach is accepted, the new AML Regulation grants various entities access to data for regular customer monitoring without clear guidelines on how these customers should be selected or the criteria used.

In conclusion, the EU's decision to exclude in-game currencies from the scope of the MiCA Regulation and, as a result, the AML regime and the departure from the risk-based approach raise concerns about the adequacy of the measures in effectively addressing the risks associated with digital currencies. The lack of transparency regarding these decisions and the potential implications for data privacy and proportionality warrant further examination.

The EU made a deliberate choice to evolve the regulation of digital currencies by introducing MiCA and expanding the list of obliged entities under the new AML regime. This decision led to the introduction of obligations for specific entities within the digital currency ecosystem under this new regime. These entities

[230] See https://secondlife.com/.

[231] EDPS Opinion 2021.

[232] Directive (EU) 2018/843 of the European Parliament and of the Council of 30 May 2018 amending Directive (EU) 2015/849 on the prevention of the use of the financial system for the purposes of money laundering or terrorist financing, and amending Directive 2009/138/EC and 2013/36/EU [2018] OJ L156/43, recital 24; Regulation (EU) 2024/1624 of the European Parliament and of the Council of 31 May 2024 on the prevention of the use of the financial system for the purposes of money laundering or terrorist financing [2024] OJ L, 2024/1624, recital 76.

are required to collect essential customer identification data and report suspicious transactions to FIUs. Additionally, they are expected to implement CDD measures to counter customer anonymity.

Under Chapter III of the AML Regulation, the CDD measures are quite straightforward. However, the new Regulation added too little to the AML regime regarding these measures. While the Regulation mandates entities offering digital currency services to collect specific data, it fails to consider whether this data is sufficient in the online environment. Based on the analysis of this chapter and recital 76, the argument is that the new Regulation classifies digital currencies as a high-risk phenomenon.[233] As a result, Article 20(2) indicates that where obliged entities identify an increased risk of money laundering, they shall apply enhanced due diligence.[234] Nevertheless, a closer look at Article 34 (scope of application of enhanced due diligence) reveals that the Article does not specify the categories of data to be collected (a concern outlined by the EDPS).[235] The only category where the Regulation provides specificity is under Article 37 regarding enhanced due diligence measures for cross-border correspondent relationships for crypto-asset service providers.[236]

Moving back to recital 76, it is implied that it is important to ensure that clearly specified categories of existing customers are also monitored on a regular basis.[237] The new Regulation includes Article 26 on the obligation of ongoing monitoring, failing, however, to clearly specify those 'categories of existing customers'.[238] In general, the new Regulation seems to roll over to the new AMLA the 'obligation' to specify the standards on the information necessary for the performance of customer due diligence.[239] However, it is not clear to what extent the AMLA will specify the categories of data to be retained, the time of retention, the categories of customers and the risk factors for the virtual environment.

The research examines digital currencies as a whole, but it is necessary to use certain cryptocurrencies as examples to analyse anonymity concerns. Bitcoin, for instance, is not entirely anonymous, but criminals can achieve a desirable level of anonymity by utilising the system in a specific manner.[240] While Bitcoin operates on a public ledger, transactions executed from the same address can be linked. However, users are not required to provide identity details to access the system, and criminals generate different addresses for each transaction to evade detection.[241]

[233] ibid.
[234] ibid Art 20(2).
[235] ibid Art 34.
[236] ibid Art 37.
[237] ibid recital 76.
[238] ibid recital 76 and Art 26.
[239] ibid Art 28.
[240] Bart Custers, Jan-Jaap Oerlemans and Ronald Pool, 'Laundering the Profits of Ransomware: Money Laundering Methods for Vouchers and Cryptocurrencies' (2020) 28(2) *European Journal of Crime, Criminal Law and Criminal Justice* 121, 135.
[241] ibid; Zijian Bao and others, 'Lockmix: a secure and privacy-preserving mix service for Bitcoin anonymity' (2020) 19 *International Journal of Information Security* 311, 312.

The challenge arises when virtual asset service providers attempt to identify users solely based on transaction history.[242] Due to the decentralised nature of cryptocurrencies, there is no central authority that can enforce CDD measures.[243] It depends on a number of entities to collect the necessary data. However, the successful implementation of these measures depends on tailoring procedures to the specific characteristics of digital currency systems.[244] Entities which are the gatekeepers of the real economy (eg exchanges between fiat currencies and digital currencies) will require clients to submit identity details before they will be able to use the services of the specific provider. Also, these entities can gather transaction information from the blockchain itself, so it is feasible to apply the CDD measures to some extent.[245]

Despite these efforts, a legal lacuna remains within the AML framework. Criminals continue to exploit the system by turning to currencies that offer higher levels of anonymity, thereby circumventing CDD measures.[246] These digital currencies aim to anonymise users by utilising obfuscated blockchains.[247] Some argue that privacy-oriented currencies provide complete anonymity, making it difficult for obliged entities to collect reliable transaction data from the public ledger.[248]

To this end, the new AML Regulation adds Article 79 to prohibit the provision of services concerning anonymous accounts and anonymity-enhancing coins.[249] However, the EU does not ban these coins or any other anonymising tools; it just prohibits obliged entities from providing such services. As a result, criminals can maintain a certain level of anonymity when exchanging privacy-oriented currencies with bitcoins, for example, without the use of an intermediary.[250] However, this is not the sole obstacle to implementing preventive measures. Perpetrators can utilise the Tor network to conceal their identity and IP address, hindering the collection of additional user data, such as geo-location information, by obliged

[242] According to the 5th AML Directive, the obliged virtual asset service providers are only exchanges between fiat currencies and virtual currencies and custodial wallet providers; Jesse Crawford and Yong Guan, 'Knowing your Bitcoin Customer: Money Laundering in the Bitcoin Economy' (2020) 13th international conference on systematic approaches to digital forensic engineering (SADFE) 38, 43.

[243] Victor Dostov and Pavel Shust, 'Cryptocurrencies: an unconventional challenge to the AML/CFT regulators?' (2014) 21(3) *Journal of Financial Crime* 249, 257.

[244] Angela SM Irwin and Adam B Turner, 'Illicit Bitcoin transactions: challenges in getting to the who, what, when and where' (2018) 21(3) *Journal of Money Laundering Control* 297, 302.

[245] Sagwadi Mabunda, 'Cryptocurrency: The New Face of Cyber Money Laundering' (2018) international conference on advances in big data, computing and data communication systems (icabcd) IEEE 3.

[246] Custers, Oerlemans and Pool (n 240) 136.

[247] Emad Badawi and Guy-Vincent Jourdan, 'Cryptocurrencies Emerging Threats and Defensive Mechanisms: A Systematic Literature Review' (2020) IEEE Access, 8, 200021-200037, 15.

[248] Alastair Berg, 'The identity, fungibility and anonymity of money' (2020) 39(2) *Economic Papers: A Journal of Applied Economics and Policy* 104, 105; these obfuscated blockchains conceal information regarding sources and destination of the transactions and amounts of currencies.

[249] Regulation (EU) 2024/1624 of the European Parliament and of the Council of 31 May 2024 on the prevention of the use of the financial system for the purposes of money laundering or terrorist financing [2024] OJ L, 2024/1624, Art 79.

[250] Custers, Oerlemans and Pool (n 240) 139.

entities.[251] In a scenario where obliged entities will expand the obligations from the CDD measures to also collect other data from users, like geo-location information, they will then inevitably face difficulties with the Tor network.

To further evade CDD measures, criminals can utilise mixing services in order to hide the illegal source of the funds they aim to launder.[252] These mixing providers can be either centralised or decentralised. Decentralised mixing providers accessed through the Tor network represent an extreme case that has not been adequately addressed by the AML regime.[253] In this scenario, there is no entity collecting data; the user's identity (along with the IP address) remains hidden, and the source of funds is obfuscated. This is a notable shortcoming of the new regime, as mixing services are highly effective and dangerous participants in digital currency money laundering.

The AML Regulation, under Article 40, takes a substantial step in considering the hindrances caused by decentralisation.[254] This provision focuses on the risks in relation to transactions with self-hosted addresses. This refers to situations where only one party to the transaction has an intermediary, and the other is decentralised. So, the Article indicates that the one intermediary shall take risk-based measures to identify, and verify the identity of, the originator or beneficiary of a transfer made from or to a self-hosted address or beneficial owner of such originator or beneficiary.[255] The issue here is how the intermediary will be able to get information concerning the other party. According to recital 39 of the travel rule Regulation, the provider should collect the information on both the originator and the beneficiary, usually from its client.[256] However, this approach is not realistic, as the client would be under no obligation or authority to reveal information of the other party that they might not even have.

Additionally, in the online environment, particularly within digital currency systems, criminals must take measures to conceal their activities. Merely relying on the Bitcoin system, for example, to hide their identities is insufficient. This highlights that even if obliged entities have access to transaction history through the blockchain, connecting suspicious transactions with real-world identities is crucial.[257]

The analysis reveals that the application of CDD measures to digital currencies is not straightforward. Collecting and analysing the necessary data to identify perpetrators in these systems is complex compared to the straightforward

[251] Tomáš Minárik and Anna-Maria Osula, 'Tor does not stink: Use and abuse of the Tor anonymity network from the perspective of the law' (2016) 32 *Computer Law & Security Review* 111.

[252] See subsection 5.5. in Chapter 1.

[253] Crawford and Guan (n 242) 39.

[254] Regulation (EU) 2024/1624 of the European Parliament and of the Council of 31 May 2024 on the prevention of the use of the financial system for the purposes of money laundering or terrorist financing [2024] OJ L, 2024/1624, Art 40.

[255] ibid Art 40(a).

[256] Regulation (EU) 2023/1113 of the European Parliament and of the Council of 31 May 2023 on information accompanying transfers of funds and certain crypto-assets and amending Directive (EU) 2015/849 (recast) [2023] OJ L150/1, recital 39.

[257] Clare Jones, 'Can You Ever Regulate the Virtual World Against Virtual Economic Crime?' (2012) 7(4) *International Commercial Law and Technology* 339, 346.

record-keeping of traditional financial institutions.[258] Obliged entities cannot solely rely on blockchain information and must gather more comprehensive details to identify users and detect suspicious transactions. However, this may result in heightened surveillance of users of the system.[259]

In a working paper on Finance and Bitcoin, the Organisation for Economic Co-operation and Development (OECD) concluded that the structure of Bitcoin and other networks is not conducive to traditional preventive measures due to the decentralised and anonymous nature of participants.[260] Moreover, due to the characteristic of decentralisation, the existing AML regime can be deemed ill-suited for these systems. Consequently, obliged entities will need to engage in enhanced due diligence, collecting a significant amount of information. However, smaller businesses may lack the capacity to comply with such measures.[261] The analysis of the AML Regulation indicates a departure from the risk-based approach in relation to digital currencies. [262] Thus, combining enhanced due diligence without a risk-based approach can impose unforeseen burdens on obliged entities in the virtual economy, as they are compelled to collect extensive data from all clients on an ongoing basis.

Conclusion

The chapter evaluates the policy option of the EU to introduce digital currencies in the AML regime and its expansion based on the newly adopted acts. The analysis shows that even if the blockchain is a public ledger and the virtual asset service providers can gather information about the transactions, this is not enough in order to acquire the whole profile of the customer. Transaction information may be helpful, but it is not always enough to track down an individual. So, the virtual asset service providers will need to gather further data.[263] To cast light onto this nebulous area, the FATF gave certain examples of this data under the enhanced due diligence measures. According to the FATF, virtual asset service providers will have to collect identity numbers and verify them with information in other databases, trace the IP address of a user (ie geo-location information), and even search the internet for information associated with the transactions of a user.[264]

[258] Dostov and Shust (n 243) 258.

[259] Minárik and Osula (n 251) 112.

[260] Adrian Blundell-Wignall, 'The Bitcoin Question: Currency Versus Trust-less Transfer Technology' (2014) OECD Working Papers on Finance, Insurance and Private Pensions No 37, 11.

[261] Perri Reynolds and Angela SM Irwin, 'Tracking digital footprints: anonymity within the bitcoin system (2017) 20(2) *Journal of Money Laundering Control* 172.

[262] Directive (EU) 2018/843 of the European Parliament and of the Council of 30 May 2018 amending Directive (EU) 2015/849 on the prevention of the use of the financial system for the purposes of money laundering or terrorist financing, and amending Directive 2009/138/EC and 2013/36/EU [2018] OJ L156/43, recital 24.

[263] Financial Action Task Force, 'Updated Guidance for a Risk-Based Approach: Virtual Assets and Virtual Asset Service Providers' (October 2021) 51.

[264] ibid 81.

Such deep research by the virtual asset service providers may cause various problems, especially data protection and privacy concerns. The information that these entities have to collect exceeds the role of the record keeper and the essence of the preventive measures. It can be argued that virtual asset service providers are obliged to undertake individual investigations into each one of their customers, considering the decrease of the threshold for the application of AML measures to transactions even below 1,000 Euros, the complete removal of the threshold for the application of the travel rule, and the departure of the EU's AML regime from the risk-based approach. The departure from the risk-based approach is a major concern as it has clear implications for fundamental rights and the implementation of the principle of proportionality.[265]

Concerning in-game currencies, the EU decided to exclude them from the AML regime.[266] The idea of obliging platforms which provide exchange services between fiat currencies and digital currencies but leaving aside in-game currencies is illogical, as there are virtual worlds and games that provide such services to their customers. Interestingly, on 27 October 2022, the European Commission published a report on the assessment of the risk of money laundering and terrorist financing affecting the internal market, admitting for the first time that 'this report considers exchangeable tokens used in video games assimilated to crypto-assets'.[267] However, the new acts mentioned above (both AML and MiCA) have in their scope only blockchain-based crypto-assets, ie excluding in-game currencies again from the AML regime.

The analysis of the 5th AML Directive, the MiCA Regulation and the newly adopted AML regime entails two significant conclusions. First, based on the AML Regulation and the transplantation of the AML regime to digital currencies, there are significant concerns about the impact of those measures on the fundamental rights of the end-user. Second, the root of the issue is not the characteristics of the technology but the inability of the providers to mitigate risks based on the existing regimes. Virtual asset service providers face numerous difficulties when applying preventive measures compared to banks. This is also the main reason why the AML regime departs from the risk-based approach, which creates a discussion concerning fundamental rights. To this end, the next chapter examines further the relationship between virtual asset service providers and their clients, having as a model the relationship between banks and clients.

[265] Regulation (EU) 2024/1624 of the European Parliament and of the Council of 31 May 2024 on the prevention of the use of the financial system for the purposes of money laundering or terrorist financing [2024] OJ L, 2024/1624; Regulation (EU) 2023/1113 of the European Parliament and of the Council of 31 May 2023 on information accompanying transfers of funds and certain crypto-assets and amending Directive (EU) 2015/849 [2023] OJ L150/1.

[266] ibid.

[267] Commission, 'Report from the Commission to the European Parliament and the Council on the assessment of the risk of money laundering and terrorist financing affecting the internal market and relating to cross-border activities' SWD(2022)344 final, 11.

5

Revisiting Anonymity and Trust under the Anti-Money Laundering (AML)Regime: Why Structural Differences Between Banks and Virtual Asset Service Providers Matter

Introduction

The extension of a centralised AML framework to decentralised digital currency systems exposes a fundamental mismatch; while the challenge of anonymity persists, its meaning and management transform entirely within a new operational landscape. The ensuing analysis casts a spotlight on the incontrovertible reality that, regardless of the stringency of the regulatory approach, it is the technology's inherent attributes and the intermediaries' capacities that ultimately dictate the practicability of implementing the regulatory regime. The development and evolution of the international and European AML frameworks have redefined banking practices. Initially directed at financial and credit institutions, the obligations arising from the AML legal framework compel banks to collect and share client information with authorities when suspicions of money laundering arise.[1] From the perspective of fundamental rights, this development significantly impacts the right to privacy of bank customers. The principles that safeguard individual privacy also apply to the digital economy. Digital currencies have the potential to eliminate the need for a trusted third party while still protecting user privacy.[2] For instance, in the Bitcoin network, there is no central authority, and transactions are verified by multiple nodes, providing protection against fraud and double-spending.[3] To

[1] Christine Lagarde, 'The role of Personal Accountability in Reforming Culture and Behavior in the Financial Services Industry' (*International Monetary Fund*, 5 November 2015), www.imf.org/en/News/Articles/2015/09/28/04/53/sp110515; Council Directive 91/308/EEC of 10 June 1991 on prevention of the use of the financial system for the purpose of money laundering [1991] OJ L166/56.

[2] Satoshi Nakamoto, 'Bitcoin: A Peer-to-Peer Electronic Cash System' (*Bitcoin*, 31 October 2008), https://bitcoin.org/bitcoin.pdf; Arvin Narayanan and others, *Bitcoin and Cryptocurrency Technologies: A Comprehensive Introduction* (Princeton University Press, 2016) 142; Primavera De Filippi and Aaron Wright, *Blockchain and the Law: The Rule of Code* (Harvard University Press, 2018) 18 and 38–39; Henri Arslanian, *The Book of Crypto: The Complete Guide to Understanding Bitcoin Cryptocurrencies and Digital Assets* (Palgrave Macmillan, 2022) 137–38.

[3] Arslanian (n 2) 51.

finalise a transaction, nodes verify that the sender possesses adequate funds, while remaining unaware of the identities of both sender and recipient.[4] Essentially, digital currencies' systems operate differently from the banking system, offering a higher level of anonymity.[5] Notably, there is no central repository of information, as the environment is decentralised, relying solely on the information recorded on the blockchain.[6]

This chapter examines the interaction between obliged entities and their clients, focusing on the principle of confidentiality, the concept of trust and the characteristics of digital currencies (ie decentralisation and anonymity). The goal is to understand the differences between banks and virtual asset service providers within the existing framework. This chapter offers a novel exposition of the unexplored relationship between the transformation of confidentiality and trust and the evolution of the digital economy. To this end, it examines how these foundational principles are progressively weakened and redefined within the digital economy. The insights gained from this analysis provide a crucial foundation for evaluating how the application of preventive AML measures has evolved, marking a shift from the traditional dynamic between bank and client to a new relationship between technology and 'client'.

The preceding chapter concluded with the argument that the existing AML framework imposes a more stringent regulatory approach on digital currencies and virtual asset service providers than on the traditional banking sector, while maintaining unchanged the requisite measures for providers. Building on this argument, the present chapter employs the 1st AML Directive as a central reference point to explain the introduction of preventive obligations into the banking system. It analyses how the banking system addressed the clash between the principle of confidentiality and the obligation to collect data from clients and report to state authorities when there is a suspicion of money laundering.[7] Subsequently, attention turns to virtual asset service providers and the newly adopted AML regime.[8] By focusing only on the 1st Directive and the new AML framework, the aim is to compare the responses of two distinct industries (namely, banks and virtual asset service providers) when the AML regime was introduced and expanded into each of their domains.

To this end, the following section looks back to 1991 to evaluate how the imposition of duties on credit and financial institutions under the 1st AML Directive affected banks. It examines the bank–customer relationship and analyses the impact of the AML regime on the principle of confidentiality using a case study

[4] Narayanan and others (n 2) 27–45; De Filippi and Wright (n 2) 20–26; Arslanian (n 2) 49–58.

[5] Arslanian (n 2) 125.

[6] ibid 51–52; De Filippi and Wright (n 2) 21–22.

[7] Council Directive 91/308/EEC of 10 June 1991 on prevention of the use of the financial system for the purpose of money laundering [1991] OJ L166/77.

[8] Directive (EU) 2018/843 of the European Parliament and of the Council of 30 May 2018 amending Directive (EU) 2015/849 on the prevention of the use of the financial system for the purposes of money laundering or terrorist financing, and amending Directive 2009/138/EC and 2013/36/EU [2018] OJ L156/43.

of Austria's secrecy regime. Afterwards, the chapter focuses on digital currencies and the shift of the business model, illustrating the practical difficulties of applying AML measures in a decentralised, trustless and pseudonymous environment. The comparative analysis of this chapter is significant as it highlights the novel challenges posed by decentralised digital currencies and demonstrates why conventional AML frameworks, designed for traditional banks, may be insufficient or ill-suited for virtual asset service providers.

1. The Preventive Side of the European Union's (EU's) AML Legislation

The AML framework has a dual purpose: first, the criminalisation of money laundering, and, second, the implementation of preventive measures to deter individuals involved in illegal activities from engaging in money laundering.[9] The former aspect mainly concerns citizens of the EU (ie natural persons).[10] The latter aspect, which is the central focus of the AML framework, applies to specified private entities. Notably, Stessens emphasises that the scope of money laundering prevention is often restricted and is particularly aimed at entities and professions susceptible to being exploited for money laundering – referred to as 'money launderettes'.[11] This statement is especially relevant when examining the more traditional forms of money laundering. An example of this is the susceptibility of banks (and other financial institutions), especially in the past, due to the secrecy policies of the banking system. However, in the case of digital currencies, the potential misuse for money laundering purposes primarily lies within the phenomenon itself rather than the entities facilitating transactions.

1.1. The Reliance of the AML Framework on Financial Institutions

The preventive measures enacted by the regulatory framework primarily impose obligations or duties upon entities within the private sector. Almost half of the Financial Action Task Force Recommendations, initially issued in 1990, concentrate on the role of financial institutions and their obligations in the fight against

[9] Directive (EU) 2015/849 of the European Parliament and of the Council of 20 May 2015 on the prevention of the use of the financial system for the purposes of money laundering or terrorist financing, amending Regulation (EU) No 648/2012 of the European Parliament and of the Council, and repealing Directive 2005/60/EC of the European Parliament and of the Council and Commission Directive 2006/70/EC [2015] OJ L141/73 (with the amendments of the 5th AML Directive), Arts 1 and 2.

[10] ibid Art 1.

[11] Guy Stessens, *Money Laundering: A New International Law Enforcement Model* (Cambridge University Press, 2009) 133.

the crime of money laundering.[12] The majority of those Recommendations were subsequently incorporated into the framework of the 1st AML Directive. Articulated within Articles 3–11 of the act, a comprehensive framework delineates the measures encapsulating the preventive ambit of the regime. Within this context, the Directive defines the term 'credit institutions' by reference to Directive 77/780/EEC as last amended by Directive 89/646/EEC.[13] Additionally, the term 'financial institution' pertains to an enterprise, distinct from a credit institution, whose principal operational focus involves conducting one or more of the operations enumerated in points 2–12 and 14 of the list annexed to Directive 89/646/EEC.[14] This expansive definition shows the extensive purview of the AML regime.[15]

From a pragmatic standpoint, the emphasis on financial institutions arises from their crucial role in the financial system.[16] Stessens points out that, as the main handlers of money, financial institutions have a significant role in money laundering activities.[17] This is due to three factors: (a) their ability to manage large amounts of money, (b) the interconnected nature of the financial system that allows for relatively easy movement of funds, and (c) the safeguarding of customer information facilitated by certain secrecy laws.[18]

However, adherence to the AML regime goes beyond a mere obligation for compliance; it also embodies a moral imperative. The imperative for universal commitment stems from the shared responsibility to uphold the stability and trustworthiness of the financial system.[19] In an opinion published regarding the

[12] ibid 134.

[13] Council Directive 91/308/EEC of 10 June 1991 on prevention of the use of the financial system for the purpose of money laundering [1991] OJ L166/77; First Council Directive 77/780/EEC of 12 December 1977 on the coordination of laws, regulations and administrative provisions relating to the taking up and pursuit of the business of credit institutions [1977] OJ L322/30; Second Council Directive 89/646/EEC of 15 December 1989 on the coordination of laws, regulations and administrative provisions relating to the taking up and pursuit of the business of credit institutions and amending Directive 77/780/EEC [1989] OJ L386/1.

[14] Second Council Directive 89/646/EEC of 15 December 1989 on the coordination of laws, regulations and administrative provisions relating to the taking up and pursuit of the business of credit institutions and amending Directive 77/780/EEC [1989] OJ L386/1.

[15] Peter Alldridge, *Money Laundering Law: Forfeiture, Confiscation, Civil Recovery, Criminal Laundering and Taxation of the Proceeds of Crime* (Hart, 2003) 97. The definition in Article 1 of the 1st AML Directive also covers insurance companies (based on First Council Directive 79/267/EEC of 5 March 1979 on the coordination of laws, regulations and administrative provisions relating to the taking up and pursuit of the business of direct life assurance [1979] OJ L63/1 as amended by Council Directive 90/619/EEC of 8 November 1990 on the coordination of laws, regulations and administrative provisions relating to direct life assurance, laying down provisions to facilitate the effective exercise of freedom to provide services and amending Directive 79/267/EEC [1990] OJ L330/50, Directive 2002/83/EC of the European Parliament and of the Council of 5 November 2002 concerning life insurance [2002] OJ L345/1 and replaced by Directive 2009/138/EC of the European Parliament and of the Council of 25 November 2009 on the taking-up and pursuit of business of Insurance and Reinsurance (Solvency II) [2009] OJ L335/1).

[16] Valsamis Mitsilegas, *Money Laundering Counter-Measures in the European Union: A New Paradigm of Security Governance versus Fundamental Legal Principles* (Kluwer Law International, 2003) 132.

[17] Stessens (n 11) 134.

[18] ibid.

[19] Mitsilegas (n 16) 132–33.

1st AML Directive, the Economic and Social Committee emphasised that 'credit institutions cannot remain insensitive to the risk of the whole financial system being destabilised or of the loss of public confidence which could result if financial channels were used for laundering money gained from serious crimes condemned by the international community'.[20] Grounded in this viewpoint, Mitsilegas concludes that, 'Not only is it thus immoral to launder money, but it is equally immoral not to participate in efforts at countering the threat.'[21] Financial and credit institutions play a crucial role in this 'moralisation crusade'.[22]

1.2. The Introduction of Non-Business Obligations

In cases of complex crimes like money laundering, law enforcement agencies and prosecutorial authorities need various financial information, such as details about the perpetrator and the trail of money. A major hurdle to the effectiveness of the AML regime is the inability of some institutions to collect this information and effectively identify customers. Consequently, the capacity to acquire specific data assumes pivotal importance within the AML regime. In pursuit of this objective, the Directive enforces a range of preventive measures upon financial institutions designed to ascertain the identification of clientele and the preservation of comprehensive transaction records.[23]

The main aim of the 1st AML Directive was to focus solely on credit and financial institutions and introduce preventing obligations which can deviate from traditional banking business principles.

To begin with, credit and financial institutions have to identify customers in the following situations:

(a) when entering into business relations, particularly when opening an account or savings accounts, or when offering safe custody facilities;[24]

(b) for any transaction with customers other than those referred to under (a), involving a sum amounting to ECU 15,000 or more, irrespective of whether the transaction is carried out in a single operation or in several operations which seem to be linked;[25]

(c) in the event of doubt as to whether the customers are acting on their own behalf or where it is certain that they are not acting on their own behalf;[26] and

[20] European Economic and Social Committee, 'Opinion on the proposal for a Council Directive on prevention of the use of the financial system for the purpose of money laundering' [1990] OJ C332/86, https://eur-lex.europa.eu/legal-content/EN/TXT/PDF/?uri=CELEX:51990AC1047.

[21] Mitsilegas (n 16) 133.

[22] ibid.

[23] All these obligations mirror the FATF Recommendations.

[24] Council Directive 91/308/EEC of 10 June 1991 on prevention of the use of the financial system for the purpose of money laundering [1991] OJ L166/77, Art 3(1).

[25] ibid Art 3(2).

[26] ibid Art 3(5).

(d) when there is suspicion of money laundering, even in cases where the amount of the transaction is lower than the threshold laid down.[27]

Article 3 introduced the foundational concept of the 'Know Your Customer' principle within its provisions.[28] The identification process covers even situations of one-off transactions with the exception of low-risk transactions.[29] A key challenge with the implementation of this principle is the lack of further guidance.[30] However, the main issue concerning the principle appeared to be in relation to Article 3(7).[31] According to Mitsilegas, 'a number of Member States . . . extend the application of Article 3(7), exempting credit and financial institutions from their identification duty when the customer is another institution . . . to include non-EC and EEA institutions.'[32] Consequently, this extension has the potential to create a gap within the identification duty.[33] Furthermore, credit and financial institutions are under an obligation to maintain records containing pertinent information available for scrutiny in any investigation involving money laundering.[34] The information kept in the records comprises:

> (a) a copy or the references of the evidence required for a period of at least five years after the relationship with their customer has ended; (b) the supporting evidence and records, consisting of the original documents or copies admissible in court proceedings under the applicable national legislation for a period of at least five years following the execution of the transactions.[35]

Although the initiation of client information gathering and identification constituted the primary phase, the establishment of a framework obligating the private sector to report potentially illicit transactions was imperative. Therefore, the second obligation concerns the reporting of suspicious transactions,[36] which has been seen as the 'cornerstone of the preventive anti-money laundering framework'.[37] As outlined in Article 6, credit and financial institutions have a dual obligation:

[27] ibid Art 3(6).

[28] Duncan E Alford, 'Anti-Money Laundering Regulations: A Burden on Financial Institutions' (1994) 19(3) *North Carolina Journal of International Law and Commercial Regulation* 437, 451–52; The principle is in line with the statement of the Basel Committee regarding Banking Supervision (December 1988, Prevention of Criminal Use of the Banking System for the Purpose of Money-Laundering); Konstantinos D Magliveras, 'The European Community's Combat Against Money Laundering: Analysis and Evaluation' (1998) 5 *ILSA Journal of International & Comparative Law* 93, 102.

[29] Council Directive 91/308/EEC of 10 June 1991 on prevention of the use of the financial system for the purpose of money laundering [1991] OJ L166/77, Art 3; Mitsilegas (n 16) 70.

[30] The Directive does not provide any methods for identification; Mitsilegas (n 16) 71.

[31] Council Directive 91/308/EEC of 10 June 1991 on prevention of the use of the financial system for the purpose of money laundering [1991] OJ L166/77, Art 3(7); Mitsilegas (n 16) 71.

[32] Mitsilegas (n 16) 71.

[33] William C Gilmore, *Dirty Money: The Evolution of Money Laundering Counter-Measures*, 2nd edn (Council of Europe Publishing, 1999) 163.

[34] Council Directive 91/308/EEC of 10 June 1991 on prevention of the use of the financial system for the purpose of money laundering [1991] OJ L166/77, Art 4.

[35] ibid.

[36] ibid Art 6.

[37] Mitsilegas (n 16) 72.

to inform authorities when there is an indication of money laundering, and to hand over all the relevant information at the request of those authorities (passive obligation).[38] A key challenge with this obligation revolves around the concept of 'suspicion' as the Directive does not provide any test regarding this concept. Consequently, Member States have had the discretion to adopt a different approach to the reporting obligation.[39]

Thus, the passive obligation creates discomfort within the banking system, necessitating the compromise of traditional bank secrecy that such institutions had historically upheld.[40] Balancing the imperative of combating money laundering with potential disruption to business relations, the Directive stipulates that: 'Information supplied to the authorities . . . may be used only in connection with the combating of money laundering. However, Member States may provide that such information may also be used for other purposes.'[41] The fundamental principle of confidentiality characterises the relationship between banks and clients, often shielded by a regime of secrecy where in some instances the bank remains unaware of the client's true identity.

Another relevant obligation concerns due diligence, as envisaged in Article 5.[42] Credit and financial institutions are mandated to 'examine with special attention any transaction which they regard as particularly likely, by its nature, to be related to money laundering'.[43] The due diligence process precedes reporting (ie before the suspicion).[44] Again, the Directive did not provide further details about the substance of the duty.[45]

The duties above underscore the pivotal role of the private sector in bolstering the efficacy of the AML framework. From the perspective of banks, the Directive imposed a substantial onus in scrutinising clients.[46] By mandating them to uncover instances of money laundering, the Directive was initially perceived as a hindrance to the free movement of capital.[47] Additionally, there would be escalated costs (borne by customers) and potential competition between banks of the Community and banks without such an obligation to detect money laundering.[48]

[38] Council Directive 91/308/EEC of 10 June 1991 on prevention of the use of the financial system for the purpose of money laundering [1991] OJ L166/77, Art 6.

[39] Mitsilegas (n 16) 73–74.

[40] Magliveras (n 28) 104–05.

[41] Council Directive 91/308/EEC of 10 June 1991 on prevention of the use of the financial system for the purpose of money laundering [1991] OJ L166/77, Art 6(3).

[42] ibid Art 5.

[43] ibid.

[44] Commission of the European Communities, 'First Commission's report on the implementation of the Money Laundering Directive (91/308/EEC) to be submitted to the European Parliament and to the Council' COM 95(54) final 12, as cited in Mitsilegas (n 16) 74.

[45] ibid; Gilmore (n 33) 163.

[46] David Kirk, 'Serious Fraud – A Banker's Perspective' in Joseph J Norton (ed), *Banks: Fraud and Crime* (Lloyd's of London Press Ltd, 1994) 22.

[47] Geoffrey W Smith, 'Competition in the European Financial Services Industry: The Free Movement of Capital Versus the Regulation of Money Laundering' (1992) 13 *University of Pennsylvania Journal of International Business Law* 101, 135

[48] ibid 132.

Moreover, the preservation of records would amplify banks' expenses. Finally, the identification process and threat to confidentiality might result in customer alienation.[49] The issues described above regarding the open-ended provisions of the 1st AML Directive could foster different approaches within the EU. While this would create incentives for customers to seek out less-stringent jurisdictions,[50] in practice, other factors such as trust, stability and legitimacy of the financial institution might outweigh cost considerations. Customers might prefer regulated jurisdictions for the credibility and security they offer, a dynamic that appears to be reflected in digital currencies, which increasingly submit to intensive regulatory scrutiny to gain legitimacy within the mainstream financial system, even though it is in direct tension with their original design principles. As a result, certain aspects of a currency's technical design are not easily reconciled with the core requirements of the AML framework.

Importantly, the AML duties were deemed burdensome for banks, which were required to serve as secret reporters, and transformed financial institutions and enterprises into law enforcement and prosecutorial authorities, thereby inculcating a sophisticated, qualitative and systematic undercover reporting ethos.[51] Consequently, rather than compelling the industry to adopt measures, the Community and Member States needed to persuade stakeholders that the advantages of a 'clean' business environment outweighed the burden.[52] The 1st AML Directive introduced a framework in which the banking sector assumes a substantial, albeit contentious, role. From the 1st AML Directive until today, the regime maintained the main obligations towards financial and credit institutions but expanded the field of application of preventive measures to further professions and entities.[53]

2. Confidentiality and Secrecy in the Bank–Customer Relationship

The evolution of AML obligations had redefined regulatory expectations, placing the long-standing principle of bank–customer confidentiality under new pressure. This shift transformed business practices, competition and financial services, arising directly from the preventive obligations imposed on financial and credit institutions, which deviate from traditional banking principles. Given the diversity of legal systems within the EU, this section examines confidentiality within both common law and civil law contexts.

[49] ibid 131

[50] ibid 136; Alford (n 28) 453.

[51] Emmanuel Ioannides, *Fundamental Principles of EU Law Against Money Laundering* (Ashgate Publishing, 2014) 24.

[52] Rowan Bosworth-Davies and Graham Saltmarsh, *Money Laundering: A practical guide to the new legislation* (Chapman & Hall, 1994) 172.

[53] Stessens (n 11) 135.

2.1. The Relationship of Confidentiality between Banks and Customers Before the Introduction of AML-related Obligations

In the context of common law, the relationship between a customer and a bank is fundamentally contractual.[54] Confidentiality is an integral aspect of the bank–customer relationship, rooted in the agency inherent in the contract.[55] The agent is entrusted with the responsibility of upholding confidentiality.[56] This relationship has broadened to encompass situations beyond the strict scope of account maintenance. The bank or its representatives offer a range of 'services' to the client. While cases such as *Lloyd's Bank Ltd v Bundy* illustrate a broader fiduciary dimension, where reliance awareness and benefit establish a relationship of confidence, this can be distinct from the contractual/agency basis of confidentiality.[57] The principle itself applies more widely, as seen in *Parry Jones v Law Society*, which recognises confidentiality in other relationships such as lawyer and client or doctor and patient.[58] The relationship between lawyer and client is further advanced in terms of legal protection, as it is covered by a privilege that safeguards the communication between the parties.[59] Such a privilege does not exist in the bank–customer relationship.[60]

The duty of confidentiality between banker and client is contractual in nature, with its parameters delineated in the *Tournier* case,[61] where confidentiality is characterised as a non-absolute obligation.[62] Bankes LJ opined that there are four limitations which justify the dissemination of information (ie breach of confidentiality): '(a) where disclosure is under compulsion by law; (b) where there is a duty to the public to disclose; (c) where the interests of the bank require disclosure; (d) where disclosure is made by express or implied consent of the customer.'[63] Mitsilegas divides these grounds into two broad categories: 'those centred on the interests of the parties in the banker-customer relationship; and those going beyond this relationship in order to address broader interest considerations'.[64]

The AML regime introduced preventive measures that run counter to the duty of confidentiality.[65] These obligations have expanded in scope and intensity

[54] Mitsilegas (n 16) 126; EP Ellinger, E Lomnicka and RJA Hooley, *Modern Banking Law*, 3rd edn (Clarendon Press Oxford, 2002) 93

[55] ibid 94 and 135–36.

[56] ibid.

[57] ibid 94 and 135–36; *Lloyd's Bank v Bundy* [1975] QB 326.

[58] *Parry Jones v Law Society* [1969] 1 Ch 1, 9; Mitsilegas (n 16) 127.

[59] *Robertson v Canadian Imperial* [1995] 1 All ER 824; [1994] 1 WLR 1493 cited by Alldridge (n 15) 270.

[60] ibid

[61] *Tournier v National Provincial Bank of England* [1924] 1 KB 461.

[62] ibid; Mitsilegas (n 16) 128; Alldridge (n 15) 270.

[63] Mark Gill, 'Banking Confidentiality' in Linda Clarke (ed), *Confidentiality and the Law* (Lloyd's of London Press Ltd, 1990) 46; *Tournier v National Provincial Bank of England* [1924] 1 KB 461 at 473.

[64] Mitsilegas (n 16) 129.

[65] Alldridge (n 15) 270; Alford (n 28) 467; Michael Levi, 'Regulating Money Laundering: The Death of Bank Secrecy in the UK' (1991) 31(2) *British Journal of Criminology* 109, 111–12.

in ways that the court in the *Tournier* case could not have anticipated, creating new tensions with the traditional duty of confidentiality in the bank–customer relationship. Alldridge argues that the duties imposed on credit and financial institutions changed the function of the banker, who is seen 'no longer as confidant, but as police informant'.[66] These duties appeared to infringe fundamental rights, which the authors of the Jack Report on Banking Services criticised by stating that 'they constitute a serious inroad into the whole principle of customer confidentiality as conceived at the time of Tournier'.[67]

The concept of confidentiality within the bank–customer relationship also finds its place within civil law countries. Nevertheless, disparities between the two legal systems are evident. In Germany (during the 1990s), this relationship was founded upon the so-called 'general banking contract'.[68] Rather than being predicated upon a singular contract, the relationship entails the formation of multiple contracts when a customer engages with the bank (such as account opening, securities, loans, etc),[69] and for those contracts, a series of instruments and principles applies.[70] Concerning the information of the individual, the bank is, in principle, obliged to maintain the confidentiality of such information.[71] This connection between the customer and the banker hinges upon mutual trust.[72]

Two arguments underpin the concept of confidentiality. First, confidentiality in the context of the bank–customer relationship exists solely due to the existence of the business relationship itself. In other words, the principle of confidentiality endures even in the absence of a contractual agreement.[73] Second, confidentiality within this relationship is intertwined with the notion of secrecy, a construct safeguarded by criminal law.[74] In French law, for instance, banking secrecy was established as a means to safeguard confidentiality.[75] Consequently, breaches of secrecy could result in criminal penalties.[76] Hence, the principle of confidentiality

[66] ibid.

[67] 'Banking Services: Law and Practice Report by the Review Committee', Chairman: Professor RB Jack CBE (1989) CM 622, 30–31; Mitsilegas (n 16) 129.

[68] Norbert Horn, 'Germany' in Ross Cranston (ed), *European Banking Law: The Banker-Customer Relationship*, 2nd edn (Routledge, 1999) 65; Canaris, *Bankvertrugsrecht* (Munich, 1988), Anm 2-3 as cited by Mitsilegas (n 16) 127.

[69] Horn (n 68) 64.

[70] For example, good faith and pre-contractual principles; ibid 65.

[71] ibid 73.

[72] Canaris, *Bankvertrugsrecht* (Munich, 1988), Anm 2-3, p 10 as cited by Mitsilegas (n 16) 127; H Jung, 'Germany' in Dennis Campbell (ed), *International Bank Secrecy* (Sweet and Maxwell, 1992) 214.

[73] ibid; O Sandrock and E Klausing, 'Germany', in Ross Cranston (ed), *European Banking Law: The Banker-Customer Relationship* (Lloyd's of London Press Ltd, 1993) 91–93.

[74] M Dostas, *General Bank Confidentiality and Confidentiality of Deposits* (in Greek) (Sakkoulas, 2000) 25–28 as cited by Mitsilegas (n 16) 12.

[75] Odile Lajoix and Marc Billiau, 'France' in Dennis Campbell (ed), *International Bank Secrecy* (Sweet and Maxwell, 1992) 188.

[76] ibid 197; Monique Contamine-Raynaud, 'Le Secret Bancaire et le Contrôle de l'État sur les Opérations de Change et sur leurs Effets Délictueux – France' in Paolo Bernasconi (ed), *Blanchiment d'Argent et Secret Bancaire (Money Laundering and Banking Secrecy)* (Kluwer Law International, 1996) 125.

was regarded as a distinct concept with connections to fundamental rights, particularly the right to privacy.[77]

In countries with civil law systems, like Germany, the idea of keeping information confidential, similar to English law, is not absolute.[78] It can be limited in certain situations, like during criminal investigations. For example, a bank in Germany may not have to share information about a client in civil legal matters, but they must do so in criminal investigations.[79] This is where banking secrecy comes into play, as it helps maintain the confidentiality between a bank and its client. However, when the AML rules were put in place, the varying levels of secrecy in different countries caused some challenges to the envisioned harmonised approach. Secrecy, being a matter of degree rather than a standard, manifested diversely. Depending on the situation, a bank might have client information but choose not to share it due to confidentiality rules, or they might not have the information at all. Client information covers more than just transaction history; it includes everything from the account holder's name to records of transactions, income, loans, and more.[80]

The AML regime was meticulously designed to compel financial institutions, particularly banks, to provide the necessary information to relevant authorities and to mitigate the prevalence of excessive secrecy. It is imperative to underscore that the premise of banking secrecy is grounded in the intention to safeguard the customer's interests. It is crucial to clarify that this commitment to banking secrecy does not infer that the customer is inherently perceived as a criminal; in other words, the rationale behind banking secrecy is rooted in legitimate purposes and is not intended to serve illicit activities.[81]

Within the realm of banks, a spectrum of secrecy levels is discernible.[82] The three main categories are (a) the classic named account, where secrecy protects information concerning the account and applies to all the employees of the bank; (b) numbered accounts with a manager for the transactions on the account (ie the manager will know certain information but not the other employees); (c) numbered accounts where even the manager might not have access to all the information about the beneficial owner.[83]

In the same context, some jurisdictions, known as secrecy havens or secrecy jurisdictions, take active steps to protect the identities and transactions of a bank's

[77] Lajoix and Billiau (n 75) 197; ibid.

[78] Mitsilegas (n 16) 129; Lajoix and Billiau (n 75) 188;

[79] Horn (n 68) 73–74.

[80] Anatoliy A Lytvynenko, 'Data Privacy and Banking Secrecy: Topical Issues in Commonwealth, Continental Europe and International Jurisprudence' (2019) 5(3) *Athens Journal of Law* 303, 304.

[81] Jack A Blum and others, 'Financial Havens, Banking Secrecy and Money Laundering' (1998) United Nations report ST/ODCCP(02)/F491, 22.

[82] ibid 16.

[83] Ingo Walter, *The Secret Money Market: Inside the Dark World of Tax Evasion, Financial Fraud, Insider Trading, Money Laundering, and Capital Flight* (Harper & Row Publishers, 1990) 39–40; Edouard Chambost, *Bank Accounts: A World Guide to Confidentiality* (Wiley, 1983) 45–52; Richard J Gagnon Jr, 'International Banking Secrecy: Developments in Europe Prompt New Approaches' (1990) 23(3) *Vanderbilt Journal of Transnational Law* 653, 661–62.

clients. They create specific secrecy laws, often designed for non-residents.[84] This kind of 'confidential' banking developed over time, especially after World War I.[85] The idea behind these laws was to keep individuals' assets safe, especially in countries facing economic instability.[86] Switzerland is a classic example of a place with secretive banking practices.[87] However, many countries were sceptical of secrecy laws.[88] After World War II, the influence of secrecy laws grew, particularly due to the profound impact of the conflict on numerous nations. In an attempt to safeguard what little they had left, individuals moved their assets to secrecy havens, inadvertently creating a loophole for illicit activities.[89] In the years that followed, many countries without strong currencies decided to adopt secrecy laws too.[90]

The principle of bank secrecy originally aimed to safeguard the privacy and security of clients, especially in countries with fragile or failing economies, providing stability and trust in the financial system rather than shielding illicit behaviour. As the fight against global financial crimes intensified, banking secrecy was forced to adapt. The international and regional (EU) AML regime diligently strived to curtail and dismantle anonymity within the banking system. Nevertheless, the eradication of secrecy does not necessarily imply that the confidentiality that underscores bank–client relationships can be exploited and circumvented without valid and compelling reasons.

2.2. The Case of Austria: Navigating the Tension between Bank Secrecy and Anti-Money Laundering

The EU faced challenges when implementing the AML regime, primarily due to the prevailing bank secrecy laws of the 1990s. One of the best examples of that era is Austria.[91] Austria, being a member of the FATF since 1990 (from the early stages of the organisation), was aware of the developments of the AML laws on the international stage.[92] However, Barbot argued that, 'The secrecy provisions of Austrian . . . laws, as of 1991, continued to be a barrier which served to shelter

[84] Joe Stephanie C Tajan, 'Emerging from Secrecy Space: Bank Secrecy to Financial Transparency' (2010) 55 *Ateneo Law Journal* 447, 450. There is a difference between secrecy havens and tax havens. Tax havens are primarily jurisdictions that aid individuals to avoid strict tax policies.

[85] Richard T Preiss, 'Privacy of Financial Information and Civil Rights Issues: The Implications for Investigating and Prosecuting International Economic Crime', (1996) 14(3) *Dickinson Journal of International Law* 525, 527; Kate Picket, 'A Brief History of Swiss Banks' (*Time*, 26 February 2009), http://content.time.com/time/subscriber/article/0,33009,1881977,00.html.

[86] ibid.

[87] Todd Jones, 'Compulsion Over Comity: The United States' Assault on Foreign Bank Secrecy' (1992) 12(3) *Northwestern Journal of International Law & Business* 454, 456–57.

[88] ibid 455.

[89] ibid 456.

[90] ibid.

[91] Magliveras (n 28) 110.

[92] See, eg, www.fatf-gafi.org/en/countries/detail/Austria.html.

and protect money launderers from detection. Such bank secrecy laws . . . made detection next to impossible.'[93]

In the early 1990s, Austria became attractive for illicit funds due to its strict secrecy regime, stable government, geographical location, and the fact that Austria at that point was not a member of the EC and, therefore, the country was not obliged to implement the 1st AML Directive.[94] Austria's secrecy laws further highlight the interplay between bank–customer confidentiality and banking secrecy, as analysed in the above section. The Kreditwesengesetz of November 1986 established this secrecy regime in section 23.[95] Based on this, confidentiality for both individual and business clients became a strict obligation.[96] The law prohibited banks and those associated with confidential relationships with the customer from revealing client information.[97]

To address international concerns, in 1992 Austria published a 'Declaration of Principles of Care of the Austrian Banking Industry' outlining guidelines to mitigate money laundering risks within the bounds of strict secrecy laws.[98] However, these guidelines were not binding and were unable to circumvent the strict confidentiality of the bank–customer relationship.[99] In the same year (1992), an Austrian banker was arrested in the US for offering to launder money through anonymous accounts in Austria.[100] Following the incident, the Austrian Chancellor and the president of the Austrian National Bank reiterated their commitment to banking anonymity.[101]

During the period prior to its entry into the European Community, the Austrian government was faced with the obligation to implement the 1st AML Directive.[102] Eventually, Austria transposed the Directive into the national legal order in 1993.[103] However, an evaluation concluded that Austria fell short of attaining the Directive's objectives.[104] Consequently, a contentious dispute emerged between Austria and the European Commission, revolving around Austria's laws permitting the establishment and maintenance of anonymous accounts.[105]

[93] Lisa A Barbot, 'Money Laundering: An International Challenge' (1995) 3 *Tul J Int'l & Compliance L* 161, 196.

[94] Bruce Zagaris and Sheila M Castilla, 'Constructing an International Financial Enforcement Subregime: The Implementation of Anti-Money-Laundering Policy' (1993) 19 *Brook J Int'l L* 871, 941.

[95] ibid.

[96] ibid.

[97] ibid.

[98] ibid 942–43.

[99] ibid 944.

[100] 'Government appeal keeps banker in jail' (*Tampa Bay Times*, 13 July 1992), www.tampabay.com/archive/1992/07/13/government-appeal-keeps-banker-in-jail/.

[101] Zagaris and Castilla (n 94) 945–46.

[102] Magliveras (n 28) 110; Council Directive 91/308/EEC of 10 June 1991 on prevention of the use of the financial system for the purpose of money laundering [1991] OJ L166/77; the Directive is the transposition of the FATF's Recommendations to the legal order of the EC.

[103] Magliveras (n 28) 110; Bundesgesetz, mit dem das Strafgesetzbuch im Zusammenhang mit der Geldwäscherei geändert wird, No 527, published in Bundesgesetzblatt für Österreich (Austrian Official Gazette), No 192, July 30, 1993, at 3885, in force 1 October 1993 as cited by Magliveras (n 28) 110.

[104] ibid 111.

[105] ibid.

The existence of numbered accounts introduced complications in terms of the identification of individuals, a paramount obligation for banks under the 1st AML Directive, particularly as delineated in Article 3(1).[106] Therefore, the Commission urged Austria to amend its national legislation in this regard, albeit without success.[107] Austria posited that banking secrecy held constitutional stature, a policy entrenched for many years, and that only Austrian citizens enjoyed the prerogative to open anonymous accounts.[108] In response, the Commission asserted that Austria should preclude complete anonymity for individuals as this would engender susceptibility to money laundering risks.[109] The situation led to the triggering of Article 169 of the EC Treaty and a referral to the European Court of Justice in 1997.[110] Simultaneously, the FATF pressed Austria to discontinue the practice of anonymous accounts.[111] Austria's reluctance prompted the FATF to wield the threat of suspension.[112] Eventually, Austria agreed to eliminate all anonymous accounts by 2002.[113]

Certain jurisdictions persist in safeguarding the principle of confidentiality through the instrumentality of secrecy regulations. In the case of Austria, anonymous accounts can be considered a problem. However, the fact that these anonymous accounts exist does not mean that all launderers use them. It might also be the case that bank secrecy raises the attention of the authorities concerning money laundering. The only effective way to achieve anonymity is not to talk about it.[114] Confidentiality within the bank–customer relationship is evident today, and this is important. The objective, therefore, is not to dismantle confidentiality but rather to find a balanced solution. This balance necessitates the establishment of distinct boundaries, the reinforcement of safeguards for the principle of confidentiality, and the avoidance of indiscriminate measures applied across the entirety of customers. Finding a balance between safeguarding client confidentiality and fulfilling AML obligations is not merely theoretical; it has direct implications for the operational workload of banks. The following section examines these burdens, considering how preventive measures extend the responsibilities of financial institutions far beyond traditional cooperation with law enforcement.

[106] Council Directive 91/308/EEC of 10 June 1991 on prevention of the use of the financial system for the purpose of money laundering [1991] OJ L166/77.

[107] Magliveras (n 28) 111; Bruce Zagaris, 'Austria Will Restrict Bank Secrecy Laws on Securities, But Not Savings Accounts' (1996) 12(3) *International Enforcement Law Reporter* 88.

[108] Helmut Fuchs, 'Gewinnabschöpfung und Geldwäscherei. Wie soll es weitergehen?' (1995) 50 *Oesterreichische Juristen Zeitung* 215 as cited by Magliveras (n 28) 111.

[109] Magliveras (n 28) 112.

[110] EC Treaty, Art 169; Magliveras (n 28) 113.

[111] Michael Allen, 'Austria Escapes Censure by Ending Secret Accounts' (*Wall Street Journal*, 16 June 2000), www.wsj.com/articles/SB961106000784088177.

[112] ibid.

[113] ibid.

[114] Jack A Blum and others, 'Financial Havens, Banking Secrecy and Money Laundering' (1998) United Nations report ST/ODCCP(02)/F491, 17.

3. How Burdensome is the AML Regime?

The complexity of the crime of money laundering necessitates a symbiotic collaboration between the private sector and law enforcement agencies. Enacting legislation which promotes the private sector as the main investigating power needs to be seriously balanced. Under the 1st AML Directive, banks have the obligation to cooperate with law enforcement agencies when asked to provide information about specific individuals.[115] Nevertheless, banks are also charged with the active investigation of their systems, coupled with the duty to report to authorities in instances of suspicion.[116] This exceeds the concept of cooperation.

3.1. The Aftermath of the AML Regime: The Death of Secrecy, Alienation of Clients and Compliance Costs

In 1991, Levi voiced concerns over the demise of bank secrecy,[117] highlighting that:

> the need for increased powers to combat money laundering serves as a nexus for a coalition between those on the political left who support inroads into bank account secrecy to 'get at' the suspected misconduct of powerful corporations, corrupt dictators . . . and those on the political right who support increased access to accounts as a necessary prelude to eliminating drug use and terrorism.[118]

Gill and Taylor, when examining the banking viewpoint,[119] asserted that the surveillance of the financial system is not aligned with the core objectives of banks (and other financial and credit institutions). Their main focus lies in maximising profits, which may occasionally involve unintentional support for illicit funds.[120] Through this interesting political approach, Levi argued that the political world agreed on the necessity of the AML regime despite the different reasons, underscoring its functionality, which hinges on the capacity of credit and financial institutions to identify clients and issue reports on suspicious activities.[121]

Nonetheless, banks' apprehension towards the AML regime extends beyond these factors. A regime such as this necessitates consensus across all European

[115] Council Directive 91/308/EEC of 10 June 1991 on prevention of the use of the financial system for the purpose of money laundering [1991] OJ L166/77.

[116] ibid.

[117] Levi (n 65) 109.

[118] ibid 111.

[119] Martin Gill and Geoff Taylor, 'Preventing Money Laundering or Obstructing Business?: Financial Companies' Perspectives on "Know Your Customer" Procedures' (2004) 44(4) *British Journal of Criminology* 582.

[120] ibid.

[121] ibid; one further argument is that the concept of money laundering is quite broad and can encompass a lot of activities.

Union members. Otherwise, it creates a competitiveness problem.[122] It fosters a race to the bottom; the lower the standards, the higher the capital. This phenomenon is pertinent at the regional level within the EU. On the global scale, if the EU upholds stringent AML rules, capital may shift to jurisdictions beyond the Union to evade these regulations.[123]

In terms of a comprehensive cost–benefit assessment, available information is limited.[124] The financial expenses associated with adherence to compliance measures can be quantified in terms of monetary outlays, encompassing operational expenditures and workforce costs devoted to sustaining the regulatory framework.[125] The benefits attributable to compliance predominantly manifest as reputational gains, which, over time, can be translated into tangible outcomes.[126] The reputational benefit of compliance is based on the fact that customers prefer respectable financial institutions to entrust with their money and businesses. The crime of money laundering is seen as a danger for financial institutions, although instances of bank insolvency directly attributed to money laundering are infrequent.[127]

The ramifications for banks are contingent upon their distinct attributes. First, it can be claimed that the impact is more noticeable among high-risk banks.[128] For this group of banks, the compliance costs will be higher.[129] Second, the impact depends on the size of the institution: larger banks are better able to cope with

[122] ibid.

[123] There are countries around the world today that did not implement the FATF Recommendations or do not have a similar approach towards money laundering, especially countries that do not have hard currencies.

[124] Jackie Harvey, 'Compliance and Reporting Issues Arising for Financial Institutions from Money Laundering Regulations: A Preliminary Cost Benefit Study' (2004) 7(4) *Journal of Money Laundering Control* 333.

[125] William Baity, 'Banking on Secrecy: The Price of Unfettered Secrecy and Confidentiality in the Face of International Organised and Economic Crime' (2000) 8 *Journal of Financial Crime* 83–86; Ioannides (n 51) 142.

[126] Anthony Saunders and Marcia Cornett, *Financial Institutions Management: A Risk Management Approach*, 4th edn (McGraw Hill Education, 2003) 372 as cited by Harvey (n 124) 337.

[127] Peter Alldridge, *What Went Wrong with Money Laundering Law?* (Palgrave Pivot, 2015) 13; Alldridge argues that 'There is little or no evidence for the claim that, leaving aside the effects of the AML regime itself, allowing banks to launder money for clients endangers the banks in question or the financial system more generally. The one exception that is sometimes mentioned is BCCI, a Bank with headquarters in Luxembourg and branches worldwide, which failed in 1991. The claim is sometimes made that BCCI became insolvent because they facilitated the laundering of Colombian drug money. BCCI was used to launder drug money, but what drove the bank into insolvency was the fact that their depositor's money was stolen.'

[128] Arjan Premti, Mohammad Jafarinejad and Henry Balani, 'The impact of the Fourth Anti-Money Laundering Directive on the valuation of EU banks' (2021) 57 *Research in International Business and Finance* 57, 59; see further Alexandra Campmas, 'How do European Banks portray the effect of policy interest rates and prudential behaviour on profitability?' (2020) 51 *Research in International Business and Finance* 51.

[129] ibid.

the costs of compliance than medium and small-sized entities.[130] To this end, the cost differential between smaller and larger banks may not be substantial, yet the resultant impact varies significantly. Gill and Taylor observe that 'while 67 per cent of banks did not regard KYC as costly, 71.4 per cent . . . of building societies and 68.4 per cent of insurance companies did consider the requirements expensive'.[131] While the authors do not explicitly state this, it can be inferred that smaller entities viewed the regulatory demands as cumbersome. This might also be based on the fact that banks have the resources to comply with the regime.

Third, Premti, Jafarinejad and Balani assert that banks engaging in non-traditional banking activities face higher exposure to money laundering risks.[132] This susceptibility emanates from unregulated operations that criminals can exploit for the purpose of laundering ill-gotten proceeds.[133] Lastly, as mentioned earlier, the rapport between customers and banks rests on the foundation of confidentiality. Numerous banks want to protect the information concerning their clients, and the clients trust that the bank will not disseminate their personal financial data. Even decades after its introduction, the AML regime carries the potential to conflict with confidentiality, raising the possibility that some clients may perceive these obligations as intrusive.[134] A study indicates that over 50% assumed that the newly founded duties of credit and financial institutions would result in client alienation.[135] Among them, there was the belief that a number of clients would also face difficulties in providing the necessary information for the identification process.[136]

3.2. A Comparison Between Banks and Virtual Asset Service Providers

This part uncovers a novel examination of the challenges posed by the trustless and decentralised architecture of digital currencies at the intersection of regulatory obligations, confidentiality and anonymity. It demonstrates that AML measures originally designed for centralised banking systems must be adapted for virtual asset service providers. The concept of money laundering emanates

[130] ibid; Aigbe Akhigbe and Anna D Martin, 'Valuation impact of Sarbanes-Oxley: Evidence from disclosure and governance within the financial services industry' (2006) 30(3) *Journal of Banking & Finance* 989; see further Marcia H Millon-Cornett and Hassan Tehranian, 'Stock market reactions to the depository institutions deregulation and monetary control act of 1980' (1989) 13 *Journal of Banking & Finance* 81; Marcia H Millon-Cornett and Hassan Tehranian, 'An Examination of the Impact of the Garn-St. Germain Depository Institutions Act of 1982 on Commercial Banks and Savings and Loans' (1990) 45 *Journal of Finance* 95.

[131] Gill and Taylor (n 119) 590; the same study also underlines that up to one-third of the tested sample agrees that the duties on credit and financial institutions were burdensome.

[132] Premti, Jafarinejad and Balani (n 128) 61.

[133] ibid

[134] Gill and Taylor (n 119) 587.

[135] ibid.

[136] ibid 588.

from the motive of criminals to legitimise the proceeds obtained through illicit activities. The crime of money laundering involves two distinct dimensions. The initial dimension encompasses the predicate offence, which constitutes the primary criminal activity yielding unlawful gains.[137] The subsequent dimension encompasses the methodology chosen to cleanse these unlawfully obtained profits. Financial institutions have the capacity to possess information concerning both dimensions. Initially, these institutions can ascertain the identities of their clients. Additionally, they are equipped to maintain comprehensive records of transaction history. This repository of data is imperative for the identification and subsequent investigation of criminal undertakings. As a result, the banking system has been positioned as a quasi-private policing entity responsible for scrutinising the financial landscape.[138] This paradigm establishes a collaboration between the private sector and public authorities, albeit one that is not without complexities. Private banks have responsibilities towards their clientele, thus leading to divergent approaches influenced by the regulations governing the relationship between banks and their customers.[139]

3.2.1. *Trust vs Trustless*

The EU's AML regime has evolved since its inception in 1991. The list of obliged entities has consistently expanded, encompassing a substantial share of the private sector. Under the existing framework, these obliged entities, which include banks and virtual asset service providers, are mandated to relay information regarding all suspicious transactions to the Financial Intelligence Units (FIUs) situated within the Member States.

Banks have transformed into *de facto* police owing to their pivotal role within the system. This role bestows banks with the prerogative to decline prospective clients at the pre-contractual stage if there is a suspicion of involvement in money laundering activities.[140] This symbiotic relationship is fundamentally grounded in trust, a factor susceptible to a multitude of dynamics. Variables such as the bank's integrity, reputation, competencies and other elements can exert influence.[141] Above all, clients require banks to exhibit discretion, underlining the essence of confidentiality within this relationship.[142]

[137] Predicate offence is the crime with which the criminal gets the illegal gains.

[138] Lloyd Himaambo, 'Role of Banks as Private Police in the Anti-Money Laundering Crusade' (2017) 9 *Bocconi Legal Papers* 157, 164.

[139] Basel Committee on Banking Regulations and Supervisory Practices, 'Prevention of criminal use of the banking system for the purpose of money laundering' (1988), www.bis.org/publ/bcbsc137.pdf.

[140] Himaambo (n 138) 168.

[141] Benedictus Renny See and others, 'Know Your Customer (KYC) Principles Relates to Bank Confidentiality as an Effort to Prevent Money Laundering Crimes' (2019) 81 *Journal of Law, Policy and Globalization* 101, 102.

[142] Anna Simonova, 'Identity Protection or Not for Employees Reporting Money Laundering? The UK Case' (2011) 8 *Macquarie Journal of Business Law* 300, 301.

The clash between the AML regime and the principle of confidentiality extends to various domains, as evident within the context of entities operating in the realm of digital currencies. Within this sphere, entities and cryptocurrencies based on anonymity confront challenges in reconciling the imperative of confidentiality. While clients might comprehend the entity's obligation to reveal personal information in instances of specific money laundering suspicions following a risk assessment, disparities arise when entities gather information irrespective of risk, even if not all details are disclosed to public authorities. Consequently, the intermediaries are faced with a dilemma. On the one hand, entities are obliged to adhere to the AML framework to avert fines and legal repercussions. On the other hand, there is the danger of liability stemming from the contract with the clients.[143] To illustrate this situation, a 2015 research study concerning the culture of compliance in the financial industry found that 21 per cent of respondents from the UK said that 'their company's confidential policies and procedures bar the reporting of the potential illegal or unethical activities directly to law enforcement or regulatory authorities'.[144]

Confidentiality constitutes a pivotal aspect of the rapport between a bank and a customer. However, confidentiality only exists when the relationship is defined by trust. Plato-Shinar explains that, 'The inferiority of the customer and his dependence on the bank . . . leaves the customer no choice but to rely on the bank and endow special trust in it.'[145] There is a mutual dependency between trust and confidentiality. The customer places trust in the bank's ability to safeguard the confidentiality of the relationship, while simultaneously upholding this confidentiality fosters the development of trust.[146] Plato-Shinar further argues that without trust, banks cannot exist, highlighting though that 'the individual customer . . . still continues to trust the bank' irrespective of past scandals which shocked the faith of the public in the banking system.[147]

Virtual asset service providers face similar dilemmas concerning the balance between adhering to regulatory requirements and preserving confidentiality.[148] In

[143] Himaambo (n 138) 182.

[144] Ann Tenbrunsel and Jordan Thomas, *The Street, The Bull and The Crisis: A Survey of the US & UK Financial Services Industry* (University of Notre Dame and Labaton Sucharow LLP, 2015) as cited by Miriam Goldby, 'Breaches of AML reporting requirements by UK bankers: Are effective enforcement choices being made by financial regulators?' in Constanza A Russo, Rosa Maria Lastra and William Blair (eds), *Research Handbook on Law and Ethics in Banking and Finance* (Edward Elgar Publishing, 2019) 333.

[145] Ruth Plato-Shinar, 'Law and ethics: the bank's fiduciary duty towards retail customers' in Constanza A Russo, Rosa Maria Lastra and William Blair (eds), *Research Handbook on Law and Ethics in Banking and Finance* (Edward Elgar Publishing, 2019) 228.

[146] ibid.

[147] ibid; Rosa Maria Lastra and Marcelo J Sheppard, 'Ethical foundations of financial law' in Constanza A Russo, Rosa Maria Lastra and William Blair (eds), *Research Handbook on Law and Ethics in Banking and Finance* (Edward Elgar Publishing, 2019) 60.

[148] Directive (EU) 2018/843 of the European Parliament and of the Council of 30 May 2018 amending Directive (EU) 2015/849 on the prevention of the use of the financial system for the purposes of money laundering or terrorist financing, and amending Directive 2009/138/EC and 2013/36/EU [2018] OJ L156/43.

contrast to banks, blockchain technology embodies a trustless paradigm.[149] The technology does not predicate trust; it guarantees it.[150] Antonopoulos argues that permissionless blockchain is a 'shift from trusting people to trusting math'.[151] This translates to virtual asset service providers occupying marginal roles, potentially affording customers greater leverage.[152] If they are not satisfied, they can continue the transactions and the exchange of digital currencies without intermediaries.[153] The issue concerning these providers is notably intricate. The 5th AML Directive and the new AML Regulation categorise the entire domain of digital currencies as high risk, aligning with a rule-based approach due to the technological attributes of these systems.[154] Consequently, virtual asset service providers are obliged to treat all customers as high risk, prompting the imposition of enhanced due diligence and the collection of data from all customers, including data generated by the system itself.[155]

In scenarios where a bank submits a Suspicious Activity Report (SAR), the assessment has already substantiated suspicions beyond mere possibilities.[156] The implication of the rule-based approach and its interaction with virtual asset service providers yields three conceivable outcomes. First, virtual asset providers might abstain from filing SARs owing to the challenges in pinpointing risk within the virtual domain of cryptocurrencies. Second, FIUs could receive an influx of SARs from virtual asset providers, who fear failure in carrying out their obligations.[157]

[149] Rosa María Lastra and Jason Grant Allen, 'Virtual Currencies in the Eurosystem: Challenges Ahead' (2018) Study requested by the ECON committee of the European Parliament, PE 619.020, 54; Primavera De Filippi, Morshed Mannan and Wessel Reijers, 'Blockchain as a Confidence Machine: The Problem of Trust & Challenges of Governance' (2020) 62 *Technology in Society* 101284; the trustless environment is based on the fact that the system is decentralised; Narayanan and others (n 2) 27–30; De Filippi and Wright (n 2) 61; Arslanian (n 2) 51.

[150] ibid.

[151] Andreas Antonopoulos, 'Bitcoin security model: trust by computation' (*Radar*, 20 February 2014), http://radar.oreilly.com/2014/02/bitcoin-security-model-trust-by-computation.html#:~:text=By%20contrast%2C%20bitcoin%20implements%20a,solving%20a%20computationally%20difficult%20problem, as cited by Silvia Semenzin and Alessandro Gandini, 'Automating Trust with the Blockchain? A Critical Investigation of "Blockchain 2.0" Cultures' (2021) 2 *Global Perspectives* 1, 2; Victoria L Lemieux, *Searching for Trust: Blockchain Technology in an Age of Disinformation* (Cambridge University Press, 2022) 57.

[152] See further Lemieux (n 151) 49–70 where it is argued that 'trust in third party intermediaries backed by trust in law, or *lex juris*, is replaced by trust in the blockchain, backed by a consensus algorithm, or lex *cryptographia*'.

[153] Lastra and Allen (n 149); De Filippi, Mannan and Reijers (n 149); Narayanan and others (n 2) 27–30; De Filippi and Wright (n 2) 61; Arslanian (n 2) 51.

[154] Directive (EU) 2018/843 of the European Parliament and of the Council of 30 May 2018 amending Directive (EU) 2015/849 on the prevention of the use of the financial system for the purposes of money laundering or terrorist financing, and amending Directive 2009/138/EC and 2013/36/EU [2018] OJ L156/43, recital 24; Regulation (EU) 2024/1624 of the European Parliament and of the Council of 31 May 2024 on the prevention of the use of the financial system for the purposes of money laundering or terrorist financing [2024] OJ L, 2024/1624, recital 76

[155] ibid.

[156] William Blair, Richard Brent and Tom Grant, *Banks and Financial Crime: The International Law of Tainted Money*, 2nd edn (Oxford University Press, 2008) 167.

[157] Daehan Kim, Mehmet Huseyin Bilgin and Doojin Ryu, 'Are suspicious activity requirements for cryptocurrency exchanges effective' (2021) 7(78) *Financial Innovation*, https://doi.org/10.1186/s40854-021-00294-6, 14.

This can be explained by the fact that the providers will collect a large variety of data from all their customers. However, this scenario entails a potential pitfall: FIUs may become overwhelmed by the sheer volume of information. Although the rule-based approach seeks to address the rapid pace of technological evolution, the process of sifting through copious data can prove time-intensive.[158] Third, virtual asset service providers could potentially target specific accounts, such as 'bitcoin whales', along with transactions involving substantial volumes of cryptocurrencies.[159]

3.2.2. *Practical Difficulties in the Application of AML Measures in the Environment of Digital Currencies*

The preventive measures delineated within the AML framework rest upon the premise that obliged entities must amass sufficient client information. Yet, the landscape of digital currencies diverges significantly from that of the traditional banking system. This divergence stems from the decentralised nature of cryptocurrencies, which is not currently addressed as a phenomenon by the AML regime nor by the MiCA Regulation.[160] Thus, a pertinent inquiry arises regarding the capacity of these entities to procure the necessary data.

Nakamoto's design of Bitcoin aimed to showcase that societies could function with payment systems operating outside the purview of closely monitored banking institutions.[161] Key attributes of this system encompass decentralisation (ie the system is not controlled by any entity and can be used without any intermediaries), instant and irreversible transactions, and anonymity (ie everyone can have bitcoins and without any limitation as to how many public keys – Bitcoin addresses – a user can have).[162]

The mainstream adoption of cyberspace coincided with heightened governmental concerns about the potential anonymity granted to users in the online realm. Cyberspace activist John Perry Barlow's 1996 declaration of cyberspace's independence embodies this sentiment: 'Governments of the Industrial World, you weary giants of flesh and steel, I come from Cyberspace, the new home of Mind. On behalf of the future, I ask you of the past to leave us alone. You are not

[158] Stan Sater, 'Do We Need KYC/AML: The Bank Secrecy Act and Virtual Currency Exchanges' (2020) 73 *Arkansas Law Review* 397, 420.

[159] 'A crypto whale is an entity that holds large amounts of cryptocurrency', from Caroline Banton, Erika Rasure and Katrina Munichiello, 'What is a Crypto Whale and How do They Affect Crypto Markets' (*Investopedia*, 11 October 2025), www.investopedia.com/terms/b/bitcoin-whale.asp.

[160] Narayanan and others (n 2) 27–30; De Filippi and Wright (n 2) 61; Arslanian (n 2) 51.

[161] Nakamoto (n 2).

[162] ibid; Directive (EU) 2018/843 of the European Parliament and of the Council of 30 May 2018 amending Directive (EU) 2015/849 on the prevention of the use of the financial system for the purposes of money laundering or terrorist financing, and amending Directive 2009/138/EC and 2013/36/EU [2018] OJ L156/43, recitals 8 and 9; Narayanan and others (n 2) 27, 138; De Filippi and Wright (n 2) 33–40, 61; Arslanian (n 2) 51–54, 138; In order to increase anonymity, users can generate a new address for each transaction they make.

welcome among us. You have no sovereignty where we gather.'[163] This statement underscores apprehensions surrounding government intervention and control over the internet, an environment perceived by many as a bastion of freedom.

Within the context of traditional banking, the term 'anonymity' signifies that an account holder's individual details remain undisclosed to bank personnel. However, this term acquires distinct connotations within the cryptocurrency realm. There should be a distinction between the anonymity of the user and the unlinkability of the transaction.[164] In the Bitcoin system, users do not provide any identification details, and they only require addresses (public keys) to make transactions. Each transaction is nonetheless recorded on the Bitcoin system's public blockchain, accessible to all blockchain users.[165] To increase anonymity, a user may generate a unique address for each transaction, enhancing unlinkability.[166] However, even with this strategy, complete anonymity remains elusive.[167]

The nature of the public blockchain renders anonymity questionable, which is why it should be perceived as pseudo-anonymity. Cryptocurrencies might be considered as the cash of the internet, because both assets have a certain level of anonymity.[168] The only difference is that the Bitcoin system can execute non-face to face transactions.[169] It can be argued that cryptocurrencies and cash have reverse characteristics. Bitcoin can execute non-face to face transactions, but every transaction can be seen on the blockchain. With cash, the identity of the 'user' is known, but the transaction is not evidenced anywhere. Thus, the Bitcoin system might offer a higher level of anonymity.[170] This is based on the pseudo-anonymity of the system and the decentralised environment. As a result, there is no central authority to, effectively, enforce any Know Your Customer (KYC) and Customer Due Diligence (CDD) measures.[171]

Building on this complexity, scholars have sought to conceptualise how different payment systems, including cryptocurrencies, operationalise anonymity within their design and purpose. The literature tries to categorise payment systems into distinct classes. On the one hand, a payment system may embody anonymity as an inherent design feature.[172] On the other hand, anonymity might not constitute the primary intent of the system.[173] The former category is notably

[163] John Perry Barlow, 'A Declaration of the Independence of Cyberspace' (Electronic Frontier Foundation, 1996), www.eff.org/cyberspace-independence.

[164] Victor Dostov and Pavel Shust, 'Cryptocurrencies: an unconventional challenge to the AML/CFT regulators' (2014) 21(3) *Journal of Financial Crime* 249, 251.

[165] ibid 252.

[166] Narayanan and others (n 2) 139–41.

[167] See also Greg Maitland and others, 'Linkability in Practical Electronic Cash Design' (2000) Information Security: Third International Workshop, ISW 2000, Wollongong, Australia.

[168] Danton Bryans, 'Bitcoin and Money Laundering: Mining for an Effective Solution' (2014) 89 *Indiana Law Journal* 441, 444.

[169] ibid.

[170] Dostov and Shust (n 164) 252.

[171] ibid.

[172] ibid 257.

[173] ibid.

contentious and has garnered extensive criticism. In contemporary times, specific cryptocurrencies assert their explicit commitment to safeguarding the anonymity of their clientele.[174] However, there is no evidence to support the argument that all digital currencies were designed solely to offer anonymity. Digital currencies are attractive due to the fact that they are decentralised, and they execute transactions instantly.[175]

The banking system and virtual asset service providers are underpinned by different business models. While the challenge remains consistent, the solution necessitates adaptation to distinct circumstances. A pivotal disparity pertains to the locus of enforcement in these two systems. Banks enforce regulations from a centralised standpoint and consequently gather necessary data. In contrast, cryptocurrencies are decentralised, lacking a singular entity to mandate individuals to provide information.[176] A second distinction pertains to the role of intermediaries. Presently, banks are indispensable for completing financial transactions. As a result, individuals are obliged to adhere to the rules imposed by banks. However, the functioning of digital currency systems does not hinge upon any single intermediary.[177] While individuals can opt to use virtual asset service providers, they are not coerced to do so.[178] The blockchain embodies a trustless ecosystem.[179] Consequently, confidentiality within these systems is contingent upon the existence of intermediaries.

Another factor to consider is that the introduction of the AML regime prompted reactions from banks, who were concerned about the potential alienation of customers.[180] Importantly, the reliance on banks precluded substantial customer alienation. However, the landscape has changed today, as virtual asset service providers are no longer necessary. As a result, these providers are aware of the precariousness of their position. Altering a fundamental feature of digital currencies, specifically, their level of anonymity, holds a true risk of alienating clients.

Furthermore, the AML regime and the MiCA Regulation exhibit a reluctance towards decentralised applications. This implies that not all transactions are executed within the regulated system. Therefore, should an individual seek to conduct a transaction via a custodial wallet provider with another individual who

[174] There is a category of cryptocurrencies which are generally called Anonymity Enhanced Cryptocurrencies. Some examples are Zcash, Monero and Dash. These three cryptocurrencies have been criticised, and they pose higher risks for money laundering and terrorist financing. See further Chapter 1 of this book.

[175] Narayanan and others (n 2) 27, 138; De Filippi and Wright (n 2) 33–40, 61; Arslanian (n 2) 51–54, 138; David Silva Ramahlo and Nuno Igreja Matos, 'What we do in the (Digital) Shadows: Anti-Money Laundering Regulation and a Bitcoin-Mixing Criminal Problem' (2021) 22(3) ERA Forum Springer Berlin Heidelberg 487, 494–96.

[176] Narayanan and others (n 2) 27–30; De Filippi and Wright (n 2) 61; Arslanian (n 2) 51.

[177] Giulio Soana, 'Regulating cryptocurrencies checkpoints: Fighting a trench war with cavalry?' (2022) 51 Economic Notes: Review of Banking Finance and Monetary Economics, https://doi.org/10.1111/ecno.12195, 7.

[178] ibid.

[179] Narayanan and others (n 2) 27–30; De Filippi and Wright (n 2) 61; Arslanian (n 2) 51.

[180] Gill and Taylor (n 119) 587.

utilises a self-hosted wallet, the former would be unable to procure the necessary data. This issue is further discussed under the travel rule Regulation, where recital 39 indicates that, for AML purposes, the provider should collect the information on both the originator and the beneficiary, usually from its client.[181]

Persistent systemic distinctions exist between banks and virtual asset service providers. Digital currencies have introduced a new business model, supported by a technological framework that allows for transaction transparency while simultaneously providing a higher level of individual anonymity. This section highlights the ongoing nature of the fundamental challenge, albeit in the transformed context of digital currencies. The AML regime, initially designed for the banking system, now grapples with specific technological characteristics that question its adequacy and effectiveness in the present environment.

A fundamental tenet of the AML regime resides in the implementation of KYC procedures. These procedures are necessary to identify customers. The significance of KYC extends beyond the mere identification of customers; it also pertains to the association of customers with specific accounts. The issue becomes apparent when this scenario is transferred to the digital currency economy. Under the new AML regime (including the MiCA Regulation), the obligations fall exclusively on centralised service providers, thereby leaving the decentralised segment of the digital economy, often regarded as more risk-prone, largely beyond regulatory reach. Consequently, a substantial part of this economy remains unregulated.

In the context of anonymity as a central issue, the utilisation of KYC procedures to de-anonymise customers constitutes merely the initial phase. Knowledge of a customer's identity does not inherently establish a link between that identity and the myriad accounts within the blockchain. The establishment of traceability through KYC is a complex undertaking. Even if FIUs acquire pertinent information, the absence of a central registry linking identities to currency wallets poses challenges.[182] Relevant authorities require comprehensive information from additional entities within this digital economy (eg crypto markets) to effectively address this. However, this becomes difficult as these systems are programmed to circumvent the involvement of third parties.[183] The analysis shows that the information collected by the obliged entities might not even be sufficient to link the identities to specific addresses.

Digital currencies and their disruptive technology have caused the separation of the economy into two spheres (the real-world economy and the digital

[181] Regulation (EU) 2023/1113 of the European Parliament and of the Council of 31 May 2023 on information accompanying transfers of funds and certain crypto-assets and amending Directive (EU) 2015/849 (recast) [2023] OJ L150/1, recital 39.

[182] Lars Haffke, Mathias Fromberger and Patrick Zimmermann, 'Virtual Currencies and Anti-Money Laundering – The Shortcomings of the 5th AML Directive (EU) and How to Address Them' (2020) 21(2) *Journal of Banking Regulation* 125, 132–34; Niels Vandezande, 'Virtual currencies under EU anti-money laundering law' (2017) 33(3) *Computer Law & Security Review* 341, 352

[183] Valentina Covolo, 'The EU Response to Criminal Misuse of Cryptocurrencies: The Young, Already Outdated 5th Anti-Money Laundering Directive' (2019) University of Luxembourg Law Working Paper No 2019-015, 14.

economy). In the beginning, digital currencies were dependent on the real-world economy.[184] Nevertheless, digital currencies are becoming mainstream day by day.[185] If the economy of digital currencies is independent, then KYC procedures will be limited to the real-world economy.[186]

Incorporating the dimension of anonymity further complicates the functional efficacy of KYC procedures. Anonymity within the context of digital currencies proves intricate to define. Different currencies provide different levels of anonymity.[187] In light of this, the efficacy of KYC procedures could be compromised, particularly when digital currencies are converted to privacy coins, which promise unlinkability and untraceability.[188] The transformation brought about by digital currencies in the landscape of online payments mirrors the nature of anonymity inherent in Austria's numbered accounts. While strong national protections once safeguarded client privacy, these measures were gradually adjusted to accommodate AML requirements. A similar trajectory is emerging for digital currencies as providers are now required to gather and disclose customer information. Unlike traditional banking, however, these regulatory measures only offer a partial solution. Despite regulation, digital currencies and their decentralised, trustless design allow transactions to circumvent intermediaries, mirroring the historic limitations of regulating informal systems such as hawala, where incorporating hawaladars had arguably limited impact on transactional flows.[189] This comparison underscores the novel regulatory challenge posed by digital currencies. While lessons can be drawn from traditional secrecy frameworks, the combination of technology and decentralisation renders the AML solution inherently partial and imbalanced.

Conclusion

The primary objective of this chapter has been to establish the distinctions between the banking industry and virtual asset service providers from the perspective of the concepts of confidentiality and trust. Following the implementation of the AML regime in 1991, credit and financial institutions were mandated to gather customer data. Some apprehensions raised by this development were ultimately unfounded, largely due to the banks' near-monopoly over payment systems. Nonetheless, a legitimate concern pertained to the competition landscape, with jurisdictions

[184] Christian Brenig, Rafael Accorsi and Günter Müller, 'Economic Analysis of Cryptocurrency Backed Money Laundering' (2015) in Twenty-Third European Conference on Information Systems (ECIS), 8, as cited by Soana (n 177) 8.

[185] David Carlisle, 'Virtual Currencies and Financial Crime: Challenges and Opportunities' (*Royal United Services Institute for Defence and Security Studies*, 27 March 2017) 14, https://rusi.org/explore-our-research/publications/occasional-papers/virtual-currencies-and-financial-crime-challenges-and-opportunities.

[186] Soana (n 177) 8.

[187] Covolo (n 183) 18; on privacy coins see further Chapter 1.

[188] ibid 19; Malte Möser, Rainer Böhme and Dominic Breuker, 'An Inquiry into Money Laundering Tools in the Bitcoin Ecosystem' (2013) APWG eCrime Researchers Summit, 1, as cited by Soana (n 177).

[189] Financial Action Task Force, 'The Role of Hawala and Other Similar Service Providers in Money Laundering and Terrorist Financing' (October 2013).

outside the EU leveraging banking secrecy and lenient regulations to attract business. Consequently, this shift had repercussions on the foundational principle of confidentiality, leading to tensions between banks and their clientele.

The advent of digital currencies marked a transformative shift. The EU designated these currencies as posing a significant threat to AML efforts. Subsequently, the EU extended the same regulatory framework to compel virtual asset service providers to dismantle anonymity within these systems. However, it is crucial to recognise that virtual asset service providers differ substantially from traditional banks. The efficacy of the AML regime is predicated on the centralised operation of banks. In contrast, digital currencies operate in a decentralised manner, wherein no single entity possesses comprehensive customer information. Furthermore, users can execute transactions without intermediary intervention.

Consequently, it is plausible to anticipate that some of the concerns voiced by banks in 1991 may indeed materialise in the case of virtual asset service providers. Notably, the argument of client alienation holds weight, as users possess the autonomy to bypass the service provider for transaction execution. The chapter culminated in an exploration of the concept of anonymity. This thematic emphasis was strategically positioned towards the chapter's conclusion rather than at its beginning. The research corroborates the existence of multiple distinctions between the banking sector and virtual asset service providers. However, it underscores that the concept of anonymity, as well as the principle of confidentiality, may be construed as analogous within both systems.

Although the issue of anonymity remains consistent, it manifests within an entirely distinct environment. It is not the issue itself necessitating a disparate approach but rather the unique operational landscape. Within the framework of the AML regime, anonymity was harmonised with a view to the centralised nature of the entities involved. Conversely, within digital currency systems, the calibration of anonymity must be revisited. In an effort to address this challenge, the EU mandated newly established entities to adhere to the AML regime. The research underscores the inherent difficulties in applying KYC and CDD to digital currencies. The belief in the effectiveness of preventive measures hinges on the perception that the real-world economy and the digital currency economy are interchangeable entities.

The truth is that 'regulators are 2–3 years behind the tech curve, are easily duped, are confused, and are terrified of losing cases, so they only go after the easy targets that don't require rethinking the laws'.[190] This assertion aptly summarises the predicament surrounding preventive measures. Anonymity within digital currencies encompasses elements of unlinkability and untraceability. The information gathered by entities at the intersection of the real-world economy and the digital economy falls short of providing comprehensive insight.

[190] Gabriel Shapiro, 'Size Does Matter – Part 1: A Philosophy of Securities Laws for Tokenized Networks' (*Medium*, 26 December 2019), https://medium.com/p/9f83b130a451.

6

The Extension of the Anti-Money Laundering (AML) Regime to Digital Currencies: A Privacy Appraisal

Introduction

The aim of this chapter is to analyse the compatibility of the extension of the AML regulatory framework to digital currencies with the right to private life and personal data protection. The concept of privacy poses a complex legal challenge, with numerous scholarly works dedicated to its definition and conceptual delineation. Divergent opinions persist regarding the constituent elements of privacy, contributing to varying degrees of privacy protection across different jurisdictions. Within the ambit of European Union (EU) law, the protection of privacy is ensured through two distinct rights set out in the Charter of Fundamental Rights. Article 7 guarantees the right to privacy, while Article 8 provides for the protection of personal data.[1]

The analysis engages with the underexplored tension at the intersection of financial regulation, privacy and data protection in the blockchain environment. By situating AML obligations within the broader framework of the EU, it reveals how digital surveillance practices challenge the proportionality of the AML regime in relation to the fundamental rights of digital currency users.

This chapter analyses privacy within the context of blockchain technology and the economy of digital currencies. Following the comparative analysis between financial institutions and virtual asset service providers, the inquiry addresses the research hypotheses, which posit that the obligations of the AML regime interfere with the rights to privacy and data protection. To achieve this, having as a basis Articles 7 and 8 of the Charter, this chapter will provide a proportionality assessment of the AML measures. A subject critical to this book and the AML Regulation is the issue of anonymity within digital currency systems. The regulatory framework employs various preventive measures aimed at mitigating anonymity, necessitating an enhancement of data collection capacities by virtual asset service providers. Notably, the newly adopted AML Regulation, particularly in the context

[1] Charter of Fundamental Rights of the European Union (2012) C326/391 ('Charter'), Arts 7, 8.

of digital currencies, departs from the conventional risk-based approach, elevating the preventive measures to blanket measures.[2]

In order to determine whether the AML regime, when applied in the blockchain environment, goes beyond what is necessary and proportionate, this research evaluates the obligations imposed on virtual asset service providers based on existing jurisprudence from the European Court of Human Rights (ECtHR) and the Court of Justice of the European Union (CJEU). Due to the lack of explicit case law relating to the interconnection of digital currencies and surveillance, this research draws on jurisprudence concerning data retention and the privatised surveillance practices of telecommunication providers. This serves as a useful comparison, as these providers are also private entities that collect and process user data. The chapter starts by distinguishing this research from existing literature, which predominantly centres on the transmission of financial information to Financial Intelligence Units (FIUs). Consequently, an analysis of the limitations surrounding the retention of such data by obliged entities is long overdue. Subsequently, the chapter scrutinises the conditions laid down by the General Data Protection Regulation (GDPR), which outlines specific principles and rules governing the retention and processing of personal data.

After establishing the basis for the infringement of fundamental rights, the chapter proceeds to investigate whether the actions taken by virtual asset service providers rely on risk assessment or if they are blanket measures affecting all customers. Building upon this, the inquiry advances to consider pertinent case law from the ECtHR and CJEU. Although the case law is not directly related to digital currencies and blockchain technology, it provides valuable insights into the retention of personal data. This is particularly relevant because the cases primarily address privatised surveillance, which is a key focus of the chapter. The analysis commences with an examination of ECtHR case law, given that the CJEU has not yet assessed the retention of financial data, particularly in the context of the AML regime. Drawing specific conclusions from this inquiry, the research subsequently transitions to an analysis of CJEU case law, as the scope of this book is rooted in EU law. In summary, the argument's conclusion hinges on an assessment of the justification for the interference, predicated on the CJEU's evaluation.

1. Financial Privacy: FIUs and Existing Literature

Concerns about privacy and data protection within the AML regime are long-standing. This chapter focuses on the retention of financial information by obliged entities, specifically virtual asset service providers. By briefly outlining the

[2] Regulation (EU) 2024/1624 of the European Parliament and of the Council of 31 May 2024 on the prevention of the use of the financial system for the purposes of money laundering or terrorist financing [2024] OJ L, 2024/1624, recital 76.

broader privacy challenges that arise after information is transferred to FIUs, this chapter situates the analysis of virtual asset service providers within the broader architecture of the AML framework, thereby offering a novel perspective on their role in the digital currency economy and demonstrating how the discussion builds upon, rather than replicates, existing research.

The fight against money laundering requires extensive financial information, as the essence of the regime is to trace financial flows.[3] The AML regime is based on the interaction between obliged entities and FIUs, constituting a collaboration between the private and public sectors. The former entities gather and retain financial information, while the latter access and process this information based on reports received from the private sector.[4] At the time of the establishment of the AML regime, there was no competence in criminal law.[5] As a result, law enforcement agencies could not have been used for the process of financial information gathering under the EU AML Directive.[6] Hence, the creation of new institutions was necessary.[7]

According to Article 19(4) of the 6th AML Directive, the FIUs are mandated to 'be operationally independent and autonomous'.[8] At the national level:

> The FIU shall be the single central national unit responsible for receiving and analysing reports submitted by obliged entities in accordance with Article 69 of Regulation (EU) 2024/1624, reports submitted by obliged entities in accordance with Article 74 and Article 80(4), second subparagraph, of that Regulation, and any other information relevant to money laundering, its predicate offences or terrorist financing, including information transmitted by customs authorities pursuant to Article 9 of Regulation (EU) 2018/1672, as well as information submitted by supervisory authorities or by other authorities.[9]

As a result, FIUs have emerged as the intelligence authorities tasked with gathering essential information.[10] Positioned between obliged entities in the private sector

[3] Foivi Mouzakiti, 'Cooperation between Financial Intelligence Units in the European Union: Stuck in the middle between the General Data Protection Regulation and the Police Data Protection Directive' (2020) 11(3) *New Journal of European Criminal Law* 351, 352.

[4] Ben Bowling and James Sheptycki, *Global Policing* (Sage Publications, 2012) 70; Anthony Amicelle and Gilles Favarel-Garigues, 'Financial Surveillance: Who cares?' (2015) 5 *Journal of Cultural Economy* 105.

[5] Mouzakiti (n 3).

[6] ibid 353.

[7] Valsamis Mitsilegas, 'New Forms of Transnational Policing: The Emergence of Financial Intelligence Units in the European Union and the Challenges for Human Rights: Part 1' (1999) 3(2) *Journal of Money Laundering Control* 147, 148; John AE Vervaele, 'Surveillance and Criminal Investigation: Blurring of Thresholds and Boundaries in the Criminal Justice System?' in Serge Gutwirth, Ronald Leenes and Paul De Hert (eds), *Reloading Data Protection* (Springer, 2013) 122.

[8] Directive (EU) 2024/1640 of the European Parliament and of the Council of 31 May 2024 on the mechanisms to be put in place by Member States for the prevention of the use of the financial system for the purposes of money laundering or terrorist financing, amending Directive (EU) 2019/1937, and amending and repealing Directive (EU) 2015/849 [2024] OJ L, 2024/1640, Art 19(4).

[9] ibid Art 19(2).

[10] Marieke de Goede, 'The chain of security' (2017) 44(1) *Review of International Studies* 24.

and law enforcement agencies, Quintel characterises FIUs as 'intermediaries'.[11] While the European AML regime partially outlines the responsibilities of these entities, they do not provide detailed guidance on their organisational structure.[12] Consequently, FIUs within EU Member states are shaped under different umbrellas.[13] EU FIUs may be administrative, police, judicial authorities, or a combination of these.[14] This diversity leads to variations in rules governing data processing and cooperation with other FIUs.[15]

Recent advancements in the area of AML law have overlooked the fundamental issue pertaining to FIU structures despite a continuous expansion of powers wielded by these intelligence units.[16] For instance, in accordance with the 6th AML Directive, 'each FIU shall be able to request, obtain and use information from any obliged entity . . . even if no prior report is filed'.[17] This unprecedented expansion of powers necessitates a clear understanding of the applicable data protection framework. As of now, the question of which data protection regulations govern FIU activities remains a subject of debate.[18]

Since FIUs engage in the processing of financial information, their operations must comply with specific data protection requirements.[19] First, the GDPR applies to both private and public entities.[20] Second, the Law Enforcement Directive (LED) comes into play.[21] For the LED to be applicable, both the material and the personal scope of the Directive must be met.[22] According to Article 1(1), personal data

[11] Teresa Quintel, 'Follow the Money, if you can: Possible solutions for enhanced FIU cooperation rules' (2019) University of Luxembourg Law Working Paper Series 1.

[12] Foivi Mouzakiti, 'Cooperation between financial intelligence units in the EU: Challenges for the right to privacy and data protection' in Katie Benson, Colin King and Clive Walker (eds), *Assets, Crimes and the State: Innovation in 21st Century Legal Responses* (Routledge, 2020) 39.

[13] ibid.

[14] ibid 39–40.

[15] Quintel (n 11) 2; Magdalena Berwczynska, 'Financial Intelligence Units: Reflections on the applicable data protection legal framework' (2021) 43 *Computer Law & Security Review* 2

[16] Teresa Quintel, 'Data protection rules applicable to Financial Intelligence Units: still no clarity in sight' (2022) 23 ERA Forum, Springer 53, 60–61.

[17] Directive (EU) 2024/1640 of the European Parliament and of the Council of 31 May 2024 on the mechanisms to be put in place by Member States for the prevention of the use of the financial system for the purposes of money laundering or terrorist financing, amending Directive (EU) 2019/1937, and amending and repealing Directive (EU) 2015/849 [2024] OJ L, 2024/1640, Art 21(4).

[18] Valsamis Mitsilegas and Niovi Vavoula, 'The Evovling EU Anti-Money Laundering Regime: Challenges for Fundamental Rights and the Rule of Law' (2016) 2 *Maastricht Journal of European and Comparative Law* 261.

[19] Quintel (n 16) 74.

[20] ibid; Regulation (EU) 2016/679 of the European Parliament and of the Council of 27 April 2016 on the protection of natural persons with regard to the processing of personal data and on the free movement of such data, and repealing Directive 95/46/EC (General Data Protection Regulation – GDPR) [2016] OJ L119/1.

[21] Directive (EU) 2016/680 of the European Parliament and of the Council of 27 April 2016 on the protection of natural persons with regard to the processing of personal data by competent authorities for the purposes of the prevention, investigation, detection or prosecution of criminal offences or the execution of criminal penalties, and on the free movement of such data, and repealing Council Framework Decision 2008/977/JHA [2016] OJ L119/89.

[22] Mouzakiti (n 3) 365

should be processed 'for the purposes of the prevention, investigation, detection or prosecution of criminal offences or the execution of criminal penalties, including the safeguarding against and the prevention of threats to public security' (material scope).[23] However, the processing must be conducted exclusively by 'competent authorities' (personal scope).[24]

The core of the debate lies in determining which instrument should be applied by FIUs. This question is inextricably linked with the organisational structure of each FIU. The LED mandates 'competent authorities'; thus, FIUs that have the status of law enforcement authorities might satisfy the personal scope of the Directive.[25] While at first glance, the material scope of the Directive may seem satisfied regardless of the status of the FIU, this is not necessarily true. The European Commission is resolute in guiding FIUs towards compliance with the GDPR, contending that the analysis conducted by FIUs may not always fall within the material scope of the Directive.[26]

Both the GDPR and the LED offer distinct levels of data protection. Mouzakiti argues that 'when an EU FIU that applies the GDPR shares personal data with an EU counterpart that applies the Directive instead, the data in question is transferred to an environment that offers, at least to some extent, watered down protections compared to those offered where the data was collected in the first place'.[27] Divergences also arise regarding data protection principles and data subject rights. Quintel and Mouzakiti present arguments in two separate papers that the suitable legal framework for FIUs is the LED as opposed to the GDPR.[28] Considering the perspective of FIUs' collaboration and adaptability, the LED appears more fitting to accomplish the objectives of the AML regime.

Nonetheless, as FIUs' powers expand alongside rapid technological developments, it remains essential to reconsider the role of privacy within this context. Although FIUs are not the primary focus of this book, aspects of their operation intersect with digital currencies, revealing potential directions for future inquiry. Notably, the 6th AML Directive authorises FIUs 'to request, obtain and use information from any obliged entity, . . . even if no prior report is filed'.[29] This enables

[23] Directive (EU) 2016/680 of the European Parliament and of the Council of 27 April 2016 on the protection of natural persons with regard to the processing of personal data by competent authorities for the purposes of the prevention, investigation, detection or prosecution of criminal offences or the execution of criminal penalties, and on the free movement of such data, and repealing Council Framework Decision 2008/977/JHA [2016] OJ L119/89, Art 1(1).

[24] ibid Art 2(1).

[25] Mouzakiti (n 3) 365.

[26] EU FIUs Platform, 'Minutes of the 37th Meeting of the EU FIUs Platform' (November 2018) 8 as cited by Mouzakiti (n 3) 365.

[27] Mouzakiti (n 3) 365.

[28] ibid 373; Quintel (n 11) 11.

[29] Directive (EU) 2024/1640 of the European Parliament and of the Council of 31 May 2024 on the mechanisms to be put in place by Member States for the prevention of the use of the financial system for the purposes of money laundering or terrorist financing, amending Directive (EU) 2019/1937, and amending and repealing Directive (EU) 2015/849 [2024] OJ L, 2024/1640, Art 21(4).

FIUs to access a broad spectrum of information collected by virtual asset service providers from the blockchain. When combined with FIUs' access to various databases, the blockchain could become a reference point for the continuous identification and surveillance of individuals through the aggregation of such data.

Even if the FIUs apply the LED (with comparatively lower standards), private sector obliged entities remain bound by the GDPR. Owing to the immutable nature of blockchain technology, virtual asset service providers may struggle to meet GDPR requirements, thereby risking encroachment upon the right to privacy (as discussed further below). While Quintel and Mouzakiti rightly argue that the LED is the appropriate framework for FIUs, technological developments complicate this relationship. If providers cannot comply with the GDPR, FIUs may nonetheless gain access to an inexhaustible, immutable pool of data governed by a less stringent legal standard. Existing scholarship primarily examines privacy and data protection concerns arising from public authorities, eg FIUs. This research instead shifts the focus to the unexplored earlier stage, the collection of information by obliged entities prior to its transfer to FIUs.

2. The Right to Privacy and the Right to the Protection of Personal Data

Engaging with the intersection of technology and privacy entails navigating through two distinct realms. While technology, particularly blockchain technology and digital currencies, may initially present challenges in comprehension, once understood, their functioning becomes clear. In contrast, privacy is a constantly debated subject, giving rise to inquiries regarding its essence, the circumstances warranting increased privacy, and the foundational principles upon which it is predicated.[30] This section offers a novel contribution by positioning privacy within the specific context of digital currencies. It builds on the argument that understanding privacy in this environment requires moving beyond the separation between privacy and data protection, offering a new perspective on how technological design reshapes fundamental rights.

Examining privacy within the framework of digital currencies is not as straightforward as comprehending the underlying technology. Solove aptly characterises it as a 'concept of disarray',[31] Gavinson acknowledges that delving into privacy law leaves one with 'a sense of uneasiness',[32] and Whittman perceives privacy as a 'slippery concept'.[33] The literature is replete with authors who grapple with privacy as an intricate and elusive construct. This chapter refrains from attempting a definitive

[30] Ruth Gavison, 'Privacy and the Limits of Law' (1980) 89(3) *Yale Law Journal* 421.
[31] Daniel Solove, *Understanding Privacy* (Harvard University Press, 2008) 12.
[32] Gavison (n 30) 421.
[33] James Q Whitman, 'The Two Western Cultures of Privacy: Dignity Versus Liberty' (2004) 113 *Yale Law Journal* 1153, 1157.

delineation of privacy. Instead, its objective is to frame privacy within the domain of digital currencies, necessitating a nuanced analysis.

2.1. The Conceptualisation of Privacy

Grasping the concept of privacy may pose challenges from a cultural perspective, as what one individual deems private may not align with another's perception.[34] In 1890, Samuel D Warren and Luis D Brandeis defined the concept of privacy as the right to be let alone, arguing that by analogy, invasion of privacy could be understood as 'an attack upon reputation' or 'a violation of honor'.[35]

While these arguments originate from the 1890s, their relevance endures to a certain extent in contemporary times. The concept of privacy as 'the right to be let alone' was spurred by apprehensions surrounding the evolution of the press in 1890 and its capacity to disseminate information about individuals' private lives. The authors also introduce a limitation to this right, positing that when individuals willingly publicise certain private information, it may diminish their claim to privacy.[36] This notion of privacy is closely linked with the concept of the personality of an individual.[37]

This perspective on privacy is contextually bound and reflects the sociocultural preoccupations of its era. To this end, the concept of privacy can undergo transformation contingent on the temporal and cultural milieu.[38] Consequently, in a culture that places significant emphasis on moral standards, privacy may be construed as a form of freedom.[39] However, modern social media, like Facebook and Instagram, have shifted the perception of privacy over time.

Returning to Warren and Brandeis' conceptualisation of privacy, it can be argued that their proposition amalgamates distinct elements.[40] The right to be let alone, as explained, introduces the idea of personal space while also emphasising the control over individuals' information.[41] According to Westin's theoretical framework, the concept of privacy is fundamentally rooted in the notion of information, wherein an individual's capacity to exert influence over the utilisation of their information holds paramount significance, especially in the context of curtailing surveillance by the state.[42]

[34] Adam Moore, 'Defining privacy' (2008) 39(3) *Journal of Social Philosophy* 411, 411.
[35] Samuel Warren and Louis Brandeis, 'The Right to Privacy' (1890) 14(5) *Harvard Law Review* 193, 198–205.
[36] ibid 199.
[37] ibid 205.
[38] Randall P Bezanson, 'The Right to Privacy Revisited: Privacy, News and Social Change, 1890-1990' (1992) 80(5) *California Law Review* 1133, 1137.
[39] ibid 1138.
[40] Warren and Brandeis (n 35).
[41] Whitman (n 33) 1208.
[42] Alan Westin, *Privacy and Freedom* (Atheneum, 1967) 315 as cited by Niovi Vavoula, *Immigration and Privacy in the Law of the European Union: The Case of Information Systems* (Brill Nijhoff, 2022) 22.

The argument that the right to privacy encompasses authority over information was criticised mainly due to the fact that it does not take into consideration the voluntary dissemination of information.[43] This criticism is even more valid when considering the concept of privacy in the virtual environment. From online banking to e-commerce and social media engagement, individuals presently engage with web-based networks for an array of activities. Thus, it is evident that this has caused a shift in the locus of control over information. Technology, broadly speaking, exerts a discernible influence on the concept of privacy. However, it is imperative to differentiate between information disseminated over the internet.

Initially, there is data that individuals willingly disclose to the public for various reasons, for instance, information shared on social media platforms, such as date of birth, place of employment, and educational background. Additionally, there is information that individuals consent to share with a third party in order to access a particular website or service, governed by the terms and services agreement with that third party.[44] Second, there is the information that individuals do not want to provide.

The latter category can encompass financial information. No one would willingly publish their financial statements and transaction history online. This brings into play the online payment services facilitated by digital currencies. Bitcoin, for instance, affords users the capacity to obscure their identities and safeguard specific information.[45] While the underlying technology (blockchain) constitutes a public ledger, and transaction history is publicly accessible, there is a certain process to trace a transaction back to an individual's identity.[46]

To 'solve' the problem of conceptualisation, Solove uses a taxonomy based on harmful activities: (1) information collection, (2) information processing, (3) information dissemination, and (4) invasion of privacy.[47] On the same pattern, Clarke argues that we need to understand privacy as a spectrum dividing the concept into four categories: (1) privacy of the person (concerned with the integrity of the individual's body), (2) privacy of personal behaviour (including all aspects of behaviour, especially sensitive matters), (3) privacy of personal communications, and (4) privacy of personal data.[48] In an attempt to update

[43] Adam Carlyle Breckenridge, *The Right to Privacy* (University of Nebraska, 1970); Niovi Vavoula, *Immigration and Privacy in the Law of the European Union: The Case of Information Systems* (Brill Nijhoff, 2022) 23; Arthur Miller, *The Assault on Privacy: Computers, Data Banks and Dossiers* (University of Michigan Press, 1971) 25; Hilary Delany and Eoin Carolan, *The Right to Privacy – A Doctrinal and Comparative Analysis*, 2nd edn (MIT Press, 2006) 8.

[44] The terms of services are basically a contract between the customer and the provider. In order for a user to access an online gaming platform or social media, the provider asks the individual to agree to certain conditions. The terms of services agreement covers a wide range of issues.

[45] The issue of pseudonymity; see further Arvind Narayanan and others, *Bitcoin and Cryptocurrency Technologies: A Comprehensive Introduction* (Princeton University Press, 2016) 138–45.

[46] ibid.

[47] Daniel Solove, 'A Taxonomy of Privacy' (2006) 154 *University of Pennsylvania Law Review* 477, 489.

[48] Roger Clarke, 'Introduction to Dataveillance and Information Privacy and Definitions of Terms' (15 August 1997), www.rogerclarke.com/DV/Intro.html.

Solove's categorisation and take into consideration technological development, Finn, Wright and Friedenwald added three new categories: (1) privacy of thoughts and feelings, (2) privacy of location and space, and (3) privacy of association.[49]

Taking into consideration the various approaches expressed for the concept of privacy, Vavoula concludes that 'privacy is a multi-level notion applicable in a cluster of contexts'.[50] Several approaches towards privacy have their merits. Considering privacy as 'control over information' will be an ideal way to move on with the analysis of privacy in digital currencies, even if this approach does not take into account the voluntary dissemination of information. Moreover, Solove's categorisation might also be useful by focusing on the harmful activities of information collection and processing. Based on this, the chapter will move on to examine the privacy of the user in the context of blockchain technology.

2.2. The Public Nature of Decentralised Public Ledgers

The control over information encompasses an individual's capacity not only to possess but also to safeguard this data from unlawful processing. However, this level of control is contingent upon an individual's autonomy.[51] Consequently, predicated on an individual's autonomy, the concept of privacy extends to include the management of personal information, which, in turn, forms a part of that individual's identity.[52] Therefore, a right to the protection of privacy suggests a certain degree of control over personal data.[53]

This entitlement establishes a delineation between the public and private spheres.[54] Within the private sphere, an individual has the agency to determine if, when, and to what extent the public will have access to their information.[55] It is doubtful, particularly in the present era of pervasive technology usage, that all an individual's information will remain entirely confidential. However, even if certain data is accessible to a third party, it does not negate the 'personal' status. Personal data comprises a broad category of information about an individual, encompassing

[49] Rachel Finn, David Wright and Will Friedenwald, 'Seven Types of Privacy' in Serge Gutwirth and others (eds), *European Data Protection: Coming of Age* (Springer, 2013) 6–8. According to Finn, Wright and Friendenwald, privacy of thoughts and feelings 'can be distinguished from privacy of the person, in the same way that the mind can be distinguished from the body', privacy of location and space entails the ability of individuals to move freely (even in public spaces) without being monitored, and privacy of association 'is concerned with people's rights to associate with whomever they wish, without being monitored'.

[50] Vavoula (n 43) 26.

[51] Gloria González Fuster, *The Emergence of Personal Data Protection as a Fundamental Right of the EU* (Springer Law, Governance and Technology Series 16, 2014) 23.

[52] Tom Gerety, 'Redefining Privacy' (1977) 12(2) *Harvard Civil Rights-Civil Liberties Law Review* 233, 236.

[53] Moore (n 34) 414.

[54] Roger Clarke, 'What's 'Privacy'?' (7 August 2006), www.rogerclarke.com/DV/Privacy.html.

[55] Moore (n 34) 420; Gerety (n 52) 272.

elements such as photographs, factual details, beliefs and ideas.[56] Broadly framed, any information an individual wishes to withhold from public knowledge can be considered personal.[57] According to the GDPR, personal data means

> any information relating to an identified or identifiable natural person ('data subject'); an identifiable natural person is one who can be identified, directly or indirectly, in particular by reference to an identifier such as name, an identification number, location data, an online identifier or to one or more factors specific to the physical, physiological, genetic, mental, economic, cultural or social identify of that natural person.[58]

Therefore, personal data includes an individual's financial information. The descriptor 'personal' conveys the inseparable link between the data and a specific individual.[59]

Technology deployment blurs the distinction between the private and public spheres. The critical concern is not solely what information is stored online but rather who possesses the capability to access it.[60] Technology complicates the preservation of control over information, encompassing aspects such as accessibility, dissemination and safeguarding. The prevailing question centres on whether this control is entirely relinquished by the data subject. Miller contends that once information is stored online, the individual forfeits control entirely.[61] While this assertion holds some validity, it is not absolute. Control is lost once a third party gains access to and processes this information. Conversely, a situation may arise in which an individual establishes a confidential relationship with a third party to store specific information. In this latter scenario, it can be argued that the individual still maintains control over the information, predicated on the confidential nature of the relationship.

Consequently, personal data pertains to information relevant to an individual, holds a certain intrinsic value, and is subject to the individual's control.[62] Through this analysis, even when data is under the control of a third party within the framework of a confidential relationship, it remains within the private sphere of the individual.[63] In general, at the time of writing, for the EU, digital currencies are not considered currencies *per se*. Nonetheless, these currencies are structured as payment services.[64] Given this framework, the system compiles specific information pertaining to transactions. Despite the EU's stance on digital currencies

[56] Raymond Wacks, *Law, Morality and the Private Domain* (Hong Kong University Press, 2000) 222.

[57] ibid.

[58] GDPR, Art 4(1).

[59] Oxford Dictionary. 'Personal' – adjective. 1) Your own; not belonging to or connected with anyone else; 2) connected with a person's private life, rather than their job or official position.

[60] Fuster (n 51) 29.

[61] Arthur Raphael Miller, *The Assault on Privacy: Computers, Data Banks, and Dossiers* (University of Michigan Press, 1971) 42; Fuster (n 51) 32.

[62] Wacks (n 56) 242.

[63] Bezanson (n 38) 1151.

[64] Satoshi Nakamoto, 'Bitcoin: A Peer-to-Peer Electronic Cash System' (Bitcoin, 31 October 2008), https://bitcoin.org/bitcoin.pdf.

lacking legal tender status, this does not alter the fact that the data stored on the blockchain can be characterised as financial information. This argument is further supported by the fact that under the new AML Regulation, the EU classifies virtual asset service providers as financial institutions.[65]

A final question revolves around whether the information generated by these systems can be classified within the broader category of personal data. Hence, it is appropriate to commence with traditional financial data entrusted by individuals to financial institutions. It is reasonable to assert that financial information is intricately linked to an individual's identity, with certain expectations regarding its usage.[66] In an ideal scenario, details such as an individual's salary, transactions and loans would remain within the private sphere.[67] This is not because they are inherently 'embarrassing' but because of their intimate association with an individual's identity, with no discernible public interest in such information. Consequently, the right to privacy can extend to encompass financial information. However, reality presents a more nuanced picture, as various interests necessitate a balanced approach to the right to privacy. Often, these interests align with the government's imperative to combat criminal activities and safeguard national security.[68]

This hole in the concept of privacy regarding financial information is expounded by Sharman, who advocated that 'the need for free and unfettered access to personal financial data in order to combat criminals and terrorists supersedes the principle of a right to privacy'.[69] This tension between the right to privacy and financial information is founded on specific situations, particularly the relationship between the individual and the trusted third-party entity holding the information. The same rationale applies to the virtual asset service providers that are now obliged under the MiCA and the new AML regime. Given the structure and technology of digital currencies, custodial wallet providers have access to and control over user funds.[70] Moreover, the transparent nature of blockchain technology means that providers have access to the complete transaction history.[71]

Under the EU AML regime, virtual asset service providers are now obliged to collect users' information.[72] This development raises two principal challenges. First, when a wallet is not linked to a traditional financial account, it remains unclear how providers can effectively verify users' identities as mandated by the

[65] Regulation (EU) 2024/1624 of the European Parliament and of the Council of 31 May 2024 on the prevention of the use of the financial system for the purposes of money laundering or terrorist financing [2024] OJ L, 2024/1624, Art 2(6)(i).

[66] See subsection 3.2.

[67] Christopher Anglim, *Privacy Rights in the Digital Era* (Grey House Publishing, 2016) 211.

[68] ibid 215.

[69] J Sharman, 'Privacy as Roguery: Personal Financial Information in an Age of Transparency' (2009) 87(4) *Public Administration* 717.

[70] See further Narayanan (n 45) 76 et seq.

[71] Primavera De Filippi and Aaron Wright, *Blockchain and the Law: The Rule of Code* (Harvard University Press, 2018) 35–39.

[72] Regulation (EU) 2024/1624 of the European Parliament and of the Council of 31 May 2024 on the prevention of the use of the financial system for the purposes of money laundering or terrorist financing [2024] OJ L, 2024/1624, Arts 2 and 3.

AML Regulation.[73] Second, digital currencies are classified as inherently high-risk, obliging providers to apply enhanced due diligence measures to all users.[74] Therefore, given the overarching perception of digital currencies as high risk, there is no risk-based approach to selecting a specific target. This could lead to a situation in which providers proactively collect extensive amounts of data (including geo-location) from all users without the users' explicit intention to share such information.

This extensive data collection inevitably brings to the forefront the question of whether an individual retains a reasonable expectation of privacy within a public space, such as the blockchain. Although the concept of 'reasonable expectation of privacy' is primarily rooted in common law jurisdictions rather than EU law, a brief analysis is necessary to contextualise the discussion.[75] In the UK, the test for determining such an expectation was articulated in *Campbell v Mirror Group Newspapers Ltd*.[76] Lord Hope considered what a reasonable person of ordinary sensibilities would feel if they were placed in the same position as the claimant.[77] Likewise, *Coco v AN Clark (Engineers) Ltd* established that confidentiality cannot be maintained for information that is already public.[78] Consequently, the case law essentially argues that the expectation of privacy is significantly diminished in public spaces.

In the USA, the courts have adopted a similar approach. In the *Tessling* case, it was held that there is no reasonable expectation of privacy where an individual has exposed information to the public.[79] Applying this reasoning to blockchain systems, the ledger can be understood as a public space, since its very purpose is to permanently record transaction data on an openly accessible network. Consistent with this view, *United States v Gratkowski* found that an individual had no reasonable expectation of privacy because the information stored on the blockchain was publicly available.[80] However, it should be emphasised that these cases concern law enforcement activities, search and seizures, where investigations are based on a degree of suspicion regarding criminal conduct.

[73] ibid Art 20; Sumit Agarwal, 'Bitcoin Transactions: A Bit of Financial Privacy' (2016) 35 *Cardozo Arts & Ent LJ* 153, 173.

[74] Regulation (EU) 2024/1624 of the European Parliament and of the Council of 31 May 2024 on the prevention of the use of the financial system for the purposes of money laundering or terrorist financing [2024] OJ L, 2024/1624, recital 76.

[75] Michael Tilbury, 'Privacy: common law or human right?' in Normann Witzleb, David Lindsay, Moira Paterson and Sharon Rodrick (eds), *Emerging Challenges in Privacy Law* (Cambridge University Press, 2014); Nicole Moreham, 'Privacy in Common Law: A Doctrinal and Theoretical Analysis' (2005) 121 *Law Quarterly Review* 628.

[76] *Campbell v Mirror Group Newspapers Ltd* [2004] UKHL 22; the subsequent case of *Murray v Express Newspapers* [2008] EWCA Civ 446 outlined several factors to be considered by the court, including the attributes of the claimant, the nature of the activity in which the claimant is engaged, etc.

[77] ibid.

[78] *Coco v AN Clark (Engineers) Ltd* [1968] FSR 415.

[79] *R v Tessling* 2004 SCC 67 at para 40.

[80] *United States v Gratowski* 964 F.3d 3017 (5th Cir, 2020).

This research diverges from those contexts by focusing instead on the unexplored area of the collection of blockchain data by private entities and their relationship with clients. As Moreham observes, individuals vary in their perceptions of what constitutes private information, and any attempt to define privacy solely by categorising information types is bound to fail.[81] Building upon this, Barendt argues that the test is objective as 'a claimant has a reasonable expectation of privacy when contemporary society considers the information to be the type ... which he or she is entitled to keep private'.[82] Following this reasoning and the existing scholarship, it could be inferred that if information is in the public space, a reasonable expectation of privacy no longer exists. A reasonable person would likely not consider blockchain-based information as inherently private, even if an individual subjectively regards it as such.

However, this argument warrants reconsideration. In a data-driven society, information cannot be viewed as isolated 'material'; rather, it forms part of an interconnected ecosystem that constitutes an individual's broader identity profile. Data recorded on the blockchain extends beyond mere transaction details. When combined with off-chain information, they can reveal significant aspects of an individual's life, particularly to third-party providers such as virtual asset service providers, who have access to such supplementary information and the capacity to link it. Furthermore, the pseudonymous nature of blockchain technology challenges the notion that no expectation of privacy exists in public spaces. While individuals may be aware that their information remains visible on the blockchain, they also rely on the system's technological architecture to protect their privacy through pseudonymity. Consequently, it is problematic to assert that no expectation of privacy exists when one of the technology's defining features is explicitly designed to preserve, at least to some extent, user privacy.

Building on this understanding of blockchain's pseudonymous and decentralised structure, it becomes necessary to consider how these characteristics shape the allocation of privacy responsibilities. Satoshi designed a space (the Bitcoin system) and gave control of its function to the system's members.[83] Due to the decentralised nature, the virtual asset service provider does not have control over the blockchain, and due to its immutable nature, even the system's members who have control cannot alter information. To this end, the protection of privacy in the bank–customer relationship is not the same as the protection in the virtual asset service provider–user relationship. On the one hand, the bank has control over the information and the power to protect the customer's privacy. On the other hand, the virtual asset service provider has no control over the blockchain, although it can access the information. In the latter situation, the individuals who have control cannot alter information, due to its immutable nature, but, as

[81] Moreham (n 75) 640–42.

[82] Eric Barendt, '"A reasonable expectation of privacy": a coherent or redundant concept?' in Andrew Kenyon (ed), *Comparative Defamation and Privacy Law* (Cambridge University Press, 2016).

[83] Nakamoto (n 64) 2; Satoshi underlined that 'To accomplish this without a trusted party, transactions must be publicly announced, and we need a system for participants to agree on a single history.'

explained in Chapters 1 and 2, they can use technological tools to anonymise their data and protect privacy. Based on this, it can be argued that the responsibility for the protection of privacy on the blockchain is shared between the individual and the provider.

As the legal framework, literature and case law frame the concept of privacy, it encompasses a broad spectrum of information. Given the relatively recent emergence of digital currencies, there have been no cases (in the EU, as of the time of writing) addressing privacy concerns and blockchain technology.[84] This subsection initiates an exploration into the categorisation of financial data as personal data. Further analysis is required to ascertain whether information on the blockchain qualifies as personal data warranting protection. Before moving to more substantial matters, the subsequent subsection provides an overview of the legal framework governing privacy and data protection.

2.3. Protection of the Right to Privacy and Data Protection: The International and the Regional Framework

Privacy is safeguarded by various international and regional instruments.[85] To begin with, on the international stage, on 10 December 1948, the United Nations General Assembly proclaimed the Universal Declaration of Human Rights (UDHR) in Paris.[86] It was the first comprehensive document to universally protect basic human rights.[87] Regarding privacy, the Declaration states in Article 12 that: 'No one shall be subjected to arbitrary interference with his privacy, family, home or correspondence, nor to attacks upon his honour and reputation. Everyone has the right to the protection of the law against such interference or attacks.'[88]

Similar wording for the protection of privacy can be found in Article 17 of the International Covenant on Civil and Political Rights (ICCPR).[89] Both of these instruments utilise broad language to encompass a wide range of considerations

[84] However, there is a recent case from the CJEU concerning the AML Directive and the access of the general public to the information on beneficial ownership: Joined Cases C-37/20 and C-601/20 *WM and Sovim SA v Luxembourg Business Registers* [2022] ECLI:EU:C:2022:912. This case will be examined later, even though it is not directly related with the collection and processing of information from obliged entities.

[85] See Lee A Bygrave, 'Data Protection Pursuant to the Right to Privacy in Human Rights Treaties' (1998) 6(3) *International Journal of Law and Information Technology* 247.

[86] Universal Declaration of Human Rights (UDHR) (1948), www.un.org/en/about-us/universal-declaration-of-human-rights; the UDHR is not a legally binding instrument.

[87] ibid.

[88] ibid Art 12.

[89] International Covenant on Civil and Political Rights (ICCPR) 1966; the Covenant was adopted by the General Assembly on 16 December 1966; see www.ohchr.org/en/professionalinterest/pages/ccpr.aspx; Article 17 of the ICCPR states that: '1. No one shall be subjected to arbitrary or unlawful interference with his privacy, family, home or correspondence, nor to unlawful attacks on his honour and reputation. 2. Everyone has the right to the protection of the law against such interference or attacks.'; the wording of the right to privacy is almost identical in the UDHR and ICCPR.

related to the right to privacy. Notably, these instruments do not provide explicit details regarding the circumstances under which the right to privacy may be restricted. In the context of the European Convention of Human Rights (ECHR), Article 8, entitled 'Right to respect for private and family life', states that:

1. Everyone has the right to respect for his private and family life, his home and his correspondence.
2. There shall be no interference by a public authority with the exercise of this right except such as is in accordance with the law and is necessary for a democratic society in the interests of national security, public safety or the economic well-being of the country, for the prevention of disorder or crime, for the protection of health or morals, or for the protection of the rights and freedoms of others.[90]

Except for the different expression of the rights in the ECHR, there is one more fundamental difference from the right to privacy under the UDHR. Article 8 ECHR clearly lays down specific limitations on the right to privacy.[91] Based on the wording of Article 8, the right to privacy can be limited in specific situations such as 'national security, public safety or . . . for the prevention of disorder or crime'.[92]

At the regional level within the European Union, several instruments address the right to privacy and data protection. One of the most important EU instruments is the Charter of Fundamental Rights of the European Union, adopted in 2000.[93] Interestingly, the protection of privacy in the Charter falls under Chapter 2: 'Freedoms'.[94] Another unique characteristic of the Charter is the fact that it protects the concept of privacy in two different articles, namely, Article 7: 'Respect for private and family life' and Article 8: 'Protection of data'.[95]

Article 7 of the Charter protects every aspect of privacy by prescribing that 'Everyone has the right to respect for his or her private and family life, home and communications.'[96] Article 8 of the Charter provides the framework for the regulation of personal data processing.[97] Article 8(2) stipulates that 'Such data must be processed fairly for specified purposes and on the basis of the consent of the person concerned or some other legitimate basis laid down by law.'[98] Two crucial points arise from this passage. First, the data can be processed, but only 'for specified purposes'.[99] Second, such processing must be based on the consent of the

[90] The European Convention on Human Rights (ECHR) was based on the Universal Declaration of Human Rights (UDHR, 1948); ECHR, Art 8.
[91] ECHR, Art 8
[92] ibid.
[93] Charter.
[94] ibid.
[95] This is also connected with the double focus of privacy within the EU. Article 7 focuses on the individual, and Article 8 focuses on personal data and the processing of that data.
[96] Charter, Art 7.
[97] Charter, Art 8.
[98] ibid.
[99] ibid.

individual concerned or another legitimate basis established by law.[100] However, the Article does not explain further what constitutes these legitimate bases.

Within the realm of EU law, the notion of personal data receives enhanced safeguards through Regulation (EU) 2016/679, commonly known as the GDPR.[101] The establishment of the GDPR, representing a significant stride in privacy protection, was made possible under Article 16 of the Treaty on the Functioning of the European Union (TFEU).[102] The advent of the new internet landscape necessitated a re-evaluation of data protection norms.[103] The Regulation stands as an evolution of Directive 95/46/EC, focusing on the safeguarding of individuals in the processing of personal data.[104] The Regulation improves the framework and introduces additional safeguards for the processing of data.[105]

In relevance to this research, data pertaining to criminal activities and convictions fall squarely within the purview of the GDPR.[106] The Regulation delineates parameters for the retention and processing of such data, incorporating appropriate safeguards. A notable innovation introduced by the GDPR lies in the clarification of the data subject's consent as a legitimate basis for data processing.[107]

The legislative framework of the EU indicates a distinction between these two concepts (privacy and data protection). However, this separation is not always explicitly evident in the jurisprudence of the CJEU, nor is it deemed obligatory in all circumstances.

2.4. Two Separate Rights Under the Same Umbrella

Theoretical approaches to the concept of privacy distinguish between two dimensions of protection, namely the protection of privacy and the protection of personal data.[108] Scholars Gutwirth and de Hert suggested that 'privacy builds a shield around the individual, creating a zone of autonomy . . . data protection puts the activity of the processor in the spotlight, gives the individual subjective rights

[100] ibid.

[101] GDPR.

[102] Treaty on the Functioning of the European Union (TFEU), Art 16, https://eur-lex.europa.eu/LexUriServ/LexUriServ.do?uri=CELEX:12012E/TXT:en:PDF; Didier Bigo and others, 'Towards a New EU Legal Framework for Data Protection and Privacy: Challenges, Principles and the Role of the European Parliament' (2011) Study requested by the European Parliament's Committee on Civil Liberties, Justice and Home Affairs, PE 453.216.

[103] Peter Hustinx, 'EU Data Protection Law – The Review of Directive 95/46/EC and the Proposed General Data Protection Regulation' (European Union Institute's Academy of European Law, 24th Session on European Union Law, 2013), https://edps.europa.eu/sites/default/files/publication/14-09-15_article_eui_en.pdf.

[104] GDPR.

[105] ibid Arts 5, 9 and 10.

[106] ibid Art 10.

[107] ibid Arts 4(11), 7, 8 and 9(2)(a).

[108] Paul De Hart and Serge Gutwirth, 'Privacy, Data Protection and Law Enforcement. Opacity of the Individual and Transparency of Power' in Erik Claes, Antony Duff and Serge Gutwirth (eds), *Privacy and the Criminal Law* (Intersentia, 2016) 61.

to control the processing of his/her personal data'.[109] At the EU level, the presence of distinct Articles in the Charter underscores the acknowledgement of data protection as a separate human right.[110] This, however, does not necessarily imply that the CJEU's jurisprudence distinguishes between the concepts of privacy and data protection. Given the rapid technological advancement of recent decades, personal data emerges as an aspect of privacy that is constantly subject to scrutiny. This prompted the EU to formally recognise the independent fundamental right to the protection of personal data.[111]

Despite the fact that there are two different Articles, the truth is that the two concepts overlap significantly.[112] This indicates that these concepts are not the same, but privacy is much broader.[113] Rodotá argues that privacy encompasses various facets of an individual's life, whereas data protection is more confined to the individual's data.[114] Others, such as Gutwirth and de Hert, perceive this new right as an avenue to safeguard specific categories of information not encompassed by privacy.[115] On the one hand, data protection has a framed playing field (ie information); on the other hand, privacy is a relatively abstract concept. Vavoula indicates that 'the structural formulation renders data protection more "tangible" than privacy . . . data protection cannot guarantee a certain level of opacity as privacy does'.[116] To illustrate, Vavoula employs the example of state surveillance, asserting that, 'Reliance on the right to data protection on its own does not suffice to determine the limits of the use of surveillance practises'.[117]

The example of surveillance given by Vavoula is accurate and proves particularly pertinent to this research. While contemporary surveillance techniques hinge on information gathering, privacy provides a more adaptable framework for protecting individuals and evaluating the impact of these measures.[118] On this subject, Mitsilegas further emphasises that the right to privacy is better equipped to address privacy threats stemming from technological progress.[119] Ultimately, while the existence of a separate right is crucial, particularly in an era overwhelmed with

[109] Serge Gutwirth and others, *Reinventing Data Protection* (Springer, 2009) preface.
[110] Lee A Bygrave, 'Privacy and Data Protection in an International Perspective' (2010) 56(8) *Scandinavian Studies in Law* 165, 182.
[111] Charter, Art 8; Fuster (n 51) 267.
[112] Antoinette Rouvroy and Yves Poullet, 'The Right to Information Self-Determination and the Value of Self-Development: Reassessing the Importance of Privacy for Democracy' in Serge Gutwirth and others (eds), *Reinventing Data Protection* (Springer, 2009) 69.
[113] Gutwirth and others (n 109)
[114] Stefano Rodotá, 'Data Protection as a Fundamental Right' in Serge Gutwirth and others (eds), *Reinventing Data Protection* (Springer, 2009) 79.
[115] Paul De Hert and Serge Gutwirth, 'Data Protection in the Case Law of Strasbourg and Luxembourg: Constitutionalisation in Action' in Serge Gutwirth and others (eds), *Reinventing Data Protection* (Springer, 2009) 8.
[116] Vavoula (n 43) 44.
[117] ibid 44; see also Rocco Bellanova, 'Data Protection, with Love' (2014) 8 *International Political Philosophy* 112, 114.
[118] Valsamis Mitsilegas, 'The Value of Privacy in an Era of Security: Embedding Constitutional Limits on Preemptive Surveillance' (2015) 8 *International Political Sociology* 107.
[119] ibid 106.

personal data on the internet, in practice, the right to data protection forms part of the comprehensive approach offered by privacy.[120] Vavoula characterises the right to privacy as a 'gateway' right because 'interference with it leads to interferences with other fundamental rights, hence its protection is vital in a broader context'.[121]

The discussion surrounding technological advancement and privacy protection naturally gravitates towards digital currencies. The transactions on the blockchain can reveal a plethora of data about the individual, especially when correlated with off-chain information. Such data consists of timestamps, IP addresses, geo-location data, financial transactions, amounts and purchase choices, preferences of the individual, and even behaviour. The question arises whether drawing a clear-cut distinction between data protection and privacy proves beneficial in this context. Based on the preceding analysis, the argument posited here is that such a differentiation is not vital for this research. While data exists on the blockchain (determining whether it qualifies as personal data worthy of protection is explored in the subsequent subsection), restricting the scope solely to data protection would diminish the essence of privacy protection in this virtual environment.

In sum, the data gathered from blockchain technology exceeds the idea of 'control over information' because it reveals multiple characteristics of the individual.[122] Therefore, employing Vavoula's terminology once more, the protection of privacy can be construed as a 'gateway' right, exemplifying the interconnectedness between data protection and privacy in cases of interference with the right.[123] In concluding this section, it is essential for the reader to retain three key points. First, the analysis leads us to assert that, for the purpose of this research, there exists no imperative to separate the right to data protection from the right to privacy. Second, interference with one right may lead to interference with the other. Third, the limitations of surveillance techniques cannot be tested based only on the right to data protection. Even though surveillance in the digital era centres around data collection, the rationale behind the interference should be assessed from a privacy perspective.

3. Blockchain: An Interference with Privacy?

This chapter analyses the protection of personal data and privacy, focusing primarily on the GDPR, the ECHR and the Charter of Fundamental Rights of the European Union. The inclusion of the ECHR and the Charter is crucial for the research to be able to apply pertinent jurisprudence to the context of digital currencies. Meanwhile, the GDPR holds paramount importance as this book seeks to clarify the boundaries of obligations incumbent upon virtual asset service

[120] Vavoula (n 43) 45.
[121] ibid.
[122] Raphael Gellert and Serge Gutwirth, 'The Legal Construction of Privacy and Data Protection' (2013) 29 *Computer Law & Security Review* 522, 525.
[123] Vavoula (n 43) 44.

providers, particularly concerning the collection and retention of data. As private entities, these providers are bound by the provisions of the GDPR. To determine the limits of the virtual asset service providers' actions, the research has to establish at which point there is an interference with the right and whether financial information falls under the concept of personal data.

The GDPR is the applicable legal instrument in the blockchain environment in relation to the retention and processing of personal data. However, a certain tension exists in the interplay between the GDPR and the AML regime. While the GDPR advocates for pseudonymity, the AML regime grapples with the risks stemming from the anonymity inherent in this technology.[124] Preventive measures mandated by the AML regime necessitate that financial and credit institutions gather data. Yet, on the internet, data is dispersed, and law enforcement agencies do not consistently attain the desired access.[125] Consequently, intermediaries are tasked with striking a balance between safeguarding personal data and mitigating money laundering risks.

This balancing exercise has proven effective in the conventional banking system. However, blockchain technology introduces complexities to this practice. The blockchain operates as a publicly accessible ledger.[126] According to the GDPR, intermediaries are required to implement pseudonymisation for such data.[127] Concurrently, these entities are compelled to dispel anonymity to mitigate money laundering risks.[128] The GDPR does not compel virtual asset service providers to anonymise the data stored on the blockchain. Nevertheless, the technique of anonymisation (ie rendering an individual unidentifiable) stands as one of the most favoured means to preserve privacy.

3.1. Anonymity, Pseudonymity and Interference with Privacy

Karasek-Wojciechowicz states that 'the GDPR . . . pushes permissionless blockchains to ensure strong pseudonymization or anonymity, while the AML combats the strong pseudonymization or anonymity with the aim of being able to analyse the ledger's content'.[129] The core objective of the GDPR is to protect individuals when their data can be traced back to them. Thus, the GDPR does not apply when

[124] GDPR, recitals 28 and 29.

[125] Harold Abelson and others, 'Keys Under Doormats: Mandating Insecurity by Requiring Government Access to All Data and Communications' (2015) 1(1) *Journal of Cybersecurity* 69.

[126] See Chapter 1, the characteristics of blockchain technology.

[127] GDPR, recitals 28 and 29.

[128] Regulation (EU) 2024/1624 of the European Parliament and of the Council of 31 May 2024 on the prevention of the use of the financial system for the purposes of money laundering or terrorist financing [2024] OJ L, 2024/1624.

[129] Iwona Karasek-Wojciechowicz, 'Reconciliation of Anti-Money Laundering Instruments and European Data Protection Requirements in Permissionless Blockchain Spaces' (2021) *Journal of Cybersecurity* 1–28, 3.

the data is truly anonymous.[130] However, there is no obligation under the GDPR to anonymise the data.

In an optimal scenario, an effective business model for safeguarding customer privacy would involve data anonymisation. Nevertheless, doing so may impede the efficacy of the AML regime. This conflict highlights that the extension of the AML regime into the digital currencies' ecosystem may not fully comprehend the intricacies of this technology. As aptly noted by Finck, 'whereas such anonymity solutions are doubtlessly desirable from a pure data protection perspective, the resulting anonymity can be problematic when examined through the lens of other policy requirements'.[131]

This observation generally holds true. Given the public accessibility of the blockchain, intermediaries are obliged to implement either pseudonymisation or anonymisation to meet the data protection standards.[132] Anonymised data refers to information that cannot be utilised to identify an individual.[133] Further guidance on anonymisation techniques was published by the Article 29 Data Protection Working Party.[134] Its opinion uses three criteria to test the efficiency of the anonymisation: '(i) is it still possible to single out an individual, (ii) is it still possible to link records relating to an individual, and (iii) can information be inferred concerning an individual?'[135] Furthermore, the opinion explains that mere pseudonymisation does not guarantee privacy.[136] It only reduces the extent to which information can be linked to a particular individual. This distinction is crucial, as transactions involving digital currencies are not anonymous.[137] The technology provides pseudonymity; thus, it is still possible to link a transaction with an individual.[138] The confusion between the two terms (anonymity and pseudonymity) is caused by the different approaches of the AML regime and data protection law.[139]

The GDPR makes a distinction between the two concepts.[140] In this context, blockchain technology can ensure pseudonymisation but not anonymity, which is essential for the research to demonstrate the applicability of the GDPR.[141] However, this distinction does not exist within the AML regime. The AML Regulation does not

[130] GDPR, recital 26.

[131] Michèle Finck, 'Blockchain and the General Data Protection Regulation: Can Distributed Ledgers be Squared with European Data Protection Law?' (2019) Study for the European Parliament, Panel for the Future of Science and Technology, PE 634.445, 35–36.

[132] ibid.

[133] Article 29 Data Protection Working Party, 'Opinion 04/2007 on the concept of personal data' (WP 136) 01248/07/EN, 21.

[134] Article 29 Data Protection Working Party, 'Opinion 05/2014 on Anonymisation Techniques' (WP 216) 0829/14/EN, 6.

[135] ibid 3.

[136] ibid.

[137] ibid.

[138] European Union Blockchain Observatory and Forum, 'Legal and Regulatory Framework of Blockchain and Smart Contracts' (2019) 15–16, www.eublockchainforum.eu/sites/default/files/reports/report_legal_v1.0.pdf.

[139] Karasek-Wojciechowicz (n 129) 3.

[140] GDPR, recital 26, Art 4(5).

[141] Abraham Hinteregger and Bernhard Haslhofer, 'An Empirical Analysis of Monero Cross-chain Traceability' (2018), https://arxiv.org/pdf/1812.02808.pdf, 1.

define the concept of pseudonymity or anonymity.[142] Therefore, for AML purposes, these two concepts are treated as closely related, if not identical. Understanding these differing approaches is crucial to grasping the distinct focuses of the AML framework and data protection law.[143]

Virtual asset service providers face a dilemma; they can either apply anonymisation to fully protect user privacy, thereby undermining compliance with the AML regime, or maintain the level of pseudonymisation inherent to blockchain technology. If they choose the latter, they must also ensure compliance with the GDPR's protective framework when collecting and retaining personal data. However, the unique attributes of the blockchain pose significant challenges to the application of the GDPR. The Regulation grants specific rights to data subjects, and one provision that proves particularly conflicting with blockchain technology and the AML regime is the 'right to be forgotten'.[144] Article 17 GDPR states that:

> The data subject shall have the right to obtain from the controller the erasure of personal data concerning him or her without undue delay and the controller shall have the obligation to erase personal data without undue delay where one of the following grounds applies:
>
> (a) the personal data are no longer necessary in relation to the purposes for which they were collected or otherwise processed; ...[145]

The blockchain is designed to be immutable, or at least to a certain extent.[146] However, under certain instances, information on the blockchain can be altered.[147] This process is difficult and requires the cooperation of different actors in the blockchain.[148] Such a characteristic is a hurdle for the 'right to be forgotten'. The research singles out this specific right, particularly Article 17(a), because it is relevant to the analysis. Article 17(a) states that the data should be erased once they 'are no longer necessary in relation to the purposes for which they were collected ...'.[149] If an intermediary collects and retains data from all its clients based on the AML Regulation, then when is this data no longer necessary? Given that digital currencies as a phenomenon are deemed high risk, the collection of data from clients lacks a specific purpose. Of course, the purpose is to mitigate the risk of money laundering, but there is no risk evaluation conducted on a case-by-case basis.

[142] Regulation (EU) 2024/1624 of the European Parliament and of the Council of 31 May 2024 on the prevention of the use of the financial system for the purposes of money laundering or terrorist financing [2024] OJ L, 2024/1624.
[143] Karasek-Wojciechowicz (n 129) 3.
[144] GDPR, Art 17
[145] ibid.
[146] Finck (n 131) 5.
[147] Daniel Conte de Leon and others, 'Blockchain: Properties and Misconceptions' (2017) 11(3) *Asia Pacific Journal of Innovation and Entrepreneurship* 286, 290.
[148] Angela Walch, 'The Path of the Blockchain Lexicon (and the Law)' (2017) 36 *Review of Banking and Financial Law* 713 cited by Finck (n 131) 5.
[149] GDPR, Art 17(a).

The immutable nature of the blockchain renders the right to be forgotten unattainable. Based on the analysis, even pseudonymised data may still lead to the data subject. The term 'erasure' used by the GDPR is highly problematic in the blockchain environment.[150] As it is difficult or impossible to delete data from the blockchain, the interpretation of the term 'erasure' should be more liberal.[151] The GDPR's scope does not include anonymous data, as it is not linked to an identifiable individual.[152] Therefore, the term 'erasure' can be interpreted as the anonymisation of the data to a level where it is impossible to identify the subject data. Karasek-Wojciechowicz argues that, 'The physical destruction of data is not required when technologies are available to ensure that there is no linkage between the particular data and the individual.'[153]

However, if intermediaries anonymise data on the blockchain (public ledger), then this goes against the purpose of the AML regime. Once the data on the blockchain is anonymous, it will not be possible to link transactions to individuals. In such cases, the AML regime prevails as it is clearly stated in the GDPR.[154] Despite the legal issues and the difficulties in protecting personal data on the blockchain, the analysis depicts a more fundamental problem between the two regimes in the blockchain environment. In all, anonymisation in the blockchain can serve the purpose of the 'erasure' of data once the retention period has expired. Nevertheless, the immutability of permissionless blockchain guarantees the unchangeable nature of data. As a result, if virtual asset service providers are not complying with the GDPR at the retention stage, then there is an interference towards privacy. Before concretely concluding that there is an interference, the research needs to establish whether the data on the blockchain constitutes 'personal data'.

3.2. The Concept of Personal Data and the Case of Financial Information

As the conceptual boundary between pseudonymisation and the qualification of information as personal data under the GDPR has been clarified, it is now possible to apply this framework to specific categories of information, such as financial data. Understanding the status of pseudonymised data provides the foundation for assessing whether financial information can be considered personal data. The purpose of this subsection is, therefore, to clarify the notion of personal data and to evaluate whether blockchain-related data falls within this classification. To address this issue, a comprehensive review of available sources has been

[150] GDPR, Art 17.
[151] Karasek-Wojciechowicz (n 129) 8.
[152] GDPR, recital 26.
[153] Karasek-Wojciechowicz (n 129) 8.
[154] GDPR, recital 19.

conducted. Notably, while the ECtHR[155] has provided relevant case law, the CJEU has had limited engagement with the issue of the retention of financial data.[156] The CJEU has focused on cases concerning the retention of telecommunications data.

Based on the GDPR's definition of personal data (set out in subsection 2.2.), the Regulation further clarifies that, 'Personal data which have undergone pseudonymisation, which could be attributed to a natural person by the use of additional information should be considered to be information on an identifiable natural person.'[157] Consequently, pseudonymised data present on the blockchain is deemed personal data. However, the GDPR does not apply to anonymous data, 'namely information which does not relate to an identified or identifiable natural person or to personal data rendered anonymous in such a manner that the data subject is not or no longer identifiable'.[158] The concept of personal data is interpreted widely by the GDPR.[159] Article 4(1) GDPR underlines that "'personal data' means any information'.[160] Therefore, arguably, this covers any category of information.[161] The definition implies that the information does not need to be about the individual.[162] Information relating to an identified or identifiable natural person will suffice.[163]

The ECtHR has ruled several times on the matter of the retention of financial information. The Strasbourg Court determined that data gathered from banking documents 'undoubtedly amounts to personal data concerning an individual'.[164] Moreover, the Court considers financial information as personal data even if such data is not sensitive in nature, denying the separation of 'business data' from the notion of 'private life'.[165] In these instances (retention of financial information), the ECtHR has identified an interference with Article 8 ECHR (the right to private life).[166]

The analysis leads to the conclusion that data relevant to an individual on the blockchain has to be considered as 'personal data'. A distinction has to be made between data relevant to the identity of an individual and data relating to the individual (ie data from the transactions). The first category contains the public keys. Finck argues that 'public keys serve as the kind of identifiers mentioned in Recital

[155] See *MN and others v San Marino*, App no 28005/12 (ECtHR, 7 October 2015); *Sommer v Germany*, App no 73607/13 (ECtHR, 27 April 2017); *Affaire Brito Ferrinho Bexiga Villa-Nova v Portugal*, App no 69436/10 (ECtHR, 1 December 2015); *GSB v Switzerland*, App no 28601/11 (ECtHR, 22 December 2015).

[156] Quintel (n 16) 20.

[157] GDPR, recital 26.

[158] GDPR, recital 26.

[159] GDPR, Art 4(1).

[160] ibid.

[161] Joined Cases C-293/12 and C-594/12 *Digital Rights Ireland Ltd v Minister for Communications, Marine and Natural Resources and others and Kärntner Landesregierung and others* ECLI:EU:C:2014:238, para 34 ('*Digital Rights Ireland*').

[162] GDPR, Art 4(1).

[163] GDPR, Art 4(1).

[164] *MN and others v San Marino*, App no 28005/12 (ECtHR, 7 October 2015) para 51.

[165] ibid.

[166] ibid para 55; *Sommer v Germany*, App no 73607/13 (ECtHR, 27 April 2017) para 48; *Affaire Brito Ferrinho Bexiga Villa-Nova v Portugal*, App no 69436/10 (ECtHR, 1 December 2015) para 44.

30 GDPR'.[167] The public key itself does not reveal the identity; thus, it falls within the concept of pseudonymised data.[168] However, the data subject can be identified through additional data.[169] Even though public keys are pseudonymised data, they are still linked with the data subject and, therefore, qualify as personal data. Similar identifiers can be 'internet protocol addresses, cookie identifiers or other identifiers such as radio frequency identification tags'.[170]

The second category encompasses all the other information on blockchain technology. Finck describes this information as 'transactional data', which covers all information relating to the transaction itself.[171] This category includes (if we take as an example the Bitcoin system) timestamps (time and date of transactions), the amount of bitcoin transferred, the transaction identifier number etc.[172] Even if transactions include a plethora of data, this does not necessarily mean that this data falls within the scope of the GDPR as 'personal data'. However, given the broad definition of 'personal data' within the GDPR, it is reasonable to assert that if the transaction entails information relevant to an individual, then this data should be considered as such.

From the analysis conducted thus far, it is evident that virtual asset service providers, especially those involved in cryptocurrencies, operate under a distinct business model compared to other industry providers. They are constrained by the immutable nature of permissionless blockchain, which precludes data alteration.[173] Consequently, these providers face challenges in fulfilling their GDPR obligations. Coupled with the fact that data on the blockchain constitutes 'personal data', it is argued that the retention of such data by the providers constitutes an interference with the right to privacy. The subsequent step involves determining if this intrusion is justifiable.

4. Surveillance on the Blockchain and Justification of Interference

In the context of the blockchain environment, the process of collecting and preserving crucial data to identify potential wrongdoers proves to be a significantly

[167] GDPR, recital 30; Finck (n 131) 26.

[168] GDPR, Art 4(5).

[169] Kelly Philipps Erb, 'IRS Tries Again To Make Coinbase Turn Over Customer Account Data' (*Forbes*, 20 March 2017), www.forbes.com/sites/kellyphillipserb/2017/03/20/irs-tries-again-to-make-coinbase-turn-over-customer-account-data/?sh=214b4a60175e.

[170] GDPR, recital 30; Frederik J Zuiderveen Borgesius, 'Singling Out People Without Knowing their Names: Behavioural Targeting, Pseudonymous Data, and the New Data Protection Regulation' (2016) 32(2) *Computer Law & Security Review* 256, 260.

[171] Finck (n 131) 28.

[172] Rakesh Sharma, Erika Rasure and Katrina Munichiello, 'What Does the Bitcoin Blockchain Record?' (*Investopedia*, 28 July 2024), www.investopedia.com/ask/answers/063015/what-does-block-chain-record-bitcoin-exchange-transaction.asp#:~:text=In%20a%20blockchain%2C%20each%20node,history%20of%20all%20Bitcoin%20transactions.

[173] Henri Arslanian, *The Book of Crypto: The Complete Guide to Understanding Bitcoin, Cryptocurrencies and Digital Assets* (Palgrave Macmillan, 2022) 53–54.

more intricate task compared to the straightforward record-keeping employed by traditional financial institutions.[174] Obliged entities find themselves unable to rely solely on blockchain-derived information. Instead, they must gather a far more extensive set of details to ascertain user identities and discern potentially suspicious transactions.[175] However, this approach may inadvertently lead to increased surveillance of users across the internet.[176]

In a working paper regarding Finance and Bitcoin, the Organisation for Economic Co-operation and Development (OECD) concluded that, regarding KYC measures, 'the structure of the Bitcoin and other networks is not well set up for this due to the decentralised and anonymous nature of the participants'.[177] Consequently, obliged entities have to collect a substantial amount of data (public keys, transactional data and IP addresses and off-blockchain data) by applying essentially enhanced due diligence measures.[178]

In June 2019, the Financial Action Task Force (FATF) issued guidance to aid countries and virtual asset service providers in understanding how the risk-based approach and preventive measures are applied to digital currencies.[179] The FATF identified that the most significant hindrances to the effectiveness of preventive measures lie in the anonymising tools available to potential criminals, such as mixers, privacy-oriented currencies, and decentralised platforms.[180] In response to these challenges, the FATF directed attention to the Interpretive Note of Recommendation 10, emphasising that in higher-risk situations, virtual asset service providers should implement enhanced due diligence measures.[181]

While the blockchain operates as a public ledger, and virtual asset service providers can gather some information from transactions, this alone is often insufficient for creating a comprehensive customer profile. While transaction information can be valuable, it does not consistently provide enough data to trace an individual. Consequently, virtual asset service providers must go further in their data collection

[174] Victor Dostov and Pavel Shust, 'Cryptocurrencies: an unconventional challenge to the AML/CFT regulators' (2014) 21(3) *Journal of Financial Crime* 249, 258.

[175] The reader should always keep in mind that the provider can collect blockchain-generated data recorded on the blockchain including the public key and transactional data. However, as highlighted by Narayanan and others (n 45) 138–68, further information can be collected (eg IP addresses) which is not recorded on the blockchain, through network analysis.

[176] Minárik Tomáš and Anna-Maria Osula, 'Tor Does not Stink: Use and Abuse of the Tor Anonymity Network from the Perspective of Law' (2016) 32(1) *Computer Law & Security Review* 111, 112.

[177] Adrian Blundell-Wignall, 'The Bitcoin Question: Currency versus Trust-Less Transfer Technology' (2014) OECD Working Papers on Finance, Insurance and Private Pensions, No 37, OECD Publishing, 11.

[178] Regulation (EU) 2024/1624 of the European Parliament and of the Council of 31 May 2024 on the prevention of the use of the financial system for the purposes of money laundering or terrorist financing [2024] OJ L, 2024/1624, Art 20(2).

[179] Financial Action Task Force, 'Guidance for a risk-based approach: Virtual Assets and Virtual Asset Service Providers' (June 2019).

[180] ibid 6 and 12.

[181] Interpretive note to Recommendation 10 (from FATF Recommendations); Regulation (EU) 2024/1624 of the European Parliament and of the Council of 31 May 2024 on the prevention of the use of the financial system for the purposes of money laundering or terrorist financing [2024] OJ L, 2024/1624, Art 20(2).

efforts.[182] To shed light on this complex area, the FATF provided specific examples of these data points under enhanced due diligence measures. According to the guidance, virtual asset service providers are required to collect identity numbers and cross-verify them with information from other databases, track the IP addresses of users (ie, geo-location information), and even conduct internet searches for information associated with a user's transactions.[183] The extent of information that these entities must collect exceeds the role of a mere record-keeper and transcends the core of preventive measures. One might argue that virtual asset service providers are compelled to conduct individual investigations for each of their customers, especially when considering the shift in the EU's AML regime away from the risk-based approach, particularly concerning digital currencies.

It is crucial to note that the research does not suggest excluding digital currencies from the scope of the AML regime. Instead, it emphasises that the traditional regime, designed to function from a centralised standpoint, faces various challenges in the context of digital currencies. The analysis presented above illustrates that service providers collect information about their clients based on their established relationships. However, the FATF recommends a proactive approach that extends beyond the conventional relationship between the individual and the service provider.[184] Clients are aware that the provider will collect data on transaction history (already public on the blockchain) and request identification details before offering services. Nonetheless, this data alone can be insufficient for effectively combating money laundering and terrorist financing.

The rule-based approach also introduces a proportionality issue. The principle of proportionality is enshrined in Article 52(1) of the Charter of Fundamental Rights of the EU.[185] Therefore, it has to be assessed whether the principle of proportionality is satisfied within the AML Regulation.[186] The Regulation asserts that a rule-based approach is more effective for the timely detection and assessment of crimes when there is a higher risk of money laundering and terrorist financing.[187] It goes on to add that it is important 'to ensure that clearly specified categories of existing customers are also monitored on a methodical basis'.[188] Nevertheless, the

[182] Financial Action Task Force, 'Guidance for a risk-based approach: Virtual Assets and Virtual Asset Service Providers' (June 2019) 41.

[183] ibid 26.

[184] ibid.

[185] Charter, Art 52(1).

[186] European Data Protection Supervisor, 'Opinion 1/2017, EDPS Opinion on a Commission Proposal amending Directive (EU) 2015/849 and Directive 2009/101/EC' (2 February 2017), 11 ('EDPS Opinion 2017'); European Data Protection Supervisor, 'Opinion 12/2021, on the anti-money laundering and countering the financing of terrorism (AML/CFT) package of legislative proposals' (22 September 2021) 16 ('EDPS Opinion 2021').

[187] Regulation (EU) 2024/1624 of the European Parliament and of the Council of 31 May 2024 on the prevention of the use of the financial system for the purposes of money laundering or terrorist financing [2024] OJ L, 2024/1624, recital 76.

[188] ibid.

Regulation does not outline how these categories will be identified if providers do not employ risk assessment.[189]

In light of the deviation from the risk-based approach in the AML Regulation, it can be contended that the collection and retention of data is evolving into a form of surveillance, particularly for virtual asset service providers. Consequently, it is argued that the obligations imposed by the Regulation amount to blanket measures. It is worth noting that this does not entail surveillance of the entire European population. Instead, it requires providers to treat digital currencies as a high-risk phenomenon, meaning they must collect and retain data from all their customers.

4.1. The Case Law of the ECtHR

The emergence of digital currencies as a potential avenue for money laundering is a relatively recent phenomenon. Research into the impact of the AML regime on the right to privacy within the blockchain environment is still in its nascent stages. Consequently, it becomes imperative to seek insights from all available sources, including the ECtHR. Article 8 of the ECHR safeguards the right to privacy.[190] Under this Article, the right has four aspects: private life, family life, correspondence and home.[191] According to the ECtHR's jurisprudence, the state should refrain from actions that encroach upon the right to private life, except in cases where Article 8(2) of the ECHR is applicable.[192] In instances of interference, the ECtHR applies an assessment known as the 'interference-justification' test.[193] This evaluation involves ascertaining whether an actual interference with the right has occurred, followed by an examination of whether the interference is justified.[194] To this end:

> There shall be no interference by a public authority with the exercise of this right except such as is in accordance with the law and is necessary in a democratic society in the interests of national security, public safety or the economic well-being of the country, for the prevention of disorder or crime, for the protection of health or morals, or for the protection of the rights and freedoms of others.[195]

From this passage, the Court examines whether the action is 'in accordance with the law' and 'necessary in a democratic society'.[196] The former encompasses two stages. Vavoula explains that the first stage includes the verification of the legality

[189] EDPS Opinion 2017, 12; EDPS Opinion 2021; see Chapter 4.
[190] ECHR, Art 8.
[191] ECHR Art 8.
[192] *Airey v Ireland*, App no 6289/73 (ECtHR, 9 October 1979) para 32; *Z and others v UK*, App no 29392/95 (ECtHR, 10 May 2001) para 4.
[193] Vavoula (n 43) 47.
[194] ibid.
[195] ECHR, Art 8(2).
[196] ECHR, Art 8(2).

of the act.[197] The second is an examination of whether the law is accessible and precise.[198] The precision criterion is the most important for the research. In the case of *Rotaru v Romania*, the Court established specific requirements for meeting the precision criterion.[199] The Court ruled that Romanian law lacked precision, primarily due to the absence of limits on data collection and storage powers, a lack of definition regarding the type of information to be gathered, uncertainty about which individuals were being targeted, the circumstances under which such collection should occur, and the duration for which the data would be retained.[200]

Applying these requirements to the issue of digital currencies reveals the problematic relationship between the AML regime and the technology. First, the Regulation does not specify what the appropriate information is to achieve the objective. Defining the type of information to be collected from the blockchain is difficult. The obliged entities have to collect all available information to be able to de-anonymise the individual. Second, there is no specific target. The AML Regulation departs from the risk-based approach, particularly for digital currencies. Therefore, every user is a target for data collection (taking into account the lower threshold and, in some cases, the removal of the minimum threshold of 1,000 Euros).[201] However, the analysis above showed that the entities handling the data on the blockchain are not able to erase the data due to the blockchain's immutable nature. If the entities decide to anonymise data to reach the GDPR threshold, then the purpose of the AML regime is void.

In law enforcement practices and surveillance, the Court has emphasised the necessity of 'reasonable suspicion'.[202] This requirement limits police surveillance powers to specific targets. However, the application of this privacy safeguard was short-lived. In the case of *Centrum för Rättvisa v Sweden*, the ECtHR justified interference (bulk interception of communications) based on national security concerns.[203] The Court reiterated that 'given the present-day threats of global terrorism and serious cross-border crime . . . Sweden had considerable power of discretion . . . to decide on setting up such a system of bulk interception'.[204] Money laundering readily falls within the category of 'serious cross-border crime', especially through digital currencies. However, it is premature to attempt to apply the same rationale to data collection from the blockchain. This specific case (and subsequent cases)[205] pertains to the interception of communication data. Data on

[197] Vavoula (n 43) 48.
[198] ibid.
[199] *Rotaru v Romania*, App no 28341/95 (ECtHR, 4 May 2000).
[200] ibid para 57.
[201] See the analysis in Chapter 4; Regulation (EU) 2024/1624 of the European Parliament and of the Council of 31 May 2024 on the prevention of the use of the financial system for the purposes of money laundering or terrorist financing [2024] OJ L, 2024/1624, Art 19(3).
[202] *Roman Zakharov v Russia*, App no 47143/06 (ECtHR, 4 December 2015) para 260.
[203] *Centrum för Rättvisa v Sweden*, App no 25252/08 (ECtHR, 25 May 2021) para 178.
[204] ibid.
[205] *Big Brother Watch and others v United Kingdom*, App nos 58170/13, 62322/14 and 24960/15 (ECtHR, 25 May 2021).

the blockchain possesses a different nature. Furthermore, it could be contended that while money laundering is a serious crime, it does not constitute a threat to national security.

In the end, the Court has to assess the 'necessary in a democratic society' criterion.[206] Regarding data collection, the case law once again employs terrorism as a justification.[207] The ECtHR, however, contends that specific safeguards must be in place to strike a balance between the necessity of the measure and the protection of the right to private life.[208] Such safeguards should mirror the nature of the measure itself, with more intrusive measures necessitating stronger safeguards.[209]

Drawing from the ECtHR's jurisprudence, it must be concluded that the Court lacks definitive standards for justifying data collection and retention, yet there are instructive lessons to be learned. Regarding collection and retention, it is vital to consider the targeted individual (reasonable suspicion).[210] One of the most common grounds for justification is 'national security'; thus, the gravity of the crime is pertinent to the assessment.[211] Lastly, it is vital to conclude whether the data can be erased (retention period). However, it must be acknowledged that this assessment hinges on the specific circumstances of each case. Blockchain technology encompasses not only 'communication' data between two individuals. Utilising aggregated data, the blockchain has the potential to reveal various information central to individuals' lives. Furthermore, the immutable nature of the technology renders data deletion exceedingly difficult, potentially leading to an unlimited retention period. The subsequent section examines the Charter of Fundamental Rights of the European Union and the jurisprudence of the CJEU with regard to the protection of the right to privacy and data protection. Given the research's focus on EU law, the ensuing subsections will apply CJEU case law to determine whether the interference with privacy can be justified.

4.2. The Case Law of the CJEU

Up to the time of writing, the CJEU has not examined the issue of retaining financial information under the AML regime. However, there exists an extensive body of cases concerning the retention of telecommunications data. All the case law analysed in this section relates to the obligations of private entities (mainly telecommunications providers) concerning the processing (including collection, retention and analysis) of their customers' data. These cases are based on the argument of privatised surveillance, which is the same argument used by this research

[206] Charter, Art 8(2).
[207] *Klass and others v Germany*, App no 5029/71 (ECtHR, 6 September 1978).
[208] ibid para 49.
[209] *MM v Netherlands*, App no 39339/98 (ECtHR, 24 September 2003) para 200.
[210] *MM v United Kingdom*, App no 24029/07 (ECtHR, 13 November 2012) paras 200–207; *MK v France*, App no 19522/09 (ECtHR, 18 April 2013) para 42.
[211] *Aycaguer v France*, App no 8806/12 (ECtHR, 22 September 2017) para 43.

concerning the obligations of virtual asset service providers. Consequently, this analysis will, by analogy, apply this case law to determine whether the infringement of the right to privacy and data protection can be justified. Relevant to this study within the Charter of Fundamental Rights of the European Union is Article 7, which pertains to 'Respect for private and family life', and Article 8, addressing the 'Protection of personal data'.[212] Much like the ECHR, both of these rights are subject to specific limitations outlined in Article 52 of the Charter.[213] The CJEU will assess the facts of each case to determine whether there is an interference with these rights and then move on to test whether Article 52 is applicable.

Article 52 states that limitations to the rights 'must be provided for by law and respect the essence of those rights and freedoms. Subject to the principle of proportionality, limitations may be made only if they are necessary and genuinely meet objectives of general interest recognised by the Union or the need to protect the rights and freedoms of others.'[214] For the proportionality test, the Court examines if the action is appropriate, necessary and proportionate.[215]

The leading data retention case is *Digital Rights Ireland*.[216] This judgment holds dual significance. First, this case signalled the demise of the Data Retention Directive.[217] Second, the Court assessed the retention of an amalgamation of data capable of revealing extensive information about the data subject (eg, identity, relationships, location, etc).[218] The Court unequivocally stated that retaining such data is a problematic practice. The conclusion was that, 'The retention of data for the purpose of possible access to them by the competent national authorities ... directly and specifically affects private life and, consequently, the rights guaranteed by Article 7 of the Charter. Furthermore, such a retention of data also falls under Article 8 of the Charter.'[219]

Following the determination of interference, the Court proceeded to the proportionality assessment. Vavoula divides the assessment of the Court into four areas: 'the personal scope of the Directive; the modalities of access and subsequent use of the data; the retention period and data security'.[220] The Court found that the Directive did not have a specific scope. It involved 'the retention of all traffic data concerning fixed telephony, mobile telephony, Internet access, Internet e-mail and Internet telephony. It, therefore, applies to all means of electronic communication.'[221] Moreover, the retention was not limited to suspected persons, and there

[212] Charter, Arts 7 and 8.

[213] Charter, Art 52.

[214] ibid.

[215] ibid.

[216] *Digital Rights Ireland*.

[217] Directive 2006/24/EC of the European Parliament and of the Council of 15 March 2006 on the retention of data generated or processed in connection with the provision of publicly available electronic communications services or of public communications networks and amending Directive 2002/58/EC [2006] OJ L105/54.

[218] *Digital Rights Ireland*, para 26.

[219] ibid para 29.

[220] Vavoula (n 43) 87.

[221] *Digital Rights Ireland*, para 56.

were no specific requirements for the retention.[222] Last, the Directive failed to include any safeguards to protect the retained data and mitigate the interference.[223]

The *Digital Rights Ireland* case highlighted the collision between technology and data protection. The Court's determination that such extensive retention equates to constant surveillance was instrumental in comprehending the adverse consequences of these practices.[224] This case serves as a guiding light for navigating uncharted territory. The application of these findings to the blockchain is of great significance. The Court condemned this pre-emptive surveillance of large numbers of people. Presently, the AML regime necessitates that obliged entities indiscriminately collect data from the blockchain.

The CJEU continued the pattern. In *Tele2*, the Court found again that the legislation

> provides for a general and indiscriminate retention of all traffic and location data of all subscribers and registered users relating to all means of electronic communication, and that it imposes on providers of electronic communications services an obligation to retain that data systematically and continuously, with no exceptions.[225]

It was also noted that combined data could essentially lead to the profiling of individuals.[226] Analogously, transactional data from the blockchain can lead to the same outcome.

Applying Article 52, the Court did not hesitate to clarify that 'the general and indiscriminate retention of all traffic and location data' cannot be justified based on the fight against terrorism and organised crime.[227] The generality of the assessed measures did not satisfy the necessity requirement of the proportionality test.[228] The *Tele2* case continued the privacy saga, expanding on the ideas of the *Digital Rights Ireland* case. The former case clarified that indiscriminate and general retention of data cannot be justified based on the fight against serious offences, limiting it to what is strictly necessary.[229]

In 2020, the CJEU delivered its decisions in the cases of *Privacy International* and *La Quadrature du Net and Others*.[230] In the first case, Privacy International (an

[222] ibid paras 57–59.

[223] ibid para 66.

[224] Valsamis Mitsilegas, *The Criminalisation of Migration in Europe: Challenges for Human Rights and the Rule of Law* (Springer, 2015) 41–42.

[225] Joined Cases C-203/15 and C-689/15 *Tele2 Sverige AB v Post- och telestyrelsen and Secretary of State for the Home Department v Tom Watson and Others* ECLI:EU:C:2016:970 ('*Tele2*') para 97.

[226] ibid para 99.

[227] ibid para 103.

[228] ibid para 107.

[229] Lorna Woods, 'When is mass surveillance justified? The CJEU clarifies the law in Privacy International and other cases' (*EU Law Analysis*, 7 October 2020), https://eulawanalysis.blogspot.com/2020/10/when-is-mass-surveillance-justified.html.

[230] Case C-623/17 *Privacy International v Secretary of State for Foreign and Commonwealth Affairs and others* ECLI:EU:C:2020:790 ('*Privacy International*'); Joined Cases C-511/18, C-512/18 and C-520/18 *La Quadrature du Net and Others v Premier Ministre and Others* ECLI:EC:C:2020:791 ('*La Quadrature du Net*').

NGO) challenged the practices of several intelligence services in the UK (GCHQ, MI5 and MI6) for the acquisition and use of bulk data.[231] The Court confirmed its previous case law and underlined that the general and indiscriminate bulk interception of data by these agencies (national authorities) is not permissible and does not satisfy the 'what is strictly necessary' requirement.[232] However, the importance of this judgment is hidden in the fact that the Court connects the actions of the service providers with the GDPR.[233]

By analogy, this also will apply to virtual asset service providers when they collect and process data from the blockchain. Nevertheless, the preceding analysis demonstrates that the GDPR is not entirely compatible with this technology. Consequently, providers will likely face challenges in meeting the GDPR's requirements and aligning with the jurisprudence.

The *La Quadrature du Net* case presents a notably intricate legal scenario.[234] This case revolves around the interpretation of Article 15(1) of Directive 2002/58/EC, a significant piece of legislation addressing the processing of personal data and safeguarding privacy within the electronic communications sector.[235] The CJEU argues that Article 5(1) of the Directive enshrines the principle of confidentiality 'of both electronic communications and the related traffic data'.[236] Notably, the Court distinguishes between traffic data and other forms, such as location data.[237] Building upon this distinction, it is determined that traffic data should solely be retained for purposes of marketing and billing, after which it must be promptly expunged. To the contrary, the processing of location data and similar information should only occur following anonymisation or in situations where the data subject has granted explicit consent.[238] However, by way of derogation, Article 15 provides the possibility to limit the principle under Article 5.[239] In this situation, such a measure must be necessary, appropriate and proportionate. The adopted measure should allow the retention of data only for a limited period and based on certain grounds.[240] The Court emphatically underscores that such measures should by no means become standard practice.[241]

A novel aspect of this case is the extensive discussion surrounding the concept of 'national security', a frequently invoked ground for justifying contentious measures. The Court highlights that, under Article 4 TEU, 'national security' falls

[231] *Privacy International*, paras 19–21.
[232] ibid paras 78–81.
[233] ibid paras 12–15.
[234] *La Quadrature du Net*.
[235] Directive 2002/58/EC of the European Parliament and of the Council of 12 July 2002 concerning the processing of personal data and the protection of privacy in the electronic communications sector (Directive on Privacy and Electronic Communications) [2002] OJ L201/37.
[236] *La Quadrature du Net*, para 107.
[237] ibid para 108.
[238] ibid.
[239] Directive on Privacy and Electronic Communications, Art 15.
[240] *La Quadrature du Net*, para 110; Such grounds might be to safeguard national security, defence and public security, and the prevention, investigation, detection and prosecution of criminal offences.
[241] *La Quadrature du Net*, para 111.

exclusively under the purview of Member States.[242] Concerns regarding national security raise the threshold to a level where Articles 7 and 8 of the Charter cannot supersede legislation permitting service providers to indiscriminately retain personal data.[243] However, the Court clarifies that the threat to national security must be 'genuine and present or foreseeable'.[244] Even in situations where such a threat exists, the retention by the providers 'must . . . be limited in time to what is strictly necessary'.[245]

It is important to note that the Court does not provide a list of threats for assessment of their severity. Nonetheless, the CJEU elucidates that combating serious crime does not validate the broad and indiscriminate retention of data.[246] Only under specific circumstances can the fight against serious crime justify serious interference with the protected rights. Yet, even in such cases, retention must be targeted and for a limited period of time.[247] Upon initial examination, the *La Quadrature du Net* case might suggest a relaxation of the stance on data retention. However, closer scrutiny reveals that the Court has not deviated from its preceding jurisprudence. It reaffirms that indiscriminate and general data retention is impermissible, as it fails the proportionality test. The case probes the concept of 'national security', which is identified as the sole grounds for justifying the widespread and indiscriminate retention of data. Nevertheless, such retention must be time limited.

The matter of data retention remains an ongoing concern. At present, there are no cases addressing blockchain technology and data retention for preventive purposes. However, drawing on the lessons from the CJEU, particularly from the *La Quadrature du Net* case, it is reasonable to contend that the rule-based approach of the AML Regulation raises significant privacy concerns. Money laundering, by definition, does not qualify as a severe 'national security' threat. Instead, it constitutes a serious crime, and as per jurisprudential standards, service providers must retain data exclusively from specific targets and for a restricted duration.

5. An Assessment of the Necessity and the Proportionality of the AML Regulation

The aforementioned cases established the existence of interference and serve as the cornerstone of the justification phase. Of particular relevance to digital currencies, due to shared characteristics such as large-scale data collection, traceability and private surveillance, are the *Digital Rights Ireland* and *La Quadrature du Net* cases. In the *Digital Rights Ireland* case, the Court notably holds that the extensive

[242] Treaty on European Union (TEU), Art 4(2); *La Quadrature du Net*, para 135.
[243] ibid para 137.
[244] ibid.
[245] ibid para 138.
[246] ibid para 141; *Tele2*, para 107.
[247] ibid para 146.

scale of data retention constitutes a particularly severe interference.[248] By analogy, the extensive data gathering undertaken by virtual asset service providers from all their clients can be characterised as a substantial infringement upon the rights of privacy and data protection.

The novelty of the present analysis rests on applying the existing body of privacy jurisprudence to the emerging digital currency economy, where the convergence of financial oversight and data governance raises unprecedented questions for the protection of fundamental rights. In this context, assessing whether such interference is justifiable necessarily entails the application of the necessity and proportionality test. For an interference to be considered justified, it must be prescribed by law; it must uphold the essence of the rights; it must serve objectives of general interest recognised by the Union; it must be necessary; and it must be proportionate.[249] According to guidelines issued by the European Data Protection Supervisor (EDPS), this translates into five separate steps:

> 1. First, it must be examined whether the law that provides for a limitation is accessible and foreseeable. . . .
> 2. Second, if the measure has passed the test of the quality of the law under point 1 above, it must be examined whether the essence of the right is respected, that is, whether the right is in effect emptied of its basic content and the individual cannot exercise the right. . . .
> 3. Third, it must be examined whether the measure meets an objective of general interest. The objective of general interest provides the background against which the necessity of the measure may be assessed. . . .
> 4. The following step consists of assessing the necessity of a proposed legislative measure. . . .
> 5. If this test is satisfied, the proportionality of the envisaged measure must be examined (proportionality test). . . .[250]

5.1. Interference with Articles 7 and 8 of the Charter

In the *WM and Sovim SA* case, the CJEU ruled that when data includes information on identified individuals, then 'the access of any member of the general public to those data affects the fundamental right to respect for private life'.[251] Furthermore, making the data available to third parties 'constitutes the processing of personal data falling under Article 8 of the Charter'. Building on this, the

[248] *Digital Rights Ireland*, para 37.

[249] Charter, Art 52(1); European Data Protection Supervisor, 'Assessing the necessity of measures that limit the fundamental right to the protection of personal data: A Toolkit' (11 April 2017) 4 ('EDPS Toolkit'); European Data Protection Supervisor, 'EDPS Guidelines on assessing the proportionality of measures that limit the fundamental rights to privacy and to the protection of personal data' (19 December 2019) ('EDPS Guidelines') 6–7.

[250] 'EDPS Guidelines' (n 249) 8–9.

[251] Joined Cases C-37/20 and C-601/20 *WM and Sovim SA v Luxembourg Business Registers* ECLI:EU:C:2022:912, para 38.

CJEU determined that the retention and subsequent analysis of data, including both metadata and content data, constitutes a violation of privacy as outlined in Article 7 of the Charter.[252] Subsection 3.2. of the analysis concluded that data stored on the blockchain can be classified as personal data, and according to the GDPR, the 'processing' of such data is interpreted widely to encompass activities such as collection and retention by third parties.[253] Consequently, the collection and retention of data by virtual asset service providers fall under Article 8 of the Charter.

Moving forward, it is essential to assess the extent of the impact on these rights using three criteria, including the number of users affected, the significance of the data and the retention period of this information. Concerning the number of users affected, the analysis will draw from the CJEU case law, specifically the *La Quadrature du Net* case, which delineates the limitations of data retention predicated on security objectives.[254] In that case, the CJEU presented various public interest objectives and delineated permissible data retention practices for each circumstance.[255] Mitsilegas and others have argued that, essentially, the CJEU established a hierarchy of objectives in *La Quadrature du Net* by evaluating the interference against three tiers: (a) safeguarding national security, (b) safeguarding public security and combating serious crime, and (c) the prevention, investigation, detection and prosecution of criminal offences.[256] Based on these objectives, the analysis will concentrate solely on the second tier of the hierarchy, ie, safeguarding public security and combating serious crime. This is because the crime of money laundering pertains to a serious crime rather than a matter of national security. The Court ascertains that activities falling under the first tier of national security involve 'activities capable of seriously destabilising the fundamental constitutional, political, economic or social structures of a country and, in particular, of directly threatening society, the population or the State itself'.[257] There is no evidence to support an assertion that the crime of money laundering can destabilise the economic structure of a state.

In *La Quadrature du Net*, the CJEU considers, among other things, legislative measures allowing for the preventive retention of traffic and location data for the purposes of combating serious crime and safeguarding public security.[258] These measures bear resemblance to the preventive measures outlined in the AML Regulation, enabling the application of the Court's conclusion by analogy. The

[252] *Digital Rights Ireland*, paras 32–37; *Tele2*, para 93; Case C-362/14 *Maximillian Schrems v Data Protection Commissioner* ECLI:EU:C:2015:650, para 94.

[253] GDPR, Art 4.

[254] *La Quadrature du Net*.

[255] ibid.

[256] Valasmis Mitsilegas and others, 'Data Retention and the Future of Large-Scale Surveillance: The Evolution and Contestation of Judicial Benchmarks' (2022) 29 *European Law Journal* 6–10.

[257] *La Quadrature du Net*, para 135.

[258] ibid para 140.

CJEU determined that it is permissible for a Member State to enact legislation (preventive measures) for the targeted retention

> of traffic and location data for the purposes of combating serious crime, preventing serious threats to public security and equally of safeguarding national security, provided that such retention is limited, with respect to the categories of data to be retained, the means of communication affected, the persons concerned and the retention period adopted, to what is strictly necessary.

However, the Court specifies that IP addresses and the civil identity of individuals are less sensitive data compared to other traffic data and, therefore, can be retained on a generalised and indiscriminate basis.[259]

In this context, 'targeted retention' is considered the retention of data of persons who 'have been identified beforehand, in the course of the applicable national procedures and on the basis of objective evidence, as posing a threat to public or national security in the Member State concerned'.[260] The Court further elaborates that:

> The limits on a measure providing for the retention of traffic and location data may also be set using a geographical criterion where the competent national authorities consider, on the basis of objective and non-discriminatory factors, that there exists, in one or more geographical areas, a situation characterised by a high risk of preparation for or commission of serious criminal offences.[261]

Concerning data retention, the analysis has to take into account the CJEU's discussion on the issue of passenger name record (PNR) data to determine the interference. In *Opinion 1/15,* the Court highlights that it does not matter whether data is sensitive; the retention of personal data with the possibility of it being subsequently transferred to public authorities alone is an interference with Article 7.[262] Moreover, the collection and retention of data also constitutes processing of personal data, which is an interference with Article 8.[263]

Information gathered from the blockchain and the user can reveal significant aspects of an individual's life, such as their civil identity, IP addresses, purchasing habits, financial details, and location. While this may not encompass the entirety of an individual's personal life, when combined, it can disclose a substantial portion.[264] Based on recital 76 of the new AML Regulation (as analysed in Chapter 4), the AML regime employs a more rule-based approach towards digital currencies, resulting in the surveillance of the totality of users and the application

[259] ibid paras 152–159; see also Case C-207/16 *Ministerio Fiscal* ECLI:EU:C:2018:788.
[260] ibid para 149.
[261] ibid para 150.
[262] Court of Justice of the European Union, 'Opinion 1/15' (26 July 2017) 20 ('Opinion 1/15').
[263] ibid; *Digital Rights Ireland*, para 36.
[264] Opinion 1/15, 20.

of enhanced due diligence measures.[265] Lastly, according to Article 77(3) of the AML Regulation, the provider has to retain the data for a period of five years after the end of the relationship (between provider and customer) or after the date of an occasional transaction.[266] This means that, for regular customers, the provider will retain the data for a considerable amount of time, especially if the customer remains in a relationship with the same provider.

5.2. The 'Provided by the Law' Requirement

The initial step in evaluating the necessity and proportionality of the preventive measures outlined in the AML Regulation involves an assessment of their legal basis. According to Article 52(1) of the Charter, 'measures that interfere with fundamental rights are provided for by law in a way that is understandable and foreseeable for the average person'.[267] The 'provided by law' requirement is straightforward, necessitating a clear legal basis.[268] However, to meet this step, it is crucial to demonstrate that the measures are also adequately accessible and sufficiently precise.[269]

'Adequately accessible' entails that 'the citizen must be able to have an indication that is adequate in the circumstances of the legal rules applicable to a given case'.[270] In the context of the AML regime, the existence of the Regulation as a legal instrument can serve as a basis for the interference, compelling virtual asset service providers to implement preventive AML measures and de-anonymise customers.[271] Ultimately, the existence of the legal basis can satisfy the 'accessibility' requirement but not the 'foreseeability' criterion.

The concept of 'foreseeability' pertains to sufficient precise measures that 'enable the citizen to regulate his conduct: he must be able – if need be with appropriate advice – to foresee, to a degree that is reasonable in the circumstances, the consequences which a given action may entail. Those consequences need not be

[265] Regulation (EU) 2024/1624 of the European Parliament and of the Council of 31 May 2024 on the prevention of the use of the financial system for the purposes of money laundering or terrorist financing [2024] OJ L, 2024/1624, recital 76. The argument in Chapter 4 is that recital 76 (recital 24 in the 5th AML Directive) categorises digital currencies as a high-risk phenomenon which might result in the application of enhanced due diligence and the surveillance of the totality of the users.

[266] Regulation (EU) 2024/1624 of the European Parliament and of the Council of 31 May 2024 on the prevention of the use of the financial system for the purposes of money laundering or terrorist financing [2024] OJ L, 2024/1624, Art 77(3).

[267] Charter, Art 52(1).

[268] The 'provided by law' requirement is similar to the 'in accordance with law' requirement in the ECHR.

[269] *Sunday Times v United Kingdom*, App no 6538/74 (ECtHR, 26 April 1979) para 49.

[270] ibid.

[271] Regulation (EU) 2024/1624 of the European Parliament and of the Council of 31 May 2024 on the prevention of the use of the financial system for the purposes of money laundering or terrorist financing [2024] OJ L, 2024/1624.

foreseeable with absolute certainty.'[272] Nevertheless, the 'foreseeability' requirement applies to both virtual asset service providers and customers. The former must comprehend how to apply the preventive measures, including what data to gather and from whom. The latter need to understand the extent of data collection and retention.

Regarding 'precision', a challenge arises from the deviation of the AML regime from the risk-based approach and its adoption of a more rule-based approach to digital currencies. As explored in Chapter 4, recital 76 of the AML Regulation underscores the importance 'to ensure that clearly specified categories of existing customers are also monitored on a regular basis' for the timely detection and assessment of the risk due to higher risk situations associated with 'certain intermediary structures'.[273] The AML Regulation, however, does not precisely define these customer categories nor explain to virtual asset service providers the basis for ongoing monitoring in the absence of prior risk assessment. However, the AML Regulation does not embody this approach in a specific Article, and the recitals of EU legislation are not legally binding, even though they can be used to clarify the instrument's objectives.

The preventive measures outlined in the AML Regulation, particularly CDD and the reporting obligations, are sufficiently precise.[274] Nevertheless, with the recent expansion of the AML regime for digital currencies, the AML Regulation does not take into account the available data on the blockchain, nor the necessary data that will lead to a successful de-anonymisation of a customer. As mentioned earlier in Chapter 3, the FATF determined that for virtual asset service providers to be able to de-anonymise customers, they have to collect additional data such as IP addresses, timestamps, geo-location data and other details.[275] The AML Regulation does not explicitly explore the risk factors of blockchain technology to determine if the provider has to collect additional information. Nonetheless, Article 20(2) of the Regulation grants obliged entities the possibility to 'determine the extent of the measures', meaning that virtual asset service providers may decide on the necessary data to achieve the objective of customer de-anonymisation.[276] One additional observation from this research is that the AML

[272] *Sunday Times v United Kingdom* (n 269) para 49; The case illustrates that it is not necessary to have absolute certainty.

[273] Regulation (EU) 2024/1624 of the European Parliament and of the Council of 31 May 2024 on the prevention of the use of the financial system for the purposes of money laundering or terrorist financing [2024] OJ L, 2024/1624, recital 76; The argument in Chapter 4 is that recital 76 mirrors the phenomenon of digital currencies by linking the speed of the transactions on the blockchain and the decentralisation of the system.

[274] Regulation (EU) 2024/1624 of the European Parliament and of the Council of 31 May 2024 on the prevention of the use of the financial system for the purposes of money laundering or terrorist financing [2024] OJ L, 2024/1624.

[275] See Chapter 3.

[276] Regulation (EU) 2024/1624 of the European Parliament and of the Council of 31 May 2024 on the prevention of the use of the financial system for the purposes of money laundering or terrorist financing [2024] OJ L, 2024/1624, Art 20(2).

Regulation no longer distinguishes between KYC and CDD measures.[277] The preventive aspect of the regime, along with the categories of data, can be found under the CDD section. To this end, the categories of data to be collected are precise to a certain extent, and the discretion to collect additional data under Article 20(2) does not negate this precision.

5.3. Assessment of the Objective of General Interest

As stipulated by Article 52(1) of the Charter, the limitation of the right must 'genuinely meet objectives of general interest recognised by the Union or the need to protect the rights and freedoms of others'.[278] Hence, this stage entails an evaluation of the AML measures to ascertain whether they align with a genuine objective of general interest.

The AML regime holds a pivotal role in the European Commission's security agenda. In 2015, the European Commission underscored the significance of developing the AML regime.[279] Furthermore, the security agenda outlined three key priorities, including addressing cybercrime and combating the illicit use of anonymising tools for money laundering purposes.[280] Building upon this strategy, the European Commission issued an action plan in 2016 aimed at bolstering the efforts against terrorist financing.[281] The Commission highlighted the absence of regulation pertaining to digital currencies and proposed extending the AML regime to encompass virtual asset service providers.[282]

Moreover, the CJEU concluded that interference serves an objective of general interest when 'the material objective of that directive is . . . to ensure that the data are available for the purpose of the investigation, detection and prosecution of serious crime. . . . The material objective of that directive is, therefore, to contribute to the . . . public security'.[283] This principle holds true for the AML Regulation as well. Recital 75 (and also recital 174) underscores that the objective of the new Regulation is to prevent the use of the Union's financial system for the purposes of

[277] KYC measures are used to identify (and verify) the customer (ie to de-anonymise the individual). So KYC entails the necessary measures for the identification of a customer before the start of the business relationship. CDD on the other hand continues during the relationship to determine the risks associated with the customer.

[278] Charter, Art 52(1).

[279] Commission, 'Communication from the Commission to the European Parliament, the Council, the European Economic and Social Committee and the Committee of the Regions: The European Agenda on Security' COM(2015) 185 final.

[280] ibid 13.

[281] Commission, 'Communication from the Commission to the European Parliament and the Council on an Action Plan for strengthening the fight against terrorist financing' COM(2016) 50 final.

[282] ibid 3–5.

[283] *Digital Rights Ireland*, para 41.

money laundering and terrorist financing.[284] This explicitly states that the retention and processing of data for money laundering purposes serve a public interest objective. Therefore, the surveillance of the blockchain aligns with the objective of public interest, specifically the safeguarding of the financial system through the fight against money laundering.

Hence, it can be contended that the AML Regulation (and the broader AML regime) fulfils objectives of general interest recognised by the EU.

5.4. Assessment of the Respect for the Essence of the Fundamental Rights

The Luxembourg Court conducts an assessment to ascertain if the interference contradicts the essence of the right, an aspect that must be respected even if the interference is deemed justified.[285] However, existing case law does not provide a definitive test for identifying whether a measure fails to respect the essence of a right. Nevertheless, the Court provides some guidance which, by analogy, can be applied to virtual asset service providers.

In the *Digital Rights Ireland* case, the Court scrutinised the essence of both rights – privacy and data protection. It was established that:

> So far as concerns the essence of the fundamental right to privacy and the other rights laid down in Article 7 of the Charter, it must be held that, even though the retention of data required by Directive 2006/24 constitutes a particularly serious interference with those rights, it is not such as to adversely affect the essence of those rights given that, as follows from Article 1(2) of the directive, the directive does not permit the acquisition of knowledge of the content of the electronic communications as such.[286]

Hence, in the context of privacy, the essence of the right remained intact as the Directive mandated only the retention of communication data, not the content of that communication.[287] Similarly, in the *Schrems* case, the Court concluded that 'permitting the public authorities to have access on a generalised basis to the content of electronic communications must be regarded as compromising the essence of the fundamental right to respect for private life'.[288] Consequently, it can be inferred that granting public authorities the power to gain generalised access to the content of communications can indeed affect the essence of the right. Concerning data

[284] Regulation (EU) 2024/1624 of the European Parliament and of the Council of 31 May 2024 on the prevention of the use of the financial system for the purposes of money laundering or terrorist financing [2024] OJ L, 2024/1624, recital 75.

[285] See Maja Brkan, 'The Concept of Fundamental Rights in the EU Legal Order: Peeling the Onion to its Core' (2018) 14(2) *European Constitutional Law Review* 332; Koen Lenaerts, 'Limits on Limitations: The Essence of Fundamental Rights in the EU' (2019) 20 *German Law Journal* 779; 'EDPS Guidelines' (n 249) 8.

[286] *Digital Rights Ireland*, para 39.

[287] ibid; the Court held the same opinion in *Tele2*, para 101.

[288] Case C-362/14 *Maximilian Schrems v Data Protection Commissioner* ECLI:EU:C:2015:650, para 94 ('*Schrems*').

protection, the Court similarly determined that the essence of the right was preserved because the Directive included specific provisions for the safeguarding of personal data.[289] However, applying the same approach by analogy to the surveillance of virtual asset service providers may lead to a different conclusion.

First, the AML Regulation requires knowledge of the financial information (ie amounts, timestamps, parties, etc). However, virtual asset service providers collect more than just financial data. As analysed earlier, information from the blockchain can offer substantial insights into an individual's daily life and activities. Second, the AML Regulation mandates the protection of data under the GDPR.[290] Nonetheless, the interference with these rights also arises from the fact that virtual asset service providers cannot fully comply with GDPR requirements.[291] Consequently, it might seem inappropriate to apply the Court's decision to the situation of virtual asset service providers. One argument could be that even if the Court were to apply its stringent approach concerning the essence of the rights to the present circumstances (ie, interference by virtual asset service providers), the outcome would differ from the *Digital Rights Ireland* case, suggesting that the interference would inevitably have a direct impact on the essence of the rights.

However, a counter-argument that the interference does not impinge on the essence of the rights can be divided into two parts. First, drawing on the conclusion of the *Digital Rights Ireland* case that the 'interference with those rights . . . is not such as to adversely affect the essence of those rights given that, as follows from Article 1(2) of the Directive, the Directive does not permit the acquisition of knowledge of the content of the electronic communications as such', it can be argued that the Court categorises data depending on the information available to third parties. For the sake of this research, we will divide the data into 'core data' and 'external data'. The former encompasses information about the individual's core life aspects and includes the 'content of communications' category outlined by the CJEU. The latter comprises information about the external sphere of an individual's life, such as location, communication metadata, hobbies, habits, buying patterns, identity, etc. The crucial distinction lies in the fact that interference with 'core data' would result in an impact on the essence of the right. However, this is not the case with 'external data'. It remains to be determined whether information on the blockchain falls under 'core data' or 'external data'. The research leads to the conclusion that even though there is a variety of information on the blockchain, the interference does not impact the essence of the right to privacy or data protection. Data gathered from a permissionless blockchain is publicly available. Even if a virtual asset service provider, during the de-anonymisation process, collects and combines information such as IP addresses, time stamps and other details, the essence of the right remains intact.

[289] *Digital Rights Ireland*, para 40.

[290] Regulation (EU) 2024/1624 of the European Parliament and of the Council of 31 May 2024 on the prevention of the use of the financial system for the purposes of money laundering or terrorist financing [2024] OJ L, 2024/1624, recital 150.

[291] See section 3.

The second part of the counter-argument is focused on the GDPR and the nature of the blockchain (more generally, on the safeguards for the protection of privacy and data protection). The fact that virtual asset service providers cannot fully adhere to GDPR requirements is not a matter of the provider's willingness to follow the rules, but rather a fundamental organisational clash between technology and the GDPR. The immutable nature of the blockchain is structured in such a way that information cannot be altered, resulting in a situation where information is pseudonymous but not anonymous. However, the de-anonymisation process is not straightforward and requires combined data from various sources. The responsibility to protect privacy in a public permissionless blockchain is shared with the individual. Once the relationship between customer and provider is over, the individual is the one who has control over the data. Therefore, it is the individual's responsibility to anonymise the data. There are various techniques that can be deployed to enhance anonymity, with the primary one being the ability to create a new address for each transaction. Thus, the research illustrates that the interference does not impact the essence of the rights.

5.5. The Necessity Test

The case law of the CJEU does not offer explicit guidance on how to conduct an assessment of necessity. Often, the Court combines the necessity and proportionality test to reach a conclusion. According to the guidance of the EDPS, 'Necessity implies the need for a combined, fact-based assessment of the effectiveness of the measure for the objective pursued and of whether it is less intrusive compared to other options for achieving the same goal.'[292]

Based on the above passage, the necessity test involves two key steps. First, it consists of determining whether the preventive measures outlined in the AML regime pertaining to digital currencies are capable of achieving the Regulation's objective. Second, it necessitates an examination of whether there exist alternative measures that are less intrusive. The term 'effectiveness' is subjective, and determining the efficacy of the AML regime is inherently challenging. Furthermore, the transplantation of the regime to digital currencies is a novel development (since the 5th AML Directive), and thus far there has been no comprehensive evaluation of its effectiveness. The effectiveness of the regime will be influenced by the inherent nature of blockchain technology. For example, in permissioned blockchains where there exists a central governing entity, the measures can be applied centrally, akin to the traditional banking system.[293] However, the problem is more profound in permissionless blockchains (eg Bitcoin), which are founded on decentralisation.[294]

[292] 'EDPS Toolkit' (n 249) 5.
[293] The issue of decentralisation; see Narayanan (n 45) 27 et seq; Arslanian (n 173) 51–53.
[294] ibid.

Narayan and others argue that:

> If anyone were ever able to link your Bitcoin address to your real-world identity, then all your transactions . . . will have been linked back to your identity. To make things worse, linking a Bitcoin address to real-world identity is often easy. If you interact with a Bitcoin business – be it an online wallet service, exchange, or other type of merchant – they usually want your real-world identity for transactions with them.[295]

In light of this, it can be contended that despite the challenges arising from the cryptocurrency environment, including decentralisation and anonymity, the implementation of the preventive measures can be considered effective to some degree. This conclusion is based on the fact that the Regulation's objective also encompasses the mitigation of the risk of money laundering, not solely the actual prevention of the crime. Regarding the question of whether the activities of the collection and the retention of data are appropriate for the objective pursued by the new AML Regulation, the research concludes that the technology necessitates the collection of additional data for the establishment of the risk and the anonymisation of the individual. As explained, providers will employ network analysis and collection of both blockchain-generated data and off-chain data for the monitoring of customers. Therefore, the collection and retention of such data can be considered appropriate for attaining the objective, which encompasses the end of anonymity within these systems to mitigate and prevent the crime of money laundering.

The second step in the necessity assessment involves examining whether less intrusive measures exist that can achieve the same objective.[296] To begin with, the regime permits the application of enhanced due diligence measures (which are more intrusive) in situations where the risk is deemed higher.[297] The Regulation's classification of the entire phenomenon as high risk, resulting in the application of these measures to all customers, pertains more to proportionality than necessity, an aspect analysed in the subsequent section. The AML Regulation does not propose alternative, less intrusive measures to attain the same objective. The obligation of the providers to mitigate the risk of money laundering is the minimum that can be done. The only alternative is to leave the standard obligation of collecting identification details on the providers and oblige law enforcement agencies to perform the blockchain analysis and monitor users. Due to the fact that blockchain is public, this suggestion is feasible, but it is not less intrusive because then we move from privatised surveillance to public surveillance. Nevertheless, a less intrusive measure would be to maintain the same threshold for the application of CDD measures. In Article 19 of the AML Regulation, by way of derogation from

[295] Narayanan (n 45) 139.
[296] 'EDPS Toolkit' (n 249) 5.
[297] Regulation (EU) 2024/1624 of the European Parliament and of the Council of 31 May 2024 on the prevention of the use of the financial system for the purposes of money laundering or terrorist financing [2024] OJ L, 2024/1624, Arts 34–46.

the general threshold, the EU obliges virtual asset service providers to apply CDD measures for crypto transactions of at least 1,000 Euros and apply at least the measures identified in Article 20(1)(a) when carrying out (even) occasional transactions where the value is below 1,000 Euros.[298] This (unjustified) measure comes without the necessity for a risk-based evaluation. Consequently, it can be argued that the necessity test might be deemed not satisfied, especially when considering the decrease in the threshold for transactions involving cryptocurrencies.

5.6. The Proportionality Test

Last, but not least, the application of the proportionality test to the interference is paramount. Under this test, the Court must scrutinise whether the actions of the EU align with being 'appropriate for attaining the legitimate objectives pursued by the legislation at issue and do not exceed the limits of what is appropriate and necessary in order to achieve those objectives'.[299] As a first step, the Court applies a number of factors to investigate whether the discretion of the legislator should be limited.[300] The CJEU established that the discretion of the legislator would be subject to stringent review based on the gravity of the interference and the fundamental nature of the rights in question.[301] The proportionality test entails a delicate balancing exercise between the negative outcome of the interference and the positive outcome of achieving the aim of the AML Regulation. The test fails if the gravity of the interference outweighs the positive outcome.

5.6.1. Targeted Surveillance

With respect to the scope of the measures for virtual asset service providers, it is troublesome that the AML Regulation seems to depart from the risk-based approach. Recital 76, which emphasises the need for continuous monitoring of 'clearly specified categories of existing customers', is not incorporated into an Article of the Regulation, making it not legally binding for virtual asset service providers.[302] Even if the Regulation were to adhere to the risk-based approach, it still does not specify how risk is assessed in blockchain technology and what data is required to identify customers.[303] Moreover, the analysis in the above section, concerning the decrease of the threshold, reinforces the argument that

[298] ibid Arts 19 and 20.

[299] *Digital Rights Ireland*, para 46.

[300] Such factors are: the area concerned, the nature of the right at issue guaranteed by the Charter, the nature and seriousness of the interference, and the object pursued by the interference; *Digital Rights Ireland*, para 47.

[301] ibid para 48.

[302] Regulation (EU) 2024/1624 of the European Parliament and of the Council of 31 May 2024 on the prevention of the use of the financial system for the purposes of money laundering or terrorist financing [2024] OJ L, 2024/1624, recital 24.

[303] The Regulation does not explain the risk factors (red flags) in the environment of digital currencies.

the AML regime applies a more rule-based approach to the phenomenon of digital currencies.

Therefore, one part of the answer to the proportionality test depends on whether virtual asset service providers retain data through targeted efforts or engage in indiscriminate customer surveillance. Drawing a parallel with the *La Quadrature du Net* case, virtual asset service providers are permitted to implement measures for targeted data retention and client monitoring in matters related to public security and combating serious crime.[304] In the recent *Ligue des Droits Humains* case (the PNR judgment), the CJEU further clarified the concept of 'targeted' surveillance, stating that 'the criteria used for the purposes of advance assessment must be determined in such a way as to target, specifically, individuals who might be reasonably suspected of involvement in terrorist offences or serious crime covered by that directive'.[305] This approach aligns with the risk-based approach, which ought to be followed under the AML regime. The provider will apply enhanced due diligence or ongoing surveillance only when faced with a high-risk situation and suspicion of money laundering.[306]

One of the central privacy concerns revolves around the indiscriminate retention of IP addresses (as recommended by the FATF for virtual asset service providers). However, as established, the IP addresses, as well as the civil identity of individuals, can be retained indiscriminately.[307] IP addresses can serve as a valuable tool to determine whether a transaction is high risk or not, resulting in a more targeted surveillance of individuals. Transactions to or from specific third countries are automatically deemed high risk without the need for further assessment.[308] Therefore, implementing ongoing surveillance for specific transactions based on location can meet the criteria for targeted data retention and monitoring. However, the geographical classifier can be bypassed with the use of VPN technology.[309]

In *Digital Rights Ireland*, the Court concluded that 'the retention of all traffic data . . . applies to all means of electronic communication, the use of which is very widespread and of growing importance in people's lives' and, therefore, 'covers, in a generalised manner, all persons and all means of electronic communication as well as all traffic data without any differentiation, limitation or exception being made in the light of the objective of fighting against serious crime'.[310] Although the judgment in the above case does not fall squarely within the context of digital currencies – since it concerned the retention of communication data affecting

[304] *La Quadrature du Net*, paras 152–159.

[305] Case C-817/19 *Ligue des Droits Humains v Conseil des Ministres* ECLI:C:2022:491, para 198.

[306] Regulation (EU) 2024/1624 of the European Parliament and of the Council of 31 May 2024 on the prevention of the use of the financial system for the purposes of money laundering or terrorist financing [2024] OJ L, 2024/1624, Art 34.

[307] ibid.

[308] See eg https://eur-lex.europa.eu/legal-content/EN/TXT/?uri=CELEX:02016R1675-20231018.

[309] VPN is the technology which creates a secure and encrypted connection by obscuring the IP address.

[310] *Digital Rights Ireland*, paras 56–57.

the entire European population – the expansion of the AML regime to include a significant range of virtual asset service providers (as defined under MiCA) is substantial.[311] This development clearly signifies that CDD measures will be applicable to all users (regardless of their individual risk profiles) engaging in cryptocurrency transactions through a service provider (ie non-decentralised applications), particularly in light of the reduced threshold for such transactions.

In conclusion, even if we consider similar identifiers such as the CJEU's 'geographical factor' as a potential justification for targeted surveillance – namely the retention is specifically aimed at users of digital currencies rather than the entire population utilising the financial system –such reasoning can be misleading. This is primarily due to the fact that the vast majority of users are likely to interact with a virtual asset service provider at some point, rendering the resulting data retention and monitoring measures effectively indiscriminate.

To this end, the structure of the AML regime, particularly as it applies to digital currencies, results in a failure to meet the criterion of proportionality *stricto sensu*. Recital 76 of the AML Regulation arguably characterises the phenomenon of digital currencies as inherently high risk, thereby enabling the application of enhanced CDD measures under Article 34.[312] Additionally, the reduced threshold stipulated in Article 19(3) significantly broadens the scope of these intrusive measures, subjecting a significant number of users to extensive surveillance, which again raises concerns regarding the indiscriminate retention of data.[313]

Further compounding this issue is the lack of specificity in the legislative framework. While recital 76 calls for continuous monitoring of clearly defined categories of users, Article 26 fails to articulate these categories, effectively extending surveillance measures to users of cryptocurrencies.[314] Moreover, with respect to transactions involving self-hosted wallets, Article 40 imposes additional data collection requirements on providers, further intensifying the regulatory burden.[315]

This discussion intersects with the so-called travel rule Regulation governing information accompanying transfers of cryptocurrencies, which forms an integral component of the AML framework. Recital 38 of this Regulation confirms that the travel rule applies to all cryptocurrency transfers, eliminating the threshold of 1,000 Euros, which is applicable to traditional funds transfers.[316] In relation to self-hosted wallets, the European Banking Authority's guidelines further mandate that

[311] This is a significant development, because under the 5th AML Directive only two types of virtual asset service providers were obliged.

[312] Regulation (EU) 2024/1624 of the European Parliament and of the Council of 31 May 2024 on the prevention of the use of the financial system for the purposes of money laundering or terrorist financing [2024] OJ L, 2024/1624, recital 76 and Art 34.

[313] ibid Art 19(3).

[314] ibid Art 26.

[315] ibid Art 40.

[316] Regulation (EU) 2023/1113 of the European Parliament and of the Council of 31 May 2023 on information accompanying transfers of funds and certain crypto-assets and amending Directive (EU) 2015/849 [2023] OJ L150/1, recital 38.

virtual asset service providers collect additional information, potentially through blockchain analytics, third-party service providers, and digital identities used in messaging systems.[317]

Taken together, these provisions indicate that the AML regime adopts an unprecedented and arguably rigid stance towards cryptocurrencies. This shift is essentially a surveillance system, which fails to satisfy the principle of proportionality. It remains to consider the existence of regulatory safeguards in the AML Regulation.

5.6.2. *Procedural Safeguards*

The proportionality test involves assessing existing procedural safeguards aimed at minimising the impact of the AML measures, specifically KYC and CDD, on users' privacy and data protection rights. According to Article 77(3) of the AML Regulation, all collected data can be retained for up to five years after the termination of the business relationship with the customer or an occasional transaction.[318] After the end of the prescribed retention period, the virtual asset service provider must delete the data of the individual.[319] This restriction ensures that data is retained solely for achieving the objectives of the AML regime. Once the purpose is fulfilled, there is no longer a legal basis for continued interference. However, considering that relationships with financial institutions tend to last for decades, it indicates that virtual asset service providers will have access to users' data for a significant period of time.

This procedural safeguard is closely tied to the requirement for virtual asset service providers to adhere to the GDPR when processing customers' data.[320] As discussed in subsection 3.1., providers face challenges in complying with the GDPR due to the immutable nature of permissionless blockchains. However, it is important to remember that the blockchain itself is not a service controlled by the provider. Therefore, there is a shared responsibility between the provider and the individual in the blockchain environment. The providers must comply with the GDPR, including anonymising or deleting information under their control. This information will include blockchain-generated data such as public keys, timestamps and amounts, and off-chain data such as civil identities, IP addresses, location etc. The latter will be deleted once the retention period is over. The former will remain on the blockchain. To this end, the individuals must take steps to safeguard their privacy within the blockchain once the relationship is over. The individuals will have to use tech-

[317] European Banking Authority, 'Guidelines on information requirements in relation to transfers of funds and certain crypto-assets transfers under Regulation (EU) 2023/1113 ('Travel Rule Guidelines')' (4 July 2024) 30.

[318] Regulation (EU) 2024/1624 of the European Parliament and of the Council of 31 May 2024 on the prevention of the use of the financial system for the purposes of money laundering or terrorist financing [2024] OJ L, 2024/1624, Art 77(3).

[319] ibid.

[320] ibid Art 76.

nology to anonymise data in order to be assured that their former provider will not be able to trace them by retrieving data from the blockchain. Consequently, the obligation of virtual asset service providers to adhere to the GDPR serves as a valid procedural safeguard to minimise the impact on users.

Additionally, under the GDPR, providers are obliged to appoint a Data Protection Officer (DPO). According to Article 37 of the GDPR, the processor has to designate an officer in the case where 'the core activities . . . consist of processing operations which, by virtue of their nature, their scope and/or their purposes, require regular and systematic monitoring of data subjects on a large scale'.[321] The DPO serves as an additional layer of data protection by overseeing the provider's compliance with the GDPR during data processing.[322] This ensures that data is processed solely for AML purposes, and it will be deleted once the objective is achieved.

The risk-based approach of the AML regime stands as the most significant procedural safeguard in minimising the impact of the measures on users' fundamental rights. It allows for a focused approach to higher-risk situations, thus addressing concerns about generalised surveillance. Subsection 5.6.1. mentions that the rule-based approach, as envisaged by recital 76 of the new AML Regulation, is not legally binding because it is not embodied in a specific Article.[323] However, the recital can assist in determining the scope of the Regulation, and one may argue that the absence of risk factors tailored to digital currencies effectively results in a rule-based AML regime for these products. If the provider cannot determine the risk, then all transactions of digital currencies can be categorised as high risk.

Annex III of the AML Regulation acknowledges that a risk factor may be the potential for a product or service to promote anonymity.[324] However, the AML Regulation (or the Annex) does not make a distinction between anonymity and pseudonymity. The lack of precise risk factors for digital currencies shows the inability of the AML regime to comprehend systemic issues of blockchain technology. This can also serve as a counter-argument in favour of the risk-based approach. If we interpret the anonymity risk factor literally, then when applying CDD measures, the virtual asset service providers will be focused on situations where the user exceeds the level of pseudonymity and enters the sphere of anonymity, an example being transactions with privacy-oriented currencies (eg Monero).[325] This is a further argument that the risk-based approach of the AML regime can be considered, to a certain extent, as a procedural safeguard.

Nevertheless, as demonstrated in the analysis provided in section 5.6.1., despite the AML regime's formal commitment to a risk-based approach, the substantive

[321] GDPR, Art 37.

[322] ibid Art 38.

[323] Regulation (EU) 2024/1624 of the European Parliament and of the Council of 31 May 2024 on the prevention of the use of the financial system for the purposes of money laundering or terrorist financing [2024] OJ L, 2024/1624, recital 76.

[324] ibid, Annex III 2(b).

[325] See Chapter 1; these types of digital currencies are designed to obfuscate transaction details, IP addresses etc.

features of the newly adopted framework – particularly concerning digital currencies – indicate a shift towards a rule-based model. The reduction, and in some cases the complete removal of the *de minimis* threshold under both the AML Regulation and the travel rule Regulation, reflects a clear intent to apply indiscriminate measures, effectively amounting to blanket surveillance.

Connected with the analysis of the risk-based approach, Article 21 of the 6th AML Directive provides that FIUs shall be able to request, obtain and use information from any obliged entity, even in the absence of a prior suspicious activity report.[326] This provision substantially expands the access afforded to public authorities, enabling them to obtain information without a case-by-case assessment or a concrete suspicion of money laundering. Such broad access inevitably increases the risk of undue interference with users' fundamental rights. Accordingly, this research concludes that the proportionality test is not satisfied, and therefore that the interference cannot be regarded as justified.

Conclusion

The analysis engages with an area that remains largely unexplored, namely the interaction between privacy and data protection rights and the expanding nature of AML obligations in the context of blockchain technology. By applying existing jurisprudence to this novel technological and regulatory environment, it advances an original perspective on how existing legal standards operate and reveal their limitations within the digital currency economy.

The final chapter has undertaken a comprehensive assessment of the right to privacy and data protection within the dynamic landscape of blockchain technology. The impact of surveillance on the right to privacy and data protection has been a longstanding subject of scrutiny. However, the intersection of privatised surveillance and blockchain technology constitutes a relatively nascent area of inquiry. The challenge lies in the scarcity of specific cases pertaining to the realm of digital currencies, necessitating the derivation of insights and conclusions from existing jurisprudence of the ECtHR and CJEU. Analysis of the GDPR at the beginning of the chapter serves as an overview of the standards that virtual asset service providers need to follow during the retention and processing of personal data. Based on the rights and principles of the GDPR, the relationship between data protection and blockchain technology is inherently flawed. The pseudonymised data falls within the GDPR's scope, although the data is destined to stay on the blockchain due to the blockchain's immutable nature. Therefore, at the stage of the retention

[326] Directive (EU) 2024/1640 of the European Parliament and of the Council of 31 May 2024 on the mechanisms to be put in place by Member States for the prevention of the use of the financial system for the purposes of money laundering or terrorist financing, amending Directive(EU) 2019/1937, and amending and repealing Directive (EU) 2015/849 [2024] OJ L, 2024/1640, Art 21.

of the data by the virtual asset service providers, there is an interference with the right to privacy and data protection.

Drawing from the jurisprudence of both the ECtHR and CJEU, this research applies analogical reasoning to arrive at certain conclusions. First, the virtual asset service providers must collect only relevant (to the objective) personal data and retain such data for as long as is strictly necessary.[327] Nevertheless, the AML regime does not specify what the relevant information is in the blockchain. As analysed before, the fact that blockchain pseudonymises data leads virtual asset service providers to proactively search for data outside the client–provider relationship in order to achieve the objective.

Central to the argument is the determination of whether the generalised and indiscriminate retention of personal data, akin to privatised surveillance, can be justified for the purposes of money laundering. The adoption of a rule-based approach in the AML Regulation initially implies that the measures may not be justified. However, the crux of the matter lies in discerning whether the retention is targeted, irrespective of the rule-based paradigm applied to digital currencies. A fundamental distinction exists between communication data and financial data. In scenarios involving communication surveillance, both the sender and receiver of an electronic message are subject to scrutiny. In contrast, financial institutions typically gather information solely from the client, with financial data predominantly centred around the individual. While the CJEU has not provided a definitive benchmark for quantifying whether the retention is indeed targeted through analogical reasoning from jurisprudential precedents, this research ultimately concludes that the interference with fundamental rights cannot be deemed justified. Essentially, the argument rests on the observation that, despite the AML regime's stated reliance on the well-established risk-based approach, the core structure of the newly adopted framework, particularly as it pertains to digital currencies, demonstrates a marked shift toward a surveillance-oriented model, as it imposes intrusive measures that are indiscriminately applicable to all users of digital currencies, regardless of individual risk.

It is evident that the new AML regime embodies conflicting objectives, as it functions not only as an instrument of crime prevention but also as a motor for the regulation of the digital currency market. The use of criminal law to pursue such dual aims renders the proportionality assessment particularly complex. Nevertheless, a more proportionate application of the AML framework to digital currencies could be achieved through supervisory and standard-setting functions of the newly established anti-money laundering authority (AMLA). Under Articles 5 and 12 of the AMLA Regulation, AMLA is empowered to publish analyses, develop risk benchmarks, and promote convergence of supervisory practices across the Union.[328] These functions could serve as *ex post* safeguards by ensuring

[327] *S and Marper v United Kingdom*, App nos 30562/04 and 30566/04 (ECtHR, 4 December 2008).

[328] Regulation (EU) 2024/1620 of the European Parliament and of the Council of 31 May 2024 establishing the Authority for Anti-Money Laundering and Countering the Financing of Terrorism and amending Regulations (EU) No 1093/2012, (EU) No 1094/2010 and (EU) No 1095/2010 [2024] OJ L, 2024/1620, Arts 5 and 12.

that obliged entities, including virtual asset service providers, collect and retain only data strictly necessary to address objectively defined money laundering risks. In particular, the periodic review of risk factors, which would be tailored for the digital currency economy, under Article 12(8), could guide authorities and providers in calibrating due diligence obligations, thereby reducing reliance on broad or indiscriminate data-gathering practices.[329] Such guidance within the AML supervisory cycle, coupled with clearly defined data categories and risk factors in the AML Regulation, would enhance proportionality in practice, ensuring that AML objectives are pursued without unjustified interference with the right to privacy and data protection.

[329] ibid Art 12(8).

Conclusion

The scenarios introduced at the beginning of this book were not rhetorical flourishes but signposts of a broader structural tension within the anti-money laundering (AML) framework of the European Union (EU), namely the augmented financial surveillance imposed on users of digital currencies. The analysis undertaken in this book demonstrates that digital currencies and blockchain technology have not merely created new regulatory challenges; they have reshaped the very terrain on which EU law must operate. The transformation of AML obligations into mechanisms of privatised surveillance, further intensified under the new AML Regulation, exposes deep structural tensions within the EU's regulatory framework.[1] It is precisely at the intersection of technological innovation and increasingly intrusive regulatory design that the balance between AML objectives and the protection of fundamental rights is tested. This book situates itself within this emerging technology and evolving regulatory landscape in order to answer the central question of whether the transplantation of the AML regime to digital currencies is compatible with the fundamental rights to privacy and data protection as enshrined in Articles 7 and 8 of the Charter of Fundamental Rights of the EU.[2] The findings underscore the challenges raised by the EU's legislative choice to utilise a criminal law instrument, ie the AML Regulation, as a tool to regulate the digital currency economy.

In this book, I have argued that the interference with the rights to privacy and data protection is unjustified when balanced against the objectives of the AML regime. To reach this conclusion, I examined the EU's policy choices on digital currencies during the negotiations and adoption of the 5th AML Directive, which remains in force at the time of writing, as well as those reflected in the new AML Regulation.[3] To mitigate the risks associated with digital currencies, the EU initially opted to incorporate them into the AML regime. However, with the recent adoption of the Markets in Crypto-Assets Regulation (MiCA) and the proposal for

[1] Regulation (EU) 2024/1624 of the European Parliament and of the Council of 31 May 2024 on the prevention of the use of the financial system for the purposes of money laundering or terrorist financing [2024] OJ L, 2024/1624.

[2] Charter of Fundamental Rights of the European Union (2012) C326/391, Arts 7 and 8.

[3] Directive (EU) 2018/843 of the European Parliament and of the Council of 30 May 2018 amending Directive (EU) 2015/849 on the prevention of the use of the financial system for the purposes of money laundering or terrorist financing, and amending Directive 2009/138/EC and 2013/36/EU [2018] OJ L156/43.

the Digital Euro, the EU is now pursuing a more comprehensive approach towards digital currencies.[4]

Understanding how the AML framework evolved helps explain why the initial regulatory strategy proved insufficient. The decision to include in the 5th AML Directive only two categories of entities, namely exchangers between fiat currencies and cryptocurrencies, on the one hand, and custodial wallet providers, on the other, left the vast majority of the digital currency system unregulated. Given the decentralised structure of these technologies, users are not compelled to rely on such providers, and even where they do, significant portions of their activity remain outside the scope of the Directive. This approach changed in the new AML Regulation, which, together with MiCA, substantially expands the list of obliged entities involved in the cryptocurrency system.

A similar regulatory gap arises in relation to in-game currencies. The 5th AML Directive expressly excludes them from its scope, yet, as discussed in Chapter 4, this book argues that it is difficult to justify the Directive's decision to regulate exchanges between fiat currencies and digital currencies while simultaneously excluding in-game currencies, particularly given the existence of online games that provide functionally analogous services. The new AML Regulation maintains this approach by defining its scope strictly in relation to cryptocurrencies and distributed ledger technology, thereby continuing to exclude in-game currencies that fall outside this category.

The most concerning issue in the 5th AML Directive, also replicated in the new AML Regulation, is the departure from the risk-based approach. According to recital 24 of the Directive (and the subsequent recital 76 of the AML Regulation), the higher risks associated with certain intermediary structures make it impossible, in the EU's view, for a risk-based approach to ensure timely detection and assessment of risks.[5] As a result, customers must be monitored constantly.[6] Therefore, I have argued that the AML regime shifts to a more rule-based approach targeting the totality of customers. By emphasising the need for rapid detection, the recitals implicitly capture the defining features of digital currencies – pseudonymity and decentralisation – which the regime treats as inherently increasing the likelihood of money laundering activities. Consequently, digital currencies are treated as a high-risk phenomenon, requiring more intrusive measures in the form of enhanced due diligence by providers.

[4] Regulation (EU) 2023/1114 of the European Parliament and of the Council of 31 May 2023 on markets in crypto-assets, and amending Regulations (EU) No 1093/2010 and (EU) No 1095/2010 and Directives 2013/36/EU and (EU) 2019/1937 OJ L150/40; Commission, 'Proposal for a Regulation of the European Parliament and of the Council on the establishment of the digital euro' COM(2023) 369 final.

[5] Directive (EU) 2018/843 of the European Parliament and of the Council of 30 May 2018 amending Directive (EU) 2015/849 on the prevention of the use of the financial system for the purposes of money laundering or terrorist financing, and amending Directive 2009/138/EC and 2013/36/EU [2018] OJ L156/43, recital 24; Regulation (EU) 2024/1624 of the European Parliament and of the Council of 31 May 2024 on the prevention of the use of the financial system for the purposes of money laundering or terrorist financing [2024] OJ L, 2024/1624, recital 76.

[6] ibid.

Both the 5th AML Directive and the new AML Regulation operate on the assumption that virtual asset service providers are capable of assessing risk and collecting customer information in the same manner as banks and other traditional obliged entities. In practice, the compliance burden on virtual asset service providers is substantially greater. To meet the AML obligation, these providers are, in fact, required to collect substantially more information (including IP addresses, device identifiers, geo-location data). To this end, I have argued that such a burden of deep blockchain analysis exceeds the essence of preventive measures and creates various concerns about the privacy of users of digital currencies. While these concerns relate directly to the impact of the AML regime on users of digital currencies, the book shows that the deeper problem lies in the inability of virtual asset service providers to mitigate risks within the parameters of the existing risk-based approach.

It is precisely this structural mismatch – the imposition of banking-style obligations on actors who lack banking-style capabilities – that provides the bridge to the book's broader comparative inquiry. To illustrate how these obligations evolved and how similar tensions were navigated in an earlier context, the book juxtaposes two regulatory moments that have remained largely unexplored in combination, namely the treatment of virtual asset service providers under the 5th AML Directive and the subsequent AML Regulation, and the inclusion of banks in the very 1st AML Directive. By analysing these developments side by side, the book evaluates for the first time how the principle of confidentiality operated in each era and how providers in both sectors responded to the introduction of AML obligations. Beginning with the principle of confidentiality in the bank–customer relationship, Chapter 5 highlighted the challenges faced by the EU during the early stages of the AML regime. As a case study, the bank secrecy regime of Austria was examined to exemplify the hurdles faced, given Austria's fierce stance on client anonymity, based on the principle of confidentiality and under the protection of strict bank secrecy rules. As Barbot argued, 'The secrecy provisions of Austrian . . . laws, as of 1991, continued to be a barrier which served to shelter and protect money launderers from detection.'[7] This passage is significant not only for understanding the Austrian case but also because its reasoning translates directly into the context of digital currencies. In the EU's AML regime, anonymity is regulated on the assumption that financial activity is handled by centralised, identifiable intermediaries – such as banks or, more recently, virtual asset service providers – whose position in the system allows the law to impose uniform, harmonised due diligence obligations on them. Therefore, despite the current AML regime imposing obligations on virtual asset service providers, inherent challenges persist in implementing AML measures within the blockchain environment.

A central claim of this book is that in order to comply with the EU's AML regime, virtual asset service providers are compelled to adopt increasingly intrusive

[7] Lisa A Barbot, 'Money Laundering: An International Challenge' (1995) *Tul J Int'l & Compliance L* 161, 196.

measures, which might lead to an interference with the end user's rights to privacy and data protection. The analysis concludes that, as a result of these requirements, the AML regime is gradually transforming into a system of surveillance. This book's original contribution lies in examining this transformation through the lens of privatised surveillance within blockchain-based AML compliance, whereby virtual asset service providers are required to perform investigative and monitoring functions traditionally associated with public authorities, despite operating in a decentralised, pseudonymous environment. Analysing this shift brought to light novel questions about the expanding regulatory role of private intermediaries and the implications of their actions for the fundamental rights of users.

The argument advanced here is informed by the jurisprudence of the European Court of Human Rights (ECtHR) and the Court of Justice of the European Union (CJEU). Once established that the interference with the rights to privacy and data protection (Articles 7 and 8 of the Charter) exists, the analysis applied Article 52 of the Charter to determine the justification of the identified interference. In the evaluation of the AML measures, a comprehensive examination was undertaken, drawing insights from a series of CJEU judgments related to the issue of data retention and privatised surveillance. Notably, in the *La Quadrature du Net* case, the Court ruled that only the targeted retention of data for the purposes of combating serious threats to public security and combating serious crime is permitted.[8] However, the analysis leads us to the argument that the AML Regulation is applying a rule-based approach that affects the totality of users of digital currencies.

In assessing necessity and proportionality, the book finds that the AML Regulation meets the 'provided by law' requirement – it is accessible, foreseeable and sufficiently precise, even though it does not expressly define the categories of information required for client monitoring. Moreover, the AML Regulation pursues an objective of clear public interest, namely, the protection of the financial system through the prevention, detection and investigation of money laundering and terrorist financing. Thus, the surveillance of users of digital currencies aligns with an objective of public interest.

The measures adopted under the AML framework also respect the essence of the rights to privacy and data protection. To reach this conclusion, I distinguished between two categories of personal data, namely 'core data' and 'external data'. Interference with the first category results in an infringement of the essence of the rights, but interference with the second category does not. Given the transparent and pseudonymised nature of blockchain transactions, the data generated by the technology and subsequently collected by providers falls within the category of external data.

Turning to necessity, the adopted measures must be suitable for achieving the objective in the absence of less intrusive measures. Despite challenges faced by virtual asset service providers, the argument is that the AML measures have a certain degree of effectiveness, particularly because the AML objective concerns

[8] *La Quadrature du Net and Others v Premier Ministre and Others* ECLI:EC:C:2020:791, para 141.

the mitigation, rather than the complete prevention, of money laundering risks. The final stage of the analysis centred on proportionality *stricto sensu,* where the AML Regulation proves most problematic. I have argued that the Regulation significantly expands the number of virtual asset service providers falling within its scope, with the result that CDD measures are applicable to all users engaging in cryptocurrency transactions through a provider. The lowering of applicable thresholds further brings within scope large volumes of low-value transactions that were previously outside the regime. Recital 76 intensifies this development by implicitly treating the defining features of digital currencies as inherently high risk, thereby pushing providers to systematically apply enhanced CDD under Article 34 of the AML Regulation.[9] The reduced threshold under Article 19 compounds this trend, significantly increasing the intrusiveness of the measures imposed on users.[10]

When this is read together with the 'travel rule' Regulation, which extends information-sharing obligations to all cryptocurrency transfers, without the 1,000 Euros threshold applied to traditional fund transfers, it becomes clear that user information can circulate extensively between providers, even for minor transactions. Taken cumulatively, these measures demonstrate that the new AML framework adopts an unprecedentedly rigid stance towards digital currencies. In practice, it constructs a surveillance system that captures almost all users and almost all transactions, ultimately failing to satisfy the proportionality test *stricto sensu.*

The findings of this book raise broader questions about the future of the AML regime. The implementation of AML measures within blockchain-based environments reveals that virtual asset service providers face structural and technological constraints that differ from those of traditional financial intermediaries. This invites reflection on whether the expectations placed upon virtual asset service providers under the EU's broader 'responsibilisation strategy' may, in fact, be excessive.[11] One alternative would be to shift the burden of analysis of permissionless public blockchains to specialised law enforcement agencies. Yet such an approach would require extensive training and the development of advanced technological expertise within public authorities.

In the case of in-game currencies, further investigation proves complicated due to their exclusion from the scope of the EU's AML regime. Nevertheless, the regulatory questions they raise are no less significant. Decisions on the regulation of in-game currencies should be made with careful consideration of their intended purpose. In-game currencies are designed to facilitate gameplay, and the primary purpose of games is entertainment – an environment predominantly populated by children and teenagers. Introducing a criminal law instrument into such a space

[9] Regulation (EU) 2024/1624 of the European Parliament and of the Council of 31 May 2024 on the prevention of the use of the financial system for the purposes of money laundering or terrorist financing [2024] OJ L, 2024/1624, recital 76 and Art 34.

[10] ibid Art 19.

[11] David Garland, 'The Limits of the Sovereign State: Strategies of Crime Control in Contemporary Society' (1996) 36 *British Journal of Criminology* 445.

risks disproportionate intrusion. A more appropriate approach would be a model of internal self-regulation within gaming ecosystems, supplemented by AML obligations only where in-game activities extend into the real economy. Building on the analysis developed in this book, a platform that enables exchanges between in-game currencies and fiat currencies effectively assumes the role of a virtual asset service provider and should accordingly fall within the personal scope of the EU's AML regime.

This aligns with the book's broader criticism of the EU's reliance on a criminal law instrument to regulate the digital currency ecosystem. The recent adoption of the MiCA Regulation, together with ongoing discussions on the Digital Euro, marks a significant step toward providing legal stability for the development of digital currency systems. The EU is intensifying its efforts to regulate digital currencies comprehensively. Under these new regulations, the EU seeks to address the phenomenon of digital currencies not only through AML law but also through financial and monetary law, thereby encompassing consumer and investor protection as well as financial stability. Given that digital currencies pose structural challenges to the traditional financial system, coherence across these normative frameworks will be essential.

Nevertheless, despite the innovations introduced by the MiCA Regulation, it remains limited in scope. The Regulation does not extend to decentralised applications, particularly those operating in the domains of Decentralised Finance (DeFi) and Decentralised Autonomous Organisations (DAOs). Their inherent decentralisation makes alignment with the AML framework exceedingly difficult. What remains, therefore, is a crucial question for future scholars and policymakers alike: can financial crime truly be addressed in a world without intermediaries, or must the regulatory imagination expand to meet the decentralised realities of digital finance?

BIBLIOGRAPHY

1. International Bodies Publications

Financial Action Task Force, ' The Forty Recommendations' (1990)

___ 'The Forty Recommendations' (1996)

___ ' The Forty Recommendations' (2003)

___ 'International Standards on Combating Money Laundering and the Financing of Terrorism & Proliferation' (2012)

___ 'Combating the Abuse of Alternative Remittance Systems' (20 June 2003)

___ 'Money Laundering Using New Payment Methods' (October 2010).

___ 'Virtual Currencies: Key Definitions and Potential AML/CFT Risks' (June 2014)

___ 'Guidance for a Risk-Based Approach: Virtual Currencies' (June 2015)

___ 'Guidance for a risk-based approach: Virtual Assets and Virtual Asset Service Providers' (June 2019)

___ 'Targeted Update on Implementation of the FATF Standards on Virtual Asset and Virtual Asset Service Providers' (June 2020)

___ 'Virtual Assets: Red Flag Indicators of Money Laundering and Terrorist Financing' (September 2020)

___ 'Second 12-Month Review of the Revised FATF Standards on Virtual Assets and Virtual Asset Service Providers' (July 2021)

____ 'Updated Guidance for a Risk-Based Approach: Virtual Assets and Virtual Asset Service Providers' (October 2021)

___ 'Report 1990' (1990)

___ 'Annual Report 1991-1992' (June 1992)

___ 'Annual Report 1997-1998' (June 1998)

___ 'FATF Cracks down on Terrorist Financing' (31 October 2001)

United Nations Office on Drugs and Crime (UNDOC) 'Estimating Illicit Financial Flows Resulting from Frug Trafficking and Transnational Organized Crimes' Research report (October 2011) UNDOC 9 <https://www.unodc.org/documents/data-and-analysis/Studies/Illicit_financial_flows_2011_web.pdf>

United Nations, 'The Impact of Organized Criminal Activities Upon Society at Large: Report of the Secretary General' UN Doc. E/CN.15/1993/3 (11 January 1993)

United Nations, 'Universal Declaration of Human Rights (UDHR)' (1948) <https://www.un.org/en/about-us/universal-declaration-of-human-rights>

United Nations, 'International Covenant on Civil and Political Rights (ICCPR)' (1966) <https://www.ohchr.org/en/professionalinterest/pages/ccpr.aspx>

Basel Committee On Banking Regulations and Supervisory Practices, 'Prevention of criminal use of the banking system for the purpose of money laundering' (1988) <www.bis.org/publ/bcbsc137.pdf>

International Institute for the Unification of Private Law (UNIDROIT), 'Principles on Digital Assets and Private Law' (April 2023)

2. National Publications

UK

Banking Services: Law and Practice Report by the Review Committee, chairman: Professor RB Jack CBE (1989) CM 622

Czech Republic

The Senate of the Parliament of the Czech Republic, '38th Resolution of the Senate on anti-money laundering package' (30 November 2016)

3. Books

Alldridge P, *Money Laundering Law: Forfeiture, Confiscation, Civil Recovery, Criminal Laundering and Taxation of the Proceeds of Crime* (Oxford, Hart 2003)

___ *What Went Wrong With Money Laundering Law?* (Palgrave 2015)

Anglim C, *Privacy Rights in the Digital Era* (Grey House Publishing 2016)

Arora A, *Cases and Materials in Banking Law* (Pitman Publishing 1993)

Arora A, *Banking Law* (Pearson 2014)

Arslanian H, *The Book of Crypto: The Complete Guide of Understanding Bitcoin, Cryptocurrencies and Digital Assets* (Palgrave Macmillan 2022)

Arslanian H and Fischer F, *The Future of Finance: The Impact of FinTech, AI and Crypto on Financial Services* (Palgrave Macmillan 2019)

Avguleas E and Marjosola H, *Digital Finance in Europe: Law, Regulation and Governance* (De Gruyter 2022)

Benson K, King C and Walker C, *Assets, Crimes and the State: Innovation in the 21st Century Legal Responses* (Routledge 2020)

Bernasconi P, *Blanchiment d' Argent et Secret Bancaire Money Laundering and Banking Secrecy* (Kluwer Law International, the Hague, London, Boston 1996)

Blair W, Brent R and Grant T, *Banks and the Financial Crime: The International Law of Tainted Money* (2nd ed, Oxford University Press 2008)

Boister N and Currie J. R, *Routledge Handbook on Transnational Criminal Law* (Routledge 2014)

Bosworth-Davies R and Saltmarsh G, *Money Laundering: A practical guide to the new legislation* (Chapman & Hall 1994)

Bowling B and Sheptycki J, Global Policing (Sage Publications 2012)

Breckenridge C. A, *The Right to Privacy* (University of Nebraska 1970)

Brummer C, *Cryptoassets: Legal, Regulatory and Monetary Perspectives* (Oxford University Press 2019)

Campbell D, *International Bank Secrecy* (Sweet and Maxwell, London, 1992)

Castronova E, *Synthetic Worlds: The Business and Culture of Online Games* (The University of Chicago Press 2005)

Chambost E, *Bank Accounts: A World Guide to Confidentiality* (Wiley 1983)

Chaum D, Rivest L. R and Sherman T. A, *Advances in Cryptology: Proceedings of Crypto 82* (Springer 1983)

Claes E, Duff A and Gutwirth S, *Privacy and the Criminal law* (Intersentia 2016)

Clarke L, *Confidentiality and the Law* (Lloyd's of London Press Ltd., London, New York, Hamburg, Hong Kong, 1990)

Cornelius K and Hermann D, *Virtual Worlds and Criminality* (Springer 2011)

Cox D, *Handbook of Anti-Money Laundering* (Wiley 2014)

Cranston R, *European Banking Law: The Banker-Customer Relationship* (Lloyd's of London Press Ltd., London, New York, Hamburg, Hong Kong 1993)

___ *European Banking Law: The Banker-Customer Relationship* (2nd ed, Rutledge 1999)

Davies G, *A History of Money* (4th edn, University of Wales Press 2016)

De Filippi P and Wright A, *Blockchain and the Law: The Rule of Code* (Harvard University Press 2018)

Delany H and Carolan E, *The Right to Privacy – A Doctrinal and Comparative Analysis* (2nd ed, MIT Press 2006)

Demetis S. D, *Technology and Anti-Money Laundering: A systems Theory and Risk-based Approach* (Edward Elgar 2010)

Dewatripont M and Tirole J, *The Prudential Regulation of Banks* (The MIT Press 1994)

DiBiasio J, *Cowries to Crypto: The History of Money, Currency and Wealth* (OANDA 2020)

Dostas M, *General Bank Confidentiality and Confidentiality of Deposits* (in Greek), (Sakkoulas 2000)

Edwards A and Gill P, *Transnational Organised Crime: Perspectives on Global Security* (Routledge 2003)

Einzig P, *Primitive Money: In its ethnological, Historical and Economic Aspects* (2nd edn, Pergamon Press 1966)

Ellinger E, Lomnicka E and Hooley R, *Modern Banking Law* (3rd ed, Clarendon Press Oxford 2002)

Ellinger E, Lomnicka E and Hare C, *Ellinger's Modern Banking Law* (5th ed, Oxford University Press 2011)
Evans M and Koutrakos P, *Beyond the Established Legal Orders: Policy Interconnections Between the EU and the Rest of the World* (Bloomsbury Publishing 2011)
Fox D and Green S, *Cryptocurrencies in Public and Private Law* (Oxford University Press 2019)
Fuster G. G, *The Emergence of Personal Data Protection as a Fundamental Right of the EU* (Springer Law, Governance and Technology Series 16 2014)
Gilmore C. W, *International Efforts to Combat Money Laundering* (Cambridge University Press 1992)
___ *Dirty Money: The evolution of money laundering counter-measures* (Council of Europe Press 1995)
___ *Dirty Money: The Evolution of Money Laundering Counter-Measures* (2nd edition, Council of Europe Publishing 1999)
___*Dirty Money: The Evolution of International Measures to Counter Money Laundering and the Financing of Terrorism* (3rd ed, Council of Europe publishing 2004)
Gleeson S, *The Legal Concept of Money* (Oxford University Press 2018)
Gutwirth S, Leenes R and De Hert P, *Reloading Data Protection* (Springer 2013)
Gutwirth S and others, *Reinventing Data Protection* (Springer 2009)
Gutwirth S and others, *European Data Protection: Coming of Age* (Springer 2013)
Harrison K and Ryder N, *The Law Relating to Financial Crime in the United Kingdom* (2nd edn, Routledge 2017)
Hopton D, *Money laundering: a concise guide for all business* (Gower Publishing Ltd. 2009)
King C, Walker C and Gurulé J, *The Palgrave Handbook of Criminal and Terrorism Financing Law* (Vol 1, Palgrave Macmillan 2018)
Lee D, *Handbook of digital currency: bitcoin, innovation, financial instruments and big data* (Elsevier/ AP 2015)
Lemieux L. V, *Searching for Trust: Blockchain Technology in an Age of Disinformation* (Cambridge University Press 2022)
Leslie D, *Legal Principles for Combatting Cyberlaundering* (Springer 2014)
Lexis® PSL TMT Team (eds), *An Introduction to Technology Law* (LexisNexis 2018)
Liaw T, *The Routledge Handbook of Fintech* (Routledge: Taylor & Francis Group 2021)
Ligeti K and Simonato M, *Chasing Criminal Money: Challenges and Perspectives on Asset Recovery in the EU* (Hart Publishing 2017)
Lipson A and Brain R, *Computer and Video Game Law: cases, statutes, forms, problems & materials* (Carolina Academic Press 2009)
Lyon David, *Surveillance Society: Monitoring Everyday Life* (Open University Press 2005)
MacQueen L. H, *Money Laundering Hume Papers on Public Policy* (vol 1(2), Edinburgh University Press 1993)
Madinger J, *Money Laundering: A Guide for Criminal Investigators* (3rd edn, CRC Press Taylor & Francis Group 2012)
Manciandaro D and others, *Black Finance: The Economics of Money Laundering* (Edward Elgar Publishing 2007)
McCarthy J. K, *The Money Laundering Market: Regulating the Criminal Economy* (Agenda Publishing 2018)
Miller A, *The Assault on Privacy: Computers, Data Banks and Dossiers* (University of Michigan Press 1971)
Mitsilegas V, *Money Laundering Counter-Measures in the European Union: A New Paradigm of Security Governance Versus Fundamental Legal Principles* (Kluwer Law International 2003)
___ *The Criminalisation of Migration in Europe: Challenges for Human Rights and the Rule of Law* (Springer 2015)
Mitsilegas V, Hufnagel S and Moiseienko A, *Research Handbook on Transnational Crime* (Edward Elgar Publishing 2019)
Mügge D, *Europe and the Governance of Global Finance* (Oxford University Press 2014)
Narayanan and others, *Bitcoin and cryptocurrency technologies: a comprehensive introduction* (Princeton University Press 2016)

Nishibe M, *The Enigma of Money: Gold, Central Banknotes, and Bitcoin* (Springer 2016)
Norton J. J, *Banks: Fraud and Crime* (LLOYD'S of London Press LTD 1994)
Pompella M and Matousek R, *The Palgrave Handbook of FinTech and Blockchain* (Palgrave Macmillan 2021)
Proctor C, *Mann of the Legal Aspect of Money* (7th edn, Oxford University Press 2012)
Reuter P and Truman E, *Chasing Dirty Money: The Fight Against Money Laundering* (Institute for International Economics 2004)
Rider B and Ashe M, *Money Laundering Control* (Round Hall Sweet & Maxwell 1996)
Ridgeway W, *The Origin of Metallic Currency and Weight Standards* (Cambridge University Press 1892)
Robinson J, *The Laundrymen: Inside Money Laundering, the World's Third-Largest Business* (Pocketbooks 1995)
Russo A. C, Lastra M. R and Blair W, *Research Handbook on Law and Ethics in Banking and Finance* (Edward Elgar Publishing 2019)
Ryder N, Turksen U and Hassler S, *Fighting Financial Crime in the Global Economic Crisis* (Routledge, 2015)
Ryder N, *Financial Crime in the 21st Century: Law and Policy* (Edward Elgar 2011)
___, *Money Laundering – An Endless Cycle? A Comparative Analysis of the Anti-Money Laundering Policies in the United Kingdom, Australia and Canada* (Routledge, 2012)
Saunders A and Cornett M, *Financial Institutions Management: A Risk Management Approach* (4th ed, McGraw Hill Education 2003)
Savona U. E, *Responding to Money Laundering: International Perspectives* (Harwood academic publishers, Australia, Canada, China, France, Germany, India, Japan, Luxembourg, Malaysia, The Netherlands, Russia, Singapore, Switzerland, Thailand, United Kingdom 1997)
___*European Money Trails* (Harwood Academic Publishers 1999)
Solove D, *Understanding Privacy* (Harvard University Press 2008) 12
Stessens G, *Money Laundering: A New International Law Enforcement Model* (Cambridge University Press 2000)
Tenbrunsel A and Thomas J, *The Street, The Bull and The Crisis: A Survey of the US & UK Financial Services Industry* (University of Notre Dame and Labaton Sucharow LLP 2015)
Van Duyne C. P, Harvey H. G and Gelemerova Y. L, *The Critical Handbook of Money Laundering: Policy, Analysis and Myths* (Palgrave Macmillan 2018)
Vandezande N, *Virtual Currencies: A Legal Framework* (KU Leuven Centre for IT & IP Law Series, Intersentia 2018)
Von Bogdandy A and others, *The Exercise of Public Authority by International Institutions: Advancing International Institutional Law* (Springer Science & Business Media 2010)
Von Mises L, *The Theory of Money and Credit* (Liberty Fund Incorporated 1981)
Vavoula N, *Immigration and Privacy in the Law of the European Union: The Case of Information System* (Brill Nijhoff 2022)
Unger B and van der Linde D, *Research Handbook on Money Laundering* (Edward Elgar 2013)
Unger B, *The Scale and Impact of Money Laundering* (Edward Elgar 2007)
Wacks R, *Law, Morality and the Private Domain* (Hong Kong University Press 2000)
Walter I, *The Secret Money Market: Inside the Dark World of Tax Evasion, Financial Fraud, Insider Trading, Money Laundering, and Capital Flight* (Harper & Row Publishers 1990)
Weatherford J, *The History of Money* (Crown Publishers 1997)
Westin A, *Privacy and Freedom* (Antheneum 1967)
Zurn M, Nolkaemper A, and Peerenboom R, *Rule of Law Dynamics: In an Era of International and Transnational Governance* (Cambridge University Press 2012)

4. Articles, Chapters in Collective Books and Studies

Abelson H and others, 'Keys Under Doormats: Mandating Insecurity by Requiring Government Access to All Data and Communications' (2015) 1(1) Journal of Cybersecurity 69
Abrams N, 'The New Ancillary Offenses' (1989) 1 Criminal Law Forum 1

Agarwal S, 'Bitcoin Transactions: A Bit of Financial Privacy' (2016) 35 Cardozo Arts & Ent. LJ 153
Akhigbe A and Martin D. A, 'Valuation impact of Sarbanes-Oxley: Evidence from disclosure and governance within the financial services industry' (2006) 30(3) Journal of Banking & Finance 989
Alford E. D, 'Anti-Money Laundering Regulations: A Burden on Financial Institutions' (1994) 19(3) North Carolina Journal of International Law and Commercial Regulation 437
Alldridge P, 'Money Laundering and Globalization' (2008) 35(4) Journal of Law and Society 437
Alvarez F, Argente D and Van Patten D, 'Are Cryptocurrencies Currencies? Bitcoin as Legal Tender in El Salvador' (2022) National Bureau of Economic Research Working Paper 29968, 1 < https://www.nber.org/system/files/working_papers/w29968/w29968.pdf>
Amicelle A and Favarel-Garigues G, 'Financial Surveillance: Who cares?' (2015) 5 Journal of Cultural Economy
Andrian T and Mancini-Griffoli T, 'The Rise of Digital Money' (2021) 13 Annual Review of Financial Economics 57
Athanassiou P, 'Impact of Digital Innovation on the Processing of Electronic Payments and Contracting: An Overview of Legal Risks' (2017) European Central Bank Legal Working Paper Services 16/2017
Badawi E and Jourdan V. G, 'Cryptocurrencies Emerging Threats and Defensive Mechanisms: A Systematic Literature Review' (2020) IEEE Access, 8, 200021-200037
Baity W, 'Banking on Secrecy: The Price of Unfettered Secrecy and Confidentiality in the Face of International Organised and Economic Crime' (2000) 8 Journal of Financial Crime 83
Bao Z and others, 'Lockmix: a secure and privacy-preserving mix service for Bitcoin anonymity' (2020) 19 International Journal of Information Security 311
Barbot A. L, 'Money Laundering: An International Challenge' (1995) 3 Tul J Int'l & Compliance L 161
Barendt E, 'A reasonable expectation of privacy': a coherent or redundant concept?' in Andrew Kenyon (ed) *Comparative Defamation and Privacy Law* (Cambridge University Press 2016)
Bellanova R, 'Data Protection, with Love' (2014) 8 International Political Philosophy 112
Berg A, 'The identity, fungibility and anonymity of money' (2020) 39(2) Economic Papers: A Journal of Applied economics and Policy 104
Berg S and McCarthy J. K, 'An introduction to the challenges of money laundering in Killian J. McCarthy (ed), *The Money Laundering Market: Regulating the Criminal Economy* (Agenda Publishing 2018)
Bergström M, 'The Global AML Regime and the EU AML Directives: Prevention and Control' in Colin King, Clive Walker and Jimmy Gurulé (eds.), *The Palgrave Handbook of Criminal and Terrorism Financing Law* (Vol 1, Palgrave Macmillan 2018)
___ 'The Many Uses of Anti-Money Laundering Regulation -Over Time and into the Future' (2018) 19(5) German Law Journal 1149
Berwczynska M, 'Financial Intelligence Units: Reflections on the applicable data protection legal framework' (2021) 43 Computer Law & Security Review
Bezanson P. R, 'The Right to Privacy Revisited: Privacy, News and Social Change, 1890-1990' (1992) 80(5) California Law Review 1133
Bigo D and others, 'Towards a New EU Legal Framework for Data Protection and Privacy: Challenges, Principles and the Role of the European Parliament' (2011) Study requested by the European Parliament's Committee on Civil Liberties, Justice and Home Affairs, PE 453.216
Blum A. J and others, 'Financial Havens, Banking Secrecy and Money Laundering' (1998) United Nations report ST/ODCCP(02)/F491
Blundell-Wignall A, 'The Bitcoin Question: Currency Versus Trust-less Transfer Technology' (2014) OECD Working Papers on Finance, Insurance and Private Pensions No. 37
Bonneau J and others, 'SoK: Research Perspectives and Challenges for Bitcoin and Cryptocurrencies' (2015 *IEEE Symposium on Security and Privacy*) 104
Borgesius J. Z. F, 'Singling Out People Without Knowing their Names: Behavioural Targeting, Pseudonymous Data, and the New Data Protection Regulation' (2016) 32(2) Computer Law & Security Review 256

Borlini L, 'Regulating Criminal Finance in the EU in the Light of the International Instruments' (2017) 36 Yearbook of European Law 553

Borlini L and Anema J. F, 'Money Laundering Regulation in the European Union' in Killian J. McCarthy (ed) *The Money Laundering Market: Regulating the Criminal Economy* (Agenda publishing 2018)

Borlini L and Montanaro F, 'The Evolution of the EU Law Against Criminal Finance: The 'Hardening' of FATF Standards within the EU' (2016) 48 Georgetown Journal of International Law 1009, 1017

Boyle A, 'Some Reflections on the Relationship of Treaties and Soft Law', (1999) 48 International and Comparative Law Quarterly 901

Brenig C, Accorsi R and Müller G, 'Economic Analysis of Cryptocurrency Backed Money Laundering' (2015) in *Twenty-Third European Conference on Information Systems (ECIS)*

Brito J and Castillo A, 'Bitcoin: A primer for policymakers' (2013) 29(4) Policy 3

Brkan M, 'The Concept of Fundamental Rights in the EU Legal Order: Peeling the Onion to its Core' (2018) 14(2) European Constitutional Law Review 332

Bryans D, 'Bitcoin and Money Laundering: Mining for an Effective Solution' (2014) 89 Indiana Law Journal 441

Bygrave A. L, 'Data Protection Pursuant to the Right to Privacy in Human Rights Treaties' (1998) 6(3) International Journal of Law and Information Technology 247

Bygrave A. L, 'Privacy and Data Protection in an International Perspective' (2010) 56(8) Scandinavian Studies in Law 165

Campbell-Verduyn M, 'Bitcoin, crypto-coins, and global anti-money laundering governance' (2018) 69(2) Crime, Law Social Change 283

Campmas A, 'How do European Banks portray the effect of policy interest rates and prudential behaviour on profitability?' (2020) 51 Research in International Business and Finance 51

Cassese S, 'Administrative Law without the State-the Challenge of Global Regulation' (2005) 37 NYU Journal of International Law and Politics 663

Chambers C, 'Can You Ever Regulate the Virtual World Against Economic Crime?' (2012) 7(4) Journal of International Commercial Law and Technology 339

Chaum D, 'Blind Signatures for Untraceable Payments' in David Chaum, Ronald L. Rivest and Alan T. Sherman (eds) *Advances in Cryptology: Proceedings of Crypto 82* (Springer 1983)

Clare J, 'Can You Ever Regulate the Virtual World Against Virtual Economic Crime?' (2012) 7(4) International Commercial Law and Technology 339

Cohen J and Sabel F. C, ' Global Democracy?' (2004) 37 NYU Journal of International Law and Policy 763

Contamine-Raynaud M, 'Le Secret Bancaire et le Contrôle de l'État sur les Opérations de Change et sur leurs Effets Délictueux – France' in Paolo Bernasconi (ed.), *Blanchiment d' Argent et Secret Bancaire Money Laundering and Banking Secrecy* (Kluwer Law International, the Hague, London, Boston 1996)

Covolo V, 'The EU response to criminal misuse of cryptocurrencies: the young, already outdated 5th anti-money laundering directive' (2020) 28(3) European Journal of Crime, Criminal Law and Criminal Justice 217

Crawford J and Guan Y, 'Knowing your Bitcoin Customer: Money Laundering in the Bitcoin Economy' (2020) 13th international conference on systematic approaches to digital forensic engineering (SADFE) 38

Cullen P, 'The European Community Directive' in Hector L. MacQueen *Money Laundering: Hume Papers on Public Policy* (vol 1(2), Edinburgh University Press 1993)

Custers B, Oerlemans J and Pool R, 'Laundering the Profits of Ransomware: Money Laundering Methods for Vouchers and Cryptocurrencies' (2020) 28(2) European Journal of Crime Criminal Law and Criminal Justice 121

Czarnecki J, 'Digital Currencies and the Anti-Money Laundering/Counter-Terrorism Financing Regulation in the EU: Imaginary Risk or Real Challenge?' in Katalin Ligeti and Michele Simonato (eds), *Chasing Criminal Money: Challenges and Perspectives on Asset Recovery in the EU* (Hart Publishing 2017)

Daley J. M, 'Effectiveness of United States and International Efforts to Combat International Money Laundering' [2000] St. Louis-Warsaw Transatlantic Law Journal 175

De Filippi P, Mannan M and Reijers W, ' Blockchain as a Confidence Machine: The Problem of Trust & Challenges of Governance' (2020) 62 Technology in Society 101284

De Goede M, 'The Chain of Security' (2017) 44(1) Review of International Studies 24

De Hart P and Gutwirth S, 'Data Protection in the Case Law of Strasbourg and Luxembourg: Constitutionalisation in Action' in Serge Gutwirth and others (eds.), Reinventing Data Protection (Springer 2009)

___, 'Privacy, Data Protection and Law Enforcement. Opacity of the Individual and Transparency of Power' in Erik Claes, Antony Duff and Serge Gutwirth (eds.), *Privacy and the Criminal law* (Intersentia 2016)

De Leon C. D and others, 'Blockchain: Properties and Misconceptions' (2017) 11(3) Asia Pacific Journal of Innovation and Entrepreneurship 286

Diver S. C, 'The Optimal Precision of Administrative Rules' (1983) 93 Yale Law Journal 65

Dostov V and Shust P, 'Cryptocurrencies: an unconventional challenge to the AML/CFT regulators?' (2014) 21(3) Journal of Financial Crime 249

Drage J, 'Countering Money Laundering: The Response of the Financial Sector' in Hector L. MacQueen (ed) *Money Laundering Hume Papers on Public Policy* (vol 1(2), Edinburgh University Press 1993)

Engle E, 'Is Bitcoin rat poison? Cryptocurrency, crime and counterfeiting' (2015) 16 Journal of High Technology Law 365

Finck M, 'Blockchain and the General Data Protection Regulation: Can distributed ledgers be squared with European data protection law?' (2019) Study for the European Parliamentary Research Service, PE 634.445

Finn R, Wright D and Friedenwald W, 'Seven Types of Privacy' in Serge Gutwirth and others (eds), *European Data Protection: Coming of Age* (Springer 2013)

Foley S, Karlsen J and Putniņš T, 'Sex, Drugs, and Bitcoin: How Much Illegal Activity Is Financed through Cryptocurrencies?' (2019) 32 The Review of Financial Studies 1798

Gagnon Jr. J. R, 'International Banking Secrecy: Developments in Europe Prompt New Approaches' (1990) 23(3) Vanderbilt Journal of Transnational Law 653

Garland D, 'The Limits of the Sovereign State: Strategies of Crime Control in Contemporary Society' (1996) 36 British Journal of Criminology 445

Gathii T. J, 'The Financial Action Task Force and Global Administrative Law' (2010) Journal of the Professional Lawyer 197

Gavison R, 'Privacy and the Limits of Law' (1980) 89(3) The Yale University Volume 421

Gellert R and Gutwirth S, ' The Legal Construction of Privacy and Data Protection' (2013) 29 Computer Law & Security Review 522

Gerety T, 'Redefining Privacy' (1977) 12(2) Harvard Civil Rights-Civil Liberties Law Review 233

Geva B, 'Cryptocurrencies and the Evolution of Banking, Money and Payments' in C. Brummer (ed), *Cryptoassets: Legal, Regulatory and Monetary Perspectives* (Oxford University Press 2019)

Gill M, 'Banking Confidentiality' in Linda Clarke (ed.), *Confidentiality and the Law* (Lloyd's of London Press Ltd., London, New York, Hamburg, Hong Kong, 1990)

Gill M and Taylor G, 'Preventing Money Laundering or Obstructing Business?: Financial Companies' Perspectives on 'Know Your Customer' Procedures' (2004) 44(4) British Journal of Criminology 582

Goldby M, 'Breaches of AML reporting requirements by UK bankers: Are effective enforcement choices being made by financial regulators?' in Constanza A. Russo, Rosa Maria Lastra and William Blair (eds), *Research Handbook on Law and Ethics in Banking and Finance* (Edward Elgar Publishing 2019)

Haffke L, Fromberger M and Zimmermann P, 'Virtual Currencies and Anti-Money Laundering – The Shortcomings of the 5th AML Directive (EU) and How to Address Them' (2020) 21 Journal of Banking Regulation 125

Harvey J, 'Compliance and Reporting Issues Arising for Financial Institutions from Money Laundering Regulations: A Preliminary Cost Benefit Study' (2004) 7(4) Journal of Money Laundering Control 333

Harvey J and Branco-Illodo I, 'Why Cryptocurrencies Want Privacy: A Review of Political Motivations and Branding Expressed in "Privacy Coin" Whitepapers' (2020) 19 Journal of Political Marketing 107

Himaambo L, 'Role of Banks as Private Police in the Anti-Money Laundering Crusade' (2017) 9 Bocconi Legal Papers 157

Horn N, 'Germany' in Ross Cranston (ed.), *European Banking Law: The Banker-Customer Relationship* (2nd edition, Rutledge 1999)

Houben R and Snyers A, 'Cryptocurrencies and blockchain: Legal context and implications for financial crime, money laundering and tax evasion' (2018) Study requested by the TAX3 committee of the European Parliament, PE 619.024

Hustinx P, 'EU Data Protection Law – The Review of Directive 95/46/EC and the Proposed General Data Protection Regulation' (European Union Institute's Academy of European Law, 24th Session on European Union Law 2013) <https://edps.europa.eu/sites/default/files/publication/14-09-15_article_eui_en.pdf>

Ioannides E, *Fundamental Principles of EU Law Against Money Laundering* (Ashgate Publishing 2014)

Irwin A and Slay J, 'Detecting Money Laundering and Terrorism Financing Activity in Second Life and World of Warcraft' (International Cyber Resilience Conference, Perth Western Australia, August 2010) 41

Irwin A and Turner B. A, 'Illicit Bitcoin transactions: challenges in getting to the who what, when and where' (2018) 21(3) Journal of Money Laundering Control 297

Isaac E and Posner A. R, 'An Economic Analysis of Legal Rule Making' (1974) 3 Journal of Legal Studies 257

Itzikowitz A, and others 'Nature of Money Laundering' in *Anti Money Laundering Guide* (Thomson Reuters, Sweet Maxwell 2017)

Johnson J, 'Is the Global Financial System AML/CFT Prepared?' (2008) 15 Journal of Financial Crime 7

Jones T, 'Compulsion Over Comity: The United States' Assault on Foreign Bank Secrecy' (1992) 12(3) Northwestern Journal of International Law & Business 454

Jung H, 'Germany' in Dennis Campbell (ed.), *International Bank Secrecy* (Sweet and Maxwell, London, 1992)

Karapatakis A, 'Virtual Worlds and Money Laundering under the EU Law: The Inadequacy of the Existing Legal Framework and the Challenges of Regulation' (2019) 10 New Journal European Criminal Law 128

Karasek-Wojciechowicz I, 'Reconciliation of Anti-Money Laundering Instruments and European Data Protection Requirements in Permissionless Blockchain Spaces' (2021) Journal of Cybersecurity 1-28

Kim D, Bilgin H. M and Ryu D, 'Are suspicious activity requirements for cryptocurrency exchanges effective', (2021) 7(78) Financial Innovation <https://doi.org/10.1186/s40854-021-00294-6>

Kingsbury B and Stewart R, 'Legitimacy and Accountability in Global Regulatory Governance: The Emerging Global Administrative Law and the Design and Operation of Administrative Tribunals of International Organizations' in S Flogaitis (ed), *International Administrative Tribunals in a Changing World* (Esperia Publications London 2008)

Kirk D, 'Serious Fraud – A Banker's Perspective' in Joseph J. Norton (ed), *Banks: Fraud and Crime* (LLOYD'S of London Press LTD 1994)

Klimmt C, 'Virtual Worlds as a Regulatory Challenge: A User Perspective' in Kai Cornelius and Dieter Hermann (eds), *Virtual Worlds and Criminality* (Springer 2011)

Krisch N and Kingsbury B, 'Introduction: Global Governance and Global Administrative Law in the International Legal Order' (2006) 17(1) European Journal of International Law

Krisch N, 'Global Governance as Public Authority: An Introduction' (2012) 10(4) International journal of constitutional law 976

Ladeur H. K, 'The Emergence of Global Administrative Law and Transnational Regulation' (2012) 3(3) Transnational legal theory 243

Lajoix O and Billiau M, 'France' in Dennis Campbell (ed.), *International Bank Secrecy* (Sweet and Maxwell, London, 1992)
Lastra M. R and Allen G. J, 'Virtual Currencies in the Eurosystem: Challenges Ahead' (2018) Study requested by the ECON committee of the European Parliament, PE 619.020
Lastra M. R and Sheppard J. M, 'Ethical foundations of financial law' in Constanza A. Russo, Rosa Maria Lastra and William Blair (eds), Research Handbook on Law and Ethics in Banking and Finance (Edward Elgar Publishing 2019)
Lenaerts K, 'Limits on Limitations: The Essence of Fundamental Rights in the EU' (2019) 20 German Law Journal 779
Levi M and Reuter P, 'Money Laundering' (2006) 34 Crime and Justice 289
Levi M, 'Regulating Money Laundering: The Death of Bank Secrecy in the UK' (1991) 31(2) The British Journal of Criminology 109
___ 'Evaluating the "New Policing": Attacking the money trail of organized crime' (1997) 30 Australian & New Zealand Journal of Criminology
Lytvynenko A. A, 'Data Privacy and Banking Secrecy: Topical Issues in Commonwealth, Continental Europe and International Jurisprudence' (2019) 5(3) Athens Journal of Law 303
Mabunda S, 'Cryptocurrency: The New Face of Cyber Money laundering' (2018) international conference on advances in big data, computing and data communication systems (icabcd) IEEE
Magliveras D. K, 'The European Community's Combat Against Money Laundering: Analysis and Evaluation' (1998) 5 ILSA Journal of International & Comparative Law 93
Maitland G and others, 'Linkability in Practical Electronic Cash Design' (2000) Information Security: Third International Workshop, ISW 2000 Wollongong Australia
Marjosola H, 'Security Tokens and the Future of EU Securities Law: Rethinking the Harmonisation Project' in Emilios Avguleas and Heikki Marjosola (eds), *Digital Finance in Europe: Law, Regulation and Governance* (De Gruyter 2022)
Miller Z, 'The Right Side of the Coin: State Approaches in Regulating Virtual Currencies' (2021) 45 Seton Hall Legis J 809
Millon-Cornett H. M and Tehranian H, 'Stock market reactions to the depository institutions deregulation and monetary control act of 1980' (1989) 13 Journal of Banking & Finance 81
___ 'An Examination of the Impact of the Garn-St. Germain Depository Institutions Act of 1982 on Commercial Banks and Savings and Loans' (1990) 45 The Journal of Finance 95
Minárik T and Osula M. A, 'Tor does not stink: Use and abuse of the Tor anonymity network from the perspective of the law' (2016) 32 Computer Law & Security Review 111
Mitsilegas V, 'New Forms of Transnational Policing: The Emergence of Financial Intelligence Units in the European Union in the European Union and the Challenges for Human Rights: Part 1' (1999) 3(2) Journal of Money Laundering Control 147
___ 'New Forms of Transnational Policing: The Emergence of Financial Intelligence Units in the European Union in the European Union and the Challenges for Human Rights: Part 2' (2000) 3(3) Journal of Money Laundering Control 250
___ 'Countering the Chameleon Threat of Dirty Money: "Hard" and "Soft" Law in the Emergence of a Global Regime against Money Laundering and Terrorist Finance', in Adam Edwards and Peter Gill (eds.), *Transnational Organised Crime: Perspectives on Global Security* (Routledge 2003)
___ 'The European Union and the Rest of the World: Criminal Law and Policy Interconnections' in Malcolm Evans and Panos Koutrakos (eds), *Beyond the Established Legal Orders: Policy Interconnections Between the EU and the Rest of the World* (Bloomsbury Publishing 2011)
___ 'Regional Organisations and Suppression of Transnational Crime' in Neil Boister and Robert J. Currie (eds.), *Routledge Handbook on Transnational Criminal Law* (Routledge 2014)
___ 'The Value of Privacy in an Era of Security: Embedding Constitutional Limits on Preemptive Surveillance' (2015) 8 International Political Sociology 107
___ 'Legal Responses to Transnational Crime: a Global Perspective' in Valsamis Mitsilegas, Saskia Hufnagel and Anton Moiseienko (eds) *Research Handbook on Transnational Crime* (Edward Elgar Publishing 2019).

Mitsilegas V and Gilmore B, 'The EU Legislative Framework Against Money Laundering and Terrorist Finance: A Critical Analysis in the Lights of Evolving Global Standards' (2007) 56 International and Comparative Law Quarterly 119

Mitsilegas V and Vavoula N, 'The Evolving EU Anti-Money Laundering Regime' (2016) 23(2) Maastricht Journal of European and Comparative Law 261

Mitsilegas V and others, 'Data Retention and the Future on Large-Scale Surveillance: The Evolution and Contestation of Judicial Benchmarks' (2022) European Law Journal 1-36

Moiseienko A and Izenman K, 'Gaming the System: Money Laundering Through Online Games' (2019) 39(9) Rusi Newsbrief < https://static.rusi.org/20191011_newsbrief_vol39_no9_moiseienko_and_izenman_web.pdf>

Moore A, 'Defining privacy' (2008) 39(3) Journal of Social Philosophy 411

Moreham N, 'Privacy in Common Law: A Doctrinal and Theoretical Analysis' (2005) 121 Law Quarterly Review 628

Möser M, Böhme R and Breuker D, 'An Inquiry into Money Laundering Tools in the Bitcoin Ecosystem' (2013) APWG eCrime researchers summit

Mouzakiti F, 'Cooperation between Financial Intelligence Units in the European Union: Stuck in the middle between the General Data Protection Regulation and the Police Data Protection Directive' New Journal of European Criminal Law 11(3) (2020) 351

___ 'Cooperation between financial intelligence units in the EU: Challenges for the right to privacy and data protection' in Katie Benson, Colin King and Clive Walker (eds.), *Assets, Crimes and the State: Innovation in the 21st Century Legal Responses* (Routledge 2020)

___ 'Financial Surveillance, Money Laundering and Terrorist Financing in the EU: The Case of Financial Intelligence Units' (PhD Thesis, Queen Mary University of London 2021)

Pauwelyn J, 'Informal International Lawmaking: Framing the Concept and Research Questions' in Joost Pauwelyn, Ramses Wessel, and Jan Wouters (eds.), *Informal International Lawmaking* (Oxford University Press 2012)

Pavlidis G, 'Financial information in the context of anti-money laundering: Broadening the access of law enforcement and facilitating information exchanges'(2020) 23(2) Journal of Money Laundering Control 369

Plato-Shinar R, 'Law and ethics: the bank's fiduciary duty towards retail customers' in Constanza A. Russo, Rosa Maria Lastra and William Blair (eds), *Research Handbook on Law and Ethics in Banking and Finance* (Edward Elgar Publishing 2019)

Preiss T. R, 'Privacy of Financial Information and Civil Rights Issues: The Implications for Investigating and Prosecuting International Economic Crime', (1996) 14(3) Dickinson Journal of International Law 525

Premti A, Jafarinejad M and Balani H, 'The impact of the Fourth Anti-Money Laundering Directive on the valuation of EU banks' (2021) 57 Research in International Business and Finance 57

Proctor C, 'Cryptocurrencies in International and Public Law Conceptions of Money' in David Fox and Sarah Green (eds), *Cryptocurrencies in Public and Private Law* (Oxford University Press 2019)

Quintel T, 'Follow the Money, if you can: Possible solutions for enhanced FIU cooperation rules', (2019) University of Luxembourg Law Working Paper Series

___ 'Data protection rules applicable to Financial Intelligence Units: still no clarity in sight' (2022) 23 ERA Forum, Springer 53

Rajesh R, 'Bitcoin-Genesis, Opportunities, Risk and Possibilities' (2018) 7(5) Global Journal for Research Analysis

Ramahlo S. D and Matos I. N, 'What we do in the (Digital) Shadows: Anti-Money Laundering Regulation and a Bitcoin-Mixing Criminal Problem' (2021) 22(3) ERA Forum Springer Berlin Heidelberg 487

Rao Mukkamala R and Vatrapu R, 'Distributed Ledger Technologies and Blockchain for Fintech' in Liaw T(ed), *The Routledge Handbook of Fintech* (Routledge: Taylor & Francis Group 2021)

Rauchs M and others, 'Distributed Ledger Technology Systems: A Conceptual Framework' (University of Cambridge Centre for Alternative Finance August 2018)

Reid S. R, 'Virtual currency in a virtual world: Virtually unstoppable?' in Nicholas Ryder, Umut Turksen and Sabine Hassler (eds) *Fighting Financial Crime in the Global Economic Crisis* (Routledge, 2015)
Reynolds P and Irwin A, 'Tracking digital footprints: Anonymity within the bitcoin system' (2017)) 20(2) Journal of Money Laundering Control 172
Riccardi M and Levi M, 'Cash, Crime and Anti-Money Laundering' in Colin King, Clive Walker and Jimmy Gurulé (eds), *The Palgrave Handbook of Criminal and Terrorism Financing Law* (Vol 1, Palgrave Macmillan 2018)
Rodotá S, 'Data Protection as a Fundamental Right' in Serge Gutwirth and others (eds.), *Reinventing Data Protection* (Springer 2009)
Rouvroy A and Poullet Y, 'The Right to Information Self-Determination and the Value of Self-Development: Reassessing the Importance of Privacy for Democracy' in Serge Gutwirth and others (eds.), *Reinventing Data Protection* (Springer 2009)
Sandrock O and Klausing E, 'Germany', in Ross Cranston (ed.), *European Banking Law: The Banker-Customer Relationship* (Lloyd's of London Press Ltd., London, New York, Hamburg, Hong Kong 1993)
Sansonnetti R, 'Money Laundering-An International Perspective from Switzerland' in Barry Rider and Michael Ashe (eds.), *Money Laundering Control* (Round Hall Sweet & Maxwell 1996)
Sater S, 'Do We Need KYC/AML: The Bank Secrecy Act and Virtual Currency Exchanges' (2020) 73 Arkansas Law Review 397
Savona U. E, 'Mafia Money Laundering versus Italian Legislation' (1993) 1 European Journal of Criminal Policy and Research 31
Savona U. E and De Feo M, 'International Money Laundering Trends and Prevention Control Policies' in Ernesto U. Savona (ed), *Responding to Money Laundering: International Perspectives* (Harwood academic publishers, Australia, Canada, China, France, Germany, India, Japan, Luxembourg, Malaysia, The Netherlands, Russia, Singapore, Switzerland, Thailand, United Kingdom 1997)
Schuppert F. G, 'New Modes of Governance and the Rule of Law' in Michael Zurn, Andre Nolkaemper, and Randall Peerenboom (eds.) *Rule of Law Dynamics: In an Era of International and Transnational Governance* (Cambridge University Press 2012)
See R. B and others, 'Know Your Customer (KYC) Principles Relates to Bank Confidentiality as an Effort to Prevent Money Laundering Crimes' (2019) 81 Journal of law, Policy and Globalization 101
Semenzin S and Gandini A, 'Automating Trust with the Blockchain? A Critical Investigation of "Blockchain 2.0" Cultures' (2021) 2 Global Perspectives 1
Sharma Z and Zhu Y, 'Platform Development in Blockchains, Risks, and Regulation' in Maurizio Pompella and Roman Matousek (eds), *The Palgrave Handbook of FinTech and Blockchain* (Palgrave Macmillan 2021)
Sharman J, 'Privacy as Roguery: Personal Financial Information in an Age of Transparency' (2009) 87(4) Public Administration 717
Sherman T, ' International Efforts to Combat Money Laundering: The Role of Financial Action Task Force' in Hector L. MacQueen (ed) *Money Laundering Hume Papers on Public Policy* (vol 1(2), Edinburgh University Press 1993)
Silva G. P, 'Recent developments in EU legislation on anti-money laundering and terrorist financing' (2019) 10 New Journal of European Criminal Law 57
Simonova A, 'Identity Protection or Not for Employees Reporting Money Laundering? The UK Case' (2011) 8 Macquarie Journal of Business Law 300
Smith W. G, 'Competition in the European Financial Services Industry: The Free Movement of Capital Versus the Regulation of Money Laundering' (1992) 13 University of Pennsylvania Journal of International Business Law 101
Soana G, 'Regulating cryptocurrencies checkpoints: Fighting a trench war with cavalry?' (2022) 51 Economic Notes: Review of Banking Finance and Monetary Economics, <https://doi.org/10.1111/ecno.12195>

Solove D, 'A Taxonomy of Privacy' (2006) 154 University of Pennsylvania Law Review 477

Stessens G, 'The FATF 'Black List' of Non-Cooperative Countries or Territories' (2001) 14 Leiden Journal of International Law 199

Tajan S. C. J, 'Emerging from Secrecy Space: Bank Secrecy to Financial Transparency' (2010) 55 Ateneo Law Journal 447

Teichmann J. M. F, 'Financing terrorism through cryptocurrencies – a danger for Europe?' (2018) 21(4) Journal of Money Laundering Control 513

Teomete Yalabik F and Yalabik I, 'Anonymous Bitcoin v enforcement law' (2019) 33 International Review of Law, Computer & Technology 34

Tilbury M, 'Privacy: common law or human right?' in Witzleb N, Lindsay D, Paterson M and Rodrick S (eds), *Emerging Challenges in Privacy Law* (Cambridge University Press 2014)

Tsingou E, 'Global Governance and Transnational Financial Crime: Opportunities and Tensions in the Global Anti-Money Laundering Regime' (2005) CSGR Working Paper No 161/05

___ 'Money Laundering' in Daniel Mügge *Europe and the Governance of Global Finance* (Oxford University Press 2014)

Van Koningsveld J, 'Money Laundering – 'You don't see it, until you understand it': rethinking the stages of the money laundering process to make enforcement more effective' in Brigitte Unger and Daan van der Linde (eds) *Research Handbook on Money Laundering* (Edward Elgar 2013)

Vandezande N, 'Virtual currencies under EU anti-money laundering law' 33 Computer law & security review 341

Verbeek A and Lundqvist M, 'Artificial intelligence, blockchain and the future of Europe: How disruptive technologies create opportunities for a green and digital economy' (2021) Report for DG Connect of the European Commission

Vervaele A.E. J, 'Surveillance and Criminal Investigation: Blurring of Thresholds and Boundaries in the Criminal Justice System?', in Serge Gutwirth, Ronald Leenes and Paul De Hert (eds.), *Reloading Data Protection* (Springer 2013)

Von Bogdandy A, Dann P and Goldmann M, 'Developing the Publicness of Public International Law: Towards a Legal Framework for Global Governance Activities' (2008) 9(11) German Law Journal 1375

Unger B 'Money Laundering Regulation: From Al Capone to Al Qaeda', in Brigitte Unger and Daan van der Linde (eds), *Research Handbook on Money Laundering* (Edward Elgar 2013)

Unger B and van Waarden F, 'How to dodge drowning in data? Rule- and Risk – Based Anti-Money Laundering Policies Compared' in Brigitte Unger and Daan van der Linde (eds) *Research Handbook on Money Laundering* (Edward Elgar 2013)

Vandezande N, 'Virtual currencies under EU anti-money laundering law' (2017) 33(3) Computer Law & Security Review 341

Walch A, 'The Path of the Blockchain Lexicon (and the Law)' 36 Review of Banking and Financial Law 713

Walker J, 'Estimates of the extent of money laundering in and through Australia' (1995) study for the Australian Transaction Reports and Analysis Centre, Queanbeyan: John Walker Consulting Services

___ 'How Big is Global Money Laundering, (1999) 3(1) Journal of Money Laundering Control 25

___ 'Money Laundering: Quantifying International Patterns' (2000) 2(6) Australian Social Monitor 139

Walker J and Unger B, 'Measuring Global Money Laundering: "The Walker Gravity Model"' (2009) 5(2) Review of Law & Economics 821

___ 'Measuring global money laundering: the 'Walker Gravity Model" in Brigitte Unger and Daan van der Linde (eds) *Research Handbook on Money Laundering* (Edward Elgar 2013)

Warren S and Brandeis L, 'The Right to Privacy' (1890) 14(5) Harvard Law Review 193

Whitman Q. J, 'The Two Western Cultures of Privacy: Dignity Versus Liberty' (2004) 113 The Yale Law Journal 1153

Zagaris B and Kingma E, 'Asset Forfeiture International and Foreign Law: An Emerging Regime' (1991) 5 Emory International Law Review 445

Zagaris B and Castilla M. S, 'Constructing an International Financial Enforcement Subregime: The Implementation of Anti-Money-Laundering Policy' (1993) 19 Brook J Int'l L 871
Zagaris B, 'Austria Will Restrict Bank Secrecy Laws on Securities, But Not Savings Accounts', (1996) 12(3) International Enforcement Law Reporter 88

5. Online Sources

Acheson N, 'Opinion, Crypto Long & Short: No, Bitcoin was not a Response to the Financial Crisis' (CoinDesk, 14 September 2021)<https://www.coindesk.com/markets/2021/01/24/crypto-long-short-no-bitcoin-was-not-a-response-to-the-financial-crisis/>
Adams S, 'Online Communities Face Money-Laundering' (The Telegraph, May 2007) <http://www.telegraph.co.uk/news/uknews/1551482/Online-communities-face-money-laundering.html>
Allen M, 'Austria Escapes Censure by Ending Secret Accounts', (The Wall Street Journal, 16 June 2000) <https://www.wsj.com/articles/SB961106000784088177>
Anderson N, 'eBay bans the auction of in-games items' (arstechnica, 30 January 2007) <https://arstechnica.com/gaming/2007/01/8731/>
Antonopoulos A, 'Bitcoin security model: trust by computation' (Radar, 20 February 2014) < http://radar.oreilly.com/2014/02/bitcoin-security-model-trust-by-computation.html#:~:text=By%20contrast%2C%20bitcoin%20implements%20a,solving%20a%20computationally%20difficult%20problem.>
Asmundson I and Oner C, 'Back to Basics: What is Money?' (International Monetary Fund, September 2012) <https://www.imf.org/external/pubs/ft/fandd/2012/09/basics.htm>
Back A, 'A Partial Hash Collision Based Postage Scheme' (1997) <http://hashcash.org/papers/announce.txt>
Baer K and others, 'Crypto Poses Significant Tax Problems – and They Could Get Worse: Tax systems need updating to cope with crypto assets, whose anonymity and decentralized nature poses challenges – not least for the value added tax' (IMF Blog, 5 July 2023) <https://www.imf.org/en/Blogs/Articles/2023/07/05/crypto-poses-significant-tax-problems-and-they-could-get-worse>
Banton C, 'Bitcoin Whale' (Investopedia, 22 July 2021) <https://www.investopedia.com/terms/b/bitcoin-whale.asp>
Barlow P. J, 'A Declaration of the Independence of Cyberspace' (Electronic Frontier Foundation 1996) <https://www.eff.org/cyberspace-independence>
Camdessus M, 'Money Laundering: the Importance of International Countermeasures' (International Monetary Fund, 10 February 1998) <https://www.imf.org/en/News/Articles/2015/09/28/04/53/sp021098>
Carlisle D, 'Virtual Currencies and Financial Crime: Challenges and Opportunities' (Royal United Services Institute for Defence and Security Studies, 27 March 2017) <https://rusi.org/explore-our-research/publications/occasional-papers/virtual-currencies-and-financial-crime-challenges-and-opportunities>
Clark A, 'AIG's $61.7bn crash sends markets plunging' (The Guardian, 3 March 2009) < https://www.theguardian.com/business/2009/mar/02/aig-insurance-loss>
Clarke R, 'Introduction to Dataveillance and Information Privacy and Definitions of Terms' (Roger Clarke's Web-site, 15 August 1997) <http://www.rogerclarke.com/DV/Intro.html>
___ 'What's 'Privacy'?' (Roger Clarke's Web-Site, 7 August 2006) <https://www.rogerclarke.com/DV/Privacy.html>
Cuen L, 'US DOJ Calls Bitcoin Mixing 'a Crime' in Arrest of Software Developer' (CoinDesk, 13 February 2020) <https://www.coindesk.com/podcasts/coindesk-podcast-network/interview-us-doj-calls-bitcoin-mixing-a-crime-in-arrest-of-software-developer>
Cuthbertson A, 'How children playing Fortnite are helping to fuel organised crime' (The Independent, 13 January 2019) <https://www.independent.co.uk/news/fortnite-v-bucks-discount-price-money-dark-web-money-laundering-crime-a8717941.html>
Dai W, 'B-money' (1988) < http://www.weidai.com/bmoney.txt>;

De Paoli L and Hill J, 'The Last of Lehman Brothers' (Bloomberg UK, 18 May 2022) < https://www.bloomberg.com/features/2022-lehman-brothers-collapse-plan-repay-after-bankruptcy/?leadSource=uverify%20wall>

Duarte F, 'How many Cryptocurrencies are there in 2025?' (Exploding Topics, 1 April 2025) <https://explodingtopics.com/blog/number-of-cryptocurrencies>

Duffield E and Diaz D, 'Dash: A Privacy-Centric Crypto-Currency' (2015) <https://www.exodus.com/assets/docs/dash-whitepaper.pdf>

Erb P. K, 'IRS Tries Again To Make Coinbase Turn Over Customer Account Data' (Forbes, 20 March 2017) <https://www.forbes.com/sites/kellyphillipserb/2017/03/20/irs-tries-again-to-make-coinbase-turn-over-customer-account-data/?sh=214b4a60175e>

Finney H, 'RPOW - Reusable Proofs of Work' (2004) <https://cryptome.org/rpow.htm>

Frankenfield J, Rasure E and Logan M, 'Dark Wallet: What it is Concerns, Future' (Investopedia, 24 July 2024) <https://www.investopedia.com/terms/d/dark-wallet.asp>

Frankenfield J, Andrerson S and Ecker J, 'Atomic Swap: Definition, How it Works With Cryptocurrency Trade' (Investopedia, 14 August 22) <https://www.investopedia.com/terms/a/atomic-swaps.asp>

Hasbi A, 'Cryptocurrencies: Potential for Terror Financing?' (CSS ETH Zurich, 23 May 2018) <https://isnblog.ethz.ch/technology/cryptocurrencies-potential-for-terror-financing>

Hinteregger A and Haslhofer B, 'An empirical Analysis of Monero Crosschain Traceability' (2018) <https://arxiv.org/pdf/1812.02808.pdf>

Kapilkov M, 'Chainalysis: Only 1% of $1 Trillion Transacted in Crypto in 2019 was Illicit' (Cointelegraph, 5 March 2020) <https://cointelegraph.com/news/chainalysis-only-1-of-1-trillion-transacted-in-crypto-in-2019-was-illicit>

Lomas U, 'Austria Agrees to Abolish Anonymous "Passbook" Accounts', (*Wolters Kluwer: Tax-News Global Tax News*, 16 June 2000) <https://www.tax-news.com/news/Austria_Agrees_To_Abolish_Anonymous_Passbook_Accounts____552.html>

Madison T, 'Privacy Coins: How Monero, Dash, and ZCash Will Enable True Privacy' (Medium, 28 March 2019) <https://blog.goodaudience.com/privacy-coins-what-you-need-to-know-975a3460d944>

Maiberg E, 'Why Is 'Second Life' Still a Thing' (Motherboard, April 2016) <https://motherboard.vice.com/en_us/article/z43mwj/why-is-second-life-still-a-thing-gaming-virtual-reality>

Manning L, 'Dutch Authorities Shut Down Bestmixer' (Bitcoin Magazine, 22 May 2019) <https://bitcoinmagazine.com/culture/dutch-authorities-shut-down-bestmixer?utm_source=chatgpt.com'

Münzer J, 'Bitcoins: Supervisory assessment and risks to users' (BaFin: Federal Financial Supervisory Authority, 17 February 2014) < https://www.bafin.de/SharedDocs/Veroeffentlichungen/EN/Fachartikel/2014/fa_bj_1401_bitcoins_en.html>

Nakamoto S, 'Bitcoin: A Peer-to-Peer Electronic Cash System' (Bitcoin, 31 October 2008) <https://bitcoin.org/bitcoin.pdf>

Partington R, 'Digital currencies pose threat to economy, warns Bank of England' (The Guardian, 7 June 2021) < https://www.theguardian.com/business/2021/jun/07/digital-currencies-pose-threat-to-economy-warns-bank-of-england>

Perez B. Y, 'US Arms Dealer Allegedly Used Bitcoin for Purchases' (Coindesk, 12 August 2015) <https://www.coindesk.com/us-arms-trader-allegedly-used-bitcoin-for-purchases>

Picket K, 'A Brief History of Swiss Banks' (Time, 26 February 2009) <http://content.time.com/time/subscriber/article/0,33009,1881977,00.html>

Purchese R, 'World of Warcraft and the battle against black market gold' (Eurogamer.net, April 2015) <http://www.eurogamer.net/articles/2015-04-29-world-of-warcraft-and-the-battle-against-black-market-gold>

Ravelli R, 'Arrest of Alleged Bitcoin Fog Operator Signals Continued DOJ Focus on Crypto "Mixers"' (Lexology, 18 May 2021) <https://www.lexology.com/library/detail.aspx?g=b46073d7-0731-42d2-b319-270bd0c17c6e>

Reiff N and Rasure E, 'B-Money: Overview, Goals, Differences from Bitcoin' (Investopedia, 25 October 2021) <https://www.investopedia.com/terms/b/bmoney.asp>

Richet J, 'Laundering Money Online: a review of cybercriminals' methods' (2013) <arXiv:1310.2368 >

Shapiro G, 'Size Does Matter – Part 1: A Philosophy of Securities Laws for Tokenized Networks' (Medium, 26 December 2019) < https://medium.com/p/9f83b130a451> - Episode 328 (transcript available) < https://epicenter.tv/episodes/328/>

Sharma R, Rasure E and Munichiello K, 'What does the Bitcoin Blockchain Record' (Investopedia, 28 July 2024) < https://www.investopedia.com/ask/answers/063015/what-does-block-chain-record-bitcoin-exchange-transaction.asp#:~:text=In%20a%20blockchain%2C%20each%20node,history%20of%20all%20Bitcoin%20transactions.>

Szabo N, 'Bit gold' (2005) <https://unenumerated.blogspot.com/2005/12/bit-gold.html>

Wagner A, 'Digital Vs Virtual Currencies', (BITCOIN Magazine, 22 August 2014) <https://bitcoinmagazine.com/articles/digital-vs-virtual-currencies-1408735507>

Wijman T, 'The Games Market in 2022: The Year in Number' (newzoo, 21 December 2022) <https://newzoo.com/insights/articles/the-games-market-in-2022-the-year-in-numbers>

Wilson T, 'Explainer:'Privacy coin' Monero offers near total anonymity' (Reuters, 15 May 2019) <https://www.reuters.com/article/us-crypto-currencies-altcoins-explainer/explainer-privacy-coin-monero-offers-near-total-anonymity-idUSKCN1SL0F0>

Woods L, 'When is mass surveillance justified? The CJEU clarifies the law in Privacy International and other cases' (EU Law Analysis, 7 October 2020) <https://eulawanalysis.blogspot.com/2020/10/when-is-mass-surveillance-justified.html>

Žemaitis E, 'Top 5 Privacy-Oriented Crypto Wallets' (Cryptonews, 10 March 2019) <https://cryptonews.com/exclusives/top-5-privacy-oriented-crypto-wallets-3490.htm>

Developer Resource Center, 'Permissioned Blockchain' (Oracle, 18 August 2022) < https://developer.oracle.com/learn/technical-articles/permissioned-blockchain>

Barclaycard <https://home.barclaycard/about-us/>

Trend Micro Forward-Looking Threat Research (FTR) Team, 'The Cybercriminal Roots of Selling Online Gaming Currency' [2016] A TrendLabs Research Paper, <https://www.trendmicro.com/vinfo/us/security/news/cybercrime-and-digital-threats/cybercriminal-roots-selling-online-gaming-currency>

Chainalysis, 'The 2020 Crypto Crime Report: Everything you need to know about cryptocurrency-based crime' (January 2020) < https://ag-pssg-sharedservices-ex.objectstore.gov.bc.ca/ag-pssg-cc-exh-prod-bkt-ex/257%20-%20001%20Appendix%20A%20-%202020-Crypto-Crime-Report%20Chainanalysis.pdf>

Chainalysis, 'The 2023 Crypto Crime Report: Everything you need to know about cryptocurrency-based crime' (February 2023) <https://go.chainalysis.com/rs/503-FAP-074/images/Crypto_Crime_Report_2023.pdf>

Chainalysis, 'The 2025 Crypto Crime Report: The rising role of cryptocurrency in all forms of crime and how its transparency is creating unique opportunities for investigation' (February 2025) <https://www.chainalysis.com/wp-content/uploads/2025/03/the-2025-crypto-crime-report-release.pdf>

European Union Blockchain Observatory and Forum, 'Legal and Regulatory Framework of Blockchain and Smart Contracts' (2019) <https://www.eublockchainforum.eu/sites/default/files/reports/report_legal_v1.0.pdf>

G7 Summit, 'The declaration of 1989' (Paris, 16 July 1989) <http://www.g8.utoronto.ca/summit/1989paris/communique/index.html>

'Global Games Market Report' (2025) < https://resources.newzoo.com/hubfs/Free%20Reports/Games%20Market%20Report%20and%20Forecasts/2025_Newzoo_Free_Global_Games_Market_Report.pdf?utm_campaign=15407504-2025%20GMRF&utm_medium=email&_hsenc=p2ANqtz--fR95582yZhdfU5t_why0YhbXriKmu7Z93LOLfem93Pz8OQUi-w8E4zsly1DfZrXbsq1gD7jIld9Vz7iAZnEPwBJdgVw&_hsmi=377586429&utm_content=377586429&utm_source=hs_automation>

'Creation of the Bretton Woods System' (Federal Reserve History, 22 November 2013) < https://www.federalreservehistory.org/essays/bretton-woods-created>

'The Story Behind the Card' (Diners Club International) < https://www.dinersclubus.com/home/about/dinersclub/story#:~:text=February%201950.,world's%20first%20multipurpose%20charge%20card.>

'1963: American Express comes to Britain' (BBC Home) <http://news.bbc.co.uk/onthisday/hi/dates/stories/september/10/newsid_3031000/3031968.stm>

'What is a Bitcoin Wallet? A beginner's guide to storing BTC' (Cointelegraph) <https://cointelegraph.com/bitcoin-for-beginners/what-is-bitcoin-wallets>

'How does Bitcoin work?' (bitcoin) <https://bitcoin.org/en/how-it-works>

'Operator of Illegal Bitcoin Exchange Coin.mx Sentenced to Prison' (Nasdaq, 30 June 2017) <https://www.nasdaq.com/articles/operator-of-illegal-bitcoin-exchange-coin.mx-sentenced-to-prison-2017-06-30>

'What is Monero (XMR)?'<https://web.getmonero.org/get-started/what-is-monero/>

'Counter-terrorists win: Financial crime through video games is on the rise' (The Economist, 9 November 2019) < https://www.economist.com/finance-and-economics/2019/11/07/financial-crime-through-video-games-is-on-the-rise>

'Permissioned blockchain vs. permissionless blockchain: Key differences' (Cointelegraph) < https://cointelegraph.com/blockchain-for-beginners/permissioned-blockchain-vs-permissionless-blockchain-key-differences>

Guarda Team, 'Custodial vs Non-Custodial Wallets: Benefits of light wallets' (*Medium*, 8 June 2018) <https://medium.com/@HaloDotSocial/custodial-vs-non-custodial-wallets-whats-the-difference-kucoin-wallet-web3-academy-3f09818c702a >

The United States Department of Justice, 'Ohio Resident Charged with Operating Darknet-Based Bitcoin "Mixer," which Laundered Over $300 Million' <https://www.justice.gov/opa/pr/ohio-resident-charged-operating-darknet-based-bitcoin-mixer-which-laundered-over-300-million>

'What is a Bitcoin Wallet? A beginner's guide to storing BTC' (Cointelegraph) <https://cointelegraph.com/bitcoin-for-beginners/what-is-bitcoin-wallets>

'Government appeal keeps banker in jail' (Tampa Bay Times, 13 July 1992) <https://www.tampabay.com/archive/1992/07/13/government-appeal-keeps-banker-in-jail/>

Europol press release, <https://www.europol.europa.eu/newsroom/news/multi-million-euro-cryptocurrency-laundering-service-bestmixerio-taken-down>

Commission 'Blockchain Strategy' < https://digital-strategy.ec.europa.eu/en/policies/blockchain-strategy>

Oxford English Dictionary Online OED Online (Oxford University Press 2014)

INDEX

alienation of clients 149–51
alternative remittance activity 75–6
AML (Anti-Money Laundering) regime
aftermath 149–51
alienation of clients 149–51
anonymity and trust 135–60
confidentiality and secrecy in bank-customer relationship 142–8
preventive side of EU legislation 137–42
application to digital currencies 1–7
bank-customer confidentiality and secrecy prior to 142–6
and banks 48, 135, 137, 142, 145
alienation from customers, risk of 157
apprehension towards regime 149–50
5th Directive 141
operational workload 148
resources to comply with regime 151
compliance costs 149–51
and data protection 8, 12, 14, 15, 161, 162, 181
evolution of European regime 95–134
extension to digital currencies 161–211
FATF influence on evolution of EU regime 97–104
fundamental rights concerns on inclusion of digital currencies and expansion 124–7
in-game currencies excluded from 9, 10, 12, 128, 129, 134, 217
inconsistent terminology 9, 26
international *see* international AML regime
introduction of digital currencies in 104–14
available policy choices 110–14
proposal for amending 4th AML Directive 108–10
realisation by European Commission 106–7
warming by EBA 105–6
MiCA Regulation *see* MiCA (Markets in Crypto-Assets Regulation)
newly adopted
5th Directive *see* 5th AML Directive
critical evaluation of limitations of new framework 127–33
defining digital currencies 116–20
fundamental rights concerns 124–7
MiCA Regulation *see* MiCA (Markets in Crypto-Assets Regulation)
proposal for an AML Regulation 120–2
shifting from risk-based to rule-based approach 7, 16, 133, 187, 188, 198, 204
travel rule Regulation (2023) 123–4
virtual asset service providers, requirements for 114–33
non-business obligations, introduction of 139–42
practical difficulties in applying measures in digital currency environment 155–9
proportionality test 15, 16
and pseudonymity 137
regional frameworks 2
Regulations *see* AML Regulation (2024/1620), newly adopted; travel rule Regulation (2024/1624)
reliance of framework on financial institutions 137–9
risk-based approach *see* risk-based approach of AML regime
and virtual asset service providers *see* virtual asset service providers
AML Regulation (2024/1620), newly adopted 3, 9, 16, 218
anonymity issue addressed by 121, 131–2, 180–1
CDD enhanced measures 122, 126, 130, 198, 206
Commission proposal for (2021) 115, 120–2
concerns/limitations
compatibility with right to respect for private life and personal data protection 7
digital currencies, regarding 7, 95, 104
EDPS opinion 126
failure to identify categories of personal data to be processed 126

AML Regulation *(continued)*
failure to provide specific categories of data or specific categories of customers to be monitored 126, 129
proportionality 16
shifting from risk-based to rule-based approach 16, 133
on decentralisation *see* decentralisation
digital currencies 104
EDPS on 126
expanding the list of obliged entities involved in the cryptocurrency system 214
expansion of 124–5
extension of obligations under 11–12
and 5th AML Directive 16
in-game currencies 10, 12
and MiCA Regulation 26, 120, 121–2
MiCA Regulation designed to align with 120
monitoring requirements to wide range of actors 12
necessity and proportionality, assessment 193–209
assessment of respect for essence of fundamental rights 200–2
interference with Arts 7 and 8 of Charter 194–7
necessity test 202–4
objective of general interest, assessing 199–200
proportionality assessment 204–9
'provided by law' requirement 197–9
negotiations for 126
powers to monitor customers on a regular basis 129
Recital 76 7, 129
and revision of AML framework 12
standardised compliance, favouring 12
turning point in AML framework 7
see also AML (Anti-Money Laundering) regime; travel rule Regulation (2024/1624)
AMLA (Anti-Money Laundering Authority) 102, 115, 130
Articles 5 and 12 of AMLA Regulation 210
anonymity
AML regime, under 135–60
AML Regulation 121, 131–2, 180–1
and Bitcoin system 8n39, 31–3, 156
concept 39
cryptocurrencies 48
and data protection 180
data protection standards 180
GDPR 179
and interference with privacy 179–82
preventive side of EU AML legislation 137–42
and pseudonymity 36, 39, 180
revision of FATF Recommendations 5
Anti-Money Laundering ***see*** **AML (Anti-Money Laundering) regime**
Anti-Money Laundering Authority ***see*** **AMLA (Anti-Money Laundering Authority)**
asset-referenced tokens 119

banks 3, 25, 43, 215
access of law enforcement agencies to centralised registries 13
and alternative remittance activity 75–6
and AML regime 48, 135, 137, 142, 145
1st Directive 148, 149, 215
5th Directive 141
alienation from customers, risk of 157
apprehension towards 149–50, 160
operational workload 148
resources to comply with 151
bank–customer relationship 87n171, 134, 136, 141, 152
confidentiality and secrecy 142–8, 151, 215
privacy protection 173
tensions 160
and Bitcoin system 24, 30
and blockchain environment 153–4
central bank digital currencies 33
central bank monopoly over money creation/monetary policy 113
centralised operation 160
compared with digital currency entities 92
compliance costs 150
core objectives not aligned with surveillance of financial system 149
data gathered from, as personal data 183
as *de facto* police 152
defining function of 23
digital currencies existing outside banking system 78, 79
dissatisfaction with, and rise of digital currencies 6
distinguished from virtual asset service providers ix, 15, 16, 87, 134, 136, 151–9, 160
expenses 142, 150
exposure to money laundering risks 151

fiat currencies and banking system 16, 23, 82, 83
high-risk 150
and KYC obligations 151
and legal tender 35
limitations of traditional bank-centred AML approach 1, 5
monopoly over payment systems 159
notes 35
obligation to detect money laundering 141
PayPal accounts 32
preservation of records 142
private 152
prohibited from revealing client information 147
and Recommendation 8 (2003) 75
secrecy laws and policies 4, 137, 142–8, 215
size of 150–1
suspicious transactions, obligation to report 152
and trust issues 153
see also ECB (European Central Bank)
barter 19–20
Bitcoin system 135
and anonymity 8n39, 31–3, 156
and banks 24, 30
Bitcoin: A Peer-to-Peer Electronic Cash System' (whitepaper) 24
blockchain technology 5, 184
and characteristics of cryptocurrencies 17–18
complete anonymity unachievable 8n39
concealing identities 132, 168
and concept of digital currencies 9
criminal potential 24
and cryptography 30
and decentralised finance 23, 27–8, 202
design of 155, 173
El Salvador giving legal tender to 24–5
foundations for 23
in-game currencies existing before 76
as a general example 29
introduction of (2008) 5
invention of 17
linking to real-world identity 203
as most well-known cryptocurrency 17
non-face to face transactions 156
OECD working paper 133, 185
operating on a public ledger 130
and other digital currencies 18
privatisation of money 24
public blockchain 156
research limitations 12
size of payment systems 24
see also Bitcoin system; blockchain
black markets 39
comparison of value 63
fiat money 39–40
in-game currencies 50, 57
peso exchange 75
and virtual worlds 57–8
blockchain
and banks 153–4
Bitcoin built on technology of 5
crypto-assets 134
data protection in environment of 161
data relevant to an individual on, as personal data 183
decentralisation 10, 156, 173
distributed ledger technology 119
information collected from 178, 196, 198, 201
interference with privacy, whether 178–84
and anonymity/pseudonymity 179–82
and money laundering 59–60
permissioned/permissionless 12, 42
pseudonymity 29, 59, 156, 173, 179–82, 183
surveillance on, and justification of interference 184–93
CJEU case law 189–93
ECtHR case law 187–9
transactions as pseudonymous 5
see also Bitcoin system; cryptocurrencies

cards, plastic 22
CDD (Customer Due Diligence) 11, 130–2
application to digital currencies, difficulties with 132–3, 160
circumventing measures 131, 132
crypto-asset service providers/transactions 122, 204, 206, 217
customer anonymity, countering 130
enhanced, under AML Regulation 122, 126, 130, 198, 206, 217
'geographical factor' 206
and KYC obligations 127, 199, 199n277
no central authority to enforce measures 131, 156
procedural safeguards 207
proportionality/necessity test 13, 207
and risk-based approach of AML regime 127
thresholds 122, 203, 204
see also KYC (Know Your Customer)
'chain of security' concept (Goede) 8

Charter of Fundamental Rights of the EU 178, 189
acknowledgement of data protection as a separate human right 177
Article 7 (right to privacy) 175, 190, 193
interference with 4, 175, 194–7
Article 8 (protection of personal data) 175, 190, 193
interference with 4, 194–7
Article 52(1) (permitted restriction of privacy/data rights) 4, 186
assessment of objective of general interest 199
proportionality assessment 161, 186
'provided by law' requirement 197
on retention of amalgamated data 190
CJEU (Court of Justice of the European Union) 14
jurisprudence of 16, 176, 177, 189, 193, 209, 210, 216
surveillance on blockchain, and justification of interference 189–93
compliance costs 149–51
confidentiality and secrecy in bank-customer relationship 142–8, 215
death of secrecy concerns 149–51
before introduction of AML-related obligations 143–6
tension between bank secrecy and AML regime 146–8
consumable commodities 20
crypto-asset service providers, concept of 118, 120, 121
crypto-assets
blockchain- and non-blockchain based 134
categories 33
concept of 118, 119, 120, 121
and electric money tokens 119, 128
and electronic money 128
impact assessment 126
new definitions 120, 128
in newly adopted AML framework 26
non-fungible tokens as 59n68
payment tokens 33
proposal for Regulation on 102
security tokens 33
services 120
shifting from risk-based to rule-based approach 126
utility tokens 33
see also crypto-asset service providers, concept of; MiCA (Markets in Crypto-Assets Regulation)
cryptocurrencies
actors 43–7
anonymity *see* anonymity
Bitcoin as most well-known cryptocurrency 17
capability to trade or transfer 80
characteristics 10, 29–33, 48
and concept of digital currencies 9
criminal potential 50
cryptography *see* cryptography
decentralisation 30–1
distinguished from in-game currencies 10
exchanges
between different cryptocurrencies and swappers 44–5
with fiat currencies 43, 44
peer-to-peer 45
feasibility of money laundering through 14
and in-game currencies 12, 27
common features 38, 39, 40, 48
distinguished from 10, 39, 40, 48
immutability 31
included in FATF definition of virtual assets 80–1
international regime 66
mixing services 47, 59–60
money laundering through 14, 50, 55, 57
and other payment tokens 33–6
privacy-oriented 18
pseudonymity 31–3, 40–1, 43, 46, 48, 55, 92
real-world value transfer 10
technology 41–2
trading platforms 45
virtual asset service providers 83
as virtual assets 92
wallet providers 45–7
see also Bitcoin system; blockchain
cryptography 9, 17, 29–30
cryptocurrencies based on 28, 29
role in Bitcoin system 30
used to conceal addresses of users 36
Customer Due Diligence *see* CDD (Customer Due Diligence)

DAO (Decentralised Autonomous Organisations) 218
data protection
acknowledged as a separate human right 177
and AML regime 8, 14, 15, 161, 162, 181
5th AML Directive 12
and anonymity 180
in blockchain environment 161

compliance with rules 121
data gathering as infringement of 194
FIU activities 164–5, 166
framework 14
fundamental rights 7, 13
GDPR, levels offered by 165
infringement, whether justifiable 190
interference with 4, 13
international and regional framework 174–8
jurisprudence of the CJEU 189
LED, levels offered by 165
and organisational structures 14
principles 165
and privacy 166, 174, 175, 177, 178
proportionality and necessity test 12
protection of personal data and right to privacy 7, 166–78
pseudonymisation or anonymisation implemented by intermediaries 180
re-evaluation of norms 176
rights of digital currency users 1
and surveillance techniques 178
and technology 191
understanding of applicable framework 164
and virtual asset service providers 134
see also personal data
Data Protection Officer *see* DPO (Data Protection Officer)
decentralisation
AML Regulation on 132
and Bitcoin system 23, 27–8, 202
blockchain 10, 156, 173
cryptocurrencies 30–1
and digital currencies 6
incompatibility of legal regulation with decentralised nature of some digital currencies, illustrating 119
MiCA Regulation inapplicable where complete 120, 128, 157
mixing services 64
public ledgers 169–74
see also DAO (Decentralised Autonomous Organisations); DeFi (Decentralised Finance)
decentralisation, in cryptocurrencies 30–1
Decentralised Autonomous Organisations *see* DAO (Decentralised Autonomous Organisations)
Decentralised Finance *see* DeFi (Decentralised Finance)
decentralised public ledgers, public nature of 169–74
DeFi (Decentralised Finance) 121, 218
digital currencies 25–41
application of CDD measures to, difficulties with 132–3
architecture of financial surveillance in systems 8–12
Bitcoin *see* Bitcoin system
compared with fiat currencies 7, 18
concept 9–10
convertible exchange platforms for conversion of fiat money 11, 85, 107, 109
regulation of 111, 112
dark side, quantification exercise 60–3
and decentralised finance 6
defining phenomenon of 116–20
and dissatisfaction with banks 6
e-money 25
existing outside banking system 78, 79
extension of AML regime to 161–211
FATF on
currency exchanges *see* 'convertible exchange platforms' above
guidance report of 2015 85
technologically neutral language 16
fundamental rights concerns on inclusion in AML regime and expansion 124–7
and in-game currencies 9–10, 12
impact of new AML Regulation and travel rule Regulation on 104
inclusion in 5th Directive 124–5
international AML framework protecting from criminals 79–83
international and regional focus 10–12
introduction in EU and international AML regimes *see* AML (Anti-Money Laundering) regime
legal definition 13
and money laundering 49–64, 90–2
pseudonymity 6
red flag indicators 89–90
see also virtual asset service providers
research limitations 12
speed 6
technological characteristics 17–48
terminology 25–7
typology 27–9
virtual *see* virtual asset service providers; virtual assets; virtual currencies
see also Bitcoin system; blockchain; cryptocurrencies; in-game currencies; money laundering; virtual currencies

DLT (Distributed Ledger Technology) 42, 119
DPO (Data Protection Officer) 208

EBA (European Banking Authority), warning by 105–6
ECB (European Central Bank)
categorisation of digital currencies 27
on closed virtual currencies 37
on defining digital currencies 116–17
opinions and reports 15
ECHR (European Convention on Human Rights) 4, 178, 190
'accordance with law' requirement 197n268
Article 8 (right to respect private/family life) 175, 183, 187
ECtHR (European Court of Human Rights) 15, 162, 183
jurisprudence of 16, 187, 189, 209, 210, 216
surveillance on blockchain, and justification of interference 187–9
EDPB (European Data Protection Board) 15
EDPS (European Data Protection Supervisor) 15
on AML Regulation 126
on Commission's approach for addressing money laundering and terrorist financing 129
on departure from risk-based approach of AML regime 125, 126, 129
justification of interference guidelines 194
on lack of specificity regarding categories of data to be collected 130
on necessity test 202
on need to monitor specified categories of existing customers 125
warnings from 126
electronic money (e-money) 25, 80, 119, 128
tokens 119, 128
European Banking Authority ***see*** **EBA (European Banking Authority)**
European Central Bank ***see*** **ECB (European Central Bank)**
European Commission
EDPS on Commission's approach to addressing money laundering/terrorist financing 129
and introduction of digital currencies in AML regime 106–7
justification of rule-based approach 125
proposal for AML Regulation 115, 120–2
travel rule Regulation, proposal for 115
European Convention on Human Rights (ECHR) ***see*** **ECHR (European Convention on Human Rights)**
European Data Protection Board ***see*** **EDPB (European Data Protection Board)**
European Data Protection Supervisor ***see*** **EDPS (European Data Protection Supervisor)**

FATF (Financial Action Task Force)
chronological overview of developments and AML legislation 103*t*
global standard-setter for AML 10
guidelines for virtual asset service providers 83–90
red flag indicators in digital currencies 89–90
risk-based approach tailored to 86–9
and international AML regime 65–93
members 69–70
as norm-making and not law-making body 72–4
purpose and structure 68–70
Recommendations *see* Recommendations (FATF)
risk-based approach
departure from traditional risk-based model 96
guidance as generic and insufficient 16, 127
'Guidance for a risk-based approach of AML regime to virtual currencies' report (2015) 85
less discretion given to private entities 93
Recommendations of 2003 86
Recommendations of 2012 87
retaining in principle 11, 15
on risks associated with digital currencies 102
on virtual asset service providers 43, 67
guidelines for 83–90
Recommendation 15 introducing 78, 79
technologically neutral language used by 16
fiat currencies/money 9
and banking system 23
black markets 39–40
compared with digital currencies 7, 18
convertible exchange platforms for conversion of 11, 85, 107, 109
regulation of 111, 112
digital representation 25

entities transacting with 44–5
evolution of 17
exchanges 9, 11, 44
bitcoin, except from VAT 35
convertible, for conversion of fiat money 11, 85, 107, 109
with cryptocurrencies 43, 44
with in-game currencies 10, 38–40, 50, 64, 218
with V-bucks 40
with virtual currencies having unidirectional flow 27
5th AML Directive 3, 6, 96, 116–20, 125, 126
adoption in 2018 101–2, 114, 121n177
perceived as premature 115
and AML Regulation 16
assumptions regarding virtual asset service providers 215
bitcoin wallet 46–7
compared with MiCA 119, 120
concerns/limitations 115, 118, 121, 126, 127, 134, 206n311
compatibility with right to respect for private life and personal data protection 7
shifting from risk-based to rule-based approach 7, 12, 16, 116, 122, 125, 214
custodial wallet providers included in 11, 131n242, 214
exclusion of in-game currencies 128
fiat currencies and digital currencies exchanges included in 11, 131n242, 214
fundamental rights issues 124
in-game currencies 10, 12, 128
impact assessment of proposal for 108
inclusion of digital currencies in 124–5
initial amendments 124
initial inclusion of digital currencies in 95
and necessity test 202
outlined measures in 114
policy options 113
and proposal for amendment of 4th AML Directive 108–10
Recital 10 128
Recital 24 7, 125, 129, 197n265
technical challenges 126–7
transformation of relevant provisions into Regulation 121
and trust issues 154
turning point in AML framework 7
and virtual asset service providers 131n242, 215
virtual currencies, use of term 26, 116n148
see also AML (Anti-Money Laundering) regime; AML Regulation (2024/1620), newly adopted
Financial Action Task Force *see* FATF (Financial Action Task Force)
financial crises 22
financial institutions, reliance of AML framework on 137–9
see also banks
Financial Intelligence Units *see* FIUs (Financial Intelligence Units)
financial privacy 162–6
1st AML Directive 215
adoption of (1991) 2
and banks 148, 149
FIUs (Financial Intelligence Units)
access to information
ability to request, obtain and use (from any obliged entity) 209
absence of regulation regarding digital currencies restricting 109
collected by virtual asset service providers from blockchain 165–6
databases 166
enhanced 108
financial 162
potential to become overwhelmed by 155
powers relating to 101
tasked with gathering essential information 163–4
applicable data protection framework 14
compliance with GDPR 165
cooperation among 13, 102
data protection regulations governing activities 164–5
enabling linkage of digital currency transactions with bank accounts 115
expansion of powers 165–6
human rights issues 14
independent and autonomous 163
information exchange 8, 13, 109
instruments applying to 165
interactions with obliged entities 163
intermediaries, seen as 164
intersection with digital currencies 165
as law enforcement authorities 165
Law Enforcement Directive, applying 166
of Member States 116, 152, 164
more detailed rules, proposals for 102
organisational structure of each 165

FIUs (Financial Intelligence Units) *(continued)*
practical difficulties in applying measures in digital currency environment 158
privacy and intersection of AML regime 13
privacy concerns 162, 163
reporting suspicious transactions to 130, 152
and right to privacy and data protection 4
6th AML Directive addressing 116, 164, 165
Suspicious Activity Reports, receiving 154
types of EU FIUs 164
4th AML Directive, amendment proposal 108–10
fundamental rights, concerns regarding inclusion of digital currencies in AML regime 124–7
funds transfers, travel rule Regulation (2023) 123–4

GDPR (General Data Protection Regulation)
anonymity 179
compliance of FIUs with 165
and IP addresses 207
and LED 14
and pseudonymity 179, 182, 202
General Data Protection Regulation (GDPR) *see* **GDPR (General Data Protection Regulation)**
global financial crisis (2008) 22

hawala system 75

ICCPR (International Covenant on Civil and Political Rights) 174
immutability, cryptocurrency 31
in-game currencies 37–41
and AML Regulation 10, 12
Bitcoin, existing before 76
black markets 50, 57–8, 63
capability to trade or transfer 80
centralised platforms 9, 39, 81, 129
challenges for AML compliance 9
characteristics 29, 39, 48
as closed virtual currencies 27, 29, 80
and concept of digital currencies 9–10, 12
control over 81
criminal potential 50
and cryptocurrencies 12, 27
common features 38, 39, 40, 48
distinguished from 10, 39, 40, 48
discrepancy in treatment 128
exclusion from AML regime 9, 10, 12, 128, 129, 134
expanding into real economy 218
fiat currency exchanges 10, 38–40, 50, 57, 64, 218
5th AML Directive 10, 12, 128
gaming industry, data shortcomings 61
ignored in AML scholarship 1, 48, 61
included in FATF definition of virtual assets 80–1
international regime 66
as medium of exchange 39
MiCA Regulation 128
'money,' whether 39, 48
money laundering through 14, 38, 50, 63, 64
offers for exchange 63
pseudonymity 40–1, 48
real-world value transfer 10
regulation shortcomings 39, 51, 214
research limitations 12
research rationale 38
as store of value 39, 40
transfer of between accounts within the game 57–8
unconfirmed value 50
virtual asset service providers 83
as virtual assets 92
as virtual currencies 27
virtual object, using 59
and virtual worlds 15, 17, 27, 57–9
Second Life 37–8, 82, 84
World of Warcraft 82
see also Second Life (in-game currency); virtual worlds; World of Warcraft (in-game currency)
international AML regime 11, 16
and FATF 65–93
introduction of digital currencies to 78
primary objective 2
protection of digital currencies from criminals 79–83
response to crime of money laundering 67–74
see also AML (Anti-Money Laundering) regime; cryptocurrencies; digital currencies; FATF (Financial Action Task Force); money laundering; Recommendations (FATF)
International Covenant on Civil and Political Rights *see* **ICCPR (International Covenant on Civil and Political Rights)**
Internet Protocol *see* **IP (Internet Protocol)**

IP (Internet Protocol) addresses 11, 47, 59, 87
blockchain transactions 178
concealing 131, 132
darknet, associated with 89
determination of a transaction's risk 205
discrepancies between 89–90
due diligence measures 185
FATF on 92–3
GDPR adherence 207
obligation of virtual asset service providers to collect 133, 186, 215
retention of data on an indiscriminate basis 196, 205
tracing/tracking 133, 186

Know Your Customer *see* **KYC (Know Your Customer)**
KYC (Know Your Customer) 11
AML regime 158
application to digital currencies, difficulties with 160
association of customers with specific accounts 158
and banks 151
and CDD measures 127, 199, 199n277
functional efficiency of procedures 159
implementation of procedures 158
limited to real-world economy 159
no central authority to enforce measures 156
OECD working paper 185
proportionality/necessity test 13, 207
traceability through 158
utilisation of procedures to de-anonymise customers 158

Law Enforcement Directive *see* **LED (Law Enforcement Directive)**
LED (Law Enforcement Directive) 14, 164–6

Markets in Crypto-Assets Regulation *see* **MiCA (Markets in Crypto-Assets Regulation)**
MiCA (Markets in Crypto-Assets Regulation) 118–20, 155, 158
adoption of 118, 213
and AML Regulation 120, 121–2
Commission excluding AML obligations from 118
compared with 5th Directive 119, 120
crypto-asset service providers, concept of 118, 120, 121
crypto-assets, concept of 118, 120, 121
defining asset-referenced tokens, electronic money tokens and utility tokens 119
defining digital currencies 119
designed to align closely with AML Regulation 120
electronic money vs crypto-assets and e-money tokens 128
exclusions from scope 121, 128, 129
expanding the list of obliged entities involved in the cryptocurrency system 214
first comprehensive regulatory framework specifically addressing digital currencies 118
in-game currencies excluded from scope 128, 129
inapplicable in case of complete decentralisation 120, 128, 157
incompatibility of legal regulation with decentralised nature of some digital currencies, illustrating 119
proposal for 115
Recital 19 128
on virtual asset service providers 171, 206
see also crypto-asset service providers, concept of; crypto-assets; MMORPGs (Massively Multiplayer Online Role Playing Games)
mixing services 43, 46, 89
cryptocurrencies 47, 59–60
evasion of CDD measures 132
pseudonymity and decentralisation 64
and wallet providers 60
MMORPGs (Massively Multiplayer Online Role Playing Games) 9n42, 37, 39
money 18–25
classification
as a medium of exchange 18, 19
as a store of value 18, 19
as a unit of account 19
concept 18–19
in-game currencies as, whether 39, 48
history 18–20
new era of 20–1
paper 21–2
plastic cards 22
money laundering 49–64
ancillary crime of 52–4
and blockchain environment 59–60
chameleon crime, as 49–50
cryptocurrencies, through 14, 50, 55, 57
and digital currencies 49–64
EU and FATF's approach to 3

money laundering *(continued)*
evolution of methods 3–4
FATF Recommendations and 'digital' money laundering 74–8
in-game currencies, through 14, 38, 50, 63, 64
international response to crime of *see* international AML regime
predicate offences 52–4
process 54–9
criminal abuse of technology during 59–60
cryptocurrencies 55, 57
stages 49
integration 55, 56*f*
layering 54, 56*f*
placement 54, 56*f*

Nakamoto, Satoshi 5
necessity test 202–4
adopted measures suitable for achieving objective, requirement for 216–17
combined with proportionality test 202
degree of intrusiveness of measures 203
first step in assessment 202–3
in-game currencies excluded from AML regime 12
how to conduct 202
justification of interference 194
KYC and CDD measures 13
'necessary in a democratic society' criterion 189
necessity requirement of proportionality test 191
'provided by law' requirement 197, 216
'reasonable suspicion' 188
second step in assessment 203–4
where not satisfied 204
see also proportionality test
non-business obligations, introduction of 139–42
non-fungible tokens (NFTs) 59n68

OECD (Organisation for Economic Co-operation and Development) 133, 185
Organisation for Economic Co-operation and Development *see* **OECD (Organisation for Economic Co-operation and Development)**

paper money, history 21–2
Passenger Name Record *see* **PNR (Passenger Name Record)**
payment tokens 33–6
see also cryptocurrencies
peer-to-peer exchange 45
personal data 16, 161
categories 126
Charter of Fundamental Rights on 161
collecting 181, 210
compatibility of 5th AML Directive and new AML Regulation with 7
concept 179, 183
control over 169
core data 216
data gathered from banking documents as 183
data relevant to individual on blockchain as 183
data stored on blockchain as 195
erasure of 181
external data 216
financial information as 15, 16, 170, 174, 182, 183
fundamental right to protection of 177
and GDPR 165, 170, 176, 183, 184
on the internet 178
and privacy 168, 175, 177
processing of 8, 124, 126, 162, 164–5, 175–7, 192, 192n235, 194, 196, 209
protecting on the blockchain 182
and protection of privacy rights 176–8
and public keys 184
qualification of information as 182
relevant to an individual 170
retention 162, 179, 181, 193, 196, 209, 210
safeguarding of and mitigating money laundering risks 179, 201
sharing of 165
subject not/no longer identifiable 183
systems classified within broad category of 171
volumes of 1
warranting protection 174
PNR (Passenger Name Record) 196, 205
predicate offences 52–4
prevention and EU AML legislation
non-business obligations, introduction of 139–42
reliance of AML framework on financial institutions 137–9
privacy
anonymity, pseudonymity and interference with privacy 179–82

blockchain, whether an interference with 178–84
conceptualisation of 167–9
and data protection 166, 174, 175, 177, 178
financial 162–6
as a fundamental human right 4
interference with right to 4
and personal data 168, 175, 177
privacy coins 36–7
and pseudonymity 180
right to, protection of
international and regional framework 174–8
and protection of personal data 176–8
proportionality test 204–9
AML regime 9, 15, 161, 194–202
and AML Regulation 16, 186
policies chosen 114
case law 190–1
Charter of Fundamental Rights of the EU 161, 186
justification of interference 16
combined with necessity test 202
compliance with 4
diverse objectives complicating application of 125
fundamental rights issues 109
in-game currencies excluded from AML regime 12
indiscriminate and general data retention failing 193
justification of interference 7, 16, 190, 194, 204
KYC and CDD measures 13
multilayer 16
necessity requirement of 191
objectives of general interest recognised by the EU 190
and privacy rights 129
procedural safeguards 207–9
'provided by law' requirement 197
and risk-based approach 124, 127
risk-based approach
and elimination of the minimum threshold for cryptocurrency transactions 127
shifting from, dangers of 12, 125, 129, 134
suitability of 124
rule-based approach 186
specificity requirement 126
targeted surveillance 204–7
see also necessity test
pseudo-identity 32
pseudonymity
and AML regime 137, 180
and anonymity 36, 39, 180
blockchain 29, 59, 156, 173, 179–82, 183
combined with TOR and mixing services 64
cryptocurrencies 31–3, 40–1, 43, 46, 48, 55, 92
data protection 180
in-game currencies 40–1, 48
and GDPR 179, 182, 202
and interference with privacy 179–82
leading to data subject 182
mixing services 64
online gaming 32
and privacy 180
public keys 183, 184
transactions as pseudonymous 5
virtual asset service providers 181
wallet providers 60
public keys 14, 155, 156, 184, 185, 207
pseudonymity 183, 184

Recommendations (FATF) 1
of 2003 75–6
of 2012 76–7
amendment of 2018 78
and 'digital' money laundering 74–8
followed by many jurisdictions 10
Recommendation 15 (R15), on virtual assets service providers 78, 79
Recommendation 16 (R16), on transfer of funds/application of 'travel rule' to digital currencies 123
response to crime of money laundering 70–2
revision of 2018 5
see also FATF (Financial Action Task Force); virtual asset service providers; virtual assets
risk-based approach of AML regime
AML regime's formal commitment to 208, 210
and CDD measures 127
collection of additional information from all clients appearing contradictory to 11, 90, 93
combining due diligence with 133
FATF
departure from traditional risk-based model 96
guidance as generic and insufficient 16, 127

risk-based approach of AML regime *(continued)*
'Guidance for a risk-based approach of AML regime to virtual currencies' report (2015) 85
less discretion given to private entities 93
Recommendations of 2003 86
Recommendations of 2012 87
retaining approach in principle 11, 15
most significant procedural safeguard for fundamental rights 208
prevalence of ix
procedural safeguard 208
and proportionality test 124, 127
shifting from risk-based to rule-based approach 12, 16, 96, 116, 122, 161–2, 205, 214
AML Regulation 7, 16, 116, 133, 187, 188, 198, 204
Commission justification of 125
and crypto-assets 126
and digital currencies, associated risks 102, 125, 126, 129, 172, 185
EDPS concerns 125, 126, 129
failure on proportionality grounds 16, 134
5th AML Directive 7, 12, 16, 116, 122, 125, 214
fundamental rights implications 134
impact assessment 126
6th AML Directive 209
3rd AML Directive 100
virtual assets/virtual asset service providers, tailored to 86–9

SAR (Suspicious Activity Report) 154
Second Life (in-game currency) 9n42
AML regime applicable to 129
fiat money transactions 10n44, 38, 40, 57, 81
'Linden Dollar' 27, 57, 81
not obliged to collect customer details 129
research rationale 38
virtual world 37–8, 82, 84
see also in-game currencies; World of Warcraft (in-game currency)
secrecy ***see*** **confidentiality and secrecy in bank-customer relationship**
security tokens 33
6th AML Directive, addressing FIUs 116, 164, 165
study of AML and money laundering
digital currencies, research limitations 12
methodology 14–15
research questions 7–8
Suspicious Activity Report ***see*** **SAR (Suspicious Activity Report)**

TEU (Treaty on European Union), on national security 4n17, 192–3
TFEU (Treaty on the Functioning of the European Union) 176
The Onion Router ***see*** **TOR (The Onion Router)**
TOR (The Onion Router) software 59, 64
trading platforms 45
transactional data 14
travel rule Regulation (2024/1624) 123–4
adoption of 123
Commission proposal for (2021) 115
digital currencies 104
elimination of the minimum threshold for cryptocurrency transactions under 127, 209
extending information-sharing obligations to all cryptocurrency transfers 217
impact on digital currencies 104
Recital 38 206–7
Recital 39 132, 158
see also AML Regulation (2024/1620), newly adopted
Treaty on European Union ***see*** **TEU (Treaty on European Union)**
Treaty on the Functioning of the European Union ***see*** **TFEU (Treaty on the Functioning of the European Union)**
trust, versus trustlessness 152–5

UDHR (Universal Declaration of Human Rights) 174, 175
Universal Declaration of Human Rights ***see*** **UDHR (Universal Declaration of Human Rights)**
utility tokens 33, 119

Vienna Convention against Illicit Traffic in Narcotic Drugs and Psychotropic Substances (1988) 2
virtual asset service providers 11, 15, 44
adding to list of obliged entities 79
and AML regime 137
capabilities and limitations 14
concept 120, 121
and data protection 134
distinguished from banks ix, 15, 16, 87, 134, 136, 151–9, 160
FATF approach to 43, 67
guidelines 83–90
Recommendation 15 introducing 78, 79
risk-based 86–9
technologically neutral language used by 16

as financial intermediaries 18
information collected from blockchain 178, 196, 198, 201
legal definition 13, 66, 81–3
MiCA Regulation 171, 206
new definitions 120
and newly adopted AML regime 114–33
operational powers and structural constraints 14
preventive measures by 11
pseudonymity 181
red flag indicators in digital currencies 89–90
regulation requirement 78
risk-based approach of AML regime tailored to 86–9
virtual assets 26
cryptocurrencies included in definition of 80–1
legal definition 66, 79–81
risk-based approach tailored to 86–9
virtual currencies 25–6
bidirectional 29
closed 27, 29
in newly adopted AML framework 26
use of term under 5th Directive 26, 116n148
see also cryptocurrencies; in-game currencies
virtual worlds 37–41
and black markets 57–8
and in-game currencies 15, 17, 27, 57–9
Second Life 37–8, 82, 84
World of Warcraft 82

wallet providers 45–7, 60
pseudonymity 60
World of Warcraft (in-game currency) 9n42
black markets 57
in-game currency 58
'gold' 27, 38, 39–40
offers for currency on a single platform 58
research rationale 38
servers not used for fiat money transactions 40, 57
transfer of in-game currencies between accounts within the game 57–8
virtual world 82
see also in-game currencies; Second Life (in-game currency)

www.ingramcontent.com/pod-product-compliance
Ingram Content Group UK Ltd.
Pitfield, Milton Keynes, MK11 3LW, UK
UKHW020251290926
15470UKWH00002B/859

9 781509 982776